The Southasian Sensibility

Thank you for choosing a SAGE product! If you have any comment, observation or feedback, I would like to personally hear from you. Please write to me at contactceo@sagepub.in

—Vivek Mehra, Managing Director and CEO,
SAGE Publications India Pvt Ltd, New Delhi

Bulk Sales

SAGE India offers special discounts for purchase of books in bulk. We also make available special imprints and excerpts from our books on demand.

For orders and enquiries, write to us at

Marketing Department
SAGE Publications India Pvt Ltd
B1/I-1, Mohan Cooperative Industrial Area
Mathura Road, Post Bag 7
New Delhi 110044, India
E-mail us at marketing@sagepub.in

Get to know more about SAGE, be invited to SAGE events, get on our mailing list. Write today to marketing@sagepub.in

This book is also available as an e-book.

The Southasian Sensibility

A HIMAL *Reader*

Edited by
Kanak Mani Dixit

 www.sagepublications.com
Los Angeles • London • New Delhi • Singapore • Washington DC

Jointly published in 2012 by

 SAGE Publications India Pvt Ltd   and   **The Southasia Trust**
B1/I-1 Mohan Cooperative Industrial Area   GPO Box 24393
Mathura Road, New Delhi 110 044, India   Patam Dhoka, Lalitpur
www.sagepub.in   Nepal

SAGE Publications Inc
2455 Teller Road
Thousand Oaks, California 91320, USA

SAGE Publications Ltd
1 Oliver's Yard, 55 City Road
London EC1Y 1SP, United Kingdom

SAGE Publications Asia-Pacific Pte Ltd
33 Pekin Street
#02-01 Far East Square
Singapore 048763

Published by Vivek Mehra for SAGE Publications India Pvt Ltd, typeset in 10/14 pt Garamond by Star Compugraphics Private Limited, Delhi and printed at Chaman Enterprises, New Delhi.

Library of Congress Cataloging-in-Publication Data Available

ISBN: 978-81-321-0900-6 (HB)

The SAGE Team: Prabha Zacharias, Pranab Jyoti Sarma and Anju Saxena

Contents

List of Abbreviations

AFSPA	Armed Forces Special Powers Act
AGP	Asom Gana Parishad
APHC	All Party Hurriyat Conference
APRC	All Party Representative Committee
ASEAN	Association of Southeast Asian Nations
BJP	Bharatiya Janata Party
BNDP	Bhutan National Democratic Party
BNP	Bangladesh Nationalist Party
BPP	Bhutan People's Party
BSF	Border Security Force
CBI	Central Bureau of Investigation
CP	Communist Party
CRPF	Central Reserve Police Force
Dantak	Indian Border Roads Organisation
DFO	Divisional Forest Officer
DGSM	Dasholi Gram Swarajya Mandal
FATA	Federally Administered Tribal Areas
GATT	General Agreement on Tariffs and Trade
GNLF	Gorkha National Liberation Front
HUROB	Human Rights Organisation of Bhutan
IARI	Indian Agriculture Research Institute
IMD	Indian Meteorology Department
IPKF	Indian Peace-Keeping Force
ISI	Inter Services Intelligence, Pakistan
JeI	Jamaat-e-Islami
JKLF	Jammu & Kashmir Liberation Front
MJF	Madhesi Janaadhikar Forum
MPLF	Manipur People's Liberation Front
MQM	Muttahida Qaumi Movement
NBA	Narmada Bachao Andolan

NEFA	North East Frontier Agency
NNC	Naga National Council
NOC	No Objection Certificate
NPL	National Physical Laboratory
NSCN	National Socialist Council of Nagaland
NWFP	North West Frontier Province
OBCs	Other Backward Castes
PFHR	People's Forum for Human Rights
PLA	People's Liberation Army
PLO	Palestinian Liberation Organisation
PREPAK	People's Revolutionary Party of Kanglaipak
PWD	Public Works Department
RAW	Research and Analysis Wing
RNA	Royal Nepal Army
RSS	Rashtriya Swayamsevak Sangh
SAARC	South Asian Association for Regional Cooperation
SAFTA	South Asian Free Trade Area
SAPTA	SAARC Preferential Trade Arrangement
SUB	Student's Union of Bhutan
ULFA	United Liberation Front of Asom
UML	Communist Party of Nepal (Unified Marxist–Leninist)
UNDP	United Nations Development Programme
UNHCR	United Nations High Commissioner for Refugees
UNHRC	United Nations Human Rights Committee
UNICEF	United Nations Children's Fund
UNLF	United National Liberation Front
UNMIN	United Nations Mission in Nepal
UNP	United National Party
UPA	United Progressive Alliance
USV	Uttarakhand Sangharsh Vahini
VHP	Vishva Hindu Parishad

Acknowledgements

Quite unexpectedly, the realisation sank in among us at the editorial desk of *Himal Southasian* that 2012 is our 25th year. This book, a collection of some of the most memorable articles we have had the privilege to publish over the years, is akin to a souvenir of that milestone. As editor of *Himal* since its founding in 1987 as a Himalayan magazine, I wish to acknowledge the efforts of so many in bringing this volume into existence.

Thanks to the contributors of the articles in this compilation, incorporating the reportage and vision that in composite make up what we call the 'Southasian sensibility'. The writers not only went through the original edits once again, but also responded promptly to queries during preparation of this volume.

I acknowledge the contribution of my colleagues at *Himal* past and present, who over the last two-and-a-half decades helped edit the articles presented here. It is this group of editors that gave the magazine its particular imprimatur, from our Himalayan era to Southasian incarnation, including Kesang Tseten, Manisha Aryal, Deepak Thapa and Thomas Mathew. Laxmi Murthy and Prashant Jha did much substantive work for this volume, including the selection of contributions. After a hiatus, the project was revived and given its final shape by Carey L Biron and Vidyadhar Gadgil. Meher Ali's assistance in monitoring progress was invaluable. Roman Gautam corrected the proofs with a keen eye.

We are grateful to the team at SAGE for their interest in this project— Dr Sugata Ghosh, Rekha Natrajan and Pranab Jyoti Sarma. They are imbued with the true Southasian sensibility!

While I may be listed as the editor of this volume, the credit for chaperoning the text and information—the wisdom—in these pages goes to the many individuals who have worked at *Himal*'s desk over the past quarter-century.

Kanak Mani Dixit
Lalitpur, Nepal
1 June 2012

Introduction

The journey to Southasia

Himal magazine started its journey 25 years ago as a Himalayan publication, hence its name. In 1996, it converted to a Southasian magazine and has since sought to develop a practical vision of regionalism in southern Asia based on economic growth, social justice, pluralism and human rights. The magazine's foundational understanding is that 'being Southasian' is an essential part of the multiple and cross-cutting identities the people of this region enjoy, from the local to the provincial, national and Subcontinental. The origins of this amorphous, penumbraic regional identity go back to the growth of Indic civilisation, and some would say earlier still. This is an identity that could have been called 'Indian', perhaps, but not once India the nation state removed that privilege after 1947. From that point, to be 'India' could no longer be synonymous with being Subcontinental.

Himal's effort over the last 15 years has focused on helping to generate a new way to conceptualise the Southasian region and its identity. Perhaps slightly ahead of its time, the magazine has particularly sought to engage the mechanical nationalism that often guides—and besets—the media in large parts when it comes to regional geopolitics and bilateral relations. The South Asian Association for Regional Cooperation (SAARC) organisation has been around for as long as *Himal* has been publishing, and many continue to vest hopes that it will prosper as a grouping that binds the heads of state and government to a regional outlook. SAARC does need to become dynamic, but this too requires a reconceptualisation of Southasia beyond the idea of a conglomeration of seven (and then eight, with the addition of Afghanistan) disparate nation states.

There would be little need to wax romantic over a Southasian identity, perhaps, if it did not affect the lives and livelihoods of the people. *Himal*'s editors certainly believe that the development of humanitarian empathy between the region's cultures and societies is at the core of 'being Southasian'—that this can and will offer direct benefit in the social and economic uplift of the people of the region. Regionalism is thus a confidence-building measure that will help to reduce military expenditure, bring down barbed-wire fences between countries and promote inter-country travel. Southasian regionalism will help to make economic growth more symbiotic, as economies of scale kick in and efficiencies help to bring down prices, generate employment and raise standards of living. In particular, the tens of millions living in deep poverty in the border regions that make up the 'arc of poverty' in the Brahmaputra-Ganga-Indus basin from Bangladesh to Balochistan would benefit if Southasian regionalism were to become a reality—an idea that is discussed from several perspectives in the articles included in this Reader.

The reason that regionalism remains a weak though well-meaning aspiration, rather than hard reality, has to do with the nationalism of newborn states—the bane of Southasia. Out of a sense of self-preservation, these nationalisms have sought to define Southasian regionalism as synonymous with 'SAARC regionalism'. Thus, the idea of working together across societies is limited to a notion of nation-state capitals cooperating, rather than peoples gathering across frontiers to debate and collaborate. Typically, then, the Southasian discourse, whether among government officials or civil-society 'track two' actors, has sought to involve representatives of all Southasian countries. While this might seem to represent an ideal, it makes for a very unreal Southasia when everyone is forced to sit together all the time regardless of theme or topic—and hence, regionalism itself fails to gain traction.

Regionalism in southern Asia has been affected by the attempt to try out a copy of the European Union, on the one hand, and Association of Southeast Asian Nations (ASEAN) on the other. However, India's overwhelming presence right at the centre of Southasia requires a very different formula. This contention is only strengthened by the fact that, other than Afghanistan-Pakistan, all other Southasian countries border India rather than one another.

Visualising a region

The proclivity to consider a particular topic as 'Southasian' only when all eight SAARC countries are involved in a conclave, initiative or concept is a primary reason why the whole conceptualisation exercise has gone awry. As the understanding has evolved among *Himal*'s editors over the years, any activity carried out across a Southasian border must be considered 'regional', to begin with. Beyond the bilateral, there are the trilateral, the quadrilateral ... onward to the octagonal Southasian definition offered by SAARC. When Nepal collaborates with Bihar and Uttar Pradesh on any issue, from tourism to flood control; when Bangladesh engages with West Bengal; or when plans are made for deeper connections between Kerala and Sri Lanka—these must be seen as Southasian activities. There is no need to see the free-trade agreement signed between India and Sri Lanka in 1998 as only a bilateral agreement: that document could well set an example for other countries of the region.

The shared history and present-day diversity of Southasia requires us to reach for an amorphous identity that is based on a number of parallel visions. One such conceptualisation would, of course, be the SAARC view of Southasia, based on the membership of eight countries. Another, however, would consider Southasia as a penumbra of cultures from Balochistan and Afghanistan eastward and southward to Tibet, Burma, Sri Lanka and the Maldives. This kind of regionalism cannot have sharp outer boundaries: Tibet, for instance, can politically be a part of China while also being a part of the greater Southasian civilisation. Burma is part of both South and Southeast Asia, just as Afghanistan is Southasian as well as Iranian and Central Asian.

It is important not to essentialise the meaning of Southasia and Southasian, while also not allowing these definitions to be so soft and broad-based that they come to be everything to everyone, and hence lose all meaning. One definition that appeals to the editors of *Himal* is to consider Southasia as a region made up of the much smaller units of governance, particularly when it comes to the larger countries—the states and provinces of India and Pakistan. The smaller countries of Southasia should contemplate developing links with these provinces and states. Likewise, the states and provinces should be interacting reasonably independent of the national government. The knee-jerk capital-based nationalisms in the smaller countries would tend to reject such a notion, so we have to add an important caveat: there is no questioning the sovereignty of any country. Why should it be seen as an anti-national statement to suggest that Nepal will build its economic future as a sovereign country by ensuring that it benefits from (and, in turn, that it benefits) the neighbouring Indian states of Uttarakhand, Bihar or Uttar Pradesh? Bangladesh's future is also tied to commerce and contact with the Indian Northeast, West Bengal and Burma's Rakhine state.

An effective implementation of the federal structures of India and Pakistan would actually be the best path to a utilitarian, effective, people-friendly form of regionalism in Southasia. Again, this does not mean challenging the sovereignty of either country, just as it does not mean challenging the sovereignty of the smaller countries to suggest that they collaborate with the neighbouring states of India or Pakistan. Instead, this vision of Southasia attempts to provide more texture to enrich the notion of living in each part of the region, such that we can collectively own our history and gain socially, culturally and economically from the continuity of history and the contiguity of geography.

Even though Southasian regionalism takes us beyond the nation state, its philosophies are actually anchored in the need for better federal units and more effective local governments throughout the region. As noted earlier, India, for the size of its population, geographical area, and economic and geo-political might, is a country that actually covers much of the region. In that sense, it truly is a subcontinent rather than a country. For now, India is governed as a centralised democracy, which is certainly better than any non-democratic alternative. On the other hand, if we are to consider the number of people in any country as representative of its importance and socio-cultural weight, India must federalise more than it has, so that its population benefits and the growing income divide is held in check. Indeed, New Delhi must devolve more power to local governments beyond the distribution allowed by federalism. Doing so would not only be considered 'Southasian' (given that India forms much of Southasia), but would also make India increasingly open to its neighbouring countries and provinces. The more the states of India open up, the better it is for economic growth and development all around.

Visualising and actualising Southasia as a region would also help to pro-vide a new framework for studying the area's emerging powers. At a time when India and China are touted as the powerhouses of Asia, an alternative vision would posit Southasia as a whole as the more logical counterpoint to the Middle Kingdom. Though such a vision might have limited geopolitical use, the Southa-sian counterpoint could be helpful in terms of comparing and contrasting the two most-populous regions of Asia, helping in cooperation between the two. A regional outlook on India, based on a regional confidence in Southasia, would help to establish a mature and supportive geopolitical foundation linking these two vital parts of Asia.

One of the weaknesses in the development of the Southasian space is that the 'track-two' arena has largely been the domain of the English-speaking sections of the national capitals. It is imperative to think of regionalism as going beyond conference rooms and airport lounges. We must 'vernacularise' the Southasian discourse, where we talk not just of Southasia but of *Dakshin Asia*. Or *Junoobi Asia* in Urdu, *Thekke Asia* in Malayalam, *Dakunu Asiyawa* in Sinhala, *Therkaasia* in Tamil, *Shumale Asia* in Kashmiri, *Dokkhin Ashia* in Bangla and *Dakhin Asia* in Sindhi—and why not *Barsageer*, the Urdu term for Subcontinent?

Regionalism must catch the imagination of the masses rather than only well-meaning elites, so that the push surges from below. Just as the campaign against the nuclearisation of Southasia has withered in the absence of a vernacular people's campaign in India, Pakistan and elsewhere in the neighbourhood, so is the need for Southasian regionalism not taken seriously because it is still an idea and ideal pushed from the top. Trickle-down Southasianism has its limits, as we have seen all too often in attempts to make it spark in the last few decades.

Southasian empathy

The editors of *Himal* have been mulling over these topics since we started as a cross-regional Himalayan magazine. We converted to a Southasian magazine when we realised that journalism must tap into the socio-economic and cultural streams, rather than merely the perceived commonalities of geographical terrain. *Himal*'s editors have sought out thinkers, writers and reporters who have, above all, the quality of empathy that makes a Southasian out of a person born in Afghanistan, Bangladesh, Bhutan, Burma, India, the Maldives, Nepal, Pakistan, Sri Lanka or Tibet. Early on, we also realised the need to seek contributors who recognise that it is important to maintain a self-questioning attitude towards one's own national establishment—a critical component if we are to reach out across borders that have, all too quickly, become frontiers guarded with concertina wire and halogen floodlights. We wanted to cover ideas that were at times difficult for country-based publications to adequately explore, and also issues that tended to receive short shrift due to the overwhelming focus on crossborder geopolitics and in-country politics.

It is with this philosophical underpinning, then, that we set out to compile a collection of some of our most thought-provoking articles, essays and ruminations from the past quarter-century. We have selected pieces that represent our vision of Southasia, both in terms of geographical spread as well as a selection of themes and topics. These contributions, vitally important in themselves, also represent the ways in which *Himal* seeks to make the concept of Southasia a strong, central part of our vision of ourselves. Hopefully, this vision will be strong enough to create an impact in each of our national capitals, such that we can move towards a Southasia notably lacking in the crossborder rancour of the past six decades. In turn, such an evolution would have the direct effect of improved lives and livelihoods for a very large portion of our region, one that houses nearly a fourth of all humanity.

It is important to remark upon *Himal*'s Kathmandu base. Due to its geographical placement, in relatively close range to the populous sub-region that is North Southasia (though, sadly, rather remote from South Southasia, including South India and Sri Lanka), its liberal visa regime, which welcomes any and all, and for being seen as the most 'neutral' nation state of Southasia, Nepal provides the ideal space for the incubation of Southasianism. And it is from this base in Kathmandu that the *Himal* family, which includes contributors, supporters, readers, editors, staff-writers and many others, has helped the magazine to remain afloat and energetic. The fact that Nepal became an open, democratic society in 1990 was a boon without which an independent magazine such as *Himal* could not have been contemplated, much less survived. On occasion, the editors of *Himal* have been forced to be increasingly active in keeping alive an open society. For the sake of the people of Nepal, as well as to keep in step with the ideals of a democratic Southasia, it is important to watchdog the pluralism currently alive in Nepal. The open border that Nepal shares with India provides a living example of how sovereignties can be protected even as frontiers are kept unlocked and unchained. However, there are today rumblings of attempts to restrict this open bilateral border—rumours that should worry the civil society throughout the region.

As editor of *Himal* since its founding, I would like to take this opportunity to thank each and every individual who has supported the magazine in this quarter-century journey from the Himalaya across Southasia. The representative articles printed in this collection provide an interesting insight into the evolution of Southasia as a whole, as well as a snapshot of how the editors of *Himal* have conceptualised the regionalism that is specific to our subcontinent. I would also like to pay special tribute to the great thinker Eqbal Ahmed, of Islamabad, who is no longer with us. His vision, as well as the knowledge and wisdom of all other writers included in this volume, is included also as a tribute to honour the countless individuals who have been part of this, *Himal*'s, journey to Southasia.

Kanak Mani Dixit
Patan Dhoka, Lalitpur, Nepal
10 July 2011

The Drukpa image of Bhutan derives from the core regions of Para, Thimphu, Punakha and Tongsa, whose 'religio-cultural and political practices were accepted as the national ones,' according to A C Sinha. There is every reason to appreciate western Bhutan's heritage and lifestyle; yet the overwhelming emphasis on the Ngalung ignores the population groups that are equally significant if not as interesting to outsiders. These include, cumulatively, the Sarchop; the Brokpa 'aborigines' of the high valleys; the multi-ethnic Nepali-speakers of the lower hills; as well as smaller Tota, Santhal, Doya and Rajbanshi communities.

The game plan

Even though Bhutan is a relatively easy country to govern, the Thimphu government is also among the more efficient in the developing world. The bureaucratic elite is almost entirely educated in the public schools of India and has a common work ethic, which also meshes with that of the king. Solidarity among the rulers, and the 'manageability' of their small, under-populated, resource-rich country, has enabled them to fine-tune development policy.

Perhaps the major accomplishment of the king's administration (there has been no prime minister since Jigme Palden Dorji was assassinated) has been its ability to keep India placated, even as Bhutan explores the boundaries of what the 1949 Treaty of Friendship allows. Today, Bhutan even has the leeway to negotiate independently with China on demarcation of its disputed northwestern boundary. While Nepal still dithers in indecision over selling hydropower to India, Thimphu is already earning from the Chukha Hydel Project. Since 1962, Bhutan has made a success of its postage stamps, which are renowned the world over for their 'thematic value and technical excellence'. The government even has the gumption to run (through agents) lotteries in India, which are said to turn in profits in the crores.

King Jigme's administration is sharp, disciplined and responsive, with a reputation of 'getting things done'. It is this administrative acumen that has been brought to bear against the Lhotshampa. The result has been devastating in its efficiency.

Somewhere along the way, a plan evolved. Its goal was to defuse the Lhotshampa demographic threat, and intricate details were worked out. A census would be taken again under more discriminatory criteria; Drig Lam Namzha would be strongly enforced; all political opponents would be termed ngolops and terrorists; schools, hospitals and services in the south would be closed;

requirement of No Objection Certificates would be slapped on the southerners; all land found to be 'illegal' would be confiscated and northerners invited in.

This is what a confidential report of a Western bilateral development agency had to say about the period July 1991 to January 1992:

> At this stage many ethnic Nepalese do not feel welcome any longer in this country. In the last year they have been treated as second rate, in principle suspect, citizens. Their participation in public life has been made extremely difficult. There were no schools, no health facilities ... sale of produce was difficult, trade licences were withdrawn, and employment opportunities were minimalised. If one then adds the fear of physical violence, it is no wonder that many families see no future in this country and decide to leave.

A well-thought-out strategy of depopulation and 'cultural cleansing' is underway, and since February 1992 it has been at its most aggressive. The picture emerges that the government's hope is to empty the country of a large number of its legitimate Nepali-speaking citizens until their proportion is brought down to a 'manageable' level. Ratan Gazmere, who is now in Jhapa, says he learned from reliable intelligence sources that the plan is to bring the Nepali-speaking population down to between 15 and 20 per cent of the country's reduced population. Foreign Minister Tshering told a visiting ambassador a few months ago that it was absolutely vital to 'balance the demographic equation'.

The plan is being sold internationally with astute diplomacy that exploits all possibilities: Nepal's fear of India, India's fear of a pan-Nepali resurgence, the West's soft spot for oriental Bhutan and a reluctance to bait India, the weakness of journalists when confronted with a kingdom in the clouds, and so on. Bhutan must rid itself of as many Lhotshampa as possible before negative international pressure builds up.

To give the benefit of doubt to the Thimphu strategists, it might all have started innocently enough, with the simple idea that Bhutan must be Bhutanese: One nation, one people. But as the various parts of the plans were implemented successfully, the enthusiasm grew and stricter implementation followed. Before long, Bhutanisation had a momentum of its own, and the strategists seem to have gained confidence in their ability—as long as the world remained silent—of 'reclaiming' their country for themselves, while the Lhotshampa were bundled off to Nepal, 'where they belonged anyway'.

The 1985 Citizenship Act, the 1988 re-census, the Drig Lam Namzha code and the language policy became the tools that began to be applied. The proof is in the silent, overgrown orchards of Samchi, where today only rhesus monkeys roam; the youths hanging around listlessly at crossroads in the townships of Jalpaiguri District in West Bengal; or the broken spirits of torture and rape victims in the refugee camps of Jhapa.

Thimphu claims that the Nepali-speakers in the camps are actually illegal migrants—labourers from work gangs brought in to build the Bhutanese roads who stayed back, or those brought in privately to man the orange groves and cardamom plantations. The argument might be called ingenuous, were it not for the fact that the international community, and even the local politicians in the refugees' own host community of Jhapa, seem to believe it.

Bhutan has always been strict about importing labour. In the past, the Dorji administrators of southern Bhutan kept close tabs on population movements, because revenue had to be collected. In building roads and development projects (including Indian labourers to build Chukha), the government ensures that there is efficient repatriation. In 1986, Nepali road labourers who had managed to remain behind were all rounded up—5,000 individuals—and trucked out of the country. The refugee leaders say that Lhotshampa supported the action against illegal migrants.

What needles the Drukpa authorities as much as the presence of illegal migrants are the marital links that Nepali-speakers insist on making with non-Bhutanese nationals. Because Nepalis of all castes and ethnicities have a limited marriage market to choose from within Bhutan, many bring brides from outside. To counter this deviation, during the golden years of cultural harmony in the 1970s, cash incentives were introduced to encourage inter-Bhutanese (primarily Nepali–Drukpa) marriages. But the process of assimilation was obviously too slow for the impatient men who had taken over the country's running.

The best non-Bhutanese spokesperson for Thimphu's present policies is Sunanda K Datta-Ray, till recently editor of the Calcutta *Statesman*. He writes:

> The kingdom has been increasingly worried not about its own subjects of Nepalese origin, but about constant flow of illegal immigrants from Nepal, Assam, Meghalaya and parts of West Bengal. Hence the 1958 cut-off date which is so bitterly resented ... Indeed, the present agitation began only when a census was carried out in 1988 to weed out clandestine migrants.

Code and census

In support of the drive towards 'One nation, one people', a royal decree was issued in 1988 demanding strict country-wide observance of Drig Lam Namzha, a code of social etiquette specific to the Ngalung community. In one stroke, many years of building towards a united Bhutanese population was destroyed. Had it been voluntary, the package sweetened with economic incentives, it is likely that the Lhotshampa would have gradually accepted at least the outward trappings of dress, etiquette and perhaps even language. But, as the king and senior officials have conceded, local officials 'misinterpreted' the decree and vehemently implemented their version. An investigation team was dispatched to bring extra-zealous officials to book, and half-hearted punishment was meted out to a few; but the code remains in force.

As Drig Lam Namzha was implemented, tailors hiked the price of *ghos* and *kiras*—traditional Drukpa male and female garments, supposedly made from locally woven Bhutanese cloth, but actually mass-produced by factories in Ludhiana, Punjab. The heavy material is inappropriate for the south's summer heat, but was made mandatory for the home, the field, office and school. While requirements are said to have been relaxed, the dress code continues to provide ample opportunity for harassment by the police. Penalty for a going without a *gho* is a week's labour or Nu 150, of which the apprehending officer is allowed to pocket half.

In Thimphu, offices come to a standstill in the late afternoons as everyone goes to learn Drig Lam Namzha. This involves tuition in Dzongkha, and training on how to wear the *kamni* scarf, how to bow with it, how to sit, how to address others, what hairstyle to keep and so on. Just as the code was introduced, the teaching of Nepali in southern schools was dropped, in February 1989.

While Drig Lam Namzha affected the Lhotshampa's cultural identity, the census made refugees out of citizens. A deliberate and well-organised policy of intimidation was set in motion to 'encourage' the Lhotshampa to leave. Walk into any refugee camp in Nepal today, and scores of refugees carrying Bhutanese citizenship identity cards will recall intimidation that ranged from being victimised by hooligans let loose on communities to the psychological distress of proving citizenship before dour officials.

A 1958 law, the first effort to define who was a 'Bhutanese', provided for citizenship by birth, registration of land holdings and naturalisation (five years' stay). A census and land survey was carried out in 1972, which served as the basis for issuing nationality certificates. In 1980, another census was conducted, and citizenship identity cards distributed; with these, 'the government completed the huge task of identifying Bhutanese citizens and distributing identity cards,' says Shiva Kumar Pradhan of the Bhutan People's Party. 'But the 1985 Citizenship Act applied new criteria of citizenship, and made them retrospective, declaring all previous government action of granting citizenship as null and void.'

The attempts to implement the 1985 Citizenship Act through a census was not begun immediately, probably because the Gorkha National Liberation Front (GNLF) in adjacent Darjeeling district had just begun its agitation. Thimphu did not want any GNLF-inspired violence ruining its careful plans. The census was begun again in 1988, just after Subhas Ghising achieved his Hill District Council.

Amidst strident opposition from the south, the Tshongdo in November 1988 expressed satisfaction with the 1985 Act. In order to assist implementation, the authorities classified Bhutanese into seven categories, F-l to F-7. Only those who had land tax receipts for the year 1958 were given F-1 status and regarded as bonafide citizens. Other categories were denied the status, including 're-immigrants' who had worked and lived outside Bhutan, children of non-Bhutanese spouses, and so on.

F-l was therefore the category to hold, but the retroactive application of citizenship back to 1958 papers was an atavistic requirement without precedent. No other proof of citizenship is accepted, including what had earlier been acceptable: the *sathram* (land registration) number, house registration number, payment of taxes, and the *goongdawoola* labour contribution.

Under the census-cum-identification exercise, Lhotshampa who had been trained abroad by the Thimphu government, who had worked for decades in the army or police, who had been Bhutanese teachers for all their working lives, who had 'non-national fathers', all were made illegal immigrants at the stroke of a pen. Citizenship cards issued in 1985 with the seal and signature of King Jigme were valueless.

Until January 1992, a No Objection Certificate (NOC) was required for all Nepali-speaking individuals who sought employment, admission in schools, trade licences, or even permission to leave the country on official work. Any whiff of an involvement in 'anti-national' activities, even by distant relatives, meant that a NOC was unavailable. The NOC requirement has now been lifted, but the point is moot as F-l status-holders are also being evicted. If there is a ngolop in the family, the whole family has to leave, if not the neighbours and the whole community. The definition of 'ngolop' varies, and can be applied loosely to all Nepali-speakers that have left the country. To some Drukpa, all southerners have become ngolops.

The confidential bilateral agency report quoted earlier says, 'Individuals are held responsible for the deeds of family members. Furthermore, there are no clear guidelines for the term "family members", and many have been forced to apply for emigration by signing the voluntary leaving certificates. Many of these families would be early settlers (1890–1930), who fall well within the 1958 census criterion.'

Recent arrivals in Jhapa say eviction is across the board, and need no longer depend on the 1985 Act criteria. Villages are being emptied regardless of whether the inhabitants have citizenship papers, 1958 land-tax documents or records of service in the bureaucracy, army or constabulary. Lately, even those who helped dungpas and dzongdas as informers (*chamches*) to identify so-called illegals, or served extra-zealously as soldiers or prison guards, are arriving as refugees. A number of refugees have identified Lhotshampa policemen who they say had tortured them in Bhutan. 'If you would turn against your own kind, what would you do to us?' the Drukpa administrators reportedly tell the *chamches* when dismissing them.

Thakur Prasad Luitel, of Danabari Block in Geylegphug, 52-years-old and born in Bhutan of a father who moved from Sikkim, says the 1988 census gave him F-1 status. He spent nine months and 12 days in Phuentsholing and Thimphu jails, during which time he says he suffered extreme mental and physical torture. Meanwhile, his teenage daughter died at home for lack of specialised care. 'When they released me I thought my punishment was over, but then the Geylegphug Dungpa called us and said we must all get out.' Luitel says the Lhotshampa prison guard who tortured him in prison has been sighted in one of the refugee camps.

The departure is carefully choreographed. Villagers of Samchi describe the dungpa and other officials sitting before voluminous records. A Lhotshampa is led in to try to prove his 1958 status, and there are any number of ways in which he can be 'found out'—for example, of having hidden a marriage with a non-Bhutanese, or having been silent about a working stint in India, and so on.

When families are declared 'illegal', they are forced to sign a 'Voluntary Leaving Certificate', which states that they are leaving of their own free will, accepting the compensation that is provided. Each family is then asked to have a black-and-white group photograph taken, and to bring in eight copies for the files before they depart. Refugees also speak of tape-recordings or video-recordings in which officials exact verbal confirmation that the departure is voluntary.

'Travel expenses' are paid out of the 'compensation' for the properties Lhotshampa leave behind. In Samchi, the 'compensation' was initially set at Nu 40,000 per acre of paddy field, but this figure was continuously scaled downwards until families got no more than Nu 4,000 per acre. In Chirang, some villagers who had been put behind bars had Nu 2,000 per month of prison stay deducted from the 'compensation' they received. A few families managed to steal away without accepting compensation or signing the government's forms, while others collected as much documentary evidence of their house and lands as they could to prove at some later date that the property was theirs.

Dal Bahadur Rai is an Indian national who works as a guard in a tea estate in Jalpaiguri district, just astride the open border. His Bhutanese neighbours are the villagers of Ahaley and Chargharey, in Ghumauney block, Samchi district. Rai says: 'In Ghumauney block, there were 684 households. Today, there are only four. They are of the mandal [headman], whose name is Komagain, Dataram Rijal, Bhakley Giri and Chandru Magar. When the rate for paddy fields was 32,000 rupees per acre, the Dahals of Ahaley sold 10 acres and made good profit. But then the rate came down and now the government gives only 3,000. Rather than take the money and give up their land forever, people like Parsuram Kafle and Sete Sanyasi sneaked away before the Dungpa could force them.'

Across from Rai's property in Jalpaiguri, the fields are empty and the villages silent. The next step is said to be the announced programme of re-settlement of northern Drukpa in the vacated lands of the south. According to the secretary of Bhutan's Department of Survey and Land Records, more than 47,000 acres of illegal land have been freed in Samchi alone; the Tshongdu, for its part, has resolved that 'illegal land holdings in the southern Districts should be allotted first to security force personnel and the Militia Volunteers.' The chief operations officer of the Royal Bhutan Army has expressed 'deep appreciation for the proposal'.

'The government's idea of a permanent solution for Bhutan's problem seems to be that of a more mixed population in the southern districts,' says the bilateral development-agency report quoted above. It adds that currently preparations are underway for the first such resettlement, in Samdrup Jonkhar district.

Thimphu high society

Drukpa society is made up of a small, educated super-elite of perhaps no more than 1,000 individuals (mostly male, even though the traditional society is matriarchal), in addition to a large peasantry. The former are all in bureaucracy or in business, with their interests intimately tied with those of the state. There is no peer support for non-conformists who might question the basis for policies of state, such as the hard-line crackdown against the Lhotshampa.

According to Rose, there is a 'virtual non-existence of competing elite groups' in Thimphu, which means that there are no dissident members from among either the traditional elite or the modernised bureaucracy. To the extent that Bhutan has 'no non-official educated elites of any size or significance,' Thimphu is an intellectual backwater. There is no one to challenge programmes designed and implemented by the administrators of the country or the conservative monastic order. The Lhotshampa civil servants who have dared to ask questions are all in exile or prison. Those that remain are increasingly marginalised, but remain silent.

Om Bahadur Pradhan, minister for trade and industry and the government's highest-ranking Lhotshampa, is son of Nyaulibabu (introduced earlier), one-time commissioner of Samdrup Jonkhar. He has served as permanent representative to the United Nations in New York. Pradhan is a student of Drukpa Kagyu philosophy, speaks fluent Dzongkha and is married to a Sarchop. Some refugees who know him well consider him 'more Drukpa than the Drukpa'. A former colleague of Pradhan is angry that he does not use his access to the king: 'Why does he not speak? He knows his father settled Nepalis in eastern Bhutan upon the express request of the Bhutanese government.'

Says Bhakti Prasad Sharma, an activist who was recently released, 'Om Pradhan is in a fix. He is disillusioned, but he is neither here nor there.' However, Pradhan did recently arrange for a group of Nepalis to approach the king with a petition detailing discriminatory treatment; and at the autumn 1991 session of the National Assembly, he did remind members that 'not all Lhotshampas were ngolops'.

The reticence of the Bhutanese civil servant is not a new phenomenon. It has been evident for decades among Bhutanese diplomats at the United Nations and at international conferences, and more recently at SAARC parleys. Today, this unwillingness to speak up has become a great asset, as inconvenient questions are never answered. The bureaucrat's extreme caution on political matters is also born of economic self-interest. The first-class gazetted officer and higher ranks have perks that beat all Southasian counterparts, including the facility to buy a new vehicle every five years, easy access to the Royal Bhutan Insurance Corporation's beneficence of low-interest loans, and duty-free liquor privileges.

Much of the real estate in Bhutanese towns is bureaucrat-owned. Pradhan is said to have four mansions besides the one he lives in, and Dawa Tshering is the second-largest real-estate tycoon in Thimphu. Tshering, who has the distinction of being the world's longest-serving foreign minister, has emerged as the spokesperson of the government's policies, even though it is said he was not part of the original coterie that planned the exercise. The *lynpo* apparently got wedded to it after his daughter married into the new royal family. Lynpo Tshering is the son of a Kalimpong Chinese and was brought up in a Nepali household there. He has a Bachelor of Laws degree and was a hostel superintendent in Kalimpong before he landed it big in Bhutan under the tutelage of late Prime Minister Dorji.

There might be little 'intellectual culture' in Thimphu, but there is plenty of high society to reap the largesse of the foreign donors and tourism, and economic policies that are increasingly tailored to suit the needs of a few. The jet-setting Drukpa are within striking distance of an exclusive Western standard of living. Druk Air's BAe 146 jet allows them instant access to New Delhi and Bangkok. The Bhutanese highways, built and maintained courtesy of the Indian Border Roads Organisation (known locally as 'Dantak'), carry Toyota Land Cruisers and air-conditioned sedans with ease. Plebeians and Indian traders drive Maruti Gypsies.

High society is almost totally Westernized. The dasho who gives a speech on cultural purity will enter the toilet cubicle of the Druk Air jet out of Paro Airport as soon as the seatbelt sign is off—to struggle out of his *gho* and emerge transformed in jacket and tie. At the border town of Phuentsholing, next to the bus stop, men and women change from traditional to Western attire, or vice-versa, jettisoning their Drukpa identity with apparent ease. In Thimphu, under cover of night, the children of the elites drive to celebrate the National Day with all-night jam sessions, in jeans and skirts.

It is a lifestyle in a dreamland that, goaded by Western and Indian plaudits, is increasingly divorced from Southasia. Thimphu's ruling class rarely visit the south, except to reach the Indian border. There is little empathy in Thimphu circles for the Lhotshampa peasantry that populates the south, and whose best and brightest actually work amongst them. As a *Kuensel* reporter admitted, it was only the lulling of a Ngalung Dungpa at Geylegphug in mid-May that 'brings to the Bhutanese people the real gravity of the disturbed situation in the kingdom,' whereas before 'reports of terrorism in remote villages were vague in their anonymity and distance.'

In Thimphu, self-righteous indignation tends to greet Lhotshampa demands for equal treatment. 'Especially in the period from October to December 1991'—around the very conservative National Assembly—'mutual distrust [between the northern and southern Bhutanese] was at a peak, with Drukpas very tense and defensive,' says one development agency report to headquarters.

A Drukpa official passing through Kathmandu in May clearly encapsulated the view from Thimphu when he said: 'You must not believe this talk of Thimphu's closed culture. Actually, the people in Thimphu are by nature open. The young intellectual group is sharp and will act. There is no racism as such, but a feeling that this thing should be allowed to take its course. A minister like Dago Tshering might seem to be hardline to outsiders, but he is articulating the threatened feelings of the Drukpa elites and commoners alike.' He continued: 'Democracy will probably come when the society is ready for it. Meanwhile, let us not bullshit the farmer. The main thing is to educate the population, which is why there is so much emphasis on education in the national budget. The southern problem has emerged not as an initiative of the government but as a response to the anti-king activities. Those that call themselves refugees are not leaving because of brutality. Their departure was voluntary.'

Ngalung individuals such as the official quoted above, when asked about their society, will emphasise its egalitarian aspects, the absence of caste and the links each family has with the home village. But it does appear that the class structure is becoming rigid to exclude not only the Lhotshampa, but also a majority of the high-mountain peasantry, which remains remote from Thimphu's bustle. Inter-marriages and enmeshing of interests among the elite families—the Wangchuks, the Dorjis or the newly ascendant family of the queens—results in a 'See no evil, hear no evil' mentality.

Opposition in absentia

So who are the ngolops? Going by government pronouncements, the most dangerous one would be Tek Nath Rizal, who was the first Lhotshampa leader to be harassed into exile. Abducted and brought back to Thimphu, he was long the seniormost ngolop in prison. Rizal was a civil servant who had impressed the king with his straight talk and dedication, and had risen to become a member of the Royal Advisory Council. In April 1988, when alarming reports arrived from Chirang of discriminatory implementation of the census, Rizal and another councillor from the south took the help of Thimphu's Lhotshampa civil servants in drafting a petition, and submitted it to King Jigme.

'The people of southern Bhutan most humbly beg Your Majesty for protection and relief,' the petition stated, asking that he disallow the retrospective effect of the 1985 Citizenship Act. The petition recalled that the review of the 1977 Citizenship Act had been done at the initiative of the southern Bhutanese, who fully shared the concern about possible settlement of illegal immigrants. '[T]o view the people with suspicion and to blame them for allegedly colluding with the immigrants to sneak them into the country is unfair and unjust.'

Rizal's action was considered treasonous; he was imprisoned for three days and his councillorship terminated. In the face of increasing harassment, he left the country at the end of 1989 with two associates and ended up in Birtamod, a junction town in Jhapa district of Nepal. There, they set up the People's Forum for Human Rights (PFHR), 'to fight for political equality in Bhutan and to inform the world about the happenings within.'

With the assistance of Ratan Gazmere, then a lecturer at the National Institute of Education in Samchi, a booklet, 'Bhutan: We want justice', was produced by the exiles. Rizal and his two companions were abducted from Birtamod by Nepali police and taken to Kathmandu. Waiting on the tarmac was a Druk Air jet with V Namgyal, King Jigme's aide-de-camp and chief of the Royal Bodyguards. They were handcuffed and taken to Thimphu. Soon after the abduction, thinking perhaps the leaderless Lhotshampa would not react, the government legislated the wearing of the *gho* and the *kira* 'for all Bhutanese at all times'.

Thereafter, the first refugees began to leave Bhutan. They were housed with the help of West Bengal's ruling party, the Communist Party of India (Marxist), at Garganda, a tea-estate community in Jalpaiguri, where large sheds belonging to tea companies were made available. In early 1990, the PFHR and the Students Union of Bhutan combined forces to establish the Bhutan People's Party (BPP) in Garganda.

Later, the refugee camps in India were dismantled and refugees who did not have relatives and friends in India moved west into Nepal, where they began to populate the banks of the Mai Khola in Jhapa. The BPP, meanwhile, established an office in Kathmandu and began a media campaign. But the Kathmandu media's reach was short, and the BPP ended up preaching to the converted. As the Bhutanese programme of depopulation progressed, not only the southern peasantry but also the high-level Lhotshampa civil servants in Thimphu started to feel the heat. Ten civil servants fled in April 1991, and others followed. The arrival of these senior bureaucrats, some of whom had helped to draft Rizal's original petition to the king, provided a degree of political articulation not previously present. Unexpectedly, however, their presence sparked infighting and rivalry among the ranks of the refugees.

The politico-bureaucrats who entered the scene first tried to carve a niche for themselves within the BPP. But they claim to have found a party that was ill-organised, lacking realistic programmes and a constitution or ideology. Above all, they criticise BPP leaders for harbouring idealistic visions of a 'free Bhutan' without searching for realistic ways by which to push forward the agenda of return. Unable to make headway with the BPP, some civil servants joined the Human Rights Organisation of Bhutan (HUROB), which, as PFHR's successor, was involved in managing the refugee camps. Others decided to form the Bhutan National Democratic Party (BNDP), as a 'democratic alternative' to the BPP. The new party was launched in the fall of 1991 in New Delhi, signifying a shift in lobbying focus.

Rightly or wrongly, the BPP is identified with the left, while the BNDP sells itself as the moderate party to which the Thimphu government will have to turn for negotiations when the time comes. King Jigme did tell Reuters that the southern problem could be solved through 'honest, sincere and genuine dialogue', but that 'dialogue had been difficult with the BPP ... because they had no clear leader.' For their part, the BPP stalwarts regard the BNDP as a party of well-to-do interlopers out to wrest away a movement that they have nurtured from the start. One European journalist, who has sympathies with the BPP, says the BNDP membership is made up of 'armchair activists' who 'tried to get the movement under their control, confused everyone, tried to divide the movement, but did not succeed.'

Pratap Subba, who presently works for HUROB as an organiser at Pathari camp, says that he left the BPP due to differences in ideology and strategy. 'The public should be the last weapon to use,' he says. 'Instead, they gave the call for mass rallies against the government with no back-up support. There was no media coverage, and a lot of false talk to mislead the people.' The BPP, says Subba, 'spends more energy fighting the other refugee organisations—SUB, HUROB and BNDP—than for the cause of return.'

S K Pradhan, BPP general-secretary, accuses the BNDP of dealing a fatal blow to opposition unity, and sowing 'absolute confusion' among the refugees. 'They want security and a comfortable stay in Kathmandu, whereas our people are on the ground, organising in the Duars, the Hill Council areas, and even within Bhutan.' Pradhan says the BPP plans to restart agitations 'within 1992', but will not divulge details as to what form they will take.

Try as they might to give a non-ethnic colour to their politics, the parties in exile have failed to enlist a single prominent dissident, either Ngalung or Sarchop, in their struggle. BPP's Pradhan claims some Drukpa membership, but they are not visible. The BNDP stated at its founding that it expected 'to dilute the allegation of ethnic-led struggle,' but the few Sarchop in exile have not yet come on board. BNDP's General-Secretary Dhakal remains hopeful that the distinct political choices presented by two parties will allow 'liberal thinkers from the Sarchops and Ngatungs to take a political stand on the crisis in Bhutan.'

What Bhutanese politics in exile lacks, clearly, is a figure to rally behind. 'Because we lack a leader, there is a dilemma in the camps,' concedes Subba. Such a figure exists in Tek Nath Rizal, but does Rizal have what it takes to lead the refugees back to Bhutan? A refugee teacher who knew Rizal since childhood says, 'He has charisma and obvious honesty. He has the ability to bring unity among the refugees. But I do not think he had the theoretical grasp to put forward the design of the new Bhutan after we go back.'

So, the BNDP and BPP are not on talking terms, neither in Kathmandu drawing rooms nor in the Jhapa camps. Regardless of their different approaches, however, neither has yet succeeded in breaking the impregnable diplomatic and media barricade that Thimphu's master diplomats have erected around themselves. 'So far, exile politics has reflected our upbringing in Bhutan. In the beginning, we had no political culture, knew nothing about forming a party, or about ideology. So we have been learning,' says Bhampa Rai of HUROB. He is concerned that, sooner or later, the refugees will become pawns in the party politics of Nepal. 'Nepali politicians must look at us refugees—not as leftists or democrats, but as Bhutanese,' he says. 'When we go back, then of course we will divide along where our ideologies lie.'

Ratan Gazmere is despondent about the state of exile politics. 'The PFHR we started was to have a non-partisan organisation fighting for human rights,' he says. 'Coming out, we find that refugee politics is steeped in power struggle. Those of us who have just come out see it as our prime responsibility to bring people together, to have unity, and to internationalise the issue.'

Bhakti Prasad Sharma, who was released in December along with Gazmere, says, 'The movement is in shambles. There is no united front because an element of ego has crept in.' The five erstwhile prisoners, he says, were 'very concerned and are talking to each other. The coming months are critical, and the priority should be to return with dignity. We can fight for reforms in Bhutan, but only after we go back. Human rights and democracy cannot go together—one has to precede the other.'

In bringing up these two issues, Sharma has put his finger on the principle issues up for discussion. The political crisis in southern Bhutan, coming as it did soon after Nepal's successful 'people's movement' for human rights and democracy of April 1990, suddenly thrust political novices forward as refugee leaders. These leaders picked up the terminology presented to them by the Kathmandu tabloids. The Bhutanese problem too became, simplistically, a movement for human rights and democracy. Whether this was realistic, however, was a different matter.

BNDP's R B Basnet, one of the senior bureaucrats who came out of Bhutan in 1991, has no doubts. 'Political reforms are necessary to guarantee human rights,' he says. 'It is not possible to have respect for human rights in the absence of democratic institutions.' This might be true, but the word *democracy* is as much anathema to Thimphu's aristocracy as it was to the ruling Rana clan of Nepal during the 1940s. It is unlikely that the Druk Gyalpo would be as amenable to opposition demands for democracy as Nepal's *Sri Panch* was in the spring of 1990.

The pages of *Kuensel* amply demonstrate how remote the Thimphu rulers are from accepting the 'one person, one vote' principle. In October last year, Foreign Minister Tshering asked the Tshongdu not to be confused with the anti-national's campaigns against dress, language, custom and religion. They had 'a much more deep-seated, long term objective', which was 'the introduction of multi-party democracy'.

Once democracy was introduced, warned Lynpo Tshering, the Lhotshampa would be in a position to form the government in Thimphu and take over the country. The combination of 'ethnic demands'—for constitutional monarchy, multiparty system and proportional ethnic representation in the National Assembly and the Cabinet—he said, would be 'a highly lethal one for the Bhutanese monarchy'.

King Jigme says that he does—ultimately, when he thinks the time is right—want to relinquish the heavy burden of monarchy. In nearly a dozen interviews over the last two years, he has said in almost identical words, 'I do not think that monarchy is the best form of government. I would not oppose democracy as long as I am fully confident that the political changes are for the greater good of our people.' Between a king who says he wants democracy—but not now—and a foreign minister who says 'never' to a multi-party democracy, there is very little room for negotiation by the parties in exile.

Militancy

The militancy in southern Bhutan, some of which took place with the apparent acquiescence of the BPP, was just the thing Thimphu needed to blow the issue out of proportion. While a few of the militants who infiltrate the border areas might have links with the BPP, others seem to have been acting independently. 'These could be unaffiliated youth who are seeking revenge for evictions, lootings and torture and rape of family members,' says Om Dhungel, a civil servant who recently came into exile.

Some of this low-intensity militancy appears to be occurring still, providing Thimphu authorities with further public relations advantage. Both the BPP and BNDP claim, however, that the *Kuensel* has gone overboard in blaming every robbery, murder and accident that occurs in Bhutan these days on the ngolops. Indeed, it seems that Bhutan no longer has crimes other than those committed by 'anti-nationals'.

'If these are infiltrators, would it not be more likely that their victims would be Drukpa? How is it that most of the crimes are against defenceless Nepali peasants?' asks BNDP's Basnet. He believes that much of the mayhem is the work of undisciplined units of the Royal Bhutan Army and the police. Many refugees in the camps maintain that the Bodo (known to them as Meche), as well as Nepali and Bengali *goonda* hooligans from India, are taking advantage of the lawless situation created by the government. Many recount reports of dungpas and chamches threatening 'to let loose the Meches' on Lhotshampa who refuse to leave.

'The use of violence by infiltrators and the burning of schoolhouses was a massive blunder,' says a Western ambassador who is accredited concurrently to New Delhi and Thimphu, and believes that Lhotshampa militants have been active in the south. 'The government might have exaggerated the threat, but we are not in a position to judge how much.'

What is intriguing about the militancy, actually, is how little of it there is considering the areas that Bhutan borders. Adjacent lies the extreme leftist hotbed of northern West Bengal; the Bodo insurgency hugs the southern jungles; and the radicalised cadres of the Gorkha National Liberation Front (GNLF) are a stone's throw away in the Kalimpong sub-division of Darjeeling district. Besides, the Duars are populated by sympathetic Nepali-speakers who could provide all the cover and protection militants might need.

In January this year, Dawa Tshering told the press in Dhaka that 'radical groups like communists, leftists and Naxalites in India and Nepal were patronis-ing terrorists against Bhutan.' This is not the picture one gets as the refugees continue to file out meekly as a government asks them to leave their land. Lynpo Tshering likes to recall the image of 'the martial Gorkhas', but the specimens arriving at the camps by the hundreds each day in cramped truckloads are members of a poor, confused peasantry that has no energy left to fight.

Nepali Police Sub-Inspector Horn Jung Chauhan has been manning the eastern Karakbhitta border checkpost since the refugees started to arrive in late 1990s. 'You cannot expect any militancy from this lot,' he says. 'These villagers come with long khukuris [knives] slung down their sides, but their *sahaas* [strength] is gone. Sometimes I ask them in exasperation, why this timidity?'

Lhotshampa militancy clearly is long on rhetoric and short on action. The 1988 pamphlet 'Bhutan: We want justice', produced by the PFHR group in Birtamod, was hardly timid when it warned that 'a whirlwind of rebellion will shake the hills of Thimphu and bring down the rising towers of terrorist power … We shall hold on to our religion, our culture, our language and our land with our "TEETH". We shall fight until we win.'

This bluster was also present in loose talk by BPP cadres of 'revolution', and the impression created of a well-organised military operation. 'We do not even have money to eat—where would we buy the guns and ammunition?' asks one member. Being a loosely run organisation, it is possible that the party has its share of 'wild cards', but BPP General-Secretary Pradhan forcefully denies that his organisation has ever espoused militant violence.

Such protestations have little effect against the proven ability of the Thimphu propagandists to reach the media with the proper 'spin'. Lynpo Tshering told *The Statesman* that sophisticated weapons were being brought 'all the way from Afghanistan and Peshawar for use by the BPP terrorists against us.' A person who was at Garganda when it still housed large numbers of refugees says that at one time he did see 100 or so guns, 'but practically all of them were antique muzzleloaders'.

Even the little Lhotshampa militancy that is occurring might peter out as the BPP, too, takes the high road of diplomacy, and as news spreads of free rations in the refugee camps in Nepal, courtesy the UN's refugee agency. But there is every likelihood that militancy bred of frustration will ignite, and much more dangerously, if a negotiated return of the refugee population looks remote.

Blind developers

Aid agencies love Bhutan because, here in the eastern Himalaya, at last, they have found the one country that might yet prove that the 'development' they propagate can work. Here is a land that is exotic, backward, under populated but with ample resources, with a benevolent monarch and a Westernised bureaucratic elite.

UN agencies, bilateral donors and international NGOs regard Bhutan as a laboratory to prove their legitimacy, and the brochures they bring out are tinged with wonder. In February 1992, the UN Development Programme's chief, William Draper, waxed lyrical about Bhutan leading in 'sustainable development' and providing a model for others, quite unmindful of the fact that the factors that come together for Bhutan (history, climate, green cover, population and geography) do not do so for most developing countries. One Western ambassador who was recently in Bhutan conceded that, 'The aid agencies have great sympathy for the Drukpa point of view, not because what they are doing is right, but because their culture is threatened.'

Bureaucratic efficiency and the buzz-phrase *absorptive capacity* does make Bhutan unique and attractive for development planners. In addition, Bhutan's well-paid bureaucracy is practically incorruptible in comparison to those of the rest of Southasia.

In the absence of resident embassies in Thimphu and the extremely controlled access to malleable media, the aid agencies are the world's ears and eyes to Bhutan. Unfortunately, they are as good as deaf and blind. Too busy praising the activities of the government, their influence on events in the south has been near zero. An aid worker, who requested anonymity for fear of losing future contracts with an aid agency, accuses the Thimphu-based international staff of United Nations Development Programme (UNDP), the World Food Programme, United Nations Children's Fund (UNICEF) and the World Health Organisation of complacency. 'If someone in the staff drafts a report on the southern problem, it is invariably diluted before it is transmitted to headquarters. I cannot fathom why development agencies, whose mandates are humanitarian, continue to act like ostriches,' she says.

Although NGOs and volunteer workers tend to be more concerned than the international civil servants of the UN, they do not speak up for fear that an irate government would terminate their programmes. The Netherlands, the United Kingdom, Australia, Switzerland, Germany and Canada all have development volunteers active in Bhutan. The international NGOs are Helvetas of Switzerland and Save the Children US and UK, while there are also several bilateral development agencies, such as DANIDA of Denmark, GTZ of Germany and FINNIDA of Finland.

The inaction out of Thimphu contrasts sharply with the development agencies in Kathmandu, which are directly and indirectly supporting the refugee efforts in Jhapa. With its commanding presence in Bhutan as the lead agency, the inaction of the UNDP office in Thimphu is curious. According to Lhotshampa counterparts as well as officials of some aid agencies in Thimphu, the current UNDP resident coordinator, Terry Jones, a Briton, has failed to be

assertive with the government. Even though he arrived in 1990 after the problems had begun, Jones has had ample opportunity to understand the nature of
the events in the south, especially when his own Bhutanese staff members leave
house and hearth to end up in the bamboo thatches of Jhapa. If there is any
back-door lobbying being done in Thimphu or at UNDP's New York headquarters, the results are not obvious.

Like Jones, practically every expatriate in Thimphu has his or her own
experience with Lhotshampa colleagues and counterparts who have been
relieved of jobs, sidelined or harassed into exile. Conversation in Thimphu
at expatriate gatherings tends to centre on the southern problem, with about
equal numbers supporting or questioning the government policies in the south.
Many of those who are disillusioned vent their frustrations when they come to
Kathmandu.

Although UNDP's efforts, if any, are still sotto voce, it did publish in 1985
a booklet entitled *The Case of Bhutan*, which identified potential problems. The
booklet, prepared by the Danish United Nations Association, speaks of 'the
danger of growing regional inequality' and calls for 'development planning in
favour of the more densely populated and poorer Southern and Eastern parts
of Bhutan … Regional differences that are connected with linguistic, ethnic
and religious differences in Bhutan might otherwise develop into a challenge to
national unity and social harmony.'

One outcome of driving out the Lhotshampa is already evident: there
is a shortage of mid-level professionals to man government services and development programmes. The projection is for an acute shortage of labour,
especially as the implementation of the major infrastructural works under the
Seventh Five Year Plan gets underway. Already, the hospitals in Thimphu are
understaffed. A plan to induct Indian workers under contract might work in
the short term, but even Drukpa administrators have been known to concede
that highlander Nepalis make better labourers in Bhutan.

One aid agency reports that the departure of a number of government
staff ('counterparts, colleagues') has affected development work in the country.
The Bhutan People's Party claims in a pamphlet that 'already 3000 civil servants
including professionals, skilled and technical manpower such as doctors,
engineers, teachers, nurses, agriculture and forestry personnel have been forced
to leave the civil service.' The party demands that international volunteers be
withdrawn as they are being used to substitute for evicted Lhotshampa.

Before the Aid Bhutan Roundtable was to meet in Geneva on 8 March
to make pledges for the Seventh Plan development projects, Foreign Minister

Tshering suggested that the southern problem not be brought up in Geneva as there would be little time and the 'technical delegation' would not be able to answer questions. Tshering asked instead that the Delhi-based representatives of the donor countries and agencies meet prior to the Roundtable to hear a report on the southern situation.

This was a master stroke, for it meant that already-sensitised Delhi-based diplomats would be present, rather than the more senior delegation in Geneva. (Even ambassadors of the same country but based in Kathmandu and New Delhi tend to have differing perceptions on Bhutan. The Delhi view generally prevails.) At the pre-Geneva meeting in Delhi, when Tshering was asked about the south, recalls a diplomat who was present, 'he replied that the problem was not very acute. He was very open in his answer, and we all went away satisfied.' In Geneva, according to a refugee who has read the Bhutanese delegation's report to the government, Switzerland and Germany did raise the matter of human-rights violations, but this apparently made no impact on the actual pledging.

Thus, at the very time that the Lhotshampa exodus was at its peak and the death rate from a meningitis epidemic was at its highest in the refugee camps, Bhutan was presented the largest aid package it has ever received. Even Lynpo Dawa Tshering expressed surprise at the windfall: 'We did not expect so much pledging.' And the lesson he drew from it, as reported by the *Telegraph*, was that 'Bhutan's image remained untarnished in the international community despite the attempts of Nepali-speaking agitators to project the Royal Government in a poor light.'

Otherwise, too, development programmes have been stepped up by the donors. New countries are offering development assistance, while others increase their commitments. GTZ is going ahead with new plans, much to the unhappiness of some Nepal-based German volunteers. According to one expatriate development worker in Bhutan, the Dutch and the Danes have significantly raised their development assistance over the past year. The Asian Development Bank has also upped its disbursements slightly, while the World Bank has started new programmes.

To give the donor governments some credit—particularly Austria, Denmark and Japan—they did shoot down the Thimphu government's funding proposal for a 'green belt' a couple of years ago. The plan was to evacuate a one-kilometre swath of forest right along the southern border with India. The plan was sold as an environmental project, but the donors got wise to the fact that the maximum concentration of Lhotshampa population is in the proposed stretch.

Nepal's problem

The refugees who come down to the roadheads in the Assam Duars and Jalpaiguri are told to turn right and to head for Nepal. For a cut, agents arrange for further passage and the families make their payment of INR 4,500 to INR 4800 per truck, inclusive of bribes to police and officials all the way to Jhapa. It is a day-long journey across fields, forest and tea plantations to the Mechi River, across the border, and to the junction town of Birtamod in Jhapa. The trucks unload their human cargo and promptly head back to Daadghari in Assam for another load.

The problem is now Nepal's—a country that most Lhotshampa regard as the original home country, but a place most have never visited and where few retain familial links. The Lhotshampa make up the largest refugee population ever to come into Nepal. For Nepal's insular elites, who have never had to confront problems of identity in the way that most Nepali-speakers outside Nepal have had to do, the Bhutanese influx has been unsettling. Here are thousands upon thousands of individuals that clearly look and speak like Nepali peasants (except for some distinctive Drukpa mannerisms and speech), but who do not regard themselves as Nepali citizens. While Nepali migrants have for long been leaving for *muglan*, this is the first time that such large numbers have returned as refugees—to a mother country that is already overpopulated.

The eastern Tarai district of Jhapa is actually made up of settlers: Nepali highlanders from Taplejung and Panchthar districts, as well as Burmese refugees who arrived in the 1960s, when General Ne Win implemented his own *bhumiputra* ('son of the soil') programme. There are already about 65,000 Lhotshampa refugees living in the Jhapa camps, and a few thousands more living outside in Nepal and in India. With assistance now available from the United Nations High Commissioner for Refugees (UNHCR), more refugees who have been staying in India are expected to arrive at the camps. If the present rate of evictions in Bhutan continues, says UNHCR, there could be between 100,000 and 130,000 refugees out of Bhutan by year-end.

Acting host to a refugee population in the most politically volatile corner of the country, Kathmandu sees it in its interest to send back the refugees as quickly as possible. Thimphu, on the other hand, seems to be banking on the hope that the longer the refugees stay away, the greater the chances that they will assimilate into Nepal's (and India's) larger population—and stay away.

Other than going to war across 100 kilometres of Indian territory, withdrawing landing rights to Druk Air at the Tribhuvan International Airport in Kathmandu, or refusing entry to Drukpa (mostly Sarchop) pilgrims to the holy places of the Kathmandu Valley, there is little that Nepal can do to directly influence Bhutanese policy. If India is not going to offer assistance, the only option available for Kathmandu is to try and blemish Bhutan's 'Shangri La' image with an international campaign. Yet even this it has been unwilling to do, for fear of ruffling India's feathers.

And so, for a year, Nepal tried Prime Minister Girija Prasad Koirala's 'Quiet Diplomacy'. Through this period, several attempts were made to discuss the matter with King Jigme and his foreign minister. Thimphu's tactic has been to sound conciliatory and ready to act, but then to let the matter languish. Even a month's inaction means another few thousand more Lhotshampa are out. Every window of opportunity must be utilised as Nepal dithers on going public.

There is, of course, no question of where the Nepali government's sympathies lie. Prime Minister Koirala has revealed that he was personally involved in the establishment of the Bhutan State Congress, which led a short-lived agitation for Nepali-speakers' rights during the early 1950s. Nepal's quiet diplomacy has involved Prime Minister Koirala and Foreign Ministry emissaries talking to their counterparts in Thimphu and Delhi. At the SAARC summit in Colombo, Koirala broached the subject with King Jigme, who was most reassuring and said the problem should be solved 'through contact'. As soon as Koirala arrived in Kathmandu, he sent off a letter stating that, as of 31 December 1991, the refugees numbered 6,000, and urged action. There was no response till March, by which time the number in the refugee camps had swelled to 25,000.

On 29 March 1992, the Nepali Foreign Secretary Narendra Bikram Shah was dispatched with a letter to King Jigme. He came back with a reply that the king would himself send an envoy, T Topgyel, who arrived the following week. By that time another 5,000 Lhotshampa had arrived, bringing the refugee figure up to 30,000. Thimphu's argument through all of this has been that the refugees come from elsewhere, not Bhutan. In response, Nepal has suggested that a joint commission be set up to investigate the authenticity of refugee nationality, with UNHCR's and India's help if Thimphu thought it necessary. Says a Nepali Foreign Ministry official, 'The basic proposal is bilateral. It can be expanded to include any other party, including India, if Bhutan so desires.'

Since Thimphu again chose to prevaricate on the proposal sent back through T Topgyel, the Nepali officials who went to the Earth Summit in Rio de Janeiro in early June had the intention of confronting the Bhutanese delegation. But the latter stalled, with the king's sister, Ashi Sonam Chheden, refusing even an informal cup of tea in between sessions. (One Bhutanese diplomat did accuse a Nepali official of being parochial, however.) In Rio itself, Koirala brought the matter of Bhutan up with Indian Prime Minister P V Narasimha

Rao, who contacted the Bhutanese king and relayed back to Koirala the response: that the king and Koirala were in close communication, and that they would solve the problem between themselves.

(When Nepali officials at one meeting referred to the presence of thousands of Bhutanese in the camps with citizenship identity cards, the Thimphu counterparts said their printers in Calcutta had proved to be crooks and were flooding the camps with fake ID cards. When the Nepalis invited the Bhutanese to discreetly bring in forgery experts to check the authenticity of samples, there was no response from Thimphu.)

In order to salvage its credibility, and with the monsoon session of Parliament coming up, Koirala's government decided finally to end the phase of quiet diplomacy. In his opening address to Parliament, King Birendra announced the government's desire to work towards a return of the Bhutanese refugees to their country 'with dignity'. An all-party meeting was held on 7 July, which agreed on a three-pronged strategy: Koirala was to continue to try to make direct contact with Thimphu; if that failed, to seek the good offices of India; and if that too failed, to internationalise the issue. Thereafter, the prime minister sent another letter to the Bhutanese monarch. A response is still awaited.

Says one Nepali official, 'If even this fails, we must remind India that Nepal is now a multi-party democracy, and this refugee problem has the potential of bringing great instability here, which is hardly in India's interest.' If India proves reluctant to use its clout in the months ahead, the official says that Nepal will reluctantly 'go international'. He says, 'Since under the Bhutan–India treaty, India is Bhutan's guide on foreign affairs, we in Nepal must respect that position and try to work through India. But if Nepal's own internal-security gets jeopardised by a hundred thousand refugees, we have to do something.'

Internationalising the issue could mean anything from quietly approaching influential Western countries, broaching the subject at the Human Rights Commission in Geneva, or bringing it up at the next SAARC Summit. Another option, which Kathmandu probably will not choose, would be to try to garner international support in order to get an item inscribed on the agenda of the UN General Assembly, when it meets in mid-September.

Western inaction

If Nepal cannot squeak for fear of India, what about the powerful Western countries that, selectively, are so keen to stand up for human rights? When human rights were trampled on in Nepal in early 1990, the international concern was enormous and decisive. Pressure was brought to bear on King Birendra: threats to cut the aid pipeline, letters from United States senators, even a warning from the World Bank. In Bhutan's case, the scale of suffering is immeasurably larger than Nepal's in 1990, and in addition there is a forced mass exodus in progress.

A senior Western diplomat in Kathmandu says that Western countries have only begun to respond to the humanitarian aspects of the Bhutanese refugees, but a policy level change has yet to occur in any of the individual capitals. 'On the merits, Bhutan would have a difficult time trying to justify its policies, but it is getting away with it,' the diplomat said. 'You have one country solving its population problem dumping refugees on another country which is not even on its borders.'

The diplomat ascribes Western inaction to several factors: 'Bhutan's isolation, the fact that it does not have diplomatic relations with many countries, the exotic aura that surrounds the country, the "Buddhist lobby" in the West, and the lack of media attention. Official visits by diplomats are strictly controlled and the Western journalists try not to be too critical because, so they say, they want to be able to get a visa when things "really get bad".'

At one time, Bhutan was keen to move out from under India's foreign policy umbrella, by inviting more resident embassies in Thimphu. That today only Bangladesh and India maintain resident embassies has become a blessing in disguise. Lack of diplomatic relations and lack of in-country representation are two main excuses for Western inaction on the southern problem.

And so, Nepal remains the only country to have broken the silence on Bhutan. Germany and the US, for all their pre-eminence in world affairs today, have less influence on Thimphu than even Norway or Switzerland. Partly this is an instance of not trying hard enough. Even without diplomatic relations, influence can be exerted through the control of UN agencies and the World Bank. The outcome could be decisive.

India's soft spot

It would be disingenuous of India to imply that the problem of overpopulated camps in Jhapa is a bilateral one between Nepal and Bhutan. The refugee population enters India before ending up in Nepal. It is also Bhutan's public claim that most of the refugees have their origins in the Indian Northeast; New Delhi has yet to accept or counter the claim. Also, interpretation of the 1949 treaty that formalised relations between India and Bhutan would indicate that India is treaty-bound to try to help sort out the problem. Article II states that 'The Government of Bhutan agrees to be guided by the advice of the Government of India in regard to its external relations.'

Neither does New Delhi seem too perturbed over the presence of refugees in India, particularly in Jalpaiguri. Nirmal Bose, a prominent politician from the district and close associate of Chief Minister Jyoti Basu, has no doubts. 'Who says there are no refugees in India?' Bose asks. 'I can tell you that there are 25,000 to 30,000 Bhutanese refugees in the Duars. And more will come—there is a serious human-rights problem. Nepal and Bhutan must sit together, and India should be associated with these discussions.'

India's support for Bhutan takes different forms. At the Geneva meeting of the Aid Bhutan Roundtable, it was after New Delhi took the lead in pledging USD 300 million that the other donor countries and agencies followed through with the additional USD 570 million. Every time King Jigme visits New Delhi, he comes back with a gift project or two. India also spends, for obvious strategic reasons, crores of rupees annually to maintain Bhutanese highways. The economic subsidies that India provides Bhutan ensure that commodities are cheaper in Bhutan, and shortages are rare. The residents of Jaigaon in Jalpaiguri regularly cross over to Phuentsholing to buy cooking gas, kerosene, sugar and other essentials. There is no rationing across the border.

Most intriguing is the question of extraterritoriality. A Bhutanese Army contingent is allowed to camp in Kalimpong to guard the Queen Mother. According to reports, in early 1992, the Queen Mother refused to renew the lease of a mansion that the liquor company Shaw Wallace was using as guesthouse. When Shaw Wallace brought up the question of tenancy rights, the Bhutanese contingent went over and had the premises vacated at gunpoint. The company has submitted a writ application in the Calcutta High Court against the Indian government for failing to provide protection.

On June 1992, a phone call from Thimphu to New Delhi was enough to activate the Indian military. An Indian Army officer and three *jawans*, all armed, entered Rumtek Monastery in Sikkim and disrupted a meeting of monks. The meeting was discussing the reincarnation of the new Karmapa to head the Kagyu order, of which the monastery has been the centre in exile since the Chinese takeover of Tibet. One of the monastic factions is known to be close to the royal family of Bhutan.

With both acts and omissions, therefore, the Indian government seems bent on keeping Thimphu happy. Why? First, it apparently has no intention of nursing another Sikkim to maturity, perhaps on account of the heavy economic burden it would entail in keeping an annexed population happy. Second, India would like to retain Bhutan as an effective buffer state on its sensitive northern border. A sedate, pliable monarchy is always preferable to a rowdy, and Nepali-dominated, democracy. Third, New Delhi is counting on Bhutan's cooperation in not providing safe haven for Bodo insurgents, who are reported to camp in the jungles of southern Bhutan.

The most important reason to want to maintain the status quo as long as feasible, however, seems to be the fear of the 'pan-Nepali' clout. While the 'Greater Nepal' bogey, as presently propagated both by Subhas Ghising of Darjeeling and Foreign Minister Dawa Tshering, is just that, New Delhi is nevertheless cautious. Says a perspicacious academic from Siliguri, 'With democracy in Bhutan, there will be one more pocket of Nepali sentiment. You already have the Nepali nation state, the district of Darjeeling, the state of Sikkim, the Duars with its concentration of Nepali-speakers—and with Bhutan you would have another Nepali-dominated nation state. Without anyone having planned it, this mix might be too volatile for New Delhi to stomach.'

B S Das, a former Indian envoy to Bhutan, warned in a 24 June article in *The Pioneer* that the dangers of 'Maha Nepal' were real: 'Bhutan's stability and the balancing structure, which its ethnicity provides, is important for India from several angles which can easily be defined but cannot be stated.' Whenever it is beneficial to stoke New Delhi's fears, Lynpo Dawa Tshering calls in the media and spins a story of illegal immigrants entering Bhutan as part of a well-planned strategy to create a 'Greater Nepal'—though the strategist is never identified.

Thimphu leaves no pebble unturned to keep Indian diplomats happy. When Indian Foreign Secretary J N Dixit and his spouse Vijaya flew into Thimphu in early June, writes Tarun Basu of *India Abroad*,

> the Bhutanese accorded him a welcome befitting a head of government [with] a ceremonial welcome complete with red carpet, siren-blaring pilot cars and a squad of crack Royal Bhutanese guards who formed a ring around him wherever he went. The State Guest House, where the Dixits stayed, was festooned with multi-coloured flags and buntings, and King Jigme Singhe Wangchuk, along with his four wives, was host to the visitors at lunch.

The *Economic Times* reported that Dixit assured his hosts that India would use its influence to stabilise the situation in its southern districts—not only by increasing policing on its border with Bhutan 'to check illegal Nepali immigration', but also to advise Kathmandu against 'doing anything to destabilise the situation in the region'.

David and Goliath

Bhutan's success in handling the media belies the fears expressed by Sunanda K Datta-Ray in a much-quoted 1990 article in *The Statesman* headlined 'The Phoney Crisis: Propaganda war against Bhutan'. Wrote Datta-Ray:

> But for all its inconsistencies, untruths and half-truths, its criminal conduct and treasonable aim, the agitation has decided advantage. With their implicit faith in the national ideal, the King and his advisers cannot match rebel stridency. Monarchies are out of political fashion today, and ethnic minorities very much in. The Bhutanese monarchy may be additionally handicapped by a conscious decision to keep the world at bay. Because of geography, compounded by the deliberate cutback on tourism, international opinion has no independent assessment to fall back on as the cry—however false—goes up of human rights in danger in yet another of the world's tucked away countries. The reality of Bhutan, serene, warm-hearted and gentle, is far less familiar even to most Indians than the raucous demonstrators … Simple trust is always a disadvantage when faced with shrill propaganda.

Datta-Ray mourned too soon. He underestimated the ability of the king and his advisers, who in retrospect hardly seem handicapped.

On the one hand there is a government that has the resources, the energy and the ability to influence world capitals. On the other is a refugee population whose voice is as feeble as its numbers are large. The refugees do not have the lobbying power of Thimphu's authorities, and the only government that would come to its aid, Nepal's, does not dare to offend India. The only media that is sympathetic, again Nepal's, has little credibility and clout worldwide, particularly on matters Bhutanese.

It is a measure of what the refugee leaders are up against that even at this late stage the question of credibility remains. Foreign diplomats in Kathmandu were still asking, in August 1992, whether it was true that most of the refugees in the camps are from Meghalaya. That Thimphu has the capability to act cruelly is considered remote.

Who is a *bhumiputra* and who is not? What makes a 'son of the soil'? If you have not invaded a territory but instead have settled unpopulated lands upon express invitation, is that enough to gain nationality? Or can you be at the mercy of later generations of rulers who decide that they have changed their minds, and they want back the territory that you developed?

Is there a chance that the Nepali-speaking refugees will assimilate and melt into the Nepali diaspora? The longer the return takes (and as hope fades), the more likely that the Nepali-speakers will be absorbed into the larger populations outside Bhutan. In the short term, however, assimilation is unlikely. Opportunities in Nepal are limited for the majority of peasant refugees. Most have lost their roots in Nepal and would not know where to go, and the Nepali economy does not hold out better prospects than would the Bhutanese economy if they were to return. There are no more forests left to clear and settle down, as was the case when the Burmese refugees came over three decades ago.

So, while a few well-to-do refugees have already bought property and a small number of professionals have gravitated towards the Indian cities and Kathmandu, where they would make do somehow in the event of no return, the bulk of the exile population will tarry in the camps, living on UNHCR rations, waiting to go home. As of this writing, it appears that a turning point on the question of the Bhutanese refugees might be reached soon. In fact, the next few months look crucial for a breakthrough. The electronic media, which is so important in these days of satellite television, has finally started showing up at the camps. With the UNHCR having certified the Lhotshampa refugee status, it will be harder for Thimphu to point the finger at 'Meghalaya, Mizoram, Arunachal…' Lynpo Tshering, when he calls in journalists for exclusive interviews, will find that the questions are harder, less fawning.

Some human-rights organisations have begun lobbying with the Human Rights Commission, and a group of eminent Southasian jurists recently issued a report that is sharply critical of Thimphu, calling for action by 'the governments and peoples of SAARC'. Even if belatedly, the refugee leaders have begun to turn their sights on New Delhi. A BPP delegation just visited the Indian capital, and the BNDP has been distributing a memorandum to Indian parliamentarians. But the going will be tough. For the refugee leaders, mostly senior to mid-level former bureaucrats and school teachers, are up against the amenable presence of King Jigme, ably supported by Dawa Tshering, a master in the art of making friends and influencing important people.

Interestingly, Thimphu itself might decide to come and sit at the negotiation table. For one thing, as the number of refugees creeps towards the 100,000 mark, it is certain that even the sleeping giants of the West will begin to sit up and take notice. One hundred thousand might also be Thimphu's secret threshold beyond which it will ease up, because that is the number of 'illegal immigrants' it claims to have discovered through its re-census programme. Also, the diplomats of Thimphu are far too astute not to know that, for the international media, it takes just a twist of the pen for the headline to change from 'The peaceful dragon' to 'The dragon breathes fire'. Exoticism is something that dissipates quickly with overuse, and ostracism must be what Thimphu's ruling elite fears most.

In February 1992, King Jigme told Reuters that he 'believed the problem would continue for at least another year but could be solved through "honest, sincere and genuine dialogue"'. If the king really thinks so, perhaps he could be persuaded not to wait till February 1993. In the refugee camps of Jhapa, there are reasonable men waiting to talk to him. Many are former officials whom he knows well. The chasm between the Drukpa and the Lhotshampa has been dug deep these past two years, but it is not unbridgeable. If the core group of Drig Lam Namzha hardliners were to be sidelined or scapegoated, the king and the refugees could probably work out an arrangement—first for a quick return, and second for a long-term formula of power-sharing in which Drukpa identity is safeguarded even as the Lhotshampa gain a satisfactory level of political freedom.

Chapter 2

Axing Chipko

Himal, January–February 1994

Manisha Aryal

The world knows it as the Chipko movement—one of the most successful environmental mass actions of the Global South, in which hill villagers fought big business. There was feminist romance in mountain women hugging trees to save them from the plainsman's axe, daring him, 'Chop me before you chop my tree.' A certain leftist nirvana of idealistic 'little folk' fighting rapacious capital also seemed to have been attained, as did the Gandhian's vision of non-violence, self-sufficiency and khadi. The overall package was good enough to bring awards to Chipko's leaders, grist for academic papers and books, and raw stock for journalists from far and wide.

Yet, the movement was much more than what has been written about it, and also much less. For a while, from the early to late 1970s, Chipko brought unprecedented energy and direction to Uttarakhand—then the Kumaun and Garhwal poor-cousin hill districts of Uttar Pradesh. Hill peasants saw possibilities of cooperative action, uniting against timber merchants and political bosses, and exploring the employment potentials in the hills. Certainly, Chipko was more than an absolutist environmental wave concerned only with trees.

Research for this article was made possible, in part, by a fellowship from the Panos Institute, London. The views expressed here are the writer's own.

However, the strengths of the movement were exaggerated, while at the same time its facets were watered down for easy consumption in Southasia, Europe and North America. Complex relationships in the mouffisil were presented by writers only as heroic standoffs between good village men/women and big, bad business/government. Soon after Chipko achieved name recognition, scholars and journalists ascended Uttarakhand—a convenient bus ride away from Delhi—and helped some Chipko leaders define their message and their image.

Historically, more than other parts of the Himalaya, the Uttarakhand hills have been oriented towards village-based activism. The villages of Kumaun and Garhwal have been resource-poor but rich in savants and sages, and have provided leadership for India at the national level. On the flip side, however, Uttarakhand continues to export menial labour to the Indian plains. Unlike the economy of neighbouring Himachal Pradesh, Uttarakhand's economy remains a lowly extension of the plains. Totalling just eight districts of Uttar Pradesh's 62 districts, there is also little political incentive for the state and central politicians and bureaucrats to try to appease the hill men and women, however demanding they may be.

For all that it might have developed into, Chipko as a definable movement was wound up too quickly, its energies sapped by excessive adulation. While study of the movement has become de rigueur in universities in India and abroad, within Uttarakhand itself Chipko is spoken of in the past tense. Before it collapsed into itself, Chipko came tantalisingly close to providing, for a corner of Southasia at least, socio-economic development through a paradigm that was self-developed.

One reason that Chipko disappeared so quickly might have been because it was so diffuse, meaning different things to different constituencies. Some of the lost momentum is obviously due to the egos of the key personalities, inflated to the bursting point and made super-sensitive by reporters, academics and urban environmentalists. No movement can sustain its spirit at the level of internecine anger and jealousy that has been present in Nainital, Almora, Chamoli, Tehri, Uttarkashi, Dehradun and Delhi.

Learn from Chipko

For whatever it was and was not, Chipko did provide a momentum and legitimacy to environmental and social activism for all of India; the real and perceived heroics of the hill people of Uttarakhand provided energy to others.

While the conditions specific to the Uttarakhand hills are obviously not to be repeated elsewhere, they find a certain kind of revival in the Appiko movement in the Western Ghats, the Narmada Bachao Andolan of Madhya Pradesh and Gujarat, and in the Chilka lake in Orissa.

Chipko has, however, singularly failed to provide a catalytic charge in other parts of the Himalaya. The forest-dwellers of the Indian Northeast, the much coddled state of Sikkim, resource-rich Himachal, violence-prone Darjeeling district and war-torn Kashmir—all of these have distinct cultural, historical, economic and political underpinnings that have given rise to different brands of protest. None, however, has been able to nurture a Chipko-like grassroots effort.

Perhaps it is in the adjacent hills of Nepal, east of Uttarakhand—where grassroots activism is most remarkable for its absence—that Chipko's legacy can be best applied. Centuries of Rana autocracy having dovetailed into three decades of an unrepresentative Panchayat regime, Nepali society's potential for grassroots activism was never tried in the modern era. With democracy's arrival in 1990, the country immediately became embroiled in party politics, all the way to the rural level. Recent years have seen the attention and energy of village-based leaders diverted and sapped by the demands of the party political machines. Rural Nepal, which contains the largest chunk of the populated and destitute midhills of the Himalayan region, still needs to learn to look away from donor organisations, international agencies, government bureaucracy and political parties, and into ways of developing from within. And Chipko, certainly, has some lessons.

The defining moment

To understand Chipko, its success and swift debilitation, one must look back to how and where it began and the personalities who were involved. In a movement that gained its momentum in part because of the sheer potency of the word 'Chipko', who uttered it first and who first hugged a tree to save it have become matters of importance. There have been arguments, and some Chipko leaders have not been above posing in front of the trunks of trees for photographers. Not everyone agrees that Chandi Prasad Bhatt, the Gandhian and social activist, was the first person to suggest the concept and use of the term 'Chipko'. Ghanashyam Raturi ('Sailani'), in a taped interview with Dehradun-based journalist Navin Nautiyal, claims that he was there first, in a song he says he wrote in December 1972 with the words *'Chipko pedo pe jangalo bachounda'*

(Stick to the trees and save the forest). The song was later to become popular in the Tehri protests.

Forest-based activism was not something that suddenly sprang up in the hills in the early 1970s. As early as 1906, when the Chandribadni forest near the town of Tehri was being surveyed to bring it under the Reserved Forest category, there had been an angry backlash in the villages. In 1930, villagers in Tiladi protested the encroachment of their rights to the forest, contrasting it to the extravagant spending of the Tehri durbar. Seventeen died in a police firing, while many more drowned in the Yamuna while trying to flee. This incident, which came to be known as the Tiladi *kand*, has had important resonance for forest movements in the years to come.

A reading of the literature, and clippings of the newspapers of Rudraprayag, Karnaprayag and Dehradun, indicates that the stage was being set for Chipko during the mid-1960s. The obvious degradation of the environment was also playing its part in developing awareness. Increasing frequency of landslides, drying-up of water sources and other trends were alerting the villagers to the fact that forests were not an unlimited resource. All over Uttarakhand, in gatherings large and small, the reference point of the growing movement came to be trees. The fact that outside forces—plains-based contractors, business and bureaucracy—were razing their forests provided the seeds of anger in students, political workers and villager elders. By the late 1960s, the villagers had started to organise themselves and to insistently question the state government's policies.

The Alaknanda topped its banks in a 1970 flash flood that devastated fields and property far downstream. The Uttarakhand inhabitants were brought head-to-head with the realisation that ecological balance had to be restored. Demonstrations were held in Purola on 11 December 1972, in Uttarkashi on 12 December and in Gopeshwar on 15 December to protest the indiscriminate logging by outside contractors.

Anand Singh Bist of Gopeshwar, the headquarters of Chamoli district of Garhwal, recalls a few early episodes of Chipko. In 1971, some elders asked the Divisional Forest Officer (DFO) in Nainital that ash trees be included in the villagers' *haque-haquooks*, their traditional rights to the forest. The DFO wrote back that ash was a 'foreign currency-earning species', which villagers could not be allowed to 'misuse' by making farmyard tools. 'Keeping the value of the tree in mind,' wrote the DFO, 'ash cannot be given to farmers to make agricultural implements.' He suggested that the farmers use pine instead. In 1973, the Dasholi Gram Swarajya Sangh—now the Dasholi Gram Swarajya Mandal (DGSM), a Sarvodaya group from Gopeshwar promoting Gandhian principles of rural development—put in a request to the DFO's office for two ash trees for its carpentry unit. This request, too, was turned down.

Meanwhile, it was learned that an Allahabad-based sports-goods manufacturer, Symonds' & Co, was given permission to fell 14 ash trees in the forest of Mandal village. The Chamoli villagers were convinced that the state government in Lucknow, once again, was out to appease the larger economic interests at the expense of the hill communities. (Ash wood is used traditionally to make *juwas*, yokes, because it is light and strong. The suggestion to use pine was considered especially obnoxious as it secretes resin and is not as sturdy.)

On 1 April, a public meeting was called in Gopeshwar to discuss a strategy to prevent the company's axes from felling the trees that had been marked in the Gaindi forest of Mandal. More than 30 *gram pradhan*s (village heads) of Dasholi block, political workers and journalists had gathered. One of those present was Anupam Mishra of the Gandhi Peace Foundation. In his 1978 book, *Chipko Movement: Uttarakhand Women's Bid to Save Forest Wealth*, Mishra writes that it was Chandi Prasad Bhatt who proposed at the meeting that the villagers hug the trees. Demonstrating what he meant, Bhatt 'locked his hands together in an embracing posture.' This, according to many, was the defining moment of the Chipko movement.

On 24 April, the day the Symonds' contractors were to fell the trees, another public meeting was called in Mandal. More than a hundred men and women came out in protest, and the contractor had to return empty-handed. In turning back the contractors, the peasants of Garhwal had notched an impressive first-time victory against plains' interests—and sparked the imagination of others in the hills.

The hills are alive

'For those of us gathered in Mandal, the only agenda was how to save our forest from the Symonds men,' says Anand Singh Bist, who was with DGSM in 1973 and today heads a Gopeshwar-based NGO. However, the ripple effect was felt beyond the Chamoli hills.

The day after pushing back the contractor and his men, Bist and a few other workers from DGSM visited the forest officer of Kedarnath division and demanded that the Symonds' deal with the Forest Department be cancelled. If not, the villagers were prepared for 'direct confrontation' with the Department. The official said that he could not override the Lucknow government's orders, but he would direct Symonds' to collect the 14 ash trees from the Rampur Phanta forests, 60 km away.

On 2 May, gram pradhans, students, party workers and journalists met in Gopeswor and put up five demands before the authorities: one, that the forest contractor system (in which Uttarakhand forests were auctioned at Dehradun or Nainital by the authorities) be abolished and a forest labourers' cooperative society be established; two, people's *haque-haqooks* be reassessed and redistributed; three, the export of raw produce from the hills be banned and villagers be provided technical training to establish small forest-based industries; four, reforestation be carried out on a war-footing; and five, that forest-dwellers themselves be involved in managing and protecting their forests.

Ghanashyam Raturi, a Sarvodaya worker and poet from Uttarkashi (popularly known as Saitani, 'adventurer' in Garhwali), sang a song of the forests, trees and people. The participants committed themselves to preventing outsiders from devastating Garhwal's woodlands. This was the beginning of the Van Bachao Andolan, the movement to save the trees, which increasingly came to be tagged simply as 'Chipko'.

On 3 May, seven activists fanned out from Gopeshwar to spread the message and save the trees. Their first stop, naturally, was Rampur Phanta in Ookhimath block, where Symonds' had been directed by the forest officer. On 5 May, they organised a gathering at Ookhimath in which Kedar Singh Rawat, the pradhan, declared that if Gopeshwar's villagers could save their forests, so could they.

That December, when the Symonds, agent arrived in the Shila Kharka forest in Rampur Phanta, he found, once again, the villagers ready and waiting. With the slogan '*Van jagey, vanvasi jagey!*' (The forests have risen, the forest dwellers have risen), the Ookhimath villagers descended on Shila Kharka. The labourers hired by Symonds' flung away their axes and ran to save themselves from the wrath of the forest-dwellers of Uttarakhand.

Twenty-five km from Joshimath, 680 hectares of the Reni Peng forest had been auctioned for INR 475,000 to one Jagmohan Bhalla, a contractor from Rishikesh. With the Gopeshwar and Ookhimath incidents fresh in memory, the contractors and the Forest Department officials lay in wait for the appropriate moment to move in. The opportunity presented itself one day when most of the menfolk had gone to Chamoli, 70 km away, to receive compensation for land they lost in Malari when the border with Tibet was closed in 1962. Thinking that they had gotten rid of the opposition, the contractors and the forestry officials, the latter in their official uniforms, reached Reni Peng with axes, labourers and rations.

The bosses had bargained without Gaura Devi, a Tolcha Bhutia widow, and other women of the village. When a young girl reported the goings-on in the forest, these women hastened to the site and implored the party to spare the trees: 'This forest is like our mother's home. Please think about your children, and leave our trees alone.' Their pleading is said to have so moved the labourers that they refused to lift their axes.

Lying within the watershed of the Rishiganga and bordering Tibet, Reni was considered not only ecologically sensitive, but politically so as well. When news of the women's activism reached New Delhi, Indian intelligence is said to have consulted with the Anthropological Survey of India about the Bhutia involvement and whether there was possibility of an ethnic movement.

Ban the logger

With the Garhwal hills becoming increasingly agitated for the forests, in April 1974 the central government set up a committee to investigate the impact of Himalayan deforestation. Virendra Kumar, a botanist from New Delhi, was named chairman and, apart from government officials, the committee also consisted of local representatives. They were Govind Singh Negi of the Communist Party of India; Govind Singh Rawat, the block pramukh of Joshimath, also with leftist leanings; and Chandi Prasad Bhatt of the DGSM.

The Forest Department's stand before what came to be known as the Reni Committee was that the Reni Peng had a mixed deciduous forest and that selective felling of conifers was appropriate. They also insisted that felling three trees for every two hectares did not cause soil erosion. The local activists responded that the actual number of trees the contractors cut always exceeded what was allowed by their permits. The Reni Committee accepted that the watersheds were damaged and that tree felling, except for the haque-haquooks of the villages, had to be stopped. Its report, completed in 1976, led to a 10-year ban on commercial felling in Reni. The ban also covered 1200 sq km of the upper catchment of the Alaknanda; in 1985, this ban was extended for an additional 10 years. The declaration of the logging ban was a major victory for the Van Bachao Andolan, and was the high point of the Chipko movement in Garhwal.

In 1975, responding to public pressure, the state government established the Uttar Pradesh Van Nigam, a corporation mandated to harvest trees itself, rather than to auction them off. The expectation that the state would be more sensitive to environmental and village requirements than to commercial interests was shattered, however, when the Van Nigam resorted to sub-contracting out its jobs. Protest against the Nigam was to be a consistent theme of activism in the ensuing years.

Even as the Reni Committee recommended the ban on tree-felling in the Alaknanda catchment, the Indian Constitution saw the addition of its 42nd Amendment, which dealt squarely with environmental protection. 'It shall be the duty of every citizen of India to protect and improve the natural environment including forest, lakes, rivers and wild life and to have compassion for living creatures,' stated Article 51 A(g). 'The State shall endeavour to protect and improve the environment and safeguard the forests and wild life of the country,' stated Article 48A. While they might not always go by the Constitution's dictates, it seemed that the national-level politicians and bureaucrats, too, were in favour of what Chipko stood for.

Kumauni auctions

Word of Garhwali activism spread, and within months Kumaun too was drawn into the circle of protest. In 1974, protestors forced the cancellation of forest auctions in Nainital, Ramnagar and Kotdwar. When 18 students of the Parvatiya Van Bachao Sangharsh Samiti were arrested, there was a wave of demonstrations in Kumaun towns. Around the time that the Chamoli hills became active, Sunderlal Bahuguna, who was the coordinator of the Uttarakhand Sarvodaya Mandal, undertook a 120-day *padayatra* in the area. His march inspired a group of students to undertake their own 700-km *yatra*, from Askot in the eastern Kumaun, adjacent to the Nepali border, all the way west to Arakot in Himachal Pradesh.

The heightened political consciousness among students was most significant. While activists had raised their voice against exploitation of forest labourers in the past, the yatra brought home to participating students—Kumaunis like Samsher Singh Bist and Shekhar Padiak, and Garhwalis like Kumar Prasoon, Pratap Shikhar and Vijay Jaddhari—the patent unfairness of forest policies and practice, as far as the hills were concerned. The 1974 yatra has continued to serve as an inspiration to successive groups of activist students from Kumaun and Garhwal.

'We were influenced by Marxism,' says Samsher Singh Bist, who was then the president of the Student Union of Kumaun University and today runs the

Chetna Printing Press in Almora. The students mobilised against the contractors' exploitation of forest labourers, and understood more than others the need for small, forest-based industries in the hills.

In October 1977, a large demonstration was organised in Nainital by activists of Uttarakhand Sangharsh Vahini (USV). This organisation was then a loose group of *pahari*s concerned about exploitation in the hills, and later became the Uttarakhand Jana Sangharsh Vahini, a political party demanding that Uttarakhand be made a separate state. Kumauni poet Girish Tiwari ('Girda') sang '*Vriskshan ka vilap*' (Lament of the trees) for the demonstrators, giving an ecological twist to a 1926 poem by Gauri Dutta Pandey. Several students were arrested in the October demonstrations in Nainital. When more than a thousand protesters surrounded the clubhouse where forest auctions were to be held, they were rescheduled for 28, 29 and 30 November. On 26 November, the Provincial Armed Constabulary marched the Nainital streets in a show of force. Altogether 53 individuals were arrested, and police sprayed teargas at the demonstrators. In the ensuing chaos, the clubhouse was gutted.

Subsequent months saw sporadic demonstrations and lathi-charges in response throughout Kumaun. On 24 February, the whole of Uttarakhand remained closed in a bandh to protest the arrests in Nainital. In January 1978, some 300 villagers camped out in the Chanchridhar forest in Dwarahat, near Almora, and prevented a contractor from the Saharanpur Star Paper Mills from entering the woods. Later, planned tree-fellings were also successfully stalled by student activists of the Uttarakhand Sangharsha Vahini.

Tehri pines

In Gopeshwar, the villagers did not have to resort to hugging the trees—the threat to do so was enough—while in Nainital the protests were mostly directed against auctions. In Tehri, however, the villagers engaged in more direct confrontation with business and authority. In early 1977, young activists in Tehri issued a pamphlet titled 'Swan song of the pines', to protest excessive resin-tapping in Henvalghati, on the way to Rishikesh. On 30 May, a crowd of villagers went up to the Adwani forest, in the same area, and pulled out the iron blades used by the tappers on chir pines. 'We were merely doing what the Forest Department was supposed to,' recalls Dhoom Singh Negi, a school headmaster who went on to become a well-known member of the Chipko pantheon. 'It was their responsibility to remove the blades if they were inserted too deep, making the pines bleed too much.'

When 640 trees from the Adwani forest and 273 trees from the Salet forest were auctioned in the Narendranagar town hall, Bahuguna went on a fast. Thereafter, the atmosphere became quite tense, and the villagers declared their intention to hug the trees to protect them from the axe. The first confrontation in Henvalghati occurred during the first week of December 1977, in the Adwani forest. On 5 December, village women tied *raksha vandan* cords around the tree trunks—the silken threads symbolised the women's determination to protect them. Negi fasted under a tree for five days, and the Henvalghati Forest Protection Committee issued a 'Declaration of rights', which equated the protection of the forests with the protection of the right to life itself.

A forest officer tried to convince the activist women of Tehri that tree-felling was an economic necessity, that it was good for the country. The officer also tried to assure them that since the felling was being done scientifically, there would be complete regeneration. The women were unconvinced, however, for they had seen all that the resin-tapping contractors were capable of. Recalls Swadesha Devi of Rampur village in Tehri, 'We told him that the trees provide *mini, pant* and *bayar*'—soil, water and pure air—'and we would not let go of them.'

Unable to convince the villagers, the contractors smuggled their Himachali labourers into the neighbouring Salet forest, where the first confirmed instance of the physical act of 'chipko-ing' is said to have occurred. 'The labourers were advancing on the trees, and there were very few of us in the forest. In desperation, I went and hugged the nearest marked tree,' recalls Dhoom Singh Negi. His activist friends joined in, hugging whichever tree the labourers made for, until finally they were forced to depart.

Later, two truckloads of the Armed Police Constabulary were sent to Henvalghati to march the trails, but the villagers would not relent. Finally, the police and contractors withdrew, and the auction grants were subsequently cancelled. There were similar cancellations elsewhere. In Ranichauri, Tehri Garhwal, a group of 200 villagers from Savli, most of them women, went into the Loital forest and tied silken threads around trunks that had been auctioned. Cancellation of the Loital auction is said to have saved some 9,500 trees, including 300 oak trees. Yet another battle was fought over Amarsar forest, near Kangar village, where about 750 trees were to have been felled by the Van Nigam. A group of high-school students arrived with Negi and Pratap Shikhar and started to hug the trees, forcing the labourers to withdraw.

The villagers of Badiyar Garh, 22 km from Srinagar in Pouri, had learnt of the planned felling of 2,500 trees in the Malgaddi woods. It was here that the last, the longest and the most violent battle was fought against the Van Nigam.

The villagers had sent a request to the activists in Henvalghati to come and help them save their forest. Kumar Prasoon and Vijay Jaddhari went to the area on 25 December 1978, a few days before the contractors arrived. They roamed the villages, spreading the Chipko message through folk songs sung to the tune of a harmonium.

Even as the contractors bribed some villagers to try to win support, the minstrel activists went from community to community, and survived by asking the villagers to contribute one chapatti each for their meals. Soon, some of the forest labourers themselves were sharing their food with Prasoon and Jaddhari, and one woodsman even claimed that he would start a Chipko movement when he returned to his village in Himachal. Once, recalls Prasoon, when Jaddhari was protecting a tree, a frustrated forest ranger snapped at two hesitant labourers, 'Why are you waiting? Saw it, chop him down. This happens here every day!' As the labourers applied their saw to the trunk, the teeth ripped Jaddhaii's pyjamas and left a mark. '*Hum ped katne aaye hai, aadmi katne nahi*' (We have come to chop trees, not men), said one of the labourers as they flung their saws away.

On 31 January, a 50-year-old villager named Saroop Singh came running with a lantern in hand, shouting '*Aaj himalaya jagega, kroor kuladha bhagega!*' (The Himalaya will rise today, the cruel axe men will be chased away). He had just heard on a radio news bulletin that the felling permits of Amarsar and Malgaddi forest had been cancelled. First, there was the ban on commercial logging in Garhwal, then the voiding of auctions in Kumaun, and now cancellation of permits in Tehri. The Chipko movement had covered the whole of Uttarakhand. The harvesting of wood was down from 62,000 cubic meters in 1971 to 40,000 cubic meters in 1981. Chipko, a villager's movement, had ensured that indiscriminate commercial forestry was ended.

Then, in April 1981, Bahuguna went on an indefinite fast, demanding a blanket ban on felling of trees above 1,000 m in the Himalaya. Even though an eight-member committee constituted to look into the demand did not feel the need to do so, the central government imposed a 15-year moratorium on commercial felling in the Uttarakhand Himalaya.

Media and khadi

The 1972 Stockholm Conference on Environment heightened international interest in ecological issues, and Chipko provided all the ingredients of a riveting story. The outside press, whether Delhi-based or overseas, took to it with alacrity. As journalist Mark Shepard wrote in 1981 in *CoEvolution Quarterly*,

'I knew I had to write about Chipko. The more I learned, the more the story seemed like a near-perfect parable of the struggle of common people against big government and business—a struggle for the control of the natural resources, that underpin survival and well-being.' Like practically every journalist who has reported and mythologised Chipko, Shepard too wrote as if what he saw and whom he met alone made up the movement. History was centred entirely on Chandi Prasad Bhatt and DGSM, with nary a passing reference to the others of Uttarakhand.

Twelve years later, it was *déjà vu* all over again. In a 1993 issue of the *Whole Earth Review*, Brian Nelson wrote:

> It is difficult to find out who started Chipko, or who is in charge of the movement today. There are no formal titles, no board of directors, not even any business cards ... There is one individual, however, whose name is mentioned at least once in every conversation about Chipko. He is the consistent presence, the overall coordinator if there is one. Chandi Prasad Bhatt is a tall, bearded man, with penetrating blue eyes and deliberate mannerisms. He is one of those rare individuals, who though remarkably gentle, somehow leave a deep and indelible impression on everyone he meets. He exudes a kind of controlled inner energy that is difficult to describe but easy to feel.

Such penetrating insights—developed on the basis of all-too-brief interviews by parachutist journalists—might automatically be suspect. But this type of analysis abounds in the mythmaking of Chipko's leadership. Indian journalists are as prone to glorifying selected Chipko superstars as Western ones. In an article entitled 'The Chipko Architect', journalist Veena Sandal wrote:

> In certain circles he is known as 'the only true Gandhian after Gandhi'. Many address him as the 'Saviour'. Yet others call him a politician. Serene and unruffled in the midst of this controversy stands Sunderlal Bahuguna ... He is the man who went to meet an applauding Kurt Waldheim, the then UN secretary general, with a bundle of firewood strapped on his back.

Journalists who rush up from Delhi to do their Chipko story rarely spare the time to visit the sites of the forest protests or meet the villagers who fought the battles of the 1970s. It is much easier to make one person the fountainhead of the movement, and not to get into detailed analyses of the complexities and contradictions of which Chipko, like any movement, has aplenty.

The vernacular media of Uttarakhand is far more realistic about Chipko. But it is also more vicious, enmeshed as these journalists are in local politics and personality clashes. Thus, while the Uttarakhand papers do cover issues at the ground level, stories of corruption, connivance with authority, international funding, etc, abound. And, unfortunately, one cannot expect much in terms of perspective or fairness.

Kumaun University historian Shekhar Pathak notes that popular movements have never received a fair deal from outside interpreters. He cites the abolition of the *begar* system of forced labour in British Kumaun as an example. 'It was the popular upsurge in the villages, rather than the initiative of a few leaders, that delivered the decisive blow to begar,' he says. 'But as time went by, the role of peasants and village activists got underplayed and it was [later] claimed that only God, Gandhi and Govind Ballav Pant were responsible for abolishing begar in Kumaun.' (G B Pant, freedom fighter and independent India's first home minister, was a Garhwali.)

Two groups that suffered from mainstream media's search for politically correct icons to represent Chipko were the Uttarakhand Sangharsha Vahini and the CPI. Their roles in the forest movement of Uttarakhand have gone virtually unremarked upon, and are unknown to most outsiders. The media's appointed Chipko exponents were, as expected, the Gandhian Sarvodaya activists Bhatt and Bahuguna. Says P C Tiwari, a lawyer in Almora and a worker with the Vahini, 'We did not have khadi personalities like Bhatt and Bahuguna. Ours was a completely political movement involving students and other young people. Our aim was to challenge the existing political system. And such an agenda naturally meant alienating the media.'

For the CPI, the protection of the exploited *kataani shramik* (saw labourers), who received poor rations and inadequate compensation, was the motivating factor. An appeal issued in July 1974 read, '*Aa gaya hai laal nishan, van sampada ke lutero savadhan*' (The red sign has arrived, beware you robbers of forest wealth). The workers of the left had several demands: that the forests be auctioned in smaller lots at prices not exceeding INR 25,000; that the contractors whose blades left deep marks on the chir trees be blacklisted; that small cottage industries based on raw materials found in the hills be established; and that technical training for forestry-based work be given to high school and college students.

'We were ready for everything, and there was violence in our Chipko,' says Kamla Ram Nautiyal, a CPI member and today the municipal head of Uttarkashi town. 'The media has never been sympathetic to the communist movement.' As time works on memory, the village activists and the more politicised facets of

Chipko—even though they were never that prominent—have begun to fade from the public record. Even as Chipko becomes part of history, it becomes increasingly identified as the creation of Bahuguna and/or Bhatt. And the two men cannot stand each other.

Bhatt and Bahuguna

Goaded by supporters, their ire fuelled by opportunistic scholars and reporters, Chipko's Big Two have been engaged in a tussle over whose work is seen to be more important and who gets the most credit. The Bahuguna–Bhatt feud is all that many know about Chipko. Bhatt was a difficult man with whom to try to arrange a meeting. 'If you had not come from as far as Kathmandu, I would not have met you,' he says to this reporter. 'Who knows, even though you are a pahari from Nepal, there is no guarantee that you will understand Chipko.'

By lantern light, Bhatt pulls out yellowed copies of early-1970s issues of Dehradun's *Yugvani* weekly and the *Rudraprayag Aniket*. Poring over two-decade-old reports, he says, 'Show me where he [Bahuguna] is. Nowhere! You have to read the early papers to know the movement.' He reaches in and brings out the first and second editions of the book *Uttarakhand mein ek sau bis din* (120 days in Uttarakhand), by Bahuguna, and points to where the author has deleted references to Bhatt in the second edition. Bahuguna 'did not want the world to know that I was associated in any way with the movement,' Bhatt says bitterly.

Ramchandra Guha, one of the academic chroniclers of Chipko, says he understands Bhatt's frustration. 'You have to give credit to Bhatt as the originator of the movement,' he says. 'He might not be as sophisticated as Sunderlal, but you cannot distort history and take away due credit. He was the one who came up with the idea of Chipko first.' According to Guha, before Chipko became prize property, Bahuguna was given to praising Bhatt for his role in the movement. 'He has called him the *mukhya sanchalak* [main organiser] of the movement.'

Anil Agarwal, environmentalist and editor of the New Delhi-based science magazine *Down to Earth*, says that when he returned from studies abroad during the early 1980s, he found Bhatt abandoned in Gopeshwar, while Bahuguna was taking all the credit for a movement he had not started. Bhatt and his supporters accuse Bahuguna of pandering to the national and international media. Says one pro-Bhatt scholar, 'The first place Bahuguna will visit when he goes to a new town is the press office. He survives on press reports.'

Whereas Bhatt is dour and tends to sound defensive, Bahuguna is suave and a quick study. 'Are you comfortable with your hotel? If you are not, you can come and stay in my guesthouse,' he says to this writer, pointing to a tent on the side of his makeshift hut on the banks of the Bhagirathi river. He is camped here at the dam-site of the Tehri project. 'You need not have wasted time waiting for me. If you had sent word, I would have come to see you,' he clucks. 'Why don't you go and meet the chief engineer of the dam? He is much more important than a simple peasant like me.'

Bahuguna, too, pulls out newspaper clippings. But what he has to show is not evidence against Bhatt but a copy of Kathmandu's *Kantipur* daily. It has a picture of the three-tonne rock that destroyed the penstock pipe of Nepal's Kulekhani hydropower station this past summer. 'The Indian papers did not carry this news,' he says 'They suppress anything that might heighten the opposition to Tehri dam. This needs to be talked about.' Indeed, Bahuguna is a stringer correspondent for the UNI news agency. Quite early in life, he says, he decided to earn his living by 'the most respected profession in the world'. Such praise, of course, intentionally or unintentionally, tends to flatter the interviewing reporter. For journalists making the two-day trip to meet him, Bahuguna makes available hard-to-get background material—reports, 'secret' government documents—as well as copies of his writings, and articles about himself.

Bahuguna is also known for his international forays, and is a master at maintaining his image as a man of the people. He insists on wearing coarse khadi, so much so that that a European researcher was astonished when he arrived in India to find that the indigenous cloth could be quite fine, too. Bahuguna, perhaps because he is a journalist himself, provides masala—crisp quotes and useful anecdotes—and takes account of the reporter's needs and deadline pressures. Tehri, which is Bahuguna's base, is much closer to Delhi than Gopeshwar, where Bhatt and the DGSM are located. Bahuguna is conversant in English, is more photogenic and laughs easily, while Bhatt is prone to moods.

As the media applauds and thrashes personalities, the tolerance level of the Chipko leaders has become razor-thin. Just after *Down to Earth* ran a Chipko story in June 1993, Bhatt resigned from the board of Centre for Science and Environment, which publishes the magazine. 'Pitaji is upset with Anil,' said Bhatt's journalist son, Om Prakash. When reminded that the article was not written by Anil Agarwal himself, he replied, 'But it is his magazine.'

This writer was advised by journalists who know (for good reason, it turned out) not to tell people in the Bahuguna camp that she had been to Gopeshwar to meet with Bhatt. Similarly, Bhatt was not to learn that she had already met

Bahuguna. When 13 representatives of a Thai NGO visited Gopeshwar in May 1993, Bhatt would not see them because their chaperone, Vir Singh of G B P University in Ranichauri, was considered close to Bahuguna.

Bhatt talks appreciatively of writers such as the late H C Kala, Anupam Mishra and Ramesh Pahari, all of whom, it turns out, have written about his pioneering role in Chipko. Mishra, in his 1978 book, practically equates Chipko with Bhatt, and Pahari, editor of *Rudraprayag Aniket*, is Bhatt's good friend and has always written glowingly about him.

Modern-day contractors

Put together, Bahuguna's public-relations skills and international appeal, and Bhatt's organising ability, might have taken the people of Uttarakhand further than where they are today. Some, such as Radha Bhatt of Laxmi Ashram in Kaushani, which promotes women's education, have tried to bring about conciliation, but without success. Most are of the view that the media's need to maintain tension and cultivate heroes, and the overzealousness of followers and hangers-on, has made the rift between the two so wide that it cannot be bridged.

It is likely that the two personalities would never have mixed anyway. 'The media might have aggravated the situation, but it certainly was not the cause of [the rift],' says Shamsher Singh Bist. According to him, Bhatt had already stopped talking to Bahuguna in 1973. 'You cannot say that there was a split,' exclaims an exasperated Bhatt. 'When were we together to begin with? Both of us are happily working in our own areas.'

While Bahuguna has been the vanguard in today's fight against the Tehri dam, Bhatt has been criticised for not showing support for the anti-dam activists. Says Dhoom Singh Negi, 'We went to Gopeshwar twice to meet him. We sent him letters and he did not reply. When Bahugunaji and I visited him, Bhattji left us standing there and went off to attend a *mahila mangal dal* [women's group] meeting.' When asked to explain his silence on the anti-Tehri dam movement, Bhatt's answer sounds lame. 'If I had gone, the media would have focused on me,' he says. 'It would not have helped the movement. I do not believe in going to an area to take credit away. If we can do things separately, we do not have to be together.'

Bahuguna, for his part, says, 'I am a dynamic person. I do not want to remain stagnant. Do you see the Bhagirathi there,' and points dramatically to the river. 'I am like this river. If my Sarvodayi friends do not want to flow with the current, I cannot force them to.'

Bhatt is today involved through the DGSM and the mahila mangal dals in reforestation and eco-development camps in Chamoli. These, he maintains, are the '*rachanatmak karya*' (creative works) required by hill society today.

Bahuguna is critical of Bhatt for going the NGO way. Calling NGOs 'modern-day contractors', he says: 'I do not want to be a contractor. People like us have to do more. NGOs segment the hill people. They try to bring development through foreign or government funds, which is never sustainable. The community has to be empowered to do things by itself. Even the interest to plant trees should come from within the community, not through external agencies and guidance.'

But how can you speak for village-based development, he is asked, when you are always travelling to Europe or North America? Bahuguna replies that he does not want to remain aloof from what is happening in the rest of the world: 'Developments that occur internationally affect what happens in this country. And it is not as if I go there on my own. They send me invitations because they want to listen to me.' There is continuing activism in the hills of Uttarakhand today—against the Tehri dam, for example, and against liquor licensing and limestone quarrying, and for better health care, education and women's rights. These, says Bahuguna, are what he and his 'friends' need to support.

Ironically, for the man who proposed hugging trees as a strategy, Bhatt insists today that the Chipko movement did not require anyone to actually hug a tree. And what of those activists who actually hugged trees? They were not really part of the Chipko movement, says Bhatt. All of which sounds a trifle disingenuous, for in the past Bhatt has fully endorsed hugging, as when he wrote in *Hugging the Himalayas: The Chipko experience*, published in 1978 by DGSM: 'The Chipko soldiers in 1973 took to the task of clinging to the marked trees in the Mandal forest, and later in Phanta-Rampur repeated the action.'

'Who told you we did not have to hug trees to protect them? Who says ours was not a movement?' retorts Swadesha Devi, the Tehri activist. 'I challenge anybody who says we did not hug. Not only us, but even our menfolk hugged the trees to protect them. Dhoom Singh Bhai did it in Adwani. When the forest ranger used his *aara* [saw] on Jaddhari, his trousers were torn and he was left with a scar.'

When pressed further about the pro-forest agitations in Tehri, Bhatt replies, 'I do not consider *that* Chipko. There the word was not powerful enough. Not only did they physically have to cling to trees, but they also had to employ methods such as reading from the Bhagwat Gita, going on fast beneath trees and getting arrested. There was a *byatha*, a story, behind the word—it was so powerful that it drove away the biggest contractor. These things to get attention cannot be called Chipko.'

Anupam Mishra agrees with Bhatt. 'Chipko was a movement born of unique circumstances,' he says. 'That it did not spread but remained localised in Chamoli is not the movement's fault.'

'Just because *your* Chipko was finished and done with in 1974, you cannot say that the movement did not happen in other places,' says Kumar Prasoon. 'Ours [in Tehri] was an organised movement. We travelled the region, convincing people that trees had value. Many of us were arrested, but we always had enough left behind to continue with the work. When things got tough, Bahugunaji would come and do a fast.'

Bhatt disagrees with this interpretation. 'The Forest Department was already asking my advice about felling trees in different areas by 1975,' he says. 'When your demands have been met, and the authority is cooperating, protest for the sake of protest is foolish.' He produces letters from as early as 1977 to prove his point. One is from the Divisional Forest Officer of Kedarnath Division, H C Khanduri, informing Bhatt that the trees of the Malari forest were to be auctioned, asking him if the area was ecologically sensitive and whether the auction should be stopped. 'The movement was not finished,' says Bhatt. 'It had only evolved.'

Decline and fall

As a group, Bhatt's DGSM is considered by some to represent most faithfully the ethos of Chipko. That the DGSM seems to be a spent force is, therefore, the prime indicator of Chipko's weakening. In an interview with this writer in November 1993, Bhatt said that all of DGSM's activities were funded with interest from the prize money he and the DGSM have received—the Ramon Magsaysay Award in 1982, the Indoman Trust Award in 1990, and the Indira Gandhi Paryavaran Puraskar in 1991.

Reports by some scholars who have studied DGSM, however, tend to paint a depressing picture. One of these scholars is Pierre-Andre Tremblay, a French-Canadian anthropologist who is studying DGSM's role in organising Garhwali villagers. He visited Gopeshwar in October 1993. 'At first, they were quite open,' he recalls. He was told about the organisation's resin and turpentine unit, the tree nurseries and the eco-development camps. A couple of cancelled appointments later, Tremblay decided to visit the DGSM work sites himself, and reports being shocked at what he saw. Other than the caretaker and his family, the resin and turpentine unit did not provide employment to anyone in the hills. The unit worked only three months a year, with the help of workers who came up from Lucknow.

'The DGSM's nursery is doing very badly and the eco-development camps are all state-funded,' says Tremblay. When he asked for the date and venue of the eco-development camp, Bhatt first cautioned Tremblay that the food in the villages would not taste good and the sanitary conditions were quite poor. When this did not deter the anthropologist, Bhatt said that DGSM had not been able to decide between two villages. 'When I asked him which two villages, Bhatt said it was a "secret" until it was decided.'

While this does not say much for Bhatt's confidence in his own group, it might also indicate his wariness of foreigners. As he was meeting Tremblay, Bhatt turned to someone else in the room and said in Garhwali, 'You have to be careful with Westerners, you know. Who knows what they will write—it might harm us ten years from now.'

If Bhatt's organisation is but a ghost of Chipko, Bahuguna too seems today a holdover from a more involved past. Today, as he camps by the Bhagirathi River and agitates against the Tehri project, one cannot help but feel that without the dam he would be a man without a cause, a following and an audience. While Bahuguna gains much-deserved credit elsewhere for standing up against the Tehri dam, within Uttarakhand he seems to be strangely alone. Says Raghunath Singh Rana, a left-leaning block *pramukh* of Jakhanidwar village, one of the villages to be submerged by the Tehri Dam Project, 'If Bahuguna understood what the people wanted, he would join us and agitate for maximum compensation for the land that is going to be submerged.'

'How can I demand compensation?' asks Bahuguna. 'I do not even believe that the dam is going to be built.' While his supporters in Delhi and Dehradun speak glowingly of 'the memory of Gandhi and the voice of Ganga', Tehri and the New Tehri residents are handed out glossy booklets like the one titled, *Silyara ke sant ka asali chehra* (The true face of the saint of Silyara, Bahuguna's village). This claims that Bahuguna is anti-development and is protesting the dam only because he has his eyes on the Nobel Peace Prize.

In his work, which is more organisational, Bhatt comes into contact with bureaucrats and participates in government committees. As a result, he is more sympathetic towards authority than the idealistic Bahuguna. Because he is an

NGO worker himself, a larger number of NGO organisers based in Delhi, Dehradun, Nainital and Almora also gravitate towards Bhatt. Bahuguna, meanwhile, has remained aloof from most other activities and NGOs.

Adopt a leader

If the media took sides in the Chipko debate in order to make a good story, the partisanship among Delhi academics has had much deeper implications. The scholars have had a role in defining the battleground itself. The villagers agitated, but it was up to the Chipko scholar to interpret their movement, establish its antecedents, anoint a leader, and provide him with a vocabulary.

One academic battle of Chipko was fought in the pages of *Seminar* in 1987. Responding to what he considered was an overly pro-Bahuguna article by the academics Jayanta Bandyopadhyay and Vandana Shiva, social-historian Ramchandra Guha wrote that Chipko was undergoing a mutilation, 'its body torn in half as environmentalists lay claim to its heritage'. An issue later, Bandyopadhyay and Shiva had a response: 'Guha displays the blinkered vision of academics ... The dynamism of movements does not exist in archives and libraries. It lives in peoples' space.' They concluded that Guha's focus on personalities was 'symbolic of the dominant view of external analysis based on fragmented reading of events and exclusive dependence on the printed word to reach the oral culture.'

Saying it was the scholar couple's effort 'to rewrite the history of Chipko from a sectarian perspective', Guha retaliated that Bandyopadhyay and Shiva's historical treatment of Chipko was 'seriously vitiated by their partisan stance in favour of Sunderlal Bahuguna'. He also wrote that the two painted 'certain groups in the brightest colours, others in darker hues, and leave still others out of the picture altogether,' and accused them of not bothering to 'elicit the views and experiences of the participants in two of the three major groupings of Chipko.'

Bandyopadhyay, who has since had an acrimonious divorce and intellectual parting of ways with Shiva, today concedes that 'Bahuguna's facility with media and researchers tends to produce biases in his favour.' When he and Shiva began research on Chipko, Bandyopadhyay says, he had addressed letters to both Bhatt and Bahuguna. True to character, Bhatt did not respond, while Bahuguna did, and his letter was welcoming. Bandyopadhyay says that he became so involved with research in Tehri that he did not attempt to contact Bhatt again.

The Chipko fault line, it seems, is deeper than the gorge of the Alaknanda. It pitches academics, journalists, activists, villagers and community leaders against each other. The situation is so tense, reported one job applicant at the G B P Institute of Himalayan Environment and Development, that when scientists are interviewed, they are likely to be asked which side of the Chipko debate they are on.

Guha does not quote Shiva in any of his works; for her part, Shiva's bibliographies contain no reference to Guha's important works on the history of social movements in Uttarakhand. Bandyopadhyay maintains today that Chipko was never a feminist movement as claimed by Shiva in her book *Staying Alive*, even though Shiva acknowledges his contribution at the front of the book. And Anil Agarwal does not think Shiva's work warrants attention.

In fact, it is surprising how little time these scholars who have defined Chipko have actually spent in the Uttarakhand hills, particularly during the critical years from 1973 to 1979. Guha's field research in Uttarakhand was all of three weeks, and he met Bahuguna only once in 1983. Agarwal was away studying in the UK when the Tehri demonstrations were taking place, and Bandyopadhyay and Shiva started their research during the latter half of the 1980s and did not go beyond Tehri, Bahuguna's home court.

Guided by their academic support groups, Chipko's acclaimed leaders have differing interpretations of the directions the movement has taken. Bahuguna says the movement became ecological after 1977, while Bhatt insists that it was an economic struggle from the start. The CPI member would define Chipko as a movement to counter 'exploitation of forest labourers and to set minimum wages', while other academics (such as Shiva) insist that Chipko was the high watermark of rural feminism.

Activist to project director

Bahuguna's criticism of NGO-based development rings true. Many of the leading activists of Chipko have, in fact, become NGO directors and coordinators. Bhatt's DGSM itself is now more a passive NGO than a grassroots initiative-taking organisation. All this means that the activists of Chipko, most of them now in their middle age or older, have transformed into managers of development projects. Under such a guise, they are less likely to politicise society in order to bring change.

What Chipko activists lacked after the forest battles were won was leadership. 'We had a meeting to discuss what was to be done after the moratorium was imposed on green felling,' says Pratap Shikhar, who now heads a Jajal-based NGO, the Uttarakhand Jan Jagriti Sansthan, which works in reforestation and drinking water. 'The movement phase was over,' Shikar continues. 'We turned to Bahugunaji for leadership. I felt that we needed to work more with the people, win their trust so that they would fend for themselves.' But Bahuguna, he says, would not listen. 'Instead', he says, 'Bahugunaji went for his Kashmir to Kohima march with Dhoom Singh Negi.'

Kumar Prasoon, who writes occasionally for newspapers, says, 'There is nobody in Uttarakhand that people can look up to; and there is nobody that the government responds to. With people involved in government-funded projects, the future of Uttarakhand looks bleak. The donors and the government money will buy us out and when the time comes, we will not be able to fight for our rights.' Samsher Singh Bist of Almora agrees with Prasoon. 'The activism in Chipko got killed,' he says. 'The activists have all started projects and got lost in the project documentations and reports.'

Some of the younger activists of Uttarakhand, meanwhile, are all too willing to give Chipko a well-deserved rest. 'Uttarakhand today faces more important issues than the 20-year-old Chipko,' says Pradeep Tamta, who stood as an Uttarakhand Kranti Dal candidate for the November 1993 Vidhan Sabha elections from Bageshwar, in Almora. 'Only when you have a house will you be able to decide how you want to decorate it. Unless Uttarakhand is a separate lull state, where we paharis can decide our own future, hundreds of Chipko and the hill society will still not develop … Policies have to be conducive to hill development, and that is impossible until Uttarakhand becomes a separate hill state.'

P C Tiwari agrees with Tamta, and cites the anti-alcohol movement of the 1980s to prove the point. 'Our three slogans then were against those who drank liquor, against those who made it and against those who sold it. We took care of the first two, but we failed when we came to the third. What could we do when the government itself was the biggest merchant?'

'Chipko died in 1980 with the moratorium,' says N C Saxena, a prominent forester who is now the director of the Lal Bahadur Shastri Institute of Administration in Mussoorie. 'This obsession with Chipko has stifled other initiatives in Uttarakhand.' Such has been the stifling effect of the real and imagined Chipko that, 14 years after the moratorium was imposed, other issues of Uttarakhand have yet to be pushed through with any degree of success. While the contractor system was abolished, and the indiscriminate felling in the hills stopped, the much-vaunted small-scale cottage industry has been a non-starter. Market penetration from the plains continues inexorably, and the hill people have not been able to tap economic well-being from, say, tourism or horticulture.

The people do have more control over the forest than before. But oddly, for a hill region so full of activists and community leaders, there has been little rise in consciousness of the responsibilities that accompany the rights. While Van Panchayats of Uttarakhand are shown to visitors as examples of how well community-managed forests do and how green and lush they are, this has often been at the expense of Reserved Forests, to which the villagers do not have rights.

Chipko's legacy also does not seem to have reduced the number of young Kumaunis and Garhwalis departing to the plains in search of employment. In fact, their numbers increase every passing year. While the demands of the hill people decorate forest policies, they are hardly implemented on the ground. Meanwhile, the Uttar Pradesh state government continues to dream of hydro-power from dams constructed in this critical seismic zone.

The most important effect of Chipko might have been in preparing the ground for the demand for a new state of Uttarakhand, but these efforts too have been stymied for the moment. As long as the hill people were fighting isolated commercial interests through a movement that had a resonant title, the central and state governments were willing to allow them the privilege. But when it comes to larger economic and political issues that are enmeshed in the demand for a separate Uttarakhand hill state, the power centres for now seem quite unwilling to rock the sluggish boat.

The political issues important for the Uttarakhand hills today outstrip the limited focus of what was Chipko, even in its widest conception. Only when the people of Uttarakhand are able to manage their own affairs will policies emerge that benefit the Kumaunis and the Garhwalis and lead towards a more sustainable economy. But then, others are not so sure. They feel that statehood is only good as a rallying cry, and much more will have to be done to make the hill economy resilient—which will mean more, not fewer, interactions with the plain's economy.

As for Chipko, it still exists. But it has migrated from the hills of its origins to seminars and conference halls further south and overseas. It lives in university courses, academic tomes and in articles like this one, which keep the controversy, but not the issues, alive.

Chapter 3

Far Eastern Himalaya
The search for distance and dignity
Himal, May–June 1995

Sanjoy Hazarika

The stretch of the Far Eastern Himalaya from Sikkim eastward is significantly different from the rest of the mountain range. The reach of the Ganga plain—of Hindu ethos and historical Muslim influence—is much more muted here. If anything, many of the animistic hill tribes have gone the other way by embracing Christianity. Unlike the cultures of the faraway flatlands, these eastern communities are more directly linked to the Tibetans of the north, or the Indo-Chinese of the south and east.

The region is also unique in its geography. Although part of the same Himalayan range, these southern latitudes nurture a lush tropical landscape drenched by one of the highest precipitation rates in the world—strikingly different from the high desert of Ladakh or the dry terraces of west Nepal. The High Himalaya itself is lower at these extremities, with the peaks descending eastward from Mount Everest (8848 m) in the Khumbu, to Kanchenjunga (8598 m) at the Nepal-Sikkim border, to Namcha Barwa (7756 m) standing guard as the great bend of the Tsangpo. About here, the Himalaya breaks southward into Burma and dwindles away eastward into the hills of the Hengduan mountains of Sichuan–Yunnan.

From Sikkim, with Tibet a constant companion to the north, the political boundary snakes across Bhutan and Arunachal Pradesh, where it makes a sharp southern twist to plunge along the edges of Yunnan province into Burma's Chili and Kachin hills. Spurs rope in Meghalaya, Nagaland, Mizoram and Manipur, before meandering through Tripura into the Chittagong Hill Tracts of Bangladesh, near the sea.

The western part of the Himalayan range is neatly packaged into a progression of states from Pakistan to Nepal to Bhutan. But here in the east, the range becomes a geopolitical jigsaw, crossing national frontiers with impunity. The rectangle of the Far Eastern Himalaya is broken up among five nation states: little Bhutan, the Northeast of India, the Chittagong Hill Tracts of Bangladesh, the Arakan region of northern Burma, the southeastern tip of Tibet and the hills of Yunnan.

Compared to the peopled Himalayan hills of Himachal Pradesh, Uttarakhand, Nepal and Sikkim, this is a region that is still underpopulated, with natural resources largely unexploited. Natural gas, petroleum, rushing water, minerals, tea, fish and timber—the wealth is there, largely unexploited due to reasons of history and geography. The bounty that was bypassed by the colonial rulers is eyed lustfully by today's market forces.

One potential source of wealth lies in the rivers that slice through the deep gorges and green valleys. Travelling eastward all the way from Mount Kailash, the great Tsangpo takes its 180-degree bend beneath Namcha Banva, descending through vertical canyons into Arunachal Pradesh before disgorging into the Assam plain. Here are some of the most powerful rivers on earth, going by volume and gradient: the Brahmaputra (Tsangpo), Chin and Dibang. In the gorge country of Burma and Southeastern China are the headwaters of the Irrawady, Salween, Mekong and the Yangtze Kiang.

Asia in miniature

While the geography and fractured frontiers of this region are fascinating in themselves, it is the population that holds even more interest: the cultural diversity and shared history, the deep animosities within and the xenophobia as far as outsiders are concerned. Ruled by the forest and inhabited by an endless procession of Tibeto-Burman tribes, the belt is a region of unceasing conflict, violence, anger and grief. Modern times seem only to have exacerbated the situation.

The multitude of languages heard along this Himalayan flow includes the guttural Tibetan and its offspring Dzongkha, the sweeter Assamese in the Brahmaputra Valley, and the lilt of Tibeto-Burman tongues in the hills of Nagaland, Manipur and Mizoram. Each step of the way, the jungles seethe with unrest and rebellion, as diminutive men and women, some in battle fatigues and others in tattered clothing, some with modern weapons, others with crude arms, fight for ideals, funds, drug profits or lost causes. They confront the military might of their respective governments.

This region is Asia in miniature, a place where the brown and yellow races meet. Taking a south–north transect, for example, you encounter the Bengali migrants in Assam, Tibeto-Burmans in the Himalayan midhills and the Khampa of the high plateau. Going west to east, the spectrum is even more diverse, from the people of Tibetan stock—the Bhutia and Lepcha of Sikkim and the Ngalong Dzongkha-speaking people next door in Bhutan—the population takes on Tibeto-Burman hues with the Sarchop of eastern Bhutan, who have affinity with the tribes of neighbouring Arunachal. Eastward, the communities become progressively less 'Tibetan' and more 'Burman'. The variety is astounding.

The tiny state of Manipur, bordering on Burma, has a population of 1.8 million, yet it shelters more than 30 separate linguistic and ethnic groups, including the Tarao whose number is down to less than 400. The forested frontier between Yunnan and Burma is host to 15 distinct groups, including the Yi, Naxi, Bai and Lisn. Several communities of Arunachal Pradesh, such as the Abhor and the Mishing, are also to be found northward in Tibet.

Straddling the ages and the mountains, the people of this winding trail form an anthropological bridge to Southeast Asia, where the roots of many can be found. The Khasi of Meghalaya are believed to have come from Kampuchea and still speak a form of Mon-Khmer, although because of British missionary influence they use the English alphabet. The Thai Ahom migrated from Thailand to Assam 600 years ago, and settled in a land they reported was as valuable as gold. The number of Thai-speakers in Assam is small, but there is a Thai Association and the community is politically active.

There are Garo in Meghalaya and in Bangladesh; there are Naga and Mizo in India and in the neighbouring hills of Burma. Festivals, liquor, dance and music shape approaches to life and habitat of the tribes. History and contemporary experiences also forge attitudes, affinity and identity, the latter being regarded as the most crucial in maintaining both distance and dignity in the face of intrusion of the larger cultures of Southasia. Convictions about the sanctity of borders are weaker here than elsewhere. Many Naga still refer to their own region as 'Western Nagaland', referring to areas with Naga communities in Burma as 'Eastern Nagaland'.

Guwahati, the capital of Assam, is closer to Hanoi than it is to Delhi. Watching graceful young women in sarongs, skirts and blouses pedal to work in Imphal, one could easily imagine being in Vientiane or Rangoon. There is a fierce pride and independence that marks the tribes. And a disdain—despite using the good things that money can buy and Central funds can achieve—for the national elites and the locals they patronise.

This bewildering medley and mosaic is dear to the social scientist, but makes administration and political control extremely complex for the faraway capitals, be it New Delhi, Rangoon or Dhaka.

What the constituent regions of the Far Eastern Himalaya also have in common is scarcity of information and difficulty of access. Southeastern Tibet, northern Burma, the Yunnan highlands, the Chittagong Hill Tracts, and the Indian Northeast—these are areas with negligible international profile. In all of Asia, there is no other region this large about which so little is known. As far as the outside world is concerned, the fierce independence, deep enmities and seemingly eternal violence all occur in a kind of a vacuum. Relegated to the far corners of each of the nation states of which they form a part, the inhabitants live in a media shadow.

The recent outflow of the Rohingya and news about the ongoing drug trade keeps northern Burma in the news pages; but on the whole this region is off the information map. The same is true for the Chittagong Hill Tracts, the sole claim to fame of which seems to be the outflow of the Chakma community. Southern Bhutan is in the news only because that is where the Lhotshampa refugees came from. Compared to the detailed social science and other research that has gone on in, say, the Uttarakhand or Nepal hills, researchers have left the Far Eastern Himalaya largely alone. Even here, however, the southeastern extremity of Tibet is unique for the absolute unavailability of information.

One of the reasons there is so little reporting and research done here is because outsiders face restrictions in travel everywhere in the Far Eastern Himalaya. Nowhere do the national authorities of Burma, Bangladesh, India, Bhutan or China allow free movement of outsiders, and in many cases there are restrictions even on citizens. Everywhere, diplomats, journalists, scholars and independent travellers face special problems. Thus have national governments successfully shielded the brutal military operations they have mounted against the locals—often rebellious minorities seeking to preserve their identities—from outside eyes. By restricting access and travel, they have obscured this region from the ears and eyes of their own people as well.

It is by the choice of the locals that Indian citizens from the 'mainland' require special permits to enter the Northeast. However, this exclusivity is a double-edged sword, for it is due to this very lack of access that information about the uniqueness and aspirations of the Northeast is kept from the larger India.

Nevertheless, more news about the Northeast gets into the press than any of the other regions. In comparison to the news blackout as far as southeast Tibet or northern Burma are concerned, the Indian Northeast comes across as a very 'open' society indeed. Perhaps, as the rest of the region struggles to catch up, these other areas too will be dogged by the problems that India's Northeast today faces. Perhaps, in that sense, the experience of the Northeast will be instructive for those elsewhere in the Far Eastern Himalaya, the rulers and the ruled alike.

Unity in adversity

A shared ecology and geography, and a history of isolation, has given rise to lifestyles and languages that link the tribes and communities behind the five frontiers. In fact, many of these tribes have more in common with each other than with the nation states of which they form distant appendages.

The cultural chasm between the people of the Indian Northeast and those of the 'mainland' is so deep, and the leap through time they have to take to catch up with the national cultural mainstream so great, that this region is unlikely to be psychologically integrated with India for some time to come. If the Sikkimese even today refer to the border point at Rongphu Bridge as the place where 'India begins', the feeling of distance is much more palpable in the hill states that lie to the east of Bhutan. Perhaps the map, too, aids in developing this mental state: every other part of India, including Kashmir, is joined integrally to the mainland, whereas the Northeast hangs on a 14 km neck of land between Nepal and Bangladesh.

The entire Far Eastern Himalaya is peopled by marginalised communities. These are peripheral groups, distant from the levers of governmental power. Much of their economic and political affairs are controlled and manipulated by all-powerful Central entities. In most cases, tiny powerful local elites have emerged, patronised by the Centre, but these are invariably alienated from their own communities. The failure to cope with change, an inability to deal with the major forces of economic and social transition that are transforming our world, is creating a deep sense of unease among this population.

A region that is used to oral traditions is being asked to turn to the newspaper and satellite television; a region which used the traditional methods of dispensing justice through village councils and chiefs is having to embrace British jurisprudence. Vibrant communities are therefore turning inwards and nurturing deep resentment towards what they perceive to be colonial behaviour by Central governments and national elites. This is true of the Northeasterner's attitude towards the Hindu-dominated and Hindi-speaking belt of the Ganga plain, of the Chakma's towards Dhaka's rulers, and of the Tibetan's towards the Han cadre who call the shots from Lhasa.

Seen in reverse, loyalties of Nepali-speakers are being questioned in Thimphu, of the Chakma in Dhaka, of the Naga in Delhi, of the Rohingya in Rangoon. The domestic policies of the national governments to the marginal peoples are almost identical, varying perhaps only in the intensity of violence with which rebellions are crushed. The problem profile of the region is also similar: a lack of industrial development, sluggish economic growth, a tattered infrastructure of roads, telecommunications and power, escalating demographic change, inadequate use of natural resources such as water, environmental degradation, low per capita income, and poor agricultural practices. Added to all this, of course, unrest and insurgency.

Because national authorities seem unable to recognise the cultural chasm, to meet basic needs, or to devise a formula for sharing the natural resources in which the region is so rich, there will be no peace in the Far Eastern Himalaya. While the people agitate for their identity, governments are perfectly willing to exploit mineral reserves, allow forests to be razed for timber, and rivers to be dammed. A withering-away of national boundaries is not in sight. But as long as the reality of separateness is not understood, the problems of the region will remain unaddressed, and the inhabitants will continue to suffer underdevelopment and violence.

Demographic change is the most immediate source of conflict in the Far Eastern Himalaya. Unwanted migrants are on the move across the region, in their tens of thousands, trailing confrontations in their wake. Mass movement in a traditionally insular area invites linguistic, ethnic and religious strife. Settlement of an alien population leads to battle over resources, particularly land.

Southasia saw its largest migration during Partition, and the Northeast was not spared. Though not on the same scale, exoduses and influxes continue, of both political refugees and economic migrants. National governments, which have their own political calculations to make, are not necessarily averse to population movements, for they can be used advantageously as vote banks, to open up frontier lands to economic exploitation, or as part of pacification and assimilation policies towards hostile local populations—as evident in the 'Han-isation' of Tibet by China.

Indeed, the best orchestrated, and ongoing, migratory pattern is to be found in north of the Himalayan divide, where people from mainland China are moving all the way into the Tibetan heartland of U-Tsang, and not just the outer provinces of Kham and Amdo. The Dalai Lama's aides maintain that the original population of six million Tibetans is being overwhelmed by the Han invasion. The official Chinese figures are far lower: Beijing puts the population within the Tibet Autonomous Region (excluding large sections who live in Kham and Amdo) at 2.1 million, and the number of Han Chinese at 79,000—but excluding the tens of thousands of troops and Chinese cadres who live without permanent-resident status.

Once the migrants or refugees arrive, the immediate cause of conflict is the question of land and its control. For host communities whose very cultures are derived from the soil and forests, the loss of land to migrant groups means a shedding of cultural identity. Population movements have affected every state in the Indian Northeast, and in two of them the original inhabitants have by now become minorities in their own land—which is the fear that impels all Northeasterners to react against migration.

One state whose indigenous inhabitants are now tiny minorities is Sikkim, where the Lepcha and Bhutia were overwhelmed over the course of the first half of the century by an inflow of Nepali-speakers. It was manipulation of the Nepali majority by New Delhi's political leadership that led to the kingdom's merger with the Indian Union in 1973.

The other state where the locals have become a minority is Tripura, the narrow thumb that juts into Bangladesh from the southeast of Assam. Once dominated by 19 Buddhist and Christian tribes, the state has been swamped by Hindu refugees from Bangladesh since the 1950s. In 1947, Tripura had a population of 600,000, of whom 93 per cent were from the indigenous tribes. By 1981, the tribes had been reduced to a minority of 28.5 per cent, out of a population of 2.06 million. Political power slipped out of the hands of the tribal communities, as they were displaced by the settlers. An insurgency began against the Bengali settlers in 1980, but it had ended by 1988.

Rejected peoples

Numerous communities in this region constitute what political scientist Myron Weiner refers to as 'rejected peoples'. Count among them the Bangladeshi migrants in Assam, Chakma refugees in Arunachal and Tripura, the Rohingya refugees from Burma now taking shelter in Bangladesh, and the Lhotshampa refugees of Bhutan.

Bangladeshi

In few regions has the impact of population movement been as vivid, painful or divisive as in Assam. Its wide and fertile valley watered by the Brahmaputra, the state has long suffered from the depredations of migration, settlement and subsequent conflict. The place of origin for most of the migrants has been Bangladesh, which has a population density of more than 800 persons per sq km—the highest in the world. The corresponding density in the Northeast is 284 for Assam, 262 for Tripura and 33 for Mizoram. The 'push' and 'pull' factors are obvious.

Even unskilled labourers find a ready market as construction workers, porters and maids in the Northeast. Language is the key factor favouring Bangladeshi migrants, for Bengali is widely spoken in Assam and understood in the hinterland. The biggest outflow of Bangladeshis took place in 1970, when a brutal Pakistan Army crackdown sent more than 10 million fleeing into India. Most went back, but more than a million stayed behind in West Bengal and Assam.

Influx into Assam continues today, largely due to economic and environmental conditions within a Bangladesh that seems to lurch through an unending cycle of flood, cyclone, drought and famine. Reaction against immigrants has exploded several times in bloodshed and rioting. Movements against 'Bangladeshis' have shaken the Northeast since 1979, particularly in Assam, which has taken the brunt of the immigration. The conflict has been exacerbated by the fact that the migrants and their descendants are predominantly Muslim, whereas the Assamese are largely Hindu. Today, the very word *Bangladeshi* has taken on a pejorative meaning in Assam.

Attempts to get the refugees to return have only resulted in more tension and violence. Meanwhile, for decades, police and high officials—and especially politicians—have actively encouraged illegal migration, due to the profits involved and the advantages of engaging in 'vote bank politics'. The price, as always, is paid by innocent people, most brutally in 1983 when more than 4,000 men, women and children, mostly Muslim settlers, were slaughtered in a series of pogroms in Assam during an election. The worst killings occurred in the rice fields of the village of Nellie, where at least 1,700 were butchered.

Land was the source of conflict. The settlers had taken over—bought or bartered—property from locals, even though such transactions were prohibited for those outside the tribal communities. However, there was poor implementation of land and tenancy laws, and there were politicians who depended on support from the Muslim vote bank. Over the years, resentment over dispossession built up in the Lalung tribe, until it finally exploded in 1983.

Although the violence against the Bangladeshi has ebbed, settlers continue to be targets of distrust and political abuse. Lately, they have fallen victim to insurgency in the region, with frequent attacks on them by armed members of the Bodo Security Force in western Assam.

Chakma

Population movements are fed by remorseless factors. Take the case of the Chakma. They seek refuge in Tripura because they are a religious minority, because their rights are being trampled upon, because their lands are being settled by Bengali-speakers in the Chittagong Hill Tracts, and because their loyalty is questioned by Dhaka. Even after decades, in some cases, the Chakma refugees have not been able to settle down in the host region, whether it is Arunachal Pradesh or Tripura.

Chittagong's Hill Tracts cover 5,093 sq miles, or 16 per cent of Bangladesh's surface area. Marked by teak forests, swift streams and undulating valleys, the area is bounded by Assam to the north, upper Burma to the east, the Arakan of Burma to the south, and Chittagong district to the west. There are 12 major tribes, largely Buddhist, who practice *jhumming*, or swidden agriculture.

When the Pakistan government completed the Kaptai hydro-electric project in 1964, the reservoir flooded about 40 per cent of the arable land in the area, and displaced more than 100,000 members of various tribal communities. An estimated 20,000, mostly Chakma but also some Mog and Jajong, moved across the frontier into Tripura. The refugees were first moved to the Lushai Hills, now Mizoram, and then offered a choice of three locations by the Indian authorities. They chose the North East Frontier Agency (NEFA), which is now Arunachal.

While lightly populated Arunachal—which was attacked and briefly annexed by China during the Indo-China war of 1962—has been one of the quieter places of the Northeast, over the past year it too has become tense. The immediate reason is that the migrant Chakma already make up seven per cent of the population of 700,000. Student organisations have started a sustained campaign to oust the migrants, who have been threatened and intimidated, thousands fleeing to the relative safety of Assam.

Among the many contradictions that remain unresolved in the Northeast is the question of nationality. While the Indian Constitution states that any child born in India is a citizen, thousands of Chakma offsprings who have been born in Arunachal since the 1960s have not been absorbed by India. On the other hand, if the children are to be accepted, where are the parents to go? The state from which they fled does not exist, and the successor state of Bangladesh does not recognise them as nationals.

The larger and more recent influx of Chakma has less to do with the Kaptai dam and more with population movements within Bangladesh. The root cause lies in Dhaka's programme to settle the Chittagong hills with Muslim Bengalis from the over-populated delta region. This concerted move to 'Bengalise' the region drew sharp reaction, culminating in an armed revolt in the 1970s by a group calling itself the Shanti Bahini. There have been several bouts of conflict in the past 20 years between the Bangladeshi armed forces and the tribal nationalists, who have received arms and training support from New Delhi's security agencies.

The Dhaka government's crackdown has been brutal. It devastated culture, kinship ties and tradition, which resulted in refugee surges across into Tripura in 1978, again in the early 1980s and yet again in 1989. While New Delhi and Dhaka have been engaged in talks and there has been some repatriation, about 50,000 refugees remain in camps on the Indian side, unwilling to believe Dhaka's assurances of security. It is not even clear that the two countries are genuinely interested in solving the problem; for Indian security agencies, particularly the Research and Analysis Wing (RAW), the Shanti Bahini remains a pawn in the power game.

Rohingya

Bangladesh plays host to its own Chakma-like situation in the case of the Rohingya. Over a quarter-century, first in 1978 and then in 1992, the Burmese military has swept into the Muslim-dominated Arakan province in drives against the Rohingya communities living there. These Arakanese are regarded as not 'sufficiently' Burmese, as more Islamic than nationalistic. The Burmese authorities, who are predominantly Buddhist, have claimed that many of those in the

Arakan area are not really Burmese and that they have illegally crossed over from Bangladesh.

The low-level Rohingya rebellion has existed for decades, but not much information is available other than that the government crackdowns were vicious. The military regime in Rangoon has always been wary of the Muslim population for having independent leanings. Its actions have led to two waves of refugees into Bangladesh, totalling more than 200,000 Rohingya each time. Not surprisingly, Rangoon claims that those driven out are Bangladeshi, a charge the Rohingya strongly deny. Efforts to repatriate them have not succeeded, although lately Burma has agreed to international monitoring of a future repatriation process.

For all their genuine grievances, the Rohingya too have been enmeshed in regional geopolitics. The troubles between the military and the Rohingya are seen by many as part of the larger confrontation between Burma and Bangladesh, which views with unease Beijing's military assistance to Rangoon. There are credible accounts of Rohingya receiving military training from Bangladeshi intelligence and military agencies.

Lhotshampa

The story of Nepali settlement in Bhutan is less than a hundred years old. Encouraged by the Bhutanese governor of western Bhutan, in the late 19th century Nepalis from the over-populated hills of the home country moved in as labourers and farmers. Over the decades, they prospered and their numbers grew in settlements and jungle clearings along the Dragon Kingdom's southern border. These frontier people, who helped create today's rich farmlands and orchards, came to be known as the Lhotshampa, the people of the south.

When a census in 1988 turned up many more Nepali-speakers than the authorities had expected, Thimphu's fears of being overwhelmed by a Nepali 'swamping', and going the way of the Chogyals' Sikkim, were heightened. In an interview in 1993, King Jigme Singye Wangchuk, Bhutan's absolute monarch, said that as many as 113,000 had been identified as illegal migrants in a newly calculated national population of 600,000. The anti-royalist agitation in Nepal, which reduced the once-absolute monarch King Birendra to a titular head of state, also clearly worried Thimphu.

Like elsewhere in the Northeast, the fear of losing their 'Drukpa' identity led the Bhutanese authorities to engage in a fierce anti-migrant reaction. Unlike the other communities of the Northeast, who were battling the establishment, however, here it was the government itself, representing the dominant community, that oversaw the process with the resources at its command.

As the pressures grew in southern Bhutan, the first refugees fled into the Jalpaiguri tea belt of India, and from there transited to eastern Nepal's Jhapa district. The first surge of exiles, of about 35,000, might be called true 'political refugees': terrorised, famished and very sick. Those who came later constitute an amorphous category, for it seems that they departed not because of political repression but because life was becoming too difficult to manage in isolated farms and hilltop hamlets.

There are today more than 110,000 Lhotshampa refugees, both in the camps of Jhapa and scattered across Nepal and neighbouring areas of India. Kathmandu has been roundly outmanoeuvred by Thimphu in bilateral talks that have gone on for several years. The Bhutanese government has managed to rid the country of a seventh of its population, and controlling the remaining Lhotshampa will be that much easier.

The process is the same everywhere: mass movement into a lightly populated region from regions of high density. The cycle consists of displacement, migration, settlement, identity loss and resentment, leading to violence on the settlers and counter-violence by settlers. It is not true, however, that conflicts have always been between hill tribal communities and invading plains' folks from outside the region. The fratricidal confrontation between the Kuki and Naga tribes is a case in point. Over the course of the past three years, more than a thousand Kuki and Naga are known to have been killed in increasingly violent attacks and counter-attacks on each other. The bitterness between the two sides, too, is linked to migration. Kuki settled traditional Naga lands several decades ago, and the memories linger.

Strategy and neglect

It is strategic compulsions that drive rulers of nation states to seek control over distant communities, and to snuff out the insurgencies and agitations that resist such control. No one has much time for critical questions relating to human rights, the sweeping powers given to the security forces, and inherent disharmony between communities of the periphery and the Central governments.

Why do nation states attach such importance to these peripheral areas? In one phrase, it is fear of disintegration of the nation state, which can never be allowed, for no national leader wants to be accused of having dismembered the motherland. Another reason is the vast natural bounty of these places: the oil, gas and other minerals, the timber, hydropower, fertile soil and biodiversity.

Men in uniform and those from security agencies swarm over the region. India, for one, justifies their presence not merely because of the insurgencies it faces, but also the presence of tens of thousands of well-equipped Chinese troops on the other side of the mountainous border. The strategic importance given to the Northeast can be seen in the fact that the large state of Arunachal Pradesh does not have a single civilian airport. Meanwhile, the military helps in the expensive task of airdropping food and consumer goods to scattered civilian communities.

It is not just Central neglect and lack of vision that is holding the Far Eastern Himalaya back. The extensive and deep-rooted insurgencies also have a role. In all cases, the earlier convictions and total commitment to independence from the nation state no longer hold true. Often, an ethos of violence for violence's sake among insurgents, coupled with the rigid stance of government, keeps moderates from finding a voice. Many insurgents stay on to fight in the jungles, simply because they know of no other way. Also, new equations have developed in these wooded hills of the Far Eastern Himalaya. Drug smuggling has become one of the major sources of funding for the guerrillas in the woods, which fuels insurgencies and maintains the circle of violence. Meanwhile, much of the righteous 'halo' of the insurgents has dimmed. Many are feared, even among their own people, as ruthless figures who will kill if the price is right.

The most enduring conflicts in India are Nagaland and Manipur, and in Burma between Rangoon's generals and the Kachin and Karen, whose rebellions have lasted half a century. In the Northeast, the Naga and Bodo of Assam present the biggest challenges to the state's security apparatus. The National Socialist Council of Nagaland (NSCN) and the Bodo Security Force have established common training camps, and often work together to ambush security forces.

The trend for the future is clear: an increasingly sharp delineation between areas of governance by the state and ungovernable areas, where the political vacuum is filled by powerful dissident groups such as the NSCN and the Bodo Security Force. The Indian state has failed to ensure stability in parts of Manipur and Nagaland, and to a lesser degree along the northwestern edge of Assam, where it touches Bhutan. As a result, the NSCN controls parts of Manipur, especially the Ukhrul and Senapati districts; it levies taxes, recruits people (often forcibly) into its army and harasses businessmen.

Likewise, the Bodo Security Force has the run of parts of Kokrajhar District of Assam, and uses the forests of southern Bhutan as a hideout. The Bhutanese are disinclined to act against the Bodo because they are outgunned, and several operations mounted by the Indian Army, with King Jigme's permission, have failed to flush them out. In recent months, the NSCN seems to have expanded its base and made inroads into the Naga-dominated district of the North Cachar hills, ambushing troops and engaging in major gun battles. It has access to funds through the fear it inspires among the tea planters, who pay protection money much as they did to the United Liberation Front of Asom (ULFA) when it held sway between 1988 and 1992.

Every state in the Indian Northeast, barring Arunachal Pradesh and Meghalaya, has seen major armed insurrections against the Indian state. The response of the state has been, as usual, to call in the army and invoke sweeping powers of search and detention. Once, it even flung the air force against Mizo rebels.

But the entire region is heavily militarised, from Tibet through the Indian Northeast and into Bangladesh and northern Burma. First, there is the military presence to guard the borders, particularly along the Indo-Tibetan frontier. Then there is the heavy military presence to maintain order over a sullen populace, as in the case of the People's Liberation Army in Tibet, or to pacify rebel groups, as with government forces in northern Burma and the Indian Army's extensive presence in the Northeast.

The role of the unfriendly neighbour, which Indians euphemistically call 'the foreign hand', is also significant in sustaining militant organisations. The Shanti Bahini operates in the Chittagong Hills with help from Indian agencies, and the rebels in northern Burma are said to receive support from Dhaka. As far as the Northeast is concerned, in the 1960s it was Pakistan and China that were providing sustenance to the Naga and Mizo rebels. This support ended with the 1971 War.

In the late 1970s and early 1980s, the Kachin Independent Army was providing support, training and weapons to the NSCN, the ULFA and to various Manipuri groups.

This backing faded after New Delhi threatened to oust Burmese refugees who had fled the repressive Rangoon regime and were staying in India. Subsequently, the NSCN, basing itself along the Bangladeshi and Burmese borders, has used its own skills to forge a leadership of the Northeast rebellions. As far as the Northeast is concerned, says one intelligence specialist, the NSCN is 'the mother of all insurgencies'.

Another pattern that seems to characterise the regional rebellions is the breakdown of 'accords', when agreements between rebel forces and governments go sour. The only successful agreement between militants and the Indian state seems to have been the Mizoram Accord of 1987, which enabled insurgents to surrender, receive an amnesty and start life afresh. Most other agreements have been fatally flawed, beginning with the Shillong Accord of 1975 between one group of Naga rebels and the Indian government, which fell apart and led to the growth of the NSCN.

The pattern of breakdown of accords tends to be similar: acceptance of accommodation by moderates and subsequent rejection by hardliners. This has happened in Tripura and in Assam, especially with regard to the Bodo. The hardcore of the ULFA leadership also rejected peace moves by their colleagues, and the organisation suffered a split from which it has yet to recover. When the Bodo struck a deal for greater autonomy with the Assamese government, in 1993, the package of promises began to unravel because the Bodo homeland's borders had been left undefined, as had been the all-important question of power-sharing. The extreme Bodo Security Force, which seeks full independence from India, struck at security forces and vulnerable targets such as unarmed Bengali settlers, in order to demonstrate its power and its rejection of the accord.

In Burma, the Rangoon government has followed a policy of punitive action against rebel groups combined with efforts to buy them out. This has worked with some groups, including a prominent communist faction, and failed with others. One of the key factors about insurgencies and governmental response in Burma is that both have their fingers in the drug trade. Over the decades, Burma has emerged as the single largest exporter of heroin to the West, and both government officials and insurgents depend on the trade for funds.

The years ahead

Amidst the crises overwhelming these fractured lands, it is difficult to envisage what the future holds for the Naga and the Mizo, the Ahom and the Mishing, the Khampa and the Chakma. Migration will continue—for, like water, no walls, laws or police forces can stop people from seeking their own survival. In a Subcontinent that will see nearly a billion Indians, 220 million Bangladeshis and 30 million Nepalis (in Nepal) by 2020, it is not feasible to hope that population flows will cease entirely.

Likewise, the nationalistic grip on the region by each of the country capitals will continue, constricting the space for autonomy and self-determination. The market forces, the state and the local elites are bound to continue to be in league, to exploit natural resources in a manner that only a few will benefit, and not necessarily the tribal communities with closest links to the land. The rebellions that have become the defining attribute of the region are also likely to continue, although individual insurgencies might tire out and disappear.

At the same time, it is doubtful that greater autonomy to economically unviable, small communities will benefit the people in the long run, except in temporarily raising hopes and creating new local aristocracies. Without outside personnel and Central funds, these states and provinces will find it difficult to fulfil modern desires that have grown over the decades. Some of these might still be forest societies, but everyone wants to modernise.

The choice for the Far Eastern Himalaya is clear. It is either to throw up one's hands in despair at the problems associated with divided geography, migration, reaction and military presence. Or it is to try to chart a path that involves joint planning for economic growth. If massive inflows of migrants and refugees are to be reduced, and people of the region are to be saved from endless rebellions, the economies of the Far Eastern Himalaya, relegated to the periphery for too long, must expand, and expand on all sides.

Economic development, rooted in the sharing of water and other natural resources, multilateral trade and assisting communities at the micro level—instead of imposing centrally sponsored schemes—seems to be the way out. A sense of inclusion and participation of local communities is critical in making programmes work. Paternalism only provokes bitterness. Locals need to be given effective control over resources, and development schemes must have their participation, not be devised and dictated by Central authorities. An example of effective local institution-building is the system of Block Development Villages in Nagaland, with locally managed schemes working where larger top-down schemes have not.

In Delhi in early May, Southasia's leaders decided to move ahead with the SAARC Preferential Trade Arrangement (SAPTA). In fact, the region of the Far Eastern Himalaya, so different from the rest of Southasia and so much like each other across the borders, would seem to make a coherent trading block in its own right. The absurdity of national boundaries that divide similar peoples and break up viable economic units is nowhere more clear than it is here, which is why this Eastern Himalayan stretch could constitute a suitable area to make regional cooperation begin to work.

A formula has to be found where it is possible to work across the borders while maintaining the sanctity of frontiers. The possibilities are endless, if the vision exists. True, it will require the national governments, which have barely begun to address some of these issues, to put their heads together, and for moderates among the regional leadership to make a show of their strength. In the end, only regionalism spurred by the search for economic possibilities will bring peace and progress to the Far Eastern Himalaya.

A network of small and medium dam projects in parts of Bhutan, Sikkim and Arunachal Pradesh would tap the explosive power of the rivers and streams disgorging from the Himalaya. The production of hydro-energy would spur economic growth in both hill and plain. The reduction of flood damage would open up new lands for cultivation and ease some of the demographic pressures in the Bengali-speaking lowlands. Power could also be exported to other parts of India and Southeast Asia, for energy hunger is destined to grow rapidly in the next decades as unshackled economies surge forward.

One can be forgiven for looking ahead to the day when workers from different parts of the region participate in economic activity under strict migration and employment laws. The economies cannot expand without better roads, railways and communication facilities, and these arteries should be intra-regional and not merely for maintaining links with the individual national mainlands. Opening up of port and transit facilities in Bangladesh and Burma would itself, in one stroke, provide economic fillip to the hinterland.

With a loosening up of border restrictions, numerous crossborder contacts would be resumed. To use just one example, the Garo and the Khasi of Meghalaya would restart their trade routes with Bangladesh, facilities that they enjoyed for centuries before Cyril Radcliffe drew the lines that divided British India. Rather than transport their goods to Assam using unreliable public transport, they would, like in the past, simply march 'down the hill' into Bangladesh.

Development of tourism and promotion of handicraft and handloom industries will also make an impact. In India, the marketing of products should involve much more than displaying local items at the state emporiums in New Delhi, and must involve a look at national and international possibilities. Improved agriculture and water-use strategies will strengthen community-based economies, and there should be a major emphasis in adding value to exported items, so that it is not only raw products such as timber and crude petroleum that exit the region.

This is not to say that insurgencies will end. Ethnic aspirations and questions of identity will remain. But at a time when the world has recognised that mere political independence does not necessarily lead to a better future, ultimate peace to the Far Eastern Himalaya will come when a measure of autonomy is accompanied by access to markets, and the definite possibilities of improving the economic conditions of one's life.

A period of education is required, both for the regional leadership as well as the national elites, in the search for peace and prosperity in the Far Eastern Himalaya. The people have spanned more than a thousand years in a lifetime, and they, more than anyone else, would like to see the creation of a new and revitalised region.

Chapter 4

A Bangladeshi looks for his country

Himal, September 1996

Afsan Chowdhury

Because of the fertility of silt, the deltaic region where the Ganga meets the Brahmaputra made possible the rise of a great agrarian population. It is a low country created by the confluence of geology and hydrology, and made for colonisation by peasantry. And peasantry it is that, today, makes up the vast majority of more than 120 million Bangladeshis.

This country of agriculturalists and a thin veneer of the gentry has always been ruled by outsiders—till as late as 1971, when they decided to do the job themselves. Over the centuries, from prehistoric through feudal times, from when colonisation gave way to a half-Pakistan and thereafter when that became the independent state of Bangladesh, Bengalees have always grappled with an identity, a personality. Even today, on the 25th year of their independence, they are not sure they have found it with the nation state that they do, at long last, have.

And whose identity are we talking about, anyway? We mostly discuss elite notions of uniqueness. The vast millions are too hungry to bother. As late as 1971, when the peasants responded, it was to the perception of the violated village rather than to calls for a nationalist war. A village was bigger than any country, and *'desh'* meant home, not much more. The identity angst is mostly reserved for the intellectual or activist who, in classrooms and tea stalls, wants to discover whether he is Bengalee or Bangladeshi. The angst is also strong among those overseas in self-exile, made melancholy by myth and memory, weeping for a land to which they will never return.

After 25 years as a nation state, can we say to whom does Bangladesh belong?

Pala to Pakistan

The rulers and the ruled have never been one. The earliest dynastic history begins with the Pala, a North Indian clan of Buddhist inclination in the ninth century. They governed from what is presently northern Bangladesh, then Pundrabardhana—the last province of Aryan India, to the east of which lay the 'impure lands'. Two hundred years after the Pala came the Sena, a rigidly Hinduistic Kshatriya-Brahmin clan from South India, who after a century of uneasy overlordship were replaced by Central Asian Muslims under Bakhtiyar Khalji, towards the end of the 12th century.

During each transition, the ruling class was changed but the peasant was left undisturbed, with his land, harvest and personal pantheons. He might change a god or two in cognisance of altered circumstances, but nothing serious. The post-12th-century rule by Turks, Afghans and Pathans is known as the Islamic period, though it is unlikely that these various rulers from different races, forever fighting each other, thought they shared anything. However, these Central Asians and Turks did not interfere with the Bangla culture or revenue collection, which kept the peasantry unruffled.

The Bengalee elites, unable to resist the invaders militarily, learned to cooperate in civil matters. This is a trait that has marked the Bengalee middle and upper classes to this day, a deep desire to please foreigners and earn salaries, because you belong to the working race, born to serve. Bangla history has forever been driven by the tyranny of limited economic choice.

It was Bengalee Hindus who mostly managed the government under the post-Sena rule, as bureaucracies developed along with the span and prosperity of the regimes. The Muslim aristocracy mostly indulged in the good life. With no resistance in sight, even the Kshatriya caste disappeared from Bengal; it was much more profitable to attend on the foreigner than to fight him. So when the British came, servers were in abundant supply. The Hindu professionals had their silent revenge as the Muslim aristocracy was displaced by the British. They got education and the jobs.

But there were also moments of cooperative pride even as the slavish mentality predominated, such as when Hindu and Muslim chieftains collaborated in a famous resistance against the Mughals. Isa Khan, who fought and defeated a Hindu agent of Akbar in a sword duel, is a legend in Bengal. There was a reason why the British, when they replaced the Mughals, began with Bengal—this was the only revenue-surplus province in the crumbling Mughal theatre. Siraj-ud-dowla, the non-Bengalee nawab who ruled over Bengal, Bihar and Orissa, fell in 1757 due to the treachery of his loyalists, both Muslim and Hindu, whom the British had bought off with money and promises. Siraj's defeat was not only the end of Muslim domination but also the end of 'independent Bengal', as understood by some. It was consumed by the India that the British began to construct with great energy.

Convenience of the alien ruler

The British, unlike previous conquerors, changed the revenue system to earn more from taxes. This ruined the peasants but created a new class of loyalists. They also introduced education, and the Bengalee babus ran hard to become clerks, teachers and lawyers, the stuff of colonial administration. The babu became the imperialist's friend and confidant, until he discovered intellectualism and militancy—but that comes later.

The Muslim upper classes, when they stopped feasting on past glories, likewise discovered the advantages of collaboration. But the seats had been mostly taken, and they had to compete with their ex-subjects, a terrible idea. Thus were the economic seeds of communal conflict sown amongst the elites. The Musalman elite had always considered themselves foreigners, and proud of it. They had the rulers' plasma. The Hindus were heathen and Bengali was, too, a heathen language.

The Bengalee Hindu, together with his other Indian co-religionists, could look at the Muslim interregnum as a thousand years of infidel rule. He could also share in the emerging Indian dream. The Muslim Bengalee elite could not do that, for they still considered themselves as the usurped ruling class. In 1857, Hindu and Muslim soldiers and many feudal lords revolted against the British. At some point, the titular leadership of the revolt was pushed unto Bahadur Shah Zafar, the last Mughal ruler. It failed, and India was passed from the Company to the Crown. The feudals, many of them Muslim, felt let down. The Muslim aristocrat, who believed in his natural right to overlordship of Hindustan and Mughal rule, was unhappy to see that the idea was not popular among Hindus.

Perhaps this was the defining moment of Bengal's and India's evolution: the response to the crushing of the 1857 uprising pointed out the great divide. The Hindus certainly had no stake in Muslim rule. By conquering India, Victoria Regina had inadvertently created two equal peoples, who now joined the race to please the rulers. It was up to the British to decide whom to reward.

The rise of the Aligarh Muslim Education Movement, a great mobilisation, fed on the fear and ambition of the Muslim, who saw the lowly Bengalee babu make away with jobs that might have been his. Research shows that his anti-Hindu feelings rose from his loathing for Bengalees, who were many and took jobs away from others. Long before America beckoned, Bengalees were creating a migration problem in Hindi- and Urdu-speaking belts of the Subcontinent. All Bengalees were seen as Hindu, and this distrust never deserted the heirs of the Muslim movement, who saw contradiction in the very term 'Bengalee Muslim'.

Muslim leaders reminded their followers that they had been hit hard by not cooperating with the British, and by lack of English education. Unless they wanted to serve out history as janitors, went the thinking, Muslims had better get educated. Thus, a newly cooperative class of Muslims joined the workforce. In Bengal, Bengali-speaking Muslims honed their English and demanded education quotas. They began to argue in courts, and began, for their part, to identify the distinctions inherent in being 'Bengalee' and 'Muslim'.

The year 1905 saw the first victory of this new identification initiative, when the province of Bengal was split into East and West Bengals. This was expected to satisfy the growing demand of the Muslim majority for some space in which to grow and catch up with the Hindus of Bengal. The Muslim League, which led the movement for the creation of Pakistan, was born in Dhaka in 1906. It was a defining moment for India: The Muslim card had emerged. The Indian National Congress had failed to develop as a national multi-communal party. The British manipulated the situation, and formalised the divide.

Under stiff pressure from the Congress, which was the natural choice of most Hindus, Bengal was reunited in 1911. The growing conflict between Hindus and Muslims, both scrambling for economic opportunities, was sharpened further. Thus in 1947, as Pakistan was coming into being as a homeland for Muslims, the demand for splitting Bengal along religious lines re-emerged, this time led by the Congress. If India was to be cut up along communal lines, why not provinces? The British agreed, and Bengal and Punjab were sliced, generating a communal carnage whose violent memory still haunts the public consciousness.

Thus, Eastern Bengal became East Pakistan, echoing the 1905 division— reflecting not an ideology but the administrative convenience of an alien ruler.

Shadow knowledge

Whether in the time of the Pala, Sena or the Turko-Afghans, the peasant culture never connected with that of the rulers. While the aristocrats and the rulers might engage in power plays based on identity, it was difficult for the rural Hindu and Muslim to be too different from each other, confronted as they were with identical challenges thrown against them by nature and society. Whatever differences there were, these were not cause for hatred but rather opportunity for multiple participation. Some customs and rituals varied, but others did not.

The peasants were brought together in the face of the same problems— floods, droughts and tax-sucking landlords. Since a Hindu peasant knew no Sanskrit and the Muslim peasant no Arabic, great theological debates were ruled out. And while doubtless there were angry moments, no cow-slaughter riots were reported. Brick constructions were few in the delta country, so there were no mosques to pull down, either.

Since they felt helpless at the hands of floods and fevers, the peasants turned to the village shaman, who used his tantric skills to unite all in some shadow knowledge of a past passed along. A peasant will rarely risk his harvest by refusing obeisance, no matter to which pantheon the gods and goddesses belonged. Water-borne diseases and swamp-nursed malaria, which wiped out tens of thousands every year, were the great unifiers of rural Bengal. Left to the peasantry, Bengal might have remained one. But the Bengalee elites, Hindu and Muslim, were brought up to believe in their differences, even though they were slightly differently posed portraits of the same person.

Islam too meant different things to the villager and the elite. The latter was closer to the formal faith, while the former had been converted by Muslim mystics and Islamic shamans. The religion was spread in rural Bengal not by the Muslim rulers but by the Sufis, whose version was syncretistic and laid-back. Togetherness, love of god and 'mind the wine and pork' would do. It was a gentle form of Islam, rather like the words of a forgiving schoolteacher, and the Muslim mystics had much in common with the Buddhist *bhikkhu* and the Hindu *sadhu*. The deity of the Bengalee peasant was not the all-powerful, strict, desert monarch but rather a singing, soulful, tropical god. His was a religion softened by a thousand monsoons.

The peasantry, Hindu and Muslim, fell behind the Sufi saints. Ignorance and illiteracy encouraged communal harmony. Till the middle of the 19th century, peasant names of both religions were interchangeable. And so the Sufi prescription and peasant theology survived for centuries, until the political variety of the faith entered with the Islamic revival, with its demand for votes and martyrs.

While the poor villagers sought divine support for day-to-day survival, the well-to-do were more worried about their pedigree. In the late 19th century, a book by one Fazle Rabbi sold well amongst the aristocratic Muslims of Bengal. It purported to show that all the leading families were 'original Muslims' from West Asia, and not low-caste Hindu converts, as common sense suggested. As the politics of representation gathered steam, this alienated group of wannabe foreigners laid claim to speak on behalf of the nearly 50 per cent of the Subcontinent's Muslims, who spoke nothing else but rustic Bengali.

The Muslim League claimed to represent all the Muslims of India, and tried to invent a uniform religious culture for them. It took its leadership almost entirely from the aristocracy. Its members dressed alike and talked in Urdu and Persian, and heartily disliked Bengalees. Casting around, the local leaders of Muslim Bengal tried the Congress but found that it was secular in tongue but communal at heart. After an initial growth, the Muslim League faltered in Bengal as the Krishak Praja Party (KPP, Peasants & Tenants Party) gained support, led by the legendary A K Fazlul Haque. The Muslim League, Mohammad Ali Jinnah included, could not possibly support the KPP's militant anti-landlord manifesto.

Fazlul Haque understood demography: there were more peasants in East Bengal, and they were mostly Muslims. The landlords were oppressive, and they were mostly Hindus. Siding with the Muslim peasants, at one go the party was able to upset the applecart of Muslim aristocracy and hit at the Hindu landlords. In reaction, the Muslim aristocracy sought support elsewhere through their upper-class cultural connections, including from the British.

As more and more Bengalee Muslims became educated and competed with Hindus for jobs, the communal divide widened. Soon, sheer numbers pushed the lowly 'Musalman Bangalees' into a position of political strength. A new brand of politician emerged from among them, one who was comfortable being both Muslim and Bengalee. With the rise of Kazi Nazrul Islam—later canonised as the national poet of Bangladesh—and the popularity of his revolutionary and love songs, urban Muslims too could now feel at home with this

Bengalee identity. Unlike their aristocratic forebears, they could claim to be part of the cultural mainstream of the Brahmaputra-Ganga delta. This new political class could both pray and sing.

Sharing only the pain

By the 1920s, Bengal was already steeped in militancy. After eons of subservience, middle-class Bengalees were finally up to resisting foreign rule. They overcame the ever-present temptation to collaborate and, instead, became part of the fight for liberation from the British. Chittagong was liberated for a week, though the revolt crumbled quickly and all the leaders were hanged. One interesting reflection of this episode is found in the work of Somerset Maugham, a serious Bengalee-hater whose Ashenden spy stories are full of Bengalee villains.

Bengalees were also unpopular with the non-Bengalees, be it the Congress leadership or that of the Muslim League. Mohammad Ali Jinnah hated Fazlul Haque; and M K Gandhi disliked Chittaranjan Das, and later his disciple Subhash Chandra Bose, founder of the Indian National Army (and, even today, Bengal's most popular hero). Das, a prominent Bengalee member of the Congress, proposed the Bengal Pact in 1923, which was to be an affirmative-action employment programme for Muslims to enhance their economic status and reduce the causes of conflict. Unfortunately, by then India was already crumbling under the weight of communal forces, and the Congress leadership rejected Das's formula. Had it decided otherwise, many historians believe, there might still be one Bengal.

After the rejection of the Bengal Pact, there were no more serious attempts made to try crafting a Bengalee identity along non-communal lines. The first general election held in Bengal in 1937 by the British under a communal voting system did prove that the Bengalee peasantry was an independent-minded force. By giving Haque's KPP more seats than the Muslim League, the rural population showed it was both 'Muslim' and 'peasant' without being 'anti-Hindu'. But after having failed to cobble together an alliance with the Congress, Haque lined up with the Muslim League. His action destroyed the KPP as a national political party that was entirely peasant-based. It also brought the peasantry firmly behind the League.

The Bengalee Muslim's sense of identity peaked during the 1940s. He was aware of his religion, felt he deserved a better chance at the job market vis-à-vis the Hindu, was willing to listen to Jinnah and the Muslim League—but he would deny neither his language nor his peasant background. For the Calcutta sophisticate, including the Muslim *bhadralok*, of course, he was a 'Bangal', the derisive term used to mean an East Bengal lout.

In 1940, the Pakistan Resolution, moved by Fazlul Haque, was passed by the Muslim League in Lahore. Bengalee scholars say the plan mentioned five independent 'states', while others claim only one state was meant, a Pakistan with two wings. All in all, by this time the Bengalee Muslim stood well and truly distant from his Hindu brother. Communalism was sharp enough to resist attempts at healing.

The partition of Bengal in 1947 was a trauma to both the Bengalee Muslim and Hindu. But while sharing a common pain, they did not share the argument; each blamed the other. Hindus said Muslims took to communal politics, which is what led to what took place in 1905 and, ultimately, in 1947. Muslims blamed the Hindus for voting for the split of Bengal. Sadly, they were both correct.

It was absurd for the Bengalee Muslim leaders to have expected support from Hindus for a united Bengal. The proposal, which was forwarded in early 1947 by Huseyn Shaheed Suhrawardy (a deputy of Das's who went on to become the prime minister of Pakistan), was a last-ditch attempt to keep Bengal intact. Suhrawardy was supported by leaders such as Abul Hashim of the Bengal Muslim League and Sarat Chandra Bose of the Congress. However, the Hindus indicated they had had enough. This had to do with the legacy of ten years of Muslim League rule in Bengal, from 1937 to 1947, which had hardly been a secular affair, having included the communal violence of the 1940s, especially the riots of 1946, and the so-called referendum for Pakistan. Bengal was torn apart for the last time.

The Bengal Provincial Muslim League represented the new citizens of East Pakistan. Resentful of Hindus and non-Bengalees—of Gandhi's Congress and Jinnah's Muslim League—they were grappling for a piece of history to call their own. Pakistan was considered a betrayal, for the Bengalees had expected an independent country rather than a 'wing' dominated by the other 'wing' from across India's vast expanse.

Song offering

Near the end, we turn to the beginning. Before there was the Bangla language, there were the people. Scholars are divided as to when Bengali evolved fully as a language, but it was probably between the eighth and tenth centuries.

Charyapad, a collection of Buddhist devotional chants discovered in a royal library in Kathmandu, is considered the earliest example of such literature, but scholars are pushing the dates further back.

The use of chants and music as a vehicle of religious expression created a close link between the language and the people. The numerous mystic cults took devotional poetry as the principal source of communication, and the rural cultural festivals were deeply rooted in oral traditions. Even today, oral poetry for reading out aloud is sold by the millions throughout rural Bangladesh. A variety of musical chants forms the bedrock of Bangla literature. Rabindranath Tagore's best poem is considered to be 'Song Offerings' (Gitanjali). The Bangla language thus binds people to perhaps the most spiritually pleasant way there is to worship.

At the first Muslim League Conference, in 1906, delegates from Muslim Bengal, while stating their loyalty to the Muslim cause, reminded the audience that Bangla would always be the vehicle of culture and communication where they came from. The Muslim aristocracy of Bengal wanted Urdu, but the Bengalees saw no reason to discard their own sturdy heritage, one that had been tended by Tagore, Nazrul and the mystic bard Lalon Shah. This would have meant discarding songs that had been sung for a thousand years. Bengalees felt that they had a right to their mother tongue, something the Pakistani elite class officially and specifically denied them as soon as independence from the British was achieved in 1947. This sparked the Language Movement, which would ultimately lead to liberation.

The quarrel between Jinnah and the Bengal Muslim League was at least a quarter-century old, and it is noteworthy that the former had always nominated Urdu-speaking Calcuttans to represent him in the party. This distrust spilled over to the newly created Pakistan. When the leaders of Pakistan, including Jinnah, insisted that Urdu alone would be the national language of Pakistan, students and cultural activists braced themselves for a fight.

The Pakistani elite and their East Pakistani friends, ill advised, refused to allow cultural freedom to the East Pakistani Bengalee Muslims and Hindus. It was also obvious that economic power was not about to be shared, and so language became the platform for the political slugfest. Matters came to a head on 21 February 1952, when the authorities fired on students demanding that Bangla be given a status equal to that accorded Urdu. Bodies fell and legend was created, as was a momentum strong enough to sustain an extended political struggle. The martyrs' memorial of Shahid Minar was constructed overnight, and became a powerful symbol. This was where the Bangladeshi nation was born as a state.

No soul brotherhood

Secret moves to splinter Pakistan began as early as 1956. The same Bengalee leadership that had ushered in Pakistan now fought for freedom for the East. The activists, including Sheikh Mujibur Rahman, said that they had never wanted the Pakistan that emerged.

Constant economic deprivation and lack of cultural freedom, including a ban on Tagore music, was not exactly the means to keep Pakistan together. But the distant rulers in Islamabad seemed unaware, or uncaring. Attempts to tinker with the Bangla script and language to make it more 'Islamic' worsened the mood. '*Pakistan zindabad*' gave way to '*Joi Bangla*', and a protest manifested through a slogan, and a language, began to undercut the foundations of an unnaturally created state.

Bengalees came to believe that Islam had been used by the Pakistan Movement leaders only to get them on their side. A deep distrust of religion in politics was sown in the 1950s and 1960s and, as the politicians became more articulate, they spoke of a secular state, with strict separation of religion and governance. In 1970, when the polls were held for the Pakistan National Assembly, with their near-total choice for the Awami League led by Sheikh Mujib, the Bengalees indicated that they wanted release from the domination of fellow Muslims of the West.

This was their finest hour, when the collective voice of Bengalees rang loud and clear: that religion had no role in government, that Pakistan had no egalitarian ideology, that there should be social equity and cultural and religious freedom. Here was identity with a belief structure, which went beyond race, language and religion. The butchery of 1971 was the final straw, which convinced the people once and for all that Islam could not be, and never was, a binding factor. That most Pakistanis thought all Bengalee Muslims were mostly Hindus was probably more disturbing than the fact that Pakistani soldiers killed Hindus before asking questions—just as Bengalees killed many Biharis after the Dhaka massacre of 26 March.

Bangladeshi or East Pakistani? The war of 1971 meant a freed 'East Pakistan' to most—a Bengalee state overcoming its past in the Pakistan Movement. It was not a soul brotherhood with the Indian who helped achieve liberation, nor with the West Bengalee Indian, as some thought. The separation of East and West Bengal achieved for the last time a quarter-century earlier had, over the period, given rise to separate identities and self-images. It was also true that the people of a united Bengal, East and West, had never together experienced a Bengalee nationalist movement. An alliance of Hindu and Muslim nationalists might have held back in 1947 when the ideological heirs of Chittaranjan Das had pushed for a United Bengal, but their proposal had been quashed by party big-wigs on both sides. Gandhi's mild support for the idea was overcome by the opposition of Sardar Vallabhai Patel and Jawaharlal Nehru.

Thus, there was no legacy of nationalist unity to fall back upon for the divided Bengalees, and it turned out that cultural affinities alone could not sustain a political movement of the kind that was required. The East had by then its own legacy of blood and death, which had generated a distinctive myth system that could not be shared with the West. This is why the presence of Bangla-speakers in West Bengal did not influence or create identity conflict or convergence in the East. The struggle remained that of a geography-driven, language-based nationalism. Not a tight construct but an original one. The 'Bangal' was going his own way.

Joi Bangladesh zindabad

Sheikh Mujib of the Awami League became the first ruler in Bengal to speak the language of the ruled, and this was the way it would be. He was a Bengalee leading Bangladesh, and nothing can wrest that distinction from him. However, after liberation, he ruled less than competently: the problems of post-war reconstruction, the ever-present crises and conspiracies, and the aroma of state power were all beyond him.

While all history had seen the struggle for identity and insistence on a national personality, now that they had their own sovereign state the Bengalee was at a loss as to what to do with it. After 1971, it was the politics of governance that took over. *Ideology, culture, nationalism*—all became one-word mantras in the hands of those seeking seats of power in Dhaka. The tussle now was for the spoils of government, and nationhood had seemingly debased the great ideals of old.

Within three years, Bangladesh had retrogressed into a one-party state. Sheikh Mujib and most of his family were brutally slain by a group of belligerent army men. Another transition of sorts began in 1975, and Sheikh Mujib's successor, General Ziaur Rahman, occupied himself with overturning everything that the Awami League had done. Socialism was diluted, and 'Islamic' initiatives promoted. To make up for the League's pro-New Delhi position, the government became piercingly anti-Indian. Friendship with India, and with Hindus, was seen as one and the same and roundly discouraged.

This was no identity crisis; it was a political reaction. India did not help matters by controlling the eternal flow of the Ganga into Bangladesh with a barrage that diverted water into the Hoogly. Much later, the evident support of the Indian masses for the Bharatiya Janata Party, which maintains a strident anti-Bengalee Muslim stance, and the Babri mosque crisis, further exacerbated matters.

Gen Ziaur Rahman was assassinated in 1981, and Gen Hussain Mohammad Ershad took charge a year later. He declared Islam the state religion, hoping to cash in on what he thought would be a popular anti-Indian move. To his surprise, Gen Ershad made lifelong enemies amongst Muslims who were—a legacy of recent history—vehemently opposed to religion cohabiting with politics. The general was thrown out by a mass agitation in 1990, after which the country's seat of power has been a seesaw between the Awami League (run by Sheikh Mujib's surviving daughter Sheikh Hasina Wajed) and the Bangladesh Nationalist Party (BNP, under Gen Ziaur Rahman's surviving spouse Begum Khaleda Zia).

Today, the Awami League supports 'Bengali nationalism' and the BNP espouses 'Bangladeshi nationalism'. However, the underlying planks of the two parties are nearly identical, the differences more cosmetic than philosophical. Party politics requires creating separate niches, however, and so Sheikh Hasina and Begum Khaleda are forever engaged in the management of perception, relating mainly to their degree of Islamic commitment and anti-Indianness. One party is probably less loud in proclaiming antipathy towards India than the other, and both are aware of the need to be seen as non-secular. Only the socialists had the seeds of a non-communal dream in their programme, but they are long since a dead movement.

The Awami League stands for secularism and socialism, along with democracy and nationalism, although it practises none very well. For its part, the BNP looks for friendship in the Islamic world, and has tinkered with the Constitution to this end. While it cannot trumpet it too loudly, the Awami League considers India its natural ally, which is to be expected, given New Delhi's support for the liberation struggle led by the League. In terms of slogans, the Awami League having appropriated *Joi Bangla*, the BNP gave official sanction to *Bangladesh Zindabad* when it came to power after 1975. There are, however, those who refuse to mouth either slogan, maintaining instead that they are Bangladeshi by citizenship and Bengalee by race.

None of this rhetorical babble touches the life of the average Muslim citizen. But it makes Hindus insecure, and they regularly remit their savings to India.

97

They get an education in Bangladesh and hunt for jobs across the border, which is also where they search for grooms for their daughters. The Hindu keeps a constant eye on the religious hate meter, just in case he has to leave on short notice.

Mishkins and unleavables

The Bangladeshi masses have been marginalised by rulers who have come from afar, and, in the latest phase, by their own kind. Such is the neglect that the peasantry has turned away from the state, seeking support instead from the development agency and NGO. A Grameen Bank loanee has much to be grateful for from the bank, for instance, while a student gets ahead with the support of BRAC, largest NGO in the country and world. Meanwhile, the distance between the peasantry and the Dhaka aristocracy, once again, only increases.

The politicians are not reliable, they only promise. So, much better to turn to the dollar-mixed sands of the Gulf, or the rubber plantations of Malaysia. A US or Canadian visa, of course, is the ultimate dream of the middle class. Not only the Hindus, but Muslims, the middle class, even the poor, have all been leaving—to Pakistan, West Asia, North America, Europe, Assam, Maharashtra, to wherever will take them. In fact, leaving Bangladesh has in itself become a way of life, and there is no nationalist pride affected when Gulf Arabs refer to Bengalees derisively as *mishkins*, beggars.

In the home country, the role of the 'donor community' becomes ever all-encompassing, and the percentage of those who believe that the country has a future declines. A major 'donor document' recently announced that most Bangladeshi professionals see a future for themselves outside Bangladesh.

But has not life always been this way? A time to survive, a time to adjust—if opportunity allows, a time to kill. We are survivors, and if it means learning a new trade or visiting a distant land and taking the lowliest job, we will. We did that as part of British India, today we do it all over the world. With Hindi channels on satellite television, we are now closer to Bombay than to Calcutta. Traditional barriers are down and old connections lost. Will they do a music video of Rabindra Sangeet on Channel V? Unlikely. Purity in diet and culture elopes with remix every day. It makes some unhappy, but many today know of no other forms.

However, fanaticism has no root in this soil. Despite funding and favour by a section of the ruling class, the support and vote base of the Islamic fundamentalists remain stagnant. Dollars were remitted, but the inter-communal cultural tradition, diluted in recent decades, remains as yet too strong to dismantle.

So, back to the question: To whom does Bangladesh belong? It probably belongs to the poor, the stay-at-homes who are forced to experience it all. It is theirs because others do not seem to want it. Those who can, leave, and society becomes more mono-cultural by the day, populated by Muslim 'Bangals', the most rustic of them all. They are the stubborn ones, the unleavables, who confront hurricanes, famine, war, pestilence and global economic shock—and emerge afterwards to face another day. Unnoticed, history has passed on to them the right to call Bangladesh their own.

Chapter 5

A Kashmiri solution for Kashmir

Himal, November–December 1996

Eqbal Ahmad

There is a conflict in Southasia that has outlasted most post-World War II disputes—the Cold War, the Vietnam War, the American–Chinese confrontation, South African Apartheid and the Israeli–Arab conflict. This long-festering dispute is the one in Kashmir. It is the primary cause of hostility between India and Pakistan, and a source for endless misery for the people of Kashmir. Two full-scale wars, an almost continuous armed confrontation at the India–Pakistan border, since 1989 a Kashmiri uprising and its repression by the Indian state, and the beleaguered Kashmiris' immense suffering have induced neither New Delhi nor Islamabad to adjust their respective stands.

New Delhi declares the matter settled. It claims that Kashmir, under its occupation, is an integral part of India, routinely denounces and occasionally threatens Pakistan for its interference in India's 'internal affairs', and has tried for years to put down—without pity, and in vain—the Kashmiri resistance. For its part, Islamabad insists that Kashmir is an unresolved international dispute and that it must be settled by a plebiscite, as originally envisaged by a UN Security Council resolution of nearly a half-century standing. These decades-old positions have not shifted, although significant transformations have overtaken the world, and Kashmir itself.

As far as the Kashmiri is concerned, the New Delhi and Islamabad governments share one key characteristic: both perceive Kashmir's realities and interests as subservient to their own. This affinity between the Pakistani and Indian positions is ironic in view of the fundamental contrast between the two in relation to Kashmir. In the language of political science, India is a 'status quo power'—that is, it actually holds the area it covets, and policies are intended to preserve the existing territorial situation. Pakistan's position, on the other hand, is that of a 'revolutionary power', one that seeks to change that status quo.

Antonio Gramsci, the 20th-century theoretician-philosopher, argued that in diplomacy and war status quo powers usually engage in 'wars of position'; they adhere to well-defined negotiating planks, battle lines and so on. Predictability is their hallmark, inflexibility their burden. By contrast, the 'revolutionary powers' are structurally better suited to waging 'wars of movement', which are characterised by tactical flexibility and a focus on process rather than fixed positions.

When a government in a revolutionary posture—that is, one seeking to change a given configuration—adopts the culture of status quo, it forfeits its primary advantage and, more often than not, loses to the adversary. Examples abound; only one should suffice. In their quest to create a Jewish state in Arab Palestine, European Zionists fought a sophisticated war of movement on multiple fronts, took calculated risks surprising enemies no less than friends, and created a Jewish state in a land where Jews had lacked all the attributes of statehood. The Arabs fought a classic war of position, and lost. After 1948, their situation shifted to a revolutionary one, that is, they aimed now at overthrowing the Israeli status quo. Yet, all actors on the Arab side, including the Palestinian Liberation Organisation (PLO) continued to fight a war of position until their morale collapsed and, wearing fig leaves, they surrendered to Israel.

Analogies are at best approximations, for no two historical situations are particularly similar. Even so, there exist frightening parallels between the ways in which Arab governments dealt with the Palestinian struggle for self-determination and the Islamabad government's policy on Kashmir. Rhetoric, strident in both cases, obstructs serious examination of realities. With Pakistan, as with the Arabs, no one tries to understand the resources, methods and strategies of the adversary. Little respect is shown for the aspirations of the people in question, Palestinian or Kashmiri, and no effort made to mobilise their resources. Their pliability and sacrifices are presumed.

Political opportunism, the exigencies of personal ambition and domestic politics shape the activities and proclamations of politicians and governments, and these pass as policy. Diplomacy is reduced to legal argumentation and references to UN resolutions. By and large, posturing substitutes for policymaking. The pressures to conform are such that the intellectual class either feeds the prevalent illusions or remains silent.

When policy is actually discussed and formulated, it is conceived mostly in military terms, and without dispassionate consideration of the adversary's or one's own political and economic capacity or will to sustain a war. Illusions substitute for analyses, bluster for planning and design. Naturally, miscalculations result and, when wars do break out, they result in defeat, as happened in 1948 and 1967 for the Arabs, and in 1971 for Pakistan, or in unfavourable stalemates as happened in 1965 for Pakistan and in 1973 for Egypt and Syria.

A notable feature in the case of both Palestine and Kashmir was the willingness of the warring sides to welcome ceasefires sponsored by superpowers and supervised by the United Nations. Obviously, neither side was keen to fight and, yet, the end of combat did not yield fruitful negotiations for peace. The vicious cycle of posturing, miscalculations and warfare finally ended for the Arabs in the abject surrender by the PLO, unequal peace for Egypt and Jordan, and a risky stalemate for Syria and Lebanon. In Southasia, Pakistan and India continue in their old ways and Kashmir remains contested betwixt.

Denial of reality

India's failures in Kashmir have been compounding since the time Jawaharlal Nehru's liberal, newly independent government chose to rely on the hated and oppressive Maharaja Hari Singh's decision to join the Indian Union. Pressed by a military confrontation with Pakistan, New Delhi took the dispute to the United Nations. It then promised to abide by the Security Council's resolution that called for a plebiscite, to allow Kashmiris to decide between joining India or Pakistan. India broke that promise.

New Delhi's only asset in those initial years had been Sheikh Mohammed Abdullah's cooperation. For his opposition to the maharaja's unpopular regime and his advocacy of reforms of land and labour in Kashmir, the sheikh and his party, the National Conference, had become the embodiment of Kashmiri nationalism. As chief minister of Kashmir, he promulgated land reforms in 1950, which further enhanced his standing with Kashmir's overwhelmingly rural and disinherited people. But this national hero was jailed in August 1953 after he began demanding greater autonomy. Except for two brief spells of freedom, he remained India's prisoner for 22 years, until February 1975, when the sheikh became chief minister after signing an agreement with Prime Minister Indira Gandhi.

Mrs Gandhi was able to defang the Lion of Kashmir, who allied with the ruling Indian National Congress. The only freedom he, and his heir apparent, Farooq Abdullah, exercised during his second term in office was the freedom to be outrageously self-indulgent and engage in corruption. Kashmiris nurtured anger and a sense of humiliation over how their vaunted 'lion' had been tamed in Indian hands. Furthermore, they had been denied not only the right of self-determination, a right affirmed by the United Nations, but were now also witnessing the disintegration of their historic Kashmiri party, the National Conference. This was taken as yet another assault on their identity and, as often happens in such circumstances, reinforced Kashmiri nationalism with regards to India.

Besides political disenchantment, the alienation of the Kashmiri from India is mired in history, economics and psychology. The problem is not communal, although sectarian Hindu and Muslim ideologues would like to view it in these terms. The latest phase of Kashmiri discontent followed significant social changes in Kashmir. The governments of Sheikh Abdullah and Ghulam Mohammed Bakhshi did free the Kashmiri from feudal controls, and helped to enlarge a middle class. In increasing numbers Kashmiri youths were educated, but their social mobility remained constricted because meaningful economic growth did not accompany land reforms or expanded educational facilities. Rebellions are normally started by the hopeful, not the abject poor.

The roots of the popular uprising in 1989 lay in the neglect of Kashmir, and New Delhi's unconscionable manipulation of Kashmiri politics. Yet India confronts the insurgency as incumbents normally do—with allegations of external subversion, brute force and unlawful machinations. Above all, it denies reality.

The reality is that New Delhi's moral isolation from the Kashmiri people is total and irreversible. It might be reversible if India were to envisage a qualitatively different relationship with Kashmir, one that meaningfully satisfied Kashmiri aspirations of self-government. So far, however, New Delhi has evinced no inclination in this direction. But can India's loss translate into Pakistan's gain?

The answer is, it cannot. Policymakers in Islamabad like to believe otherwise, and this is not unusual. It is quite common for rival countries to view their contest as a zero-sum game, whereby a loss for one side translates into a gain for the other. However, history shows this assumption to be false, and rival losses and gains are rarely proportional; they are determined by circumstances of history, politics and policy. India's Kashmir record offers a chronicle of failures, yet none of these have accrued to Pakistan's benefit. Rather, Pakistan's policy has suffered from its own defects.

Three characteristics made an early appearance in Islamabad's Kashmir policy. One, although Pakistani decision-makers know the problem to be fundamentally political, since 1948 they have approached it in military terms. Two, while the military outlook has dominated, there has been a healthy unwillingness to go to war over Kashmir. Three, while officially invoking Kashmiris' right to self-determination, Pakistan's governments and politicians have pursued policies that have all but disregarded the history, culture and aspirations of Kashmir's people. One consequence of this has been a string of grave Pakistani miscalculations regarding Kashmir. Another has been to alienate Kashmiris from Pakistan at crucial times such as 1948–49, 1965 and the 1990s.

Success has eluded Pakistan's Kashmir policy, and the costs have added up. Two wars, in 1948 and 1965, have broken out over Kashmir; annual casualties have mounted during the 1990s across the UN-monitored Line of Actual Control; and the burden of defence spending has not diminished. A study of recent Kashmiri history will help put Islamabad's blunders in perspective. In 1947–48, Kashmiri Muslims were subject to contrasting pulls. The partition of India, the communal strife that accompanied it, and Kashmir's political economy, which was linked to the Punjab, disposed them towards Pakistan. However, the people's political outlook was rooted in Kashmiri nationalism, which had been mobilised earlier by the National Conference led by Sheikh Abdullah. The latter was drawn towards the men and the party with whom he had worked closely since 1935—Nehru, Abul Kalam Azad and the Indian National Congress. (He did not meet Mohammad Ali Jinnah until 1944.) There was also a tradition of amicable relations between Kashmiri Hindus and Muslims, despite general Muslim antipathy towards the maharaja's rule.

What Kashmiris needed was time, a period of peaceful transition to resolve their ambivalence. This, they did not get. Owing to Louis Mountbatten's mindless haste, the Subcontinent was partitioned and power was transferred in a dizzying sequence of events that left little time to attend to complex details in far corners of the region. The leadership of the Muslim League, in particular, was preoccupied with the challenges of power transfer, division of assets, civil war and mass migration. The League was short on experienced leaders, and squabbling squandered their meagre skills. Quaid-i-Azam Jinnah was terminally ill.

In this climate of crisis and competition, Kashmir received scant attention. The little attention it did attract was from those who did not comprehend

Kashmiri aspirations, ambiguities or the extraordinary risks and temptations that lay in waiting. In a peculiar expression of distorted perspective, self-serving officials such as Ghulam Mohammed, a colonial bureaucrat who later wormed his way into becoming the governor-general of Pakistan, paid more attention to the undeserving and hopeless case of Hyderabad (Deccan) than to Kashmir.

When India's Home Minister Sardar Vallabhai Patel sent feelers about a possible give-and-take on Hyderabad and Kashmir, Ghulam Mohammed is said to have spurned this opportunity and carried on his lucrative dealings with Hyderabad's nizam. Pakistan also welcomed the accession of Junagadh and Manavadar, even though an overwhelming majority in both states (as well as Hyderabad) were Hindu.

In effect, Pakistan held three divergent positions on the question of accession: in favour of the Hyderabad nizam's right to independence, Junagadh's right to accede to Pakistan against the wishes of the populace, and, in Kashmir, for the right to self-determination. Double standards constitute a common enough practice in politics, but doing so invariably harms the actor who lacks the power to avert consequences. The nawab of Junagadh tried to deliver his Hindu-majority state to Pakistan, which set the precedent for the maharaja of Muslim-dominated Kashmir choosing India. Pakistan did not have the power to defend either the nawab or the nizam, nor the will to punish the maharaja. So India, practising double standards during its turn, took it all.

India's policies have been no less riddled with blunders than Pakistan's. Its moral isolation on Kashmir is nearly total, and unlikely to be overcome by military means or political manipulation. New Delhi commands not a shred of legitimacy among Kashmiri Muslims. Ironically, even as India's standing in Kashmir appears increasingly untenable, Kashmiris today appear farther from the goal of liberation than they were in the years 1989–92.

Pakistan's engagement in Kashmir is indirect and unacknowledged. As such, it enjoys greater tactical and political flexibility than either the Indian or the Kashmiri leaders. The diversity and nuances of informed opinion in Pakistan also render Islamabad more elastic than New Delhi, where the Hindutva right is powerful and breathes heavy over weak liberal shoulders. Furthermore, for a number of reasons—its popular standing in large segments of the Kashmiri population, material support of militant groups, international advocacy of Kashmir's cause—Pakistan's leverage in Kashmir is greater than what most observers assume. Yet beyond repeating tired shibboleths about 'our principled stand', Islamabad lacks a functioning policy capable of exploiting its advantages.

To date, the governments of Pakistan and Azad Kashmir have spent millions of dollars to mobilise international support behind the question of Kashmir. Islamabad's jet-setting, patronage-soaked lobbying for a UN-recommended plebiscite has elicited no significant international support during the last seven years of Kashmir insurgency. Cumulatively, Pakistan's score has been a pathetic zero. A few months ago, the Security Council even dropped Kashmir from its agenda, and it was only retroactive Pakistani lobbying that was able to obtain a temporary reprieve. The most that Pakistan has been able to achieve are favourable resolutions from the Organisation of Islamic Countries, an entity about as influential in world politics as an Arabian camel. Kashmir's cause therefore serves merely as one big pork barrel for Pakistani carpetbaggers and patronage-seekers, religious and secular, parliamentary and private.

In sum, Pakistan continues to wage a half-hearted 'war of position' replete with private doubts, symbolic posturing and petty opportunism. Its support has not helped to unify or energise the insurgency in Kashmir into a winning movement. The resulting stalemate appears 'stable', and unlikely to be upset in the absence of a conventional India–Pakistan war. Since war is not an option, Pakistan's policy is reduced to bleeding India; and India's to bleeding the Kashmiris, and to hit out at Pakistan whenever a wound can be inflicted.

Divided resistance

A study of liberation struggles of the 20th century shows that they have been victorious mainly due to seven primary and four secondary factors. The primary factors are: popular support for the liberation movement amidst increasing moral isolation of the incumbent; a dominant and unified rebel leadership and organisation; primacy of politics and subordination of the military to the political leadership; ability of the rebel organisation to 'out-administer' the incumbent, rather than merely outfight it; clarity of goals on the part of the rebels and consensus on objectives; harmony between the ideology and functioning of the movement and the inherited culture of the population; and, lastly, support from foreign countries to sustain morale and mobilise international opinion. The secondary factors refer to the logistics of waging protracted struggles: favourable terrain, availability of food, supply of arms and dependable external sanctuaries.

Movements that tend to succeed normally have the primary attributes but not the secondary ones. The *mujahideen*'s struggle against the Soviet intervention in Afghanistan, considered successful, was unique in that it was exceptionally well endowed in secondary resources, and deficient in the areas of primary requirements. However, the weaknesses were offset by generous support from the United States, Saudi Arabia, Iran and, above all, Pakistan. Even so, the mujahideen fragmented and fell apart when the Soviet Union withdrew, and President Najibullah continued to rule in Kabul. A senior diplomat in Delhi observed that the 'failure to comprehend the uniqueness of the Afghan experience and Kashmir's contrasting patterns have contributed to Pakistani blunders in the Valley.'

A look at the Kashmiri environment today suggests some unhappy conclusions. When the uprising began in 1989, it was popular, politically rooted, and converging around one dominant party—the Jammu & Kashmir Liberation Front (JKLF). Today there are upwards of 30 groups, ideologically diverse, competing, often undercutting each other. In this free-for-all, India's counter-insurgency operatives have introduced their own players, the most notorious and powerful of these being the group led by Kuka Parray, which has cut significantly into some strongholds of Kashmiri resistance.

Militarism has penetrated the resistance movement to the point that armed groups have gained primacy over the political wing. The parallel hierarchies—administrative organs, justice and policing—which were developed during 1989–92, have all but disintegrated as militarisation has grown and resistance groups have multiplied.

Appearances notwithstanding, the Kashmiri resistance is deeply divided over the question of objectives. The pro-Pakistan and pro-independence groups, the Islamists and secularists, have little in common except their opposition to India. Cooperation and coordination is difficult, if not impossible. With few exceptions, the ideologies and styles of the resistance groups, some of them linked to Pakistan's Islamic parties, run counter to the Kashmiri political culture, which is by and large temporal and pluralistic, with roots deeper in mystical than in theological Islam.

As disheartening to Kashmiris' morale as the situation at home is the news from Pakistan. The violence in Karachi—murders in government custody, siege of *mohallas* (neighbourhoods), incarceration without charge and trial, and extortion by militia—parallels the experience in the Valley today. In Islamabad, a prominent Kashmiri intellectual with a five-decade record of pro-Pakistan militancy talks ruefully of the Kashmiris' sense of alienation from Pakistan: 'All that ethnic warfare, stories of corruption, sectarian violence and political squabbles have rendered Pakistan an unattractive option. Also, Azad Kashmir is not the model for which 40,000 young Kashmiris have given their lives.'

One Srinagar intellectual, on a visit to Delhi, said, 'Riaz Khokar Sahib [Pakistan's High Commissioner to New Delhi] has Karachi thrown at him whenever he speaks of Kashmir.' Said another, a professor, 'India has been a bitter experience for us. Pakistan looks no better now. So we want a third option.'

Kashmiri aspirations have, thus, converged around a single slogan, of *azadi*. Pakistan's policymakers and Pakistani partisans of the Kashmiri struggle ought to acknowledge that this slogan translates as 'independence' for Kashmir. There exists little enthusiasm among the Kashmiri-speaking people for a plebiscite that would confine them to exchanging life under Indian sovereignty for one under Pakistan's sovereignty.

I have found no Kashmiri among the many I have interviewed inside or outside Pakistan who accepts Kashmir as an 'unfinished agenda' of the 1947 Partition. In the US, a Kashmiri academic from Srinagar asked, 'East Pakistan has violently separated from the west. The Muslim nation of the Quaid-i-Azam is now divided between three sovereign states. So what "unfinished agenda of Partition" are we Kashmiris to complete?'

Further, there is little possibility of fraternity and amity with Kashmir if it were miraculously one day to become part of Pakistan. This is because nationalism is deeper in Kashmir than in Sindh, Balochistan, or among Pashtuns or Urdu-speakers. It would assert itself in relation to the Pakistani state sooner and more furiously than Pakistani politicians imagine. At that point, Pakistan would find itself wearing the shoes India has on today. Actually, the stage for Act One of that potential strife is already set—in Azad Kashmir, which is viewed by most Kashmiri-speaking people as a Punjabi-dominated state that has shut out 'true Kashmiris' from power and privilege. Few Kashmiris can identify with Azad Kashmir. Said a retired bureaucrat who served the Muzaffarabad government in senior positions, 'To add insult to injury, Pakistani officials at the highest levels display colossal ignorance of Kashmiri history and culture. This deeply injures our sensibilities.'

Kashmiris had one more occasion to consider their alienation from Islamabad during the crisis over the Hazrat Bal mosque, when the Indian army besieged it to capture some militants. Former Prime Minister Benazir Bhutto repeatedly referred to the shrine as 'Hazrat Baal'. Said the former bureaucrat, 'I suppose she thinks the shrine is so called because the Prophet's hair is preserved there. *Bal* is a Kashmiri word meaning "neighbourhood". People are dying there and she does not know how to pronounce it nor what it means.'

In Pakistan, there is a growing though insufficiently articulated recognition of flaws in the government's Kashmir posture. In 1994, an association of retired civil and military officials in Islamabad invited M P Bhandara, a prominent Pakistani businessman and former member of Parliament, to speak on this and related issues in Islamabad. As summarised later in the media, he told the group that to let Kashmir bleed as it is now doing was 'the moral equivalent of seeing a person die in a traffic accident for want of police formality.' Islamabad's policy to end Kashmiri suffering must be sensitive to Kashmiri aspirations, he argued, adding that the policymakers must consider the impact of such a policy on the overall safety and well-being of India's Muslims. Bhandara also expressed interest in Indian journalist Kuldip Nayar's suggestion of a 'Trieste-type' solution that would confer greater autonomy upon the two Kashmirs, roughly along the Line of Actual Control.

These were not the normal terms of Pakistani discourse on Kashmir, and one would have expected some pushback from an audience of former government officials. Instead, the responses were moderate, thoughtful and generally in agreement with Bhandara's assessment. 'Our thinking rhetoric on Kashmir is old,' said one person. As to the disposition to term Kashmir as the 'unfinished agenda of Partition', this gentleman asked, 'Do we reflect on the implications of this repeated claim? What would happen if the Kashmir agenda is finished Partition-style? Will Kashmir be divided along religious lines? Will there be migrations of people trapped on the wrong side of Kashmir's partition, massacres and all? How will all that contribute to peace in this region? Will that enhance Pakistan's security?'

Said a former army officer, 'We ought to do our homework, which we do not do. India's position is less frozen than ours. It is readying now to offer Kashmir internal autonomy. In time this could become an attractive alternative to worn-out Kashmiris. India's governing elite should not be underestimated: it is sophisticated, capable of planning and executing a policy, and its political system is stable.' This was back in 1994. Such views are widespread in Pakistan today, though not widely articulated.

Shame and the burden

The first step towards a solution to the Kashmir tangle is to comprehend the ambitions and fears of the three parties—India, Pakistan and the Kashmiris. India's ambition is territorial; its aim, to exercise sovereignty over the Valley,

Jammu and Ladakh. Its strategic concerns vis-à-vis China reinforce the territorial imperative. New Delhi feels it cannot let pro-China Pakistan take over its strategic underbelly.

There are other reinforcements: India is politically polarised, and this polarisation will undoubtedly escalate if a centrist government accepts a formula to partition Kashmir. Also, India is a multi-religious state with a Muslim population as large as Pakistan's. New Delhi cannot afford another partition along religious lines without risking massacres and riots led by the strident Hindu nationalists.

Pakistan's ambition is also territorial. It is reinforced by a deeply held sense of injustice. After all, Mountbatten and his judicial minions did conspire to give India access to Jammu & Kashmir. Strategically, India's military presence in Kashmir stretches Pakistan's dangerously large defence parameters, and cuts it off from the source of its lifeline of rivers. To acquiesce in India's illegal occupation is to submit to the bullying of a big neighbour. Furthermore, Kashmiri protests and rebellions against India will not allow Pakistan to forego its advocacy of the Kashmiri right to self-determination.

As for the Kashmiri-speaking majority, the driving force among them is a well-founded sense of victimhood, a feeling historically rooted but greatly nourished since 1989 by New Delhi's brutal repression, the excesses of its security forces, and the collapse of Kashmir's economy. Furthermore, Kashmiri nationalism enjoys strong objective bases in a distinct language and culture, common historical memory, and unique geographical and environmental conditions. Kashmiris also view themselves as a divided and dispersed people, a perception that nourishes the yearning for re-unification and independence.

Since a large majority of Kashmiri-speakers live under Indian occupation, they see India as their tormentor and Pakistan as their potential rescuer. Their aspirations, however, are largely for freedom. This quest is not defined in terms of the 'two-nation' theory. The Valley is a classic environment for nurturing nationalism, home of Kashmiriyat. India cannot suppress it. Pakistan cannot absorb it. It must be accommodated.

All three sides are in a blind alley, back to back. India and Pakistan have the capacity, and apparently the inclination, to stay this course indefinitely. Out of frustration and fatigue they might swing around one day and come to blows. The Kashmiris, being the weakest and most vulnerable party, have a Hobson's choice: either give in to India and settle for what symbolic concessions they can get from the tormenting giant, or continue with resistance, however sporadically. History is replete with examples of oppressed peoples who have done just that, and their sacrifices have always been awesome. The shame and moral burden was always on the oppressors.

If one views as important the distinction between governing a society and coercing a multitude, India has ceased to govern Kashmir. Its options, then, are three-fold: one, keep its coercive presence in Kashmir and hope that some day Kashmiris will tire and throw in the towel. Two, negotiate with Kashmiri leaders on terms the latter could live with. Or three, negotiate seriously with Pakistan and Kashmiri insurgents who are grouped in the All Party Hurriyat Conference (APHC). There is also a fourth option, another India–Pakistan war, which is unrealistic as far as settling the question of Kashmir is concerned.

India's current policy is to stick with the first option while giving it a facelift. This entailed holding two elections in Kashmir while making vague promises of greater autonomy. Although the US supported the ploy, it did not attract a single leader of the APHC because Kashmiri leaders distrusted India's tenuous promise, and because Pakistan encouraged their rejection of it. So, two shotgun elections—for the Indian Parliament and for Kashmir's Legislative Assembly—have yielded the return to Srinagar, as chief minister, of Farooq Abdullah. The old Lion's ageing and discredited son is held by the people in high contempt for his earlier reign of corruption and collaboration with New Delhi.

India's electoral ploy is likely to fail. As happened in Algeria and Vietnam, within months these elections will yield India another harvest of bitterness and alienation. Pakistani and Kashmiri leaders are likely, then, to get another opportunity to engage in the politics and diplomacy of movement. If they fail to avail yet another opportunity, they will remain holding unused and archaic cards in frozen hands. Such failures rarely harm the leaders—only the people are hurt.

The present level of low-intensity warfare and large-scale repression will continue to inflict great hardships on the Kashmiri people. India, for its part, can absorb the material and political costs indefinitely. Pakistan's own non-diplomatic options are narrow. War with India, as already noted, is not a viable option. For a variety of reasons, Islamabad cannot upgrade its logistical support to Kashmiri militants substantially enough to compensate for their steady depletion in arms, men and morale. Islamabad's quest for resolving the Kashmir conflict in accordance with the United Nations resolution has become unattainable. There exists no significant support for it internationally. Nationalism has taken root in Kashmir, so most Kashmiris will prefer independence to affiliation with Pakistan.

Neither India nor Pakistan has tried the option of negotiated settlement. This would require the two adversaries to abandon their positions, fixed half a century ago, and acknowledge three fundamental realities. The first is that Kashmir's future is a matter of dispute between Pakistan, India and the Kashmiri people. Its settlement must involve and satisfy all three parties. Second, that no matter how forcefully they are promoted, unilateral solutions will not work. Kashmir is too large, populous and strategic a place for a unilateral solution to be sustained. Third, that in this instance the benefits of a historic compromise are much greater than the profits or pride of territorial acquisition.

Divided sovereignty

It is difficult for nations not ravaged by war, as were Germany and Japan at the end of World War II, to shift easily from one state of mind to another. A period of transition, during which assumptions can be tested, trust is engaged, and new bonds are built across boundaries, is often preferable to precipitous peace of the kind the Arabs of Egypt, Palestine and Jordan have entered into with Israel. In Southasia, it is important to proceed step by careful step so that shocks can be absorbed while confidence is built among the parties.

Peace, however gradual, must be based on common commitment to principles that have to be spelt out. One basic principle is that the ultimate arbiters of the Kashmir dispute are the people of Kashmir. A settlement that does not restore the natural, millennial flow of Kashmiri history, culture and geography is not likely to satisfy either Kashmiri aspirations or the requirements of durable peace between India and Pakistan. It has to be acknowledged, too, that the notion of sovereignty has changed in the last half-century, and is about to transform some more, whereby divided sovereignties are not synonymous with divided frontiers.

If these principles are understood, diplomacy might be aimed at reaching an agreement to be implemented in three stages: autonomy, open borders and 'unification with divided sovereignty' over historic Kashmir. Under an arrangement whereby Jammu and Ladakh exercise a great measure of autonomy, India might claim sovereignty over them. Similarly, Azad Kashmir might be assured fuller autonomy and freedom from the federal government at Islamabad while Pakistan continues to remain the sovereign power. Whereupon the Valley—the historical and geographical heart of Kashmir and home of Kashmiriyat—can be invested with the attributes of sovereignty.

This last needs to be accomplished in a manner that readies the Valley to serve three related purposes: as the repository and beacon of Kashmiriyat, as the insurer and facilitator of Kashmir's unity, and as a bridge between India and Pakistan. To diminish the risk of civil strife and demographic instability, and also to allow time for this new arrangement to become workable, the Valley could be guided through a period of transition under a United Nations trusteeship.

A peace plan along these lines is likely to encounter opposition from hard-liners on all three sides. Diehard Kashmiri nationalists would want sovereignty over all of the erstwhile maharaja's domain, regardless of whether it is desired by the inhabitants concerned. Similarly, the Islamists would want to make an Islamic state of it all. Fortunately, these individuals are few in number and are dependent on Pakistan's government agencies. Those who are committed to the 'Kashmir *banega* Pakistan' proposition will also oppose loudly; but it is a fortuitous though rarely acknowledged fact that given an opportunity of sincere expression, wise and farsighted views predominate in the higher ranks of the military and bureaucracy in Pakistan, and this is also true of India.

Nevertheless, India is where resistance to the proposed step-by-step solution is going to be strongest. India is a 'status quo power', and a status quo abhors change. India is also where the militant right is ascendant, and it is most powerful in the Hindi-speaking belt where Kashmir is a live issue. Furthermore, India's decision-making elite appears largely persuaded that India must cast itself in the image of a great power. Typically, great powers are less susceptible to compacts of equality and compromise, especially with smaller neighbours. The challenge of Pakistani and Kashmiri diplomacy is to persuade Indian opinion, as well as persuade the big powers and international opinion, and to bring multiple pressures on India's government to opt in favour of a sane and lasting settlement.

This is a difficult challenge, but the time is ripe. Thinking Indians and Pakistanis know that history moves on, rendering fixed positions obsolete. Any good soldier, engineer, physician, philosopher or historian understands the high cost of obsolescence, and new realities are rapidly enveloping Southasia. Globalisation is creating transnational assembly lines, breaking boundaries, forcing enemies to trade, creating transnational centres of power and circumscribing sovereignties. Southasia's governments are eager participants in the process.

Prime ministers proudly claim MOUs as their achievements, cite figures of foreign investments, sign international trade agreements and join regional cooperation treaties. India and Pakistan are members of SAARC and the World

Trade Organisation, and signatories of General Agreement on Tariffs and Trade (GATT) and the South Asian Free Trade Area (SAFTA). Ironically, they cross swords in these councils of collaboration. New realities lead them to enter into pacts of amity, and tired instincts and vested interests compel them to rake up the bile and bitterness of an earlier time.

One hand, stretched towards the future, is chopped off by another anchored in the past. This is but one, possibly the most harmful manifestation, of disorganic growth in the body politics of India and Pakistan. Yet such distortions will continue to grow as long as the two governments do not restore to this region its natural state of ecology and production, and commerce and culture.

To become prosperous and normal peoples, we must make peace where there is hostility, build bridges where there are chasms, heal where there are wounds, feed where there is hunger, prosper where there is poverty. Kashmir is the finest place to start, and not merely because it is the core of the Indo-Pakistan conflict. Our histories, cultures and religions have converged in Kashmir. Our rivers begin there, mountains meet there, and our dreams rest there.

Chapter 6

The fractured image of Muhammad Ali Jinnah

Himal, February 1998

Khaled Ahmed

Muhammad Ali Jinnah's party, the Pakistan Muslim League, is in power, and it has no doubt that he would have approved of the process of Islamisation and the imposition of Sharia law. The Quaid-e-Azam's entire career is today explained as given over to the struggle for the establishment of an Islamic state in which only Muslims would be full citizens. In fact, Jinnah has been harnessed to a version of Islamic ideology that was not his own. In order to maintain Jinnah in this ideological posture, the Pakistani state has had to modify many known details of the man's life—his beliefs, family relationships, eating habits, religiosity, his attitude towards Partition and towards India, and his views on minority rights.

In India, Jinnah has been reviled as a malevolent, humourless, politically ambitious man who wrecked the dream of a united, secular India. Authors such as H M Seervai have tried to put the record straight, but Jinnah-bashing continues in India, which has had an impact on how the larger world views the Quaid. Gandhi was Jinnah's contemporary rival, but it was young Jawaharlal Nehru who was responsible for demonising him. Shortly before his death, Louis Mountbatten called Jinnah a 'bastard' in his interview with the writers Dominique Lappiere and Larry Collins while they were researching for *Freedom at Midnight*. Richard Attenborough's film *Gandhi* has castigated Jinnah while deifying the Mahatma.

Just as he has been misrepresented outside the country, the Quaid's image has been manipulated within Pakistan. His country today struggles with internal crises, made possibly worse because it has deviated so far from the path that Jinnah charted. Indeed, the falsification of Jinnah hits at the very soul of Pakistan. It has been easier for the state to tinker with Jinnah's historic portrait because his family is not around to challenge the version that has emerged. In fact, Pakistanis today know virtually nothing about his kin, his marriage or his only child, a daughter still alive who has never been officially invited to visit Pakistan. It is now taken as the truth that the Quaid turned against his daughter when she married a Christian, considering her an apostate. However, this stands without evidence.

As for Jinnah's attitude towards India, unlike what the average Pakistani has been led to believe, Jinnah never thought that India and Pakistan would be hostile neighbours. The fact that three institutions in India—including the Aligarh Muslim University—were named beneficiaries in Jinnah's will clearly goes against the state-sponsored version of his life. Jinnah could have changed his will any time after he made it in 1929, more so after 1947, but he did not. It is a different matter that none of the three institutions in the end received money from the Jinnah Trust, which looks after the Quaid's estate—funds that were instead diverted to Pakistani institutions.

Perhaps the most drastic redrafting of Jinnah's worldview has been in how he saw minority communities, for Jinnah's vision of Indo-Pakistani relations itself was based on a bilateral regard for the minorities in each country. However, particularly within Pakistan, it was not a vision anyone cared much for. Jinnah's colleagues in the Muslim League were not willing to treat non-Muslims equally, especially not the Hindus of East Pakistan, who formed one-fourth of the population there.

The re-moulding of Jinnah's persona began even before the birth of Pakistan. On 11 August 1947, addressing the Constituent Assembly in Karachi, Jinnah said:

> You are free to go to your temples, you are free to go to your mosques or to any other place of worship in this state of Pakistan. You may belong to any religion or caste or creed ... that has nothing to do with the business of the state ... We are starting in the days when there is no discrimination, no distinction between one community and another, no distinction between one caste or

creed or another. We are starting with this fundamental principle that we are all citizens and equal citizens of one state.

The Muslim League bureaucracy, which did not agree with Jinnah's vision of a secular Pakistan, asked the press in Karachi not to print the statement. In later years, the statement was not even allowed to feature in official publications. Under General Zia ul-Haq, historians were even commissioned to state that Jinnah was not completely in his senses when he addressed the Constituent Assembly.

Gen Zia also banned Stanley Wolpert's book *Jinnah of Pakistan* (1984) because it contained descriptions of Jinnah's dietary habits. Wolpert quoted M C Chagla's book *Roses in December: An autobiography* (1974), in which it is mentioned that Jinnah drank alcohol and ate ham sandwiches. (Chagla, later chief justice at the Bombay High Court, was Jinnah's private secretary and also the Muslim League secretary. He left the League following differences with Jinnah over the Nehru Report of 1928, which envisaged a secular nationalist India and went against the Muslims because it denied them separate electorates, which would have meant assured representation in the legislatures.) On the whole, Wolpert's book is probably the most effective defence of Jinnah's secular credentials, but it has remained banned in Pakistan.

The author, who went on to write a debunking biography of Nehru titled *Nehru: A tryst with destiny* (1996), is also not as welcome in Pakistan as he might have been. It is said that Gen Zia, who acquired numerous copies of Wolpert's book on Jinnah, was in the habit of presenting it to his guests with the offending page marked to show the 'difference' between himself, as the Muslim messianic leader, and Jinnah, who had founded the country wrong. The Quaid's daughter, Dina, living in New York, was secretly asked to deny that her father ever drank alcohol or ate ham. When she refused to oblige, she was threatened with 'disclosures' about her private life if she ever made it public that she had been approached.

Islamic objectives

It is often said that Pakistan's Constitution was not framed till as late as 1956, because the West Pakistani elite was not willing to share power with the East Pakistani majority. Any constitutional dispensation would have tilted in favour of East Pakistan because its population was larger. Nevertheless, the first

Constitution of 1956 favoured West Pakistan by creating the myth of parity between East Pakistan and a West Pakistan formed into one unit after abolishing the four provinces.

Another reason for postponing the constitutional exercise, however, was that Jinnah was not willing to allow a religion-based document. It was immediately after his death in 1948 that Prime Minister Liaquat Ali Khan formed a committee of the *ulema* to decide the Islamic guidelines for it. In 1949, when the recommendations were tabled in the Constituent Assembly as the Objectives Resolution, the East Pakistani Hindu members objected, but neither did the draft please the Islamists in the Muslim League. Constitutional historian G W Chaudhry and others actually complained that the Objectives Resolution was not Islamic enough.

It is to his credit that Liaquat Ali Khan did not allow the Objectives Resolution to become as abrasively Islamic as would have been preferred by his secretary-general, Chaudhry Muhammad Ali, a close friend of Maulana Syed Abu Ala Maududi, the founder of Jamaat Islami. The reason was that Pakistan had signed the Universal Declaration of Human Rights in 1948, whose Article 18 provides that minorities should be allowed to practise their religion freely. Hence, the Objectives Resolution stated that 'adequate provision would be made for the minorities freely to profess and practise their religion and develop their cultures.'

With time, the Objectives Resolution became the Preamble to the Constitution of Pakistan. In 1985, Gen Zia decided to make the Preamble an operative part of the Constitution, and his Eighth Amendment included it as an annex to the Constitution. But without pointing it out, he removed the term 'freely' from the text. The situation today is that the Objectives Resolution, as an inoperative preamble to the Constitution, promises minorities that they can practise their religion freely, but the operative annex inside takes away this freedom. After the death of Gen Zia, in 1988, successive elected governments could have restored the original text in the annex, simply by declaring it a printing error—but they did not.

In his book on Gen Zia, *Working with Zia: Pakistan's Power Politics 1977–1988* (1996), General Khalid Mahmood Arif writes that the text of the Eighth Amendment was agreed at the army general headquarters through a consensus among the corps commanders. However, the actual job of changing the 1973 Constitution to make it 'Islamic enough' for Gen Zia was probably done by historian and lawyer Syed Sharifuddin Pirzada, a former secretary and devotee of Jinnah and his assistants. Pirzada was the one responsible for making public the ideological rift between Jinnah and his trusted lieutenant, Liaquat Ali Khan, and also wrote extensively to show that in his last days Jinnah had lost trust in Liaquat.

The Eighth Amendment—through a section known as Article 51(4)—introduced separate electorates for Muslims and non-Muslims, thus nullifying Jinnah's 11 August 1947 address to the Constituent Assembly. Non-Muslims could no longer vote together with Muslims for the general seats; they would instead stand for elections and vote only for special seats set aside for them in the federal and provincial legislatures. The amendment was made so ham-handedly that the phraseology of Article 51(4) relating to the National Assembly was not repeated in Article 106 relating to the provincial assemblies. When a Christian candidate went to court to make the Election Commission accept his candidature for the general seats in a provincial assembly, the judges interpreted Article 106 tendentiously to reject the petition. (In 1997, outgoing Chief Election Commissioner Sardar Fakhre Alam did recommend that joint electorates be resumed because separate electorates were tantamount to denial of representation to non-Muslims in Pakistan.)

Pakistan's first constitution, in 1956—prepared by Chaudhry Muhammad Ali, who was to become Pakistan's first prime minister under it—had sought to impose separate electorates on both wings of Pakistan. But East Pakistan rejected the idea, after which the matter was left to the discretion of the provinces. West Pakistan accepted the separate electorates under the Muslim League government but failed to form constituencies for non-Muslims, because its geography was clearly seen to deny representation to the minorities. As Rafi Raza wrote in *Pakistan in Perspective 1947–1997* (1997), 'Eventually, in April 1957, joint electorates were reintroduced throughout Pakistan because the task of delimiting separate electorates proved too complex.'

Since the adoption of the Eighth Amendment in 1985, Pakistan has been forcing non-Muslims to vote for special seats under a system of constituencies that are geographically so spread out that voters are most often completely unacquainted with their leaders. The minorities have been agitating against separate electorates, which have now been elevated by Islamabad to the realm of ideology.

Political package

The issue of separate electorates has been given a clear religious colour, with non-Muslims not allowed to vote together with Muslims. However, Jinnah's campaign for separate electorates in united India was of a different nature, and had nothing to do with religion. (And his two-nation proposal came much later, after he was repeatedly snubbed by the Congress.) In united India, it was the Muslim minority asking for separate electorates; in contemporary Pakistan, the minorities are not asking for separate electorates, but rather for joint electorates.

Separate electorates were initially recommended to the Indian government in 1908 by Gopal Krishna Gokhale, India's great liberal leader who was a source of inspiration to Jinnah. In 1916, in a joint session in Lucknow, Jinnah was able to get the Muslim League and Congress to accept the principle of special seats for the Muslim minority on the basis of Gokhale's liberal vision. At the joint session, Bal Gangadhar Tilak, who had eclipsed Gokhale in popularity with the use of religious symbols and extremist nationalism, voted in favour of separate electorates for Muslims. The same year, he had been successfully defended by Jinnah in a case of sedition against the Raj. Jinnah, who had been called the 'ambassador of Hindu–Muslim unity' by Gokhale, got along nicely with Tilak's religious rhetoric—both were politicians who had an eye on the opportune moment.

In 1928, replying to the Nehru Report, which had gone back on the Lucknow compact over separate electorates, Jinnah issued his Fourteen Points, in which separate electorates were claimed not as a religious demand but as a political package that could be modified. In Punjab province, the cross-communal Unionist Party of Muslims, Hindus and Sikhs ruled on the basis of separate electorates, which gave Muslims a permanent majority. When Jinnah began negotiating with the Congress over his demand for separate electorates, the Unionists convened an All-India Muslim Conference in 1929 denouncing his abandonment of the cause. The Unionists were able to get the support of the Aga Khan and Allama Iqbal, the Muslim League leader from Punjab who is perhaps better known outside Pakistan as the poet Muhammad Iqbal.

While all this was going on, Gandhi took over the Khilafat Movement—organised against the British for dismembering the Turkish Empire—which the Muslim League was reluctant to support. Gandhi thus became a leader of Muslims (that is, until he called off the Movement). Through support for the Movement, Gandhi eased Jinnah out of the Congress centre-stage. During this period, besides being in political limbo, Jinnah was personally devastated due to his having become estranged from his wife. Her death, in 1929, caused him to migrate to England, where he bought a house and settled down to legal practice, and was not to return to India till 1934.

Back in India, the Nehru Report compounded the hurt the conservative anti-Jinnah Muslims had felt by Gandhi's calling off the Khilafat Movement in 1924. Thereafter, separate electorates emerged as the foremost political issue in Muslim politics. The principle established in united India was: if the minorities want them they should be allowed as affirmative action, but it should not be imposed on the minorities by the majority population. In Pakistan, the minorities are so few (about one per cent of the national population) and scattered all over so thinly that they would prefer to vote together with the Muslims, for they would then form a vote bank for Muslim leaders. The Pakistani state has violated this principle by forcing the minorities to accept a system that effectively disempowers them. Jinnah would never have allowed it.

Apart from separate electorates, there are other laws that make non-Muslims in Pakistan second-class citizens. The law of evidence in force under the Sharia discriminates against them because their testimony is not equal to that of Muslims; the *gustakh-e-rasul* (Insult to the Prophet) law targets non-Muslims and has serious legal defects; conversion to Islam by non-Muslim women has been exploited by Muslims because Christian and Hindu marriages stand automatically annulled after the wife converts to Islam. Under another law, non-Muslims are not allowed to compete freely with Muslims for seats in educational institutions and for government employment; under the law on *zakat* (a religious tithe for charity), non-Muslims are not allowed treatment in institutions run by Islamic charity.

Nothing, it can be said, has damaged Pakistan's position on the Kashmir dispute in the 1990s more than the laws passed against the non-Muslims. The 1949 UN Security Council resolutions asking for a plebiscite in Kashmir were passed when Pakistan was still Jinnah's Pakistan. Today, it would be morally wrong to even propose that nearly two million Hindus and Buddhists of Jammu and Ladakh live under the draconian anti-minorities laws that exist in Pakistan.

Pakistan's Gettysburg

Jinnah was driven to separatism by the Congress and its dynamic leader, Nehru, who personally disliked Jinnah. While in exile in London, Jinnah attended the two Round Table Conferences convened in 1930 and 1931 to decide the future Constitution of India. He heard the name 'Pakistan' in London among Muslim activists residing there, in particular Chaudhry Rehmat Ali, who had thought up a scheme for Muslim homelands in India. The Muslim delegates of the Round

Table Conference, however, ignored Ali's theory, mainly because they had been handpicked by the Unionist chief Fazle Hussain, who in 1930 had become the first Indian member of the Viceroy's Council. The Unionists were against the Pakistan proposal because they wanted a united non-communal Punjab opposed to the politics of both the Congress and the Muslim League.

In 1940, when the All-India Muslim League approved the Lahore Resolution, the Punjab Unionist premier, Sikandar Hayat, saw to it that Pakistan was not mentioned. The resolution also mentioned separate states 'to be created for the Muslims instead of one state' in order to ensure Punjab and Bengal their separate identities. After the 1937 election, which was held on the basis of separate electorates under the Government of India Act 1935, and in which the Congress won overwhelming victories in all provinces except Punjab and Bengal, Jinnah approached the Congress once again for an agreement on power-sharing with the Muslim League. But he was snubbed by Nehru, then the Congress president. Jinnah was perforce pushed into embracing a scheme for which he had no stomach, as a liberal-secularist.

Today in Pakistan, one cannot openly call oneself a secularist. The term *liberal* is also seen as a secular giveaway, condemned by religious parties. When President Muhammad Rafiq Tarar called himself a 'liberal Muslim', he was challenged by the clergy. Jinnah could not have survived in this environment. To maintain him in the national pantheon, the state is at pains to describe him as a non-secular, non-liberal leader who had promised the Sharia as part of his political programme.

According to author Akbar S Ahmed, Jinnah's two speeches at the Constituent Assembly constitute his Gettysburg Address. They are: the 11 August speech in which he declared Pakistan a secular state, and the 14 August speech in which, in answer to Mountbatten's reference to Akbar the Great as the model for the new Muslim state, he pointed to the greater example of the Prophet of Islam, Muhammad. Additionally, while addressing the Karachi Bar Association on 25 January 1948 on the occasion of the Prophet's birthday, Jinnah said: 'Some are misled by propaganda. Islamic principles are as applicable to life as they were 1,300 years ago. The Constitution of Pakistan will be made on the basis of the Sharia.'

These two references to Islam are used by social conservatives to claim Jinnah for themselves, but they make Jinnah a fundamentalist, as aggressively claimed by New Delhi editor-journalist M J Akbar in his book *India under Siege* (1986). Jinnah had learnt his politics in India the hard way. He had objected to Gandhi's use of religion but he had also seen, without protest, Tilak doing it blatantly to establish himself as *lokmanya*, the title prefixed to his name, which means 'respected by the people'. Nothing worked on the masses more than nationalist extremism and divisive religious sloganeering. He was forced to use Islam in Punjab where the cross-communal Unionism was finally brought down by the mullahs.

But the concept of Sharia was different in the minds of Jinnah and Allama Iqbal, after they corresponded in 1937–38 to clarify what later came to be known as the vision of Pakistan. Both had endured abusive opposition from the pro-Congress Khilafat Committee headed by the Ali brothers, Muhammad and Ali. (In *The world of Fatwas: Or the Shariah in action*, New Delhi journalist Arun Shourie quotes Gandhi's diarist to show how the Ali brothers were devoted to Gandhi after 1919, kissing his feet and expressing their opposition to the Muslim League. Akbar S Ahmed notes the violent opposition faced by Jinnah from Shaukat Ali. Ashiq Hussain Batalvi, perhaps the best historian of the Pakistan Movement, speaks of virulent journalistic attacks made on Jinnah by Muhammad Ali.)

Allama Iqbal, steadfast in his opposition to the concept of Khilafat, defended the 'liberal' model of Turkish Islam in his famous lectures. The book Jinnah gave Dina to read was on Kemal Ataturk, the secular founder of modern Turkey who had abolished the Caliphate (Khilafat) in 1924. In his sixth and final lecture delivered at Aligarh in 1929, Allama Iqbal opposed the *hudood* (Quranic punishments) today in force in Pakistan. As quoted in *Reconstruction of Religious Thought in Islam* (1977), he said:

> The prophetic method of teaching according to Shah Waliullah is that, generally speaking, the law revealed by a prophet takes especial notice of the habits, ways and peculiarities of the people to whom he is specially sent. The prophet who aims at all-embracing principles, however, can neither reveal different principles for different people, nor leave them to work out their own rules of conduct. His method is to train one particular people and to use them as a nucleus for the building up of a universal sharia. In doing so he accentuates the principles underlying the social norms of all mankind in the light of the specific habits of the people immediately before him. The sharia values resulting from the application (e.g. rules relating to the penalties for crimes) are in a sense specific to that people; and since their observance is not an end in itself they cannot be strictly enforced in the case of future generations.

In December 1986, Justice Javid Iqbal, the son of Allama Iqbal, confronted Gen Zia at a seminar and, referring to the Iqbal-Jinnah correspondence, told him that Islamic punishments had not been envisaged by the two Muslim leaders for the Islamic state. While Justice Iqbal denied that the two had planned a secular state, he declared that it was an ideal secular state they had in mind. Gen Zia ignored the point, and the Hudood, including the cutting of hands and stoning to death, remained in place. Justice Iqbal has retired and today is a member of the Muslim League in the Senate, and supports the ruling party's opposition to the secular state while continuing to adhere to the view of Allama Iqbal on the question of Hudood.

The tashakhus identity

Jinnah was the most incorruptible Muslim of his times, even though his integrity originated from his Western orientation. Today, Pakistanis continue to idealise him even as their Islamic politicians plunder the country. Pakistan has reached the acme of Islam, but has become one of the most corrupt countries in the world. In a series of interviews during the recent Ramadan, almost all political leaders said that they keep the fast and, after breaking it, say the special after-dinner prayers called *travih*. They also pray five times a day and say the special *namaz* called *tahajjud*, meant for the extremely pious. The interviews are poignant because almost all these leaders face charges of dodging taxes and gouging the banks for loans they have not paid back.

Jinnah has had to be transformed because Pakistan has gradually set its face against his legacy. As author Akbar S Ahmed says, 'his behaviour reflected Anglo-Indian sociology', but he was also a Muslim. The tendency has been to emphasise the Quaid's Muslim identity by juxtaposing it with the 'Hindu-ness' of the Congress, as the Pakistani historian saw it. What Jinnah and Allama Iqbal had in mind was a modern Islamic state, the 'modern' referring to a secular state in which all religions could coexist. Contest with India, and the need at all times to separate Pakistan's identity from India's, caused the Muslim League politicians to firm up the Islamic attributes of Pakistan till their prescription broke away from Jinnah's vision. The new identity, which Gen Zia called *tashakhus*, inducted into the task of law-making the very Islamic clergy that had condemned Jinnah for visualising a separate state.

Today, the break from Jinnah has plunged Pakistan into sectarian chaos. The Shia–Sunni conflict, lying buried in old books, has been exhumed by the extremist clergy and made into a new ideology, a natural journey of 'purification' that began after Jinnah's death. Conservative Urdu columnists, who have lent their powerful rhetoric to the transformation of Jinnah into a fundamentalist, are now warning about the possibility of secularism becoming a popular slogan.

Pakistan's relations with Iran, always friendly in the past, are now judged increasingly along sectarian lines. After India's Prime Minister Inder Kumar Gujral made friendly overtures, Iran is now held out as the major enemy of Pakistan for threatening its western frontiers through interference in Afghanistan. The Central Asian states, ruled by secular elites, are gradually revising their traditionally favourable attitude towards Pakistan, and are seeing it as a threat to their own security.

Relations with India became hostile in 1947 because of what Pakistan saw as an invasion of Kashmir after Mountbatten cleared the way through a fraudulent boundary award. But Jinnah, just before his death, envisaged normal relations with India despite the Indian leadership's conviction that Pakistan would not survive and would, instead, 'relapse'. It is difficult to see how India–Pakistan relations could have been normalised, since the singular reason for Islamising Pakistan beyond Jinnah's vision was the fact that India had not 'reconciled' itself to the existence of Pakistan. However, there is no doubt that, had Pakistan remained secular, it would have consolidated itself and persuaded India to accept it on the basis of its viability.

Today, Pakistan has cut itself off from the world. Its indoctrinated leaders seem to challenge the global order, presenting Pakistan as an increasingly recalcitrant and unstable country where non-Muslim minorities are at risk. Jinnah's vision of a 'modern' state would have saved Pakistan from international isolation and made it easy for the world to deal with it. This isolation has complicated Pakistan's relations with India, and Indians seem less interested in normalising ties with a country that will soon be punished by the world. Getting rid of Jinnah's legacy has been Pakistan's greatest tragedy, the consequences of which are being felt as the country hurtles down towards ideological chaos.

Chapter 7

Generals as governors
The parallel political systems of Northeast India
Himal, June 2001

Sanjib Baruah

'Isn't there a brigadier in Shillong?' This was how Sardar Vallabbhai Patel, India's deputy prime minister, responded in 1949 to reports that the 'native state' of Manipur might be reluctant to merge fully with the Indian Union. In September of that year, the governor of Assam, Sri Prakasa, accompanied by his adviser for Tribal Areas, Nari Rustomji, flew to Bombay to apprise Patel of the situation. The fate of Manipur and other indirectly ruled 'native states' presented a significant constitutional problem when British rule of India ended in 1947. Indeed, the decision of the Kashmiri maharaja to accede to India was the beginning of the Kashmir conflict between India and Pakistan. Patel and other senior Indian officials might perhaps have pondered more on the potential difficulties that could arise from decisions by major 'native states' such as Kashmir and Hyderabad on the postcolonial dispensation in the Subcontinent. But the thought that tiny and remote Manipur, on India's border with Burma, might hesitate about fully joining India had probably never crossed their minds. The meeting of Sri Prakasa, Rustomji and Patel was brief. As Rustomji recalls in his memoir, *Enchanted Frontier*, apart from asking whether there was a brigadier stationed in the region, Patel said little else. It was clear from his voice what he meant, wrote Rustomji, and the conversation did not go any further.

Within days the maharaja of Manipur, on a visit to Shillong, found himself virtually imprisoned in his residence. The house was surrounded by soldiers, and under the pressure of considerable misinformation and intimidation, the maharaja—isolated from his advisers, council of ministers and Manipuri public opinion—was made to sign an agreement fully merging his state with India. When the ceremony to mark the transfer of power and the end of this ancient kingdom took place in Imphal on 15 October 1949, a battalion of the Indian Army was in place to guard against possible trouble.

The circumstances attending Manipur's merger with India haunt the politics of the state to this day. A number of insurgent groups regard the merger as illegal and unconstitutional, and many among the Manipuri intelligentsia are bitter about the way it took place. While Manipur today has an elected chief minister and an elected state legislature—like other states in the Indian Union—there is also a de facto parallel structure of governance directly controlled from New Delhi that manages counter-insurgency operations. Visitors to Manipur cannot but notice the strong military presence. Even historic monuments such as the Kangla Fort of the old Manipuri kings, and parts of the complex in Moirang that commemorates the rebel Indian National Army, are occupied by Indian security forces.

It is not hard to see why there is such a massive security presence in the state. Manipur, today, has numerous insurgent groups with ethnically based support among the Meitei, Naga and Kuki communities. In recent years, smaller ethnic groups such as the Paite, Vaiphei and Hmar have also formed their own armed organisations. The official count of lives annually lost in insurgency-related incidents in Manipur in recent years is in the hundreds. And somewhat independent of the activities of these insurgent organisations is the ethnic conflict between Naga and Kuki and, more recently, between Kuki and Paite. Many of these conflicts appear intractable, and some of them are attributable to the profound social transformation that these societies are undergoing.

Yet unless one believes that a coercive state is a necessary instrument to manage change, it is hard to avoid a question. Were the symbols and practices of the traditional Manipuri state, despite the significant erosion of its authority and power under British colonial rule, better equipped to achieve social cohesion? Was Patel's readiness to use force—just as the rest of India was setting off on a path of democratic rights and liberties—an early acknowledgement that Indian democracy in the Northeast would necessarily have an authoritarian accent?

Manipur is not unique. Except for Arunachal Pradesh and Mizoram, five of the seven states of Northeast India today—Assam, Manipur, Meghalaya, Nagaland and Tripura—have insurgent movements of varying levels of activity and intensity. Some of them, such as the United Liberation Front of Assam (ULFA); Nagaland's National Socialist Council of Nagalim (NSCN), now divided into two factions; and the Manipur People's Liberation Front (MPLF), which consists of the United National Liberation Front (UNLF), the People's Liberation Army (PLA) and the People's Revolutionary Party of Kanglaipak (PREPAK), have separatist agendas. Other ethnically based groups are typically dressed up as national fronts, defending this or that minority ethnic group.

As a response to those insurgencies and to the inclination by Pakistan's Inter Services Intelligence (ISI) to fish in these troubled waters, there are many more brigadiers in Northeast India today than Patel could have imagined. Military formations much larger than brigades—corps headed by lieutenant generals and divisions headed by major generals—are now stationed in this part of the country. In Vairengte, a Mizoram village, there is even a counter-insurgency and Jungle Warfare School for training officers to fight the militants. And the Indian Army is only one of the security forces deployed in the region. Other paramilitary units controlled by the central government, such as the Central Reserve Police Force (CRPF), the Border Security Force (BSF), the Assam Rifles, various intelligence bureaus and the police forces of each state, are also involved in counter-insurgency operations. And overseeing these operations is a parallel political structure that works outside the rules and norms that govern India's democratic political institutions.

Political violence—murders, bombings, kidnappings, extortion by militants and killing of militants by security forces in actual or staged encounters—has become a routine part of news from the Northeast. True, there is also news of elections, ceasefires and talks—or prospects of talks—with insurgents. But these two kinds of news and images co-exist with disturbing ease. No one finds the image of democratic elections being conducted under massive military presence anomalous. Nor does anyone expect talks with insurgents to bring about sustained peace. Indeed, in some ways, insurgencies themselves have become incorporated into the democratic political process. Good political reporters of the Northeast know the precise role that insurgent factions play in elections, or the ties that these factions have with particular mainstream politicians.

For politicians, the use of the army to fight insurgencies has by now become something of a habit. For instance, in the spring of 2000, after attacks on Bengalis by tribal militants in Tripura, political parties belonging to the state's

Left Front government observed a 12-hour bandh to pressure the central government to send in the army to deal with the situation. Chief Minister Manik Sarkar complained that even though 27 police-station areas in the state had been declared 'disturbed', the Indian Army had not yet arrived. One would hardly guess from such statements that the law that these democratic politicians were relying on—the law that permits army deployment in 'disturbed' areas—is a law that contravenes all conceivable human-rights standards.

According to the Armed Forces Special Powers Act (AFSPA), in an area that is proclaimed as 'disturbed', an officer of the armed forces has powers: (*a*) to fire upon or use other kinds of force even if it causes death; (*b*) to arrest without a warrant and with the use of 'necessary' force anyone who has committed certain offences or is suspected of having done so; and (*c*) to enter and search any premise in order to make such arrests. Army officers have legal immunity for their actions. There can be no prosecution, suit or any other legal proceeding against anyone acting under this law. Nor is the government's judgment on why an area is found to be 'disturbed' subject to judicial review.

As Ravi Nair of the South Asia Human Rights Documentation Centre in New Delhi has pointed out, the AFSPA violates several provisions of the Indian Constitution: the right to life; the right against arbitrary arrest and detention; the rules of the Indian Criminal Procedure Code relating to arrests, searches and seizures; and almost all relevant international human-rights principles. There was a time when reports of rights violations in the Northeast were taken seriously. But most Indians now regard human-rights organisations as, at best, naive, or at worst sympathisers of insurgents masquerading under the flag of human rights. The violation of rights in the Northeast is seen as the necessary cost of keeping the country safe from its enemies inside and outside.

Thus, in 1991, when the United Nations Human Rights Committee (UNHRC) asked the attorney-general of India to explain the constitutionality of the AFSPA in terms of Indian law, and to justify it in terms of international human-rights law, he defended it on the sole ground that it was necessary in order to prevent the secession of the northeastern states. The Indian government, he argued, had a duty to protect the states from internal disturbances, and that there was no duty under international law to allow secession.

State within a state

In the insurgency-hardened Northeast, democratic India has developed a de facto political system, somewhat autonomous of the formal democratically elected governmental structure. This parallel system is an intricate, multi-tiered reticulate, with crucial decision-making, facilitating and operational nodes that span the region and connect New Delhi with the theatre of action.

The apex decision-making node is the Home Ministry in New Delhi, housed in North Block on Raisina Hill. The operational node, which implements the decisions, consists of the Indian Army and other military, police and intelligence units controlled by the central and state governments, and involves complex coordination. This apparatus also involves the limited participation of the political functionaries of insurgency-affected states. Elected state governments, under India's weak federal structure, can always be constitutionally dismissed in certain situations of instability. But New Delhi has generally preferred to have them in place while conducting counter-insurgency operations. Since the insurgencies have some popular sympathy—albeit not stable or stubborn—the perception that the operations have the tacit support of elected state governments is useful for their legitimacy.

Consequently, the command structure might include some state-level politicians and senior civil servants. This is perceived to be the weakest link in the chain, due to the fear that the presence of these 'locals' might potentially subvert the counter-insurgency operations. Consider the following news reports:

1. In December 2000, the central government asked the Manipur government to investigate links between at least five ministers and insurgent groups. The Home Ministry forwarded a report to the state authorities that included evidence of such a nexus between the ministers and insurgents. Manipur's caretaker chief minister, Radhabinod Koijam, just before the fall of his government, dropped six ministers from his cabinet. Koijam was in the middle of a political battle for survival, and there were other reasons for their removal. But he defended his action by saying that their names appeared in the Home Ministry's list of 'tainted' politicians.

2. In January 2001, the Union Home Ministry proposed the setting up of a judicial enquiry commission to probe into the allegations and counter-allegations of the insurgent-politician nexus in the northeastern states.

3. In the May 2001 elections, former Chief Minister Prafulla Kumar Mahanta repeatedly accused the Congress party of having a nexus with ULFA. The Congress dismissed the charge as election propaganda, and claimed that its victory proved that the electorate did not believe the accusation. In the elections of 1996, the roles were reversed: the

Congress had made similar charges against Mahanta's party, the Asom Gana Parishad (AGP).

There are, of course, many reasons why democratically elected politicians of a particular area—particularly one in which insurgent groups and mainstream political parties might share the same social, political and cultural space—would sometimes know and have ties with each other. Pervasive corruption also leads politicians to cultivate ties with insurgent groups. They, like others with a reputation for making illegal money, consider it prudent to try to keep the insurgent groups happy, by sharing parts of their illicit income with them. Rather than a hard boundary separating insurgents and mainstream politicians, in these circumstances a nexus between some of them becomes inevitable, despite the fact that such ties might cost these politicians in terms of their credibility, as far as New Delhi is concerned.

A former home minister of Nagaland, Dalle Namo, who had been part of the Naga 'underground', once movingly acknowledged his debt to the pioneers of the movement for Naga independence. He told journalist Nirmal Nibedon that he was conscious of the fact that he lived 'in this big bungalow because men like Phizo and Imkongmeren and many others once lived in caves. All these chandeliers and lights [are there] because for them the stars were their only light; [I have] these expensive wall-to-wall carpets because they walked on moss and grass.' Nibedon recalls this conversation in a foreword to Namo's autobiography, *The Prisoner from Nagaland*.

Of course, such sentiments connecting insurgents with mainstream politicians are far from universal. It is unlikely, for instance, that Prafulla Kumar Mahanta of Assam, or Nagaland Chief Minister S C Jamir, whom militants have tried to kill more than once, would share similar idealised views about stalwarts of the Assamese or the Naga 'underground'. However, even these leaders have not always been free of ties with militants. The Khaplang-led faction of the NSCN, for instance, is reputed to have enjoyed the patronage of Jamir.

This is the paradox of counter-insurgency. On the one hand, it must draw on the legitimacy of the elected establishment. On the other, it must protect itself from this establishment's susceptibilities. Namo's account and the repeated charges of a link between northeastern politicians and insurgents underscore why India's security establishment would want a parallel structure of governance that is as autonomous as possible from the democratic politics of the state in question. For instance, in the case of the Indian government's

131

allegation of a nexus between the five Manipuri politicians and insurgents, if the Home Ministry had provided evidence of such a nexus to the 'authorities' in Manipur, it is unlikely that this report would go to the elected members of the state government—some of whom were themselves the objects of suspicion. The most likely person to have received that report from New Delhi, one can reasonably speculate, was the governor of Manipur.

However, bending the rules of constitutional democracy, and building and maintaining a parallel structure, is not always easy. Not all elected state governments have been willing to give up their constitutional prerogatives. For instance, in Assam, thanks to the consent of former Chief Minister Mahanta, counter-insurgency operations since 1997 have been conducted by a Unified Command under which all forces, including the state police, come under the operational command of the army. Tarun Gogoi, in one of his first statements as Assam's chief minister, said that he would like to see the Assam police play more of a role in the Unified Command because of its superior knowledge of local conditions. It is unlikely that Gogoi will seek to end the use of Uniform Command structure in Assam. On the other hand, elected politicians in Manipur have so far resisted pressures from the Home Ministry and the Indian Army to have a Unified Command structure. Former chief minister of Manipur, W Nipamacha, for instance, had maintained that since, legally speaking, the army was deployed in the state only to assist the civil administration, it should remain under the command of the state government.

Such potential conflicts between the compulsions of the civil dispensation and the concerns of the security establishment make the governors of these states crucial nodes in the counter-insurgency network. The management of this difficult equation, in fact, confers on the governor's office a role that far exceeds the more ceremonial functions to which it is constitutionally restricted elsewhere and in normal circumstances. The career profiles of the incumbents in the Northeast provide an index of the importance of the gubernatorial office to the parallel political system. Each of the seven governors of the north-eastern states today has either occupied high and sensitive positions in India's security establishment or has had close ties to it.

- Arunachal Pradesh: Arvind Dave, former chief, Research and Analysis Wing (RAW)
- Assam: Lieutenant General (retired) S K Sinha
- Manipur: Ved Prakash Marwah, retired Indian Police Service officer
- Meghalaya: M M Jacob, former central minister and deputy chairman of the Rajya Sabha

- Mizoram: A R Kohli, former businessman with political ties
- Nagaland: O P Sharma, retired Indian Police Service officer
- Tripura: Lieutenant General (retired) K M Seth

Two are retired military men, two are retired police officers, and one is the former head of India's espionage agency, RAW, engaged in clandestine operations abroad and at home. Of the two without any ostensible ties with the security establishment, Governor Jacob, of Meghalaya, was once minister of state for home affairs in New Delhi; and A R Kohli, recently appointed governor of relatively peaceful Mizoram, has strong ties with the RSS, suggesting proximity to Home Minister L K Advani. The fact that all the appointees have had fairly intimate connections with the security establishment cannot be mere coincidence. As appointees of the central government and as facilitating agents in the counter-insurgency regime, such antecedents serve very practical ends, particularly in ensuring that the demands of security override the rules of democracy.

Governor as judge

Instances of gubernatorial interventions point to the role they play in insulating counter-insurgency operations from democratic processes and scrutiny. Governors often act in ways that not only stretch constitutional propriety but also sacrifice democratic procedures at the altar of security expediencies. A case of what can be called counter-insurgent constitutionalism took place in Assam in 1998, when the governor, Lt Gen Sinha, intervened to stop the Central Bureau of Investigation (CBI) from prosecuting then-Chief Minister Mahanta on a serious corruption charge. Mahanta's acquiescence in the Unified Command structure was clearly important to the security establishment. At the same time, the legal pursuit of a credible corruption charge against an elected chief minister could have significantly raised the legitimacy of India's democratic government institutions in the public eye. There was a choice between two sets of values: the perceived political requirements of counter-insurgency versus an opportunity to raise the public esteem of India's democratic institutions in a region where those institutions lack legitimacy.

The corruption charge against Mahanta went back to what is commonly referred to as the 'Letters of Credit scam', involving at least INR 2 billion between 1986 and 1993. Mahanta was not chief minister at the time. Fake letters of credit were issued by the state's animal-husbandry and veterinary departments to draw money from the treasury, and a number of politicians of both the then-ruling Congress and the opposition AGP were implicated. It was also suspected that a part of the money found its way to the ULFA.

The CBI investigated a number of politicians. The case against Mahanta was that the kingpin of the scam, Rajendra Prasad Borah, had paid him INR 4 million during the 1991 elections, and that Mahanta's air travels during the campaign had been financed by Borah. According to the CBI, in that election Borah had distributed house-building material to purchase votes in Mahanta's electoral constituency. Bank drafts distributed by Mahanta in his electoral district, according to the CBI, were paid for by Borah.

For a governor—a former military general—to make a legal judgment on whether a chief minister should be prosecuted pushes the limits of constitutional propriety. To be sure, this power of Indian governors is not limited to the Northeast and, as the Delhi-based magazine *India Today* pointed out in an editorial, 'there is something profoundly undemocratic about a mechanism which requires the governor's permission to even begin legal proceeding against a chief minister seen as corrupt.' In the Northeast, given the parallel power structure in place, the potential for abuse of that power—or, perhaps, its use—as a means of securing support for the security regime from a corrupt chief minister is enormous.

The governor's reasons for disallowing the CBI's prosecution of Mahanta involved a number of legal rationalisations. Sinha pointed to the lack of evidence, and questioned the reliability of the witnesses who formed the basis of the CBI's case. The CBI, according to the governor, had not established Mahanta's 'criminal culpability'. The governor rejected the charge that Mahanta had entered into a criminal conspiracy with Borah to defraud the state, claiming that 'no evidence of such conspiracy has been provided'.

Obviously, governors enjoy extraordinary powers to influence chief ministers in the interests of the parallel regime. In this particular case, it is difficult to avoid speculating on a very obvious connection. In Assam since 1997, the Unified Command structure has been possible because of the consent given by Mahanta. That was a year before the governor was called upon to make this crucial judgment in the corruption case. Was there a *quid pro quo* in the governor's decision to protect Mahanta from legal prosecution, so as to ensure his continued support for the Unified Command structure? Did the perceived needs of counter-insurgency trump the value of achieving greater transparency in government? More importantly, what has this entire edifice and its strategies achieved by way of ending insurgency and restoring peace?

Why is peace so elusive?

This counter-insurgency apparatus and its modus operandi are geared fundamentally, and more or less exclusively, to containment. So long as insurgencies
are only contained, and no sustainable peace processes are in place, democracy
in the Northeast is likely to continue to co-exist with the use of authoritarian
modes of governance. With the significant exception of the Mizo movement,
most insurgencies in the Northeast have been transformed, or are currently
transforming, into long-term, low-intensity conflicts. The perceived need for
counter-insurgency operations never seems to go away. Even in Mizoram, at
least if one goes by the military presence in that state, the end of the insurgency
has not meant that the state within the state has been dismantled.

There are three reasons why most northeastern insurgencies turn into protracted conflicts of attrition: (*a*) the goal of counter-insurgency is limited to creating conditions under which particular insurgent groups or factions surrender
weapons, come to the negotiation table on the government's terms, and make
compromises in exchange for personal gain; (*b*) counter-insurgency operations
do not dramatically change the conditions on the ground that breed and sustain
the insurgent political culture and lifestyle; and (*c*) the political initiatives that
accompany and supplement counter-insurgency operations try to utilise former
militants in the war against insurgents, thus creating a climate of mistrust and
a cycle of violence and counter-violence between anti-government and pro-
government insurgents.

The need for a powerful security presence can hardly disappear under
these conditions. Assam's growing violence—which includes a large number of
secret killings by death squads—exemplifies the results of a counter-insurgency
strategy that, in fact, transformed an insurgency into a wider and more drawn-
out conflict. The bloody elections of May 2001, in which scores of people lost
their lives, were at odds with Lt Gen Sinha's euphoric claim of the 'ballot having
won against the bullet'.

The Mizoram exception, of course, is important. In 1986, Laldenga, the
leader of the Mizo National Front, signed an accord with Prime Minister Rajiv
Gandhi, and this remains the only instance of an accord successfully bringing about an end to insurgency in the Indian Northeast. Laldenga became the
chief minister of Mizoram, and when he lost elections two years later there
was no call for a return to insurgency. Among the factors that accounted for
the successful end of the Mizo insurgency were the following: the undisput-
ed leadership of the insurgency in the hands of a single individual who was

willing to compromise and who could deliver his part of the deal; the feasibility of offering Laldenga the chief-ministership of Mizoram in exchange for ending the insurgency; the existence of large and organised church-related civil-society institutions that were actively involved in creating and supporting the consensus for peace; and a political climate in New Delhi, during the Rajiv Gandhi years, that was relatively open to making significant political compromises with insurgents.

To date, however, the Mizo case has been the only exception, and insurgency refuses to die down despite the sophistication and resources of the counter-insurgency establishment and the leeway given it to use the governor as political administrator. In seeking to understand why peace continues to elude Northeast India, it is important to study how insurgencies are able to sustain themselves in the face of such enormous military action. It is critical to keep in mind the fact that while the security establishment runs parallel administrations that circumscribe civil administrations politically, insurgent movements run similar parallel fiscal administrations at the ground level through illegal tax collection and extortion.

One perspective on the longevity of armed civil conflicts focuses attention not so much on the grievances that are articulated by insurgent groups, but to the ability of these groups to finance their activities. For example, economist Paul Collier, in an article looking at the global patterns of armed civil conflicts, concluded that the most significant factor of civil conflicts is the ability of rebel organisations to be financially viable. He also found a strong correlation with a specific set of economic conditions, such as a region's dependence on exports of primary commodities and low national income.

It is not that poverty breeds armed civil conflicts, Collier surmises. Instead, certain economic conditions are conducive to the mobilisation of revenue by armed insurgent groups. Primary commodities are highly lootable, primary production centres located in conflict-zones are easily accessible, and production cannot be moved elsewhere. Unlike a manufacturing unit, which is not worth much once production ceases, owners and managers of such centres continue to be dependent on existing production sites, making them vulnerable to extortion. Low national income, Collier argues, is co-related with armed civil conflicts not because the objective condition of poverty sustains rebellion, but because in a context of poverty and unemployment, an insurgent group that is able to raise enough money can recruit new members quite inexpensively.

The Collier thesis is useful to explain the resilience of the Northeast insurgencies. It draws attention to the conditions that permit illegal tax collection.

For instance, in those areas of large countries where the state's presence is weak, it is easier for rebel organisations to establish illegal taxation structures that resemble official ones. The availability of foreign material support also becomes an important factor in explaining the persistence of armed civil conflicts. The civil war in Sierra Leone perhaps most dramatically supports the Collier thesis: the control over diamond mining and international diamond smuggling is clearly what has allowed the armed rebels to continue the fight.

While northeastern India is no Sierra Leone, it is nevertheless striking that the region is both poor and a primary-commodity-producing region. These are factors that, according to Collier, make an area conducive to illegal tax-collection and to the persistence of armed civil conflicts. Indeed, the production and transportation of the primary commodities that Northeast India produces and exports—tea, timber, coal and so on—have been a major source of legal taxation by governments, a source of extortion by officials, and the favourite source of illegal taxation by insurgent groups and, increasingly, by pro-government insurgent groups that collaborate in counter-insurgency operations.

Indian *taka*, Naga *taka*

During 1994–95, Sanjoy Ghose, the social activist who was kidnapped and killed by ULFA in 1997, travelled extensively in the Northeast. His travel diaries have been published posthumously as *Sanjoy's Assam*. In his travels through Nagaland, Ghose found a formalised system of tax-collection imposed by the NSCJSI. 'Everybody' paid, and in the case of the state government's Public Works Department (PWD)—perceived as highly corrupt—Ghose found that there was a progressive system of illegal taxation in place. Those of the rank of executive engineers and above paid a third of their net salary. This percentage might seem high to someone unfamiliar with the culture of corruption in the region, but the fact is that the formal, departmental salary is only a small part of the actual income of an engineer. A senior police officer of Nagaland confided to Ghose that, even though he himself was not paying, most of his colleagues did 'contribute'. Such stories about systems of illegal taxation—perhaps not equally formalised everywhere—are heard all through the Northeast. Indeed, it is not merely insurgent organisations, but mainstream political parties, student organisations and corrupt officials—all resort to coercive and illegal modes of 'tax collection' from businesses big and small.

Pervasive corruption and the preponderance of 'outsiders' in the economy of the region make the climate especially illegal–taxation-friendly. Indeed, as

Sanjoy Ghose found in the case of PWD engineers in Nagaland, unlike government tax collectors who could target only what is officially declared as income, insurgents—drawing on popular perceptions and credible rumour—can impose higher taxes based on more realistic assessments of income. It is in no one's interest to report extortion demands or payments that involve mostly illegal income to law-enforcement officials.

Krishnan Saigal, a former Indian civil servant who was Assam's planning-and-development commissioner and who is familiar with the process of development finance in the Northeast, has written about the way development funds allocated to the region are a bonanza for a group of contractors and license holders—mostly from outside the region—whose 'main ambition is to make a fast buck and get out of the area as quickly as possible'. As the Indian state has increased development expenditures in response to the voices of discontent in the Northeast, he writes, there has been an even 'quicker siphoning off of funds to the heartland with the few benefits accruing to those in power through the usual corrupt forces'. Saigal believes this has led to increasingly corrupt regimes in the northeastern states. And the people of the region, he believes, even see them as representing central power in order to keep their state underdeveloped.

The perception that New Delhi is throwing money away in order to buy peace gives an aura of legitimacy to tax collection by insurgents. The manifesto of the NSCN is a case in point: 'The pouring in of Indian capital in our country for political reasons has shattered the Naga people into a society of wild money,' creating a parasitic, exploiting class of 'reactionary traitors, bureaucrats, a handful of rich men and the Indian vermin'. Such a view of the politics underlying New Delhi's development expenditures allows Naga insurgents to take the moral high ground: it is only fair that such ill-gotten wealth be shared with an organisation that works for the greater good of the Naga community. To give another example of the consequence of this perception, in Nagaland it is said that during elections when political parties distribute money to buy votes, acceptance of that money is seen as legitimate since it involves only 'Indian *taka*' (Indian money), not 'Naga *taka*'.

In order to discredit militants in the eyes of their supporters, military and intelligence officials have in recent years started speaking about the luxurious lifestyles of insurgent leaders, or of the insurgents being nothing more than bandits seeking 'easy money'. While all this is not news to anyone living in the Northeast, whether such statements from security officials involved in counter-insurgency operations increase the legitimacy of governmental institutions with regards to the rebels is a different matter. Despite some highly publicised successes, such as unearthing evidence that one of India's major business houses (the Tatas) was providing support to Assamese rebels, it is doubtful that the focus on the expropriative aspect of insurgencies has led to any systemic change affecting the illegal tax-collection capacity of insurgent groups.

Here are two recent newspaper reports that illustrate how routine the taxation systems of insurgent organisations are and how impervious they have been to decades of counter-insurgency operations.

In February 2001, the NSCN (Isaac-Muivah) announced, and Indian newspapers routinely published the news of, a 'tax break' for industries. According to the *Times of India*, the NSCN (I-M) announced an exemption of 'loyalty taxes' for two years on certain categories of businesses—some of them even state-owned businesses. Quoting the organisation's information secretary, V Horam, the news report said that the tax break was given in order to boost economic activities in the Naga areas of the Northeast. The 'tax exemption', said the notification applied to enterprises that were less than two years old. However, the taxes on other businesses and the income tax on salaried people would continue.

In March 2001, militant groups demanded INR 40 lakhs from eight Christian missionary schools in Imphal. When the schools expressed their inability to pay, the militants imposed a fine of INR 2 crores and ordered them to close down. The matter was raised in the Manipur State Assembly. The press reported that security in and around the missionary schools was increased. The chief minister of Manipur told the state legislature that cases were registered with the police in connection with the extortion demands and were being investigated. But no one expected such investigations to go very far. Last month, three Christian missionaries were murdered by militants, apparently because of non-payment of those levies.

There seems to be little evidence that in these two states, years of counter-insurgency have had any significant impact on the conditions that have bred and sustained insurgency—i.e., the relative incapacity of civil administration to provide protection (despite its strong military presence) and the continued ability of insurgent organisations to collect illegal taxes. It appears that insurgent groups can guarantee security and collect tax better than the state can. It is hardly surprising then that many people—politicians, traders, government officials and even major corporations—make their uneasy peace with insurgent groups, just as they learn to live with counter-insurgency operations without high expectations of an end to the fighting.

What, then, accounts for this fundamental failure? It must be that New Delhi's Northeast policy has yet to come to grips with the dense social networks of northeastern societies, and the ideas and values that animate the insurgencies.

Passionate about history

How can the Northeast ever hope to get out of this quagmire, in which a larger democracy lives comfortably with the most arbitrary of powers in 'disturbed' areas? There might be occasional doubts in India about what counter-insurgency itself can achieve. But one idea that enjoys widespread acceptance is that, once the problem of the region's economic backwardness is taken care of, the main source of political turmoil will go away. Indeed it would probably be hard to find a more diehard group of economic determinists than Indian bureaucrats and politicians engaged with the Northeast.

This faith in economic development contrasts sharply with the vision of insurgent groups in the Northeast. While those who try to solve the 'insurgency problem' mainly talk about economic development and modernisation, the insurgents hark back to history. Thus ULFA speaks of Assam's lost independence when the Yandabo Treaty was signed between the British and the Burmese kings in 1826; Manipuri rebels raise questions about the constitutionality of the merger agreement of 1949; and Naga rebels query 'how these long stretches of frontiers which were neither Burmese nor Indian territories could simply disappear into India and Burma after 1947?', according to Kaka D Iralu's *Nagaland and India: The Blood and the Tears*.

True, militant groups, political parties and public opinion in northeastern states do complain about the region's economic underdevelopment. But their primary grouse appears to be perceived injustices grounded in the history of how the Indian postcolonial constitutional order came into being. Still, what is striking is that the bureaucrats, politicians and military officers who make Northeast policy are either oblivious of the historical issues that insurgencies raise, or consider them too trivial to merit substantive engagement. Thus, exploring different ways of granting greater constitutional autonomy as a response to these historical claims is not at all part of the Indian policymaker's basket of solutions.

In the history of ideas there are numerous examples of the authoritarian consequences of dealing with places and people only in terms of their supposed future—framed in terms of ideas about backwardness and progress—without taking into account their past. After all, that is how an entire generation of liberal and progressive English thinkers (Jeremy Bentham, James Mill, John Stuart Mill and Thomas B Macaulay) managed to endorse empire as a legitimate form of government, and even to justify its undemocratic and unrepresentative structure. The key to understanding this paradox of the liberal defence of empire, writes Uday Singh Mehta in his book *Liberalism and Empire*, lies in the reforms proposed by the liberals. Developmentalism, according to Mehta, had been an integral feature of liberalism. Liberal thought identified India's backwardness, so imperial rule could be justified by the initiation of endless projects for economic development, social reforms, etc.

By contrast, the conservative Edmund Burke had a harder time accepting British rule of India. Of course, Burke did not oppose empire; he argued for good government, not Indian self-government. Yet his was a sharper critique of empire because he saw India in terms of its existing established communities, and he did not want to see them threatened. And unlike liberals who worried about whether India was to be regarded as a nation or just a conglomeration of innumerable castes and tribes, Burke assumed that peoples living in one place for generations had to be regarded as political communities. Most importantly, unlike liberals, Burke, in Mehta's words, never presumed a 'foreknowledge of other people's destiny'. Indian bureaucrats would do well to take more seriously the histories of the peoples of the Northeast, and to give up the assumption of foreknowledge of their destinies that is implied in the talk about bringing development and modernisation to remote tribal societies.

Recognising the Northeast as a region where the people have histories does not, of course, mean that the region's history will have ready answers to its contemporary problems. But taking history seriously can have important implications. There is the example of the recent negotiations between Naga leaders and the Indian government where both sides have failed to arrive at a common ground—the Naga idea of a 'Nagalim', or greater Nagaland, is a source of anxiety to a number of neighbouring northeastern states, especially Manipur.

It is tempting to think of the issue entirely in terms of ethnic anxieties. But the history of the political formations of the region suggests otherwise. The political history of the region has more interconnections and continuities than the idea of bounded and demarcated ethnic homelands might suggest. In the 19th century, James Johnstone, a colonial official, described political rituals of the Manipuri kings that were remarkably inclusive. The investiture ceremony of the Manipuri kings required the queen to appear in Naga costume; the royal palace always had a house built in Naga style; and when the king travelled, he was attended on by two or three Manipuri with Naga arms, dress and ornaments.

The interconnections between the Naga and Manipuri communities suggested by the practices and rituals of the Manipuri court might not provide ready answers to resolve the Nagalim issue today. But one thing is clear: rather than secretive deals between Indian bureaucrats and leaders of one or the other insurgent organisation, these questions are best addressed by debates that take seriously the passionate interest in history that animates the northeastern insurgencies, and by taking into confidence the people of the region.

Rather than trying to contain insurgencies, India needs to raise its expectations of what is possible. Even the most protracted of armed civil conflicts in the world—Northern Ireland—is today closer to resolution than ever before. Establishing a blue-ribbon committee to examine the accomplishments and failures of the last five decades of India's strategy and tactics of counter-insurgency in the Northeast might be a good place to start. The Armed Forces Special Powers Act is almost as old as the Indian Constitution. It was introduced to deal with the Naga insurgency. Four and a half decades later, not only has peace remained elusive in Nagaland, insurgencies have enveloped formerly peaceful parts of the Northeast. The extension of this law to the entire region has compromised Indian democracy in the Northeast in unacceptable ways.

Surely half a century is a long-enough period for honest stocktaking and reassessment of goals and achievements. Until such rethinking takes place, withdrawing the AFSPA, appointing as governors those whose accomplishments are in fields other than national security, and removing the military presence from historical monuments such as the Kangla Fort and the INA memorial will be powerful symbols to indicate the desire for a new beginning that would shape a fully democratic Northeast in the 21st century.

Unfortunately, these are civil measures substantially at variance with the 'military-economic' solution that currently finds favour. The question that remains is whether an honest review of options is at all possible, given the extraordinary influence of the security establishment and the interests it has acquired in the 'disturbed' Northeast. The appointment of 'military governors' to oversee the dilution of civil political authority seems to suggest that democratic alternatives will not merit even passing consideration. After all, if a lasting peace is restored in the region, generals will no longer be governors. And there will be no need for so many brigadiers.

Chapter 8

Eating with our fingers, watching Hindi cinema and consuming cricket

Himal, March 2002

Sirivayan Anand

·

'Caste devitalises a man. It is a process of sterilisation.'
— Dr B R Ambedkar, *Philosophy of Hinduism*

'Why all this hullagulla about some remarks and f words used. So what's the big deal? As though Indians are the holy saints without abusive words. Actually Indians are the most racist people on earth. India is the only country where we have schedule caste system. Is this not racism??? We have Bungis and untouchables. Who has coined these names? The very Indian Brahmins who play cricket and want to be treated with respect. Piss on you all cricketers of India.'

— *Indian Express*, e-mail discussion forum on 'racism', 20 November 2001

India is a billion-weak nation thirsting for truly international sporting glory. Every four years, the fact that Olympic success eludes the country is lamented

---

Some of these reflections on cinema were triggered by a conversation with Ravikumar, president of PUCL Tamil Nadu-Pondicherry. I owe the point on disability and cricket players to N U Abhilash, researching cricket in the UK, who also helped to compile the teams. By way of clarification on the quote at the beginning of the essay, Ambedkar, like other male writers of his time, uses 'man' in the generic sense to refer to all of humankind, and not in the sexual masculine sense.

in public fora. Karnam Malleswari's weightlifting bronze in the 2000 Olympics, P T Usha's almost-bronze many Olympics ago, and fading memories of the men's hockey team's successive golds offer little consolation. But the last two decades have seen a phenomenal hard-sell of cricket. Though cricket is truly an uninternational sport—played by hardly 12 countries, all of them former colonies of the British empire—India's success in the 1983 World Cup, followed by the hosting of the Reliance Cup in the Subcontinent, and the subsequent television boom spurred by the policy of 'liberalisation' (a very clever word), corporate sponsorship and subsidisation, resulted in cricket effectively being marketed as the game that mattered. Cricket, like popular cinema, became a product of mass consumption, especially after one-day games became a regular fixture. More-physical sports such as hockey and football have been effectively jettisoned for 'the gentleman's game'.

The celebration and success of the movie *Lagaan* as a nice little good-vs-evil, David-vs-Goliath tale must be understood in this context. *Lagaan* has won an Oscar nod for inclusion in the 'best foreign film' line-up. After a year of hype and accolades in the Indian media and deft packaging for select Western festival circuits and in Hollywood, producer-actor Aamir Khan seems to have almost pulled off what he set out to achieve.

About the same time that *Lagaan*'s nomination for the Oscar made news, Indian newspapers and television channels devoted more than the usual space to some unusual cricket news. In Madras, Karnataka had won the Hong Kong and Shanghai Bank Corporation National Cricket Championship for the Blind, defeating Delhi. A 'liberal-secular' newspaper that has no qualms calling itself *The Hindu* (13–14 February 2002) extensively reported the tournament and even carried two-column pictures. Tamil television channels covered it as the 'soft story' of the day in their news bulletins. It looks as though the World Cup for the blind will be hosted by Madras in December 2002. Some multinational corporation, driven by late-capitalist guilt and the 'we-care' spirit, might sponsor that event too.

As I begin this, I feel weighed down by the burden of addressing (the 'liberal'?) readers of *Himal* on the regressiveness of a film such as *Lagaan*, and even more weighed down by the prospect of convincing them that cricket in India has been a truly casteist game—a game best suited to Hinduism. Burdened because even those most critical of overriding nationalism jump with joy when their national team wins. In fact, as a friend points out, 'apart from eating with our fingers, unfortunately both cricket and Hindi films unite Southasians'. For a Subcontinent that so obsessively watches cricket and Hindi cinema,

Lagaan offers cinema-as-cricket and cricket-as-cinema. In the Hyderabad of the mid-1990s, as a university-bound hostelite watching a one-day match in the common room, I saw all groups and communities 'cheering for India'. Telugu-speaking Dalits, Oriyas, Malayalis, Brahmins, Kannadigas and MTech students alike would all come in identifiable gangs, reserve seats, and be 'united' by cricket—even if they had battles to fight outside the common room. The other programmes that drew huge collective viewership were film-song countdowns in Hindi and Telugu.

To understand the vulgarity of *Lagaan*, one needs to be alive to who actually plays cricket in India, even as the myth is fabricated that everybody can participate in the game—you open a can of Coke and a sixer materialises or a wicket falls, so you keep consuming Coke for the team and the nation's good, as Aishwarya Rai leads by example during commercial breaks between overs. Even as direct participation in cricket seems an impossibility for most Indians— one half of the population, women, are effectively excluded—it encourages them to become consumers of the game irrespective of their caste, class, gender and religion. You consume cricket like Aishwarya consumes Coke in the advertisement.

Quite the same happens with cinema produced in Madras or Bombay. Even when the hero—be it Rajinikant, M G Ramachandran, Chiranjeevi or Aamir Khan—is on most occasions discoursing against the Dalits, Other Backward Castes (OBCs), women and Muslims ('subalterns'), there are millions of fans from these very groups who identify with their filmic presence: consumption, with the illusion of participation. And, in a country of one billion people, only 14 can make it to the 'national' team. Yet during a one-day match even the poor who cannot afford a TV (or, when they can, are unable anyway to afford the pay channel that broadcasts the match) congregate outside electronics shops and watch the game, even as pockets get picked. *Lagaan*, which partakes of and perpetuates this folklore of cricket as universal social solvent, lends itself very eminently to a 'casteist' reading precisely because of its thematic inflections and its choice of things to celebrate and suppress.

Millennial *purana*

Lagaan is like one of those many Hindu *purana*s—literally, 'stories of old'—that have scant regard for historicity, and which in fact revel in their ahistoricity. Puranas are mostly Brahmin-written mythologies that dwell upon the imagined feats and lore of Brahminical gods and goddesses. Like all else in Brahminic Hinduism's self-representation, puranas excel in obfuscation and mythmaking —all towards keeping the (Aryan-vedic) caste and patriarchal status quo intact. *Lagaan* is one such purana of the new millennium, an accretion to the quintessentially Brahminic mythmaking tradition. That *Lagaan*'s story and direction are by a Brahmin (Ashutosh Gowarikar) is not incidental, though a Muslim (Aamir Khan) parades as the most public face of the film.

Set in 1893, *Lagaan* is the story of how the residents of Champaner, a village in Awadh (modern-day Uttar Pradesh), master the game of cricket in three months and defeat the British cantonment team. The wager is that the British would not impose tax (*lagaan*) for the next three years if Champaner wins the match; if it loses, the entire province would have to pay a triple levy. Approaching cricket as the white man's pompous version of *gilli-danda*, the Champaner XI wins the game under the leadership of Bhuvan (Aamir Khan), aided by a 'fair-minded' white lady (Elizabeth, sister of the villainous British officer Russell, who challenges Bhuvan).

Lagaan is being celebrated by secularists, nationalists, subalternists, leftists, pseudo-secularists, members of the Bharatiya Janata Party (BJP), academics, critics and filmgoers alike. Columnists and academicians distanced themselves from the loud and jingoistic *Gadar*, and tested their analytical abilities on the subtleties of *Lagaan*. (The film has generated three articles, and counting, in *Economic and Political Weekly*.) Profiling Aamir Khan soon after the Oscar call, the *Indian Express* (17 February 2002) suggested that *Lagaan* 'won the battle of the imagination in a way that *Gadar* didn't.' The film, 'brimming with nationalism and the charm of cricket', was the right one for the Oscars, the report said. In post-Hindutva India, *Lagaan* (unlike *Gadar*) seems to offer the liberal-secular brigade something to cheer about.

Fretting over the prolonged marginalisation of 'the rural' and 'the peasantry' in Hindi cinema, Sudhanva Deshpande in a recent *Himal* article (see August 2001, 'Hindi films: The rise of the consumable hero') sees hope in *Lagaan*. Deshpande looks for 'the banished peasant' in Hindi cinema of the 1980s and 1990s, and nostalgically mourns the absence of 'the rural or urban labouring classes dancing and singing with the hero(ine)'. He concludes, 'This is why Aamir Khan's home production, *Lagaan*, is so refreshing'. (And it is Sunny Deol-Gadar who makes him run into the arms of Aamir Khan, who, never mind, may well have campaigned for the BJP in Uttar Pradesh had he not been busy with the Oscar lobbying.) As if the rural/the peasantry was ever portrayed in all its feudal and casteist–patriarchal ugliness by Hindi cinema from the 1950s to 1970s. In this framework, anything rural seems to be desirable from a class perspective. Hence we can forgive the fact that women have to bear the markers of rurality and 'tradition': 'Hindi cinema has never been naturalistic, so there is no point complaining that the girls look anything but peasant. But today, the heroes do not have any peasantry watching their passage.'

Deshpande also selectively forgets the utterly feudal leitmotif that is not just confined to Hindi, but also extends to Telugu and Tamil cinema: where the very-rural hero (played with masculine aggression by MGR, Sivaji Ganesan, Rajinikant, Vijaykanth, Akkineni Nageswar Rao, N T Rama Rao, Chiranjeevi, Balakrishna and other worthies) is pitted against the urban-educated heroine dressed in 'trendy, tight' clothes. Invariably, she rides a car, confronts the bullock-cart-driving hero, abuses him in English in the presence of his and her friends, but ultimately (after some songs and dances) is tamed/rescued and ends up in the final frame in a sari, touching the feet of her husband and the in-laws. (Alternatively, in cases where the male character is a city-bred 'modern' and the female rural/rustic, she is raped by the man. The man would be the villain, and the 'victimised' woman, the hero's sister who, 'unable to bear the shame, commits suicide'. Or, if the film is 'progressive', the hero ensures that his sister marries the now-sheepish rapist after making him see reason in a macho way.)

This trend has continued till the 1990s in South India. Even Govinda as *Coolie No. 1* (a remake of a Telugu 1990s film starring Venkatesh and Tabu), whom Deshpande celebrates for his 'proletarian image' teaches the pride (*guroor*)-filled heroine a lesson, tames her, puts her in her place. In such a reading, Manmohan Desai becomes 'the original postmodernist Bombay director, with a thorough (and often delightful) contempt for logic and meaning.' Just as much as all Hindu mythologies are the first magical-realist texts (we did it all first/it is all in the Vedas). Marquez and Lyotard can take a walk.

Coming back to *Lagaan*, it is not such a great hit in box-office terms. 'In industry lingo it is an A-class hit,' reports the *Indian Express*, meaning its popularity is confined to metros and urban pockets. (I watched it reluctantly in December 2001 in Madras, some six months after it was released. It was playing only during the morning show in a cinema that accommodates about 180 people, but whose cheapest ticket is INR 80.) Deshpande notes that 'the economics of film production has altered dramatically, and those who now account for the profits of the industry are simply not interested in watching sweaty peasantry. Why, then, has *Lagaan* succeeded? It must have been the cricket theme which, as in real life, manages to unite passions across classes and international

147

borders.' But this modern Gandhian purana is dangerous as far Dalits and women are concerned.

Take Champaner, the village from where our caste-Hindu hero, Bhuvan, leads the banner of revolt. For a long stretch in the film, Champaner—where men wear kurtas and vests ordered fresh (by Oscar-winning Bhanu Athaiya) from the nearest Khadi Gramodyog Bhandar and women are dressed in ethnic Rajasthani colours (starched spotless white if they happen to be widows)—is presented as some caste-free utopia. There is religion, of course: temple rituals, the Radha–Krishna myth, some *namaz*-doing Muslims with fez caps, and the visiting Sardarji.

Suddenly, when Bhuvan's team is training under the supervision of the white *mlechcha* woman, we spot Kachra, the untouchable, standing on the margins—literally—as the ball rolls before him. Bhuvan asks Kachra to throw the ball back. A petrified Kachra with a small broom in his right hand, his left hand handicapped, is sweating. Hero Bhuvan goads him to throw the ball, and Kachra does it with his disabled left hand. The ball spins wildly. Bhuvan is terribly impressed and wants to rope Kachra in as the 11th man they have been looking for. Predictably, the entire village from *mukhiya* (chief) to *vaid* (doctor) to *jyotish* (astrologer) opposes the move to induct an *achchut* (untouchable). They say: 'Fight the British with a silly game if you please, but don't commit *dharam-bhrasht* (sacrilege). Meaning, keep your hands off religion, kid. When the British tread on your toes, you can justifiably fight them, but practices such as untouch-ability are legacies not to be questioned.' Surprisingly, while Kachra poses a problem, being tutored in the game by a mlechcha white woman (Elizabeth) is not problematic.

Bhuvan assumes the reformer's role and launches into a speech, saying even Bhagwan Ram had eaten the fore-bitten fruit of Sabari and that he had decried untouchability. While most versions of the *Ramayana* refer to the epi-sode where Ram beheads the *shudra* Sambhuka for daring to recite the Vedas despite being ordered to stop; in Ashutosh Gowarikar's 2001 recall of the tale, there is selective forgetting. From being an upholder of the patriarchal caste system, Ram refigures here as someone who was against caste discrimination. This is of a piece with even apparently progressive elements in modern India refusing to reckon with caste. In fact, at the intellectual level there is an effort to defend 'good Hinduism' with regards to the 'bad Hinduism' (Hindutva) of the BJP and its affiliates.

In this defence of 'good Hinduism' by a range of intellectuals (explicitly by Ashis Nandy and implicitly by 'left-secular-liberal' anti-BJP voices) an issue such as caste hardly ever figures. When it does, caste has something to do with others—OBCs to Dalits. Caste is not something that you have, since it is always what others embody. In such a reconstruction, Gandhian *ramarajya* and Gandhi's Rama continue to be defended by even communist ideologues such as A B Bardhan, an MP, in the context of the Babri Masjid demolition. Thus, in a Communist Party of India booklet, 'Sangh Parivar's Hindutva versus the real Hindu ethos' (December 1992), Bardhan, immediately after noting that 6 December is Ambedkar's death anniversary, quotes Dasarath, Ram's father in the *Ramayana*: '*Raghukul reet sada chali aaye pran jaaye par vachan na jaaye*' (This is the eternal law of the Raghu clan. Life may be forfeited, but never the word once given.) Ram honoured his pledge to the letter, says Bardhan, who then accuses RSS-VHP-BJP Ram-*bhaktas* of not behaving like Ram, and proceeds to refer to Golwalkar, the former chief of the RSS, as 'Guruji', approvingly quotes Vivekananda, and invokes M K Gandhi's *sanatana dharma*—and even Sardar Patel and Bankim Chandra Chattopadhyay.

Selling 'good Hinduism' and its decencies is more than just a passing issue in *Lagaan*. A gauge of its significance is that the sequence following Kachra's entry is the only moment when an internal problem forces a confrontation in the film. All other filmic confrontations are with the external 'Other'—the white, British male. Here again, Bhuvan effects a selective reordering of the mythic past (Ram is no historical figure, anyway) in quite the same way that A B Bardhan defends 'Gandhi's Rama' as opposed to the Ram of L K Advani, the BJP leader who led the *rath yatra* that some years later culminated in the demolition of the Babri mosque. It was in a similar vein that Gandhi, when confronted by a well-read Ambedkar who threw the book(s) at him, defended both the caste system and Ram in a personalised interpretation, and in fact swore to establish *ramarajya*—a Dalit's and woman's nightmare. Again, this is a selective imagining of the past, dodging issues such as caste and patriarchy.

In the *Lagaan* purana, since wasting too much time on the Dalit's token entry would be futile, the villagers are easily won over by Bhuvan's falsified invocation of the *maryada purushottam* ('ideal superman', as Ram is referred to fondly). Besides sounding apologetic, the Dalit here is wordless, almost as if he is also dumb. The subaltern cannot speak. Completely stripped of agency, Kachra (in Hindustani, this also means 'waste' or 'garbage') simply has to follow caste-Hindu Bhuvan's words. He never exercises a choice. Kachra—someone excluded from every other social-cultural-religious aspect of village life—is never asked whether he would like to be included in such a game. It is not clear whether this Dalit, portrayed so pathetically, is even aware of why the game is being played.

Until the introduction of this Dalit character, Dalits (and, indeed, caste generally) never figure in the cinematic village. The Brahmin is conspicuous by his absence, except as the priest in the background with no dialogue. In fact, no character seems to be caste-marked in the pristine village—the Gandhian ideal. It is only Kachra who bears the burden of caste identity. From the raja to Bhuvan, we are not made aware of anybody's caste. Now, do the untouchables of Champaner live in separate quarters? Who are the other untouchables in the village? (There can't be just one!) Do they approve of Kachra being part of the team? The rest of the villagers—Bhuvan, Lakha and others—are constantly referred to as 'farmers/peasants' who own land (though they are never shown participating in any farmerly activity). Hence the lagaan (double, triple levy, whatever) affects them. But what about the landless and rightless untouchables? How does the lagaan, or the cricket match that will liberate Champaner and Awadh from this burden, affect the Dalits? What is the problem that Dalits have with the white coloniser-state? Are not their problems more linked to the caste-colonialism sustained by the raja and the caste Hindus of the village?

Gandhian concepts are liberally sprinkled in the film. In the scene where Bhuvan is introduced, he is shown trying to save a deer from falling prey to the British officer's bullets. In 1893, in a village untouched by the material aspects of modernity and modern notions of conservation, we have reason enough to believe that venison could be eaten by villagers too. It is not as if deer were not killed by anyone till the white sahibs went on *shikaar* (hunting for sport) expeditions. Just as you wonder if the local raja would not have indulged in similar hunting adventures, the construct of the caste-unmarked villager upholding vegetarianism and *ahimsa* (non-violence) lays the ground for a later scene in which the raja espouses veggie power. In a scene where Captain Russell (once again) plays the arrogant white man who challenges an effete raja to eat meat, the latter refuses on the grounds that it would be against his religious beliefs. If the raja eats the meat, the lagaan would be waived, says Russell. Whoever has heard of vegetarian kings in late 19th century? But as in other convenient obfuscations of caste in the film, the raja never identifies himself as Kshatriya. His vegetarianism and his tendency to avoid violence simply mean a double tax burden on the peasants.

The forcible inclusion of the Dalit-Kachra in the team also comes across as a Gandhian moment. While Ambedkar was a votary of the 'direct action' method—where Dalits would physically assert their civic rights and democratise public spaces, even if this resulted in temporary violence—Gandhi wanted caste Hindus to feel remorse and guilt, and thus asks them voluntarily to let untouchables participate in the general village life, from accessing Brahminic temples to water tanks. In *Lagaan*, this translates into caste Hindus, led by Bhuvan, repenting their casteism in a sudden moment of awakening. The *vaid*, an elderly character who initially opposes Kachra's entry, thanks Bhuvan for 'opening their eyes'. This scene lends credence to the much-repeated journalistic inanity: that cricket is a religion in India, and that cricket unites the nation—acknowledging by default that there are a thousand factors that actually divide the nation!

Disability and untouchability

Irrespective of the result of the game and Kachra's performance in it, the status of Dalits will remain the same. Bhuvan's impassioned plea to the 'village elders' is limited to Kachra's inclusion in the team—and this is decided by accident—and is not about the larger social exclusion of the untouchables. What comes across as being most obnoxious is that, after all the drama over Kachra's inclusion, we are told that he is a good spinner not because of ability, but because of his disability. The token Dalit is further Dalitised. When Kachra wants to throw the ball with his 'normal' hand, know-all Bhuvan insists he use the disabled hand. Kachra's ability being an untouchable is hardly significant; his disability is. Kachra's talent is not based on merit, the will to excel or the determination to defeat an enemy, like Bhuvan's is. It, like untouchability, comes with birth. And it is Bhuvan who discovers this 'innate' talent. Kachra knows nothing.

Kachra's character is supposed to be based on Baloo Palwankar, the first world-class spinner the country produced (in the 1910s, 1920s). Baloo, a left-armer, was a Dalit and an inspiration to the young Ambedkar. Baloo, however, went on to become a Congressman, was member of the Harijan Sevak Sangh, and part of the Gandhian team that forced Ambedkar to sign the Poona Pact. (This was the agreement by which Ambedkar gave up his demand of separate electorates for Dalits following an indefinite fast undertaken by Gandhi.) Baloo later went on to contest an election against Ambedkar. But *Lagaan* is an insult to Baloo and Dalits in general. The way the film manipulates Kachra is representative of how mainstream society, histories and nationalisms have dealt with Dalits. It is also reflective of how cricket has dealt with Dalits. Independent India has produced not one Dalit cricketer. (Vinod Ganpat Kambli and Doddanarasiah Ganesh, both with short-lived careers, are being talked about as the only post-1947 Dalit cricketers, but Kannadiga friends inform me that Ganesh could be a backward caste '*gowda*', and Kambli, it appears, is from a fisherman caste and technically not Scheduled Caste.)

It is not as if cricketers have not had deformities. There have been spinners—such as India's B S Chandrasekhar, Australia's John Gleeson (called the 'mystery spinner' by the English) and Sri Lanka's best-known non-Sinhalese player, Muttiah Muralitharan—who have had deformities; Chandra was stricken by polio in childhood, and both Gleeson and Murali have congenitally bent elbows. But, the juxtaposition of disability and untouchability is very disturbing.

Such a rationalising of a Dalit's ability, coming as it does in the post-Mandal post-'liberalisation' phase in which the Brahminical/statist mood is pronouncedly anti-affirmative action, is an ontological and epistemological assault on Dalits and disabled people. It makes a mockery of Dalit 'merit'. Not only is an untouchable forced into the team on caste-Hindu terms, his ability is seriously undermined by his lack of self-control over his talent. Kachra spins the ball not because he knows how to, but because his (polio-afflicted?) hand is 'not normal'. Normally, Dalits are not talented. But Kachra's inclusion gets celebrated as 'a triumph of meritocracy', according to writings by Boria Majumdar, the sport historian. This is just salt in the wound.

Would *Lagaan* sans Kachra-the-handicapped-Dalit have made it less of a success or the great film it is said to be? Since there have anyway been only two alleged Dalits in post-British Indian cricket, would the absence of Kachra have made a difference to the script? Despite the Dalit issue figuring in the World Conference Against Racism at Durban last September, the generally racist Oscar committee is unlikely to have heard of it; but it is these little clever touches that make *Lagaan* what it is. According to Tamil filmmaker Rajiv Menon and cricket historian Majumdar, *Lagaan* is supposed to herald the arrival of the Dalit in Hindi cinema. For the first time, a Dalit is being positively portrayed in colour cinema, they feel. It is the acknowledgement of caste (in passing) and its negotiation/accommodation on casteist/Brahminic terms that makes *Lagaan* the darling of the liberal-seculars. Moreover, it is Kachra's socially and physically disabled presence that offers an ideal foil to Bhuvan's sheer physicality (well-toned body, clean-shaven looks, a doting girlfriend, and overall leadership qualities). *Lagaan* had to have a Dalit. But it also had to make his talent a congenital physical problem.

At the end of the one-hour-42-minute climax of the film, and of the cricket match in it, Kachra with a bat presents an abject picture: someone utterly useless to the team when it matters (while he is not using his disabled arm to turn the old ball). Since both Bollywood cinema and Hindu puranas thrive on the miraculous and the fantastic, we could have had the disabled Kachra pulling off a six off the last ball. But the Dalit cannot be given such definitive history-making agency. Such things are best left to caste Hindus. By sheer accident, a no-ball and a single result in hero-Bhuvan taking control to hoist the winning six.

Kachra's derogatory inclusion is not the only token moment in the film. There are many such concerning women. When Bhuvan's team is preparing for the match ahead, heroine Gauri (essayed by Gracy Singh) keeps pestering the players to eat. She is unaware of being the frivolous woman who does not understand the significance of the match. (Though in an earlier scene she offers the sole moral support to Bhuvan when he is beleaguered.) The white woman Elizabeth knows better. Gauri also shows other 'typical' female behavioural traits, established in the tradition of Hindu mythologies and epics—jealousy, envy, pettiness, the ability to sing and dance, make good food, pine—and all reinforced by popular cinema.

The women of the village contribute to the game by sewing up pads and gloves and other cricketing paraphernalia. And of course they cook, serve food, and cheer the home team. If indeed the film offers several Bakhtinian moments of inversion—unconventional bowling action, dress and general behaviour considered unsuitable to the game, and finally the fantastic triumph of the oppressed (if you will) possible only in the sporting arena and not in politics—why are such inversions and role reversals not genuinely extended to women and Dalits? Why could we not have had a *Lagaan* where a few talented women—someone who can bowl because of her skill in keeping the birds away from the drying grain in the courtyard with well-aimed stones, and some other who invents the sweep shot from endless practice in sweeping the house, and a third who makes an excellent slip fielder because she catches all that a drunk husband throws at her, and suchlike—too entered the team?

This is where caste and patriarchy limit the filmic imagination. And *Lagaan* becomes a 'success'. Aamir plays the true macho male who teases his obvious object of romantic love—the classic village belle. Bhuvan's Ram-like character has shades of the mythic Krishna too. While Gauri is alive to the sexual tension between Bhuvan and Elizabeth—who even expresses it—the hero is blissfully unaware of these dynamics though he sings of himself as Kanha (the folksy Krishna) in the song '*Radha kaise na jale?*' In yet another of those token moments, Elizabeth, besides her crush on Bhuvan, is shown developing respect for local traditions—she stealthily participates in the Holi celebrations, prays at the village temple, and even applies sindoor on her forehead.

Lagaan, while claiming to recreate a piece of imagined history, ends up being yet another clever Brahminical tale that offers no progressive relief. But for a genuine understanding of how *Lagaan* uses cricket, and how a Dalit is abused by *Lagaan's* cricket, we need to look at cricket in India, and sport as such, with a caste lens.

Cricket, Brahminism, bodies

Who really plays cricket in India? I am not a historian of the game, but it does not require much disciplinary training to infer that cricket is a game that best suits Brahminical tastes and bodies, and that there has been a preponderance of Brahmin cricket players at the national level. Bored princes and Parsis bent on mimicking the white sahibs might have been the first to take to the game in the Subcontinent, and we eventually had the Bombay Pentagular—communal cricket as it was called till 1946, where teams called Hindus, Mohammedans, Parsis, Europeans and Rest played against each other. But post-1947 it has been a game monopolised by Brahmins and Brahminical castes. Little wonder that Ashis Nandy, chronicler of modern Hinduism who dedicated one of his books to V D Savarkar, thinks cricket is a game naturally suited to Hinduism. Some commentators see cricket as truly vedantic. As Nandy has it, it is less Victorian/British and more Indian/Hindu.

Maybe we need to take this considered view seriously. Compared to other modern team sports such as hockey or football, cricket hardly involves much physical activity. A cricketer can stay put in one place for a long time. Even a fast bowler expends energy in short spells and cools off at the boundary. Besides, fast bowlers are not what India is known for, except for Kapil Dev, a meat-eating Jat. We do not need too much statistical backing to assert that Indian cricketers have excellent personal records at the expense of the team. Sachin Tendulkar might top the batting averages in Test and one-day cricket, but as a team India would be in some low-down position. The more Sachin scores centuries, the less India wins—to be precise, only two centuries of Sachin's ten result in an Indian test win. (In a February 2002 Wisden list of 100 all-time best one-day innings, Sachin, who has more one-day runs than anyone else, figures at 23rd place.) Such a strange statistic is unlikely to be available in, say, hockey: Dhanraj Pillay scoring the maximum goals during a tournament and the team being in the dumps.

No sport will tolerate such neglect of bodies as cricket in India. Take Sunil Gavaskar or Gundappa Vishwanath, conservative Brahmins both, who could not have afforded their Brahmin priest-like paunches and dormant slip-fielding if they had been playing a more physical game like hockey. Not surprisingly, hockey, which has been called 'the de jure national game' of India (cricket being the de facto national game post-1983), has drawn players predominantly from Dalit, Adivasi, OBC, Muslim and Sikh communities. (India's most celebrated hockey player, Dhyan Chand, though, was a Brahmin who joined the First Brahmin Regiment at Delhi in 1922 as a 'sepoy'.)

Moreover, a game like cricket involves a colossal waste of time. Historically, it was a sport only the leisured class could indulge in. Before the advent of the one-day form, which purists continue to smirk at, it would take a full six days for a match to be played (rest day included). At the end of it, in many cases there is not even a result to show for the time spent. Spectators too must have surplus time on their hands—one must be able to waste five whole days on a Test match. Even in the result-oriented one-day format, a whole day still needs to be spared (even to watch the game on television). But such has been the craze for cricket that, for the recent one-day fixture at Madras between India and the visiting England team, the local government declared a public holiday to enable its citizens to watch the match. Such gestures have of course become common.

In sharp contrast, a hockey match is likely to yield results in about two hours. And despite the Indian hockey team's recent wonderful performances, the game is never likely to recapture the public imagination. Most important, Dhanraj, Thirumavalavan, Dilip Tirkey, Jude Menezes, Lazarus Balra or Pargat Singh are unlikely to win the confidence of the publicity managers of Pepsi or Coke. They are also unlikely candidates for promoting credit cards. And add to this the fact that cricket players tend to be a fairer lot compared to hockey players—and TV and cinema have always promoted an Indian brand of racism that excludes the darker-looking majority.

This marginalisation also owes to the social backgrounds of hockey players, and they are unlikely to make much headway in Brahmin-dominated cricket. After the monopoly of Maharashtra Brahmins during the 1970s and 1980s, the 1990s saw Karnataka send in its Brahmin pack of Anil Kumble, Sunil Joshi, Rahul Dravid, Javagal Srinath (dubbed 'the world's fastest vegetarian bowler') and Venkatesh Prasad (a fast bowler who runs all the way only to off-spin the ball). Dodda Ganesh and David Johnson were their non-Brahmin contemporaries whose careers, not surprisingly, were short-lived. While Johnson played just one international match, Ganesh did hang around for some time. Sunil Joshi persisted longer than Ganesh, but the four other Karnataka Brahmins have been mainstays in the 'national 11'—there have been several occasions when up to nine out of 11 players have been Brahmins on the team. Let me substantiate this with a quote by Shekhar Gupta, editor of the *Indian Express*: 'Harbhajan is seen as the fighting new Indian, non-English speaking, definitely non-Brahmin (in a team usually boasting 8 of them) and not from Bombay or Bangalore, the nurseries of Indian cricket, but from a small town in Punjab from where most immigrants to Britain come. So you know where that never-say-die spirit of the Southhall Sikh comes from.'

Having too many Brahmins means that you play the game a little too softly, and mostly for yourself. Let's get a Gupta sound-byte again:

> After he [Alan Donald] bowled the heart out of this, the so-called best batting line-up in the world, at Port Elizabeth in December 1992, he said the Indians were nice guys. But they were not very good at fighting. 'They don't want to handle pace. They hit a few shots and then get out,' he said. This team lost twice in Australia, South Africa, West Indies, and England and at home to both Pakistan and South Africa. They lost even the old label of tigers at home. They were not prepared for close finishes, cracked up in crunch matches and were so easily overawed by the rivals' aggressive body language. There was no other reason for them to lose to Pakistan at Madras and Calcutta (1999) and to South Africa at Bombay and Bangalore last year.

Harbhajans and Kamblis are exceptions. We are not going to see cricket at the national level being taken over by meat-eating Dalits, Muslims and Sikhs, and some much-needed team spirit ushered in. But how does a game, which I argue is inherently Brahminical and which draws upon such a small social base, continue to hijack the national imagination? In most modern nation states, sport has been one arena which marginalised groups have used to showcase their talent. Be it Maradona or Pele, Mike Tyson or Magic Johnson and Michael Jordan, or in more recent times the fantastic success of Venus and Serena Williams in a game typically dominated by rich whites, or the several athletic successes from poor African countries, or the case of gymnasts from East European countries, sport has been an avenue for making one's way up from slums and ghettoes to podiums. But in India, the caste system forecloses such possibilities. While academic studies by African–American scholars compare basketball and jazz as truly black sites of creative expression, in India one cannot even posit something like a Dalit or un-Brahmin sport (though the very thought of a sport dominated by Brahmins sounds funny). We are forced to merely record how many Dalits ever got into the 'Indian 11'. This begins to look similar to how many Dalits sing Carnatic music or dance the Bharatanatyam.

The hegemony of cricket in India not only eclipses other team sports, such as hockey, but makes the media, state and public very quickly dump and forget a Malleswari or a Limba Ram (the well-known Adivasi archer of the mid-1990s). But invoking caste and casteism in sport begs the question: If cricket is a game where unfit Brahmin men simply amble along, why is it that in other modern sports, non-Brahmin Indian men and women seem to lag behind? Why does Olympic glory seem to be a larger Subcontinental problem? For answers, I suggest that we understand how the caste system, prevalent in Southasia and most explicitly in the Subcontinent, could possibly disable the emergence and formation of 'bodies' that could physically rise up to competition from the best. This might seem quite a 'racist' and politically or scientifically wrong proposition to make, but consider what Ambedkar wrote some seven decades ago:

> If caste is eugenic, what sort of a race of men should it have produced? Physically speaking the Hindus are a C3 people. They are a race of pygmies and dwarfs stunted in stature and wanting in stamina. It is a nation 9/10ths of which is declared to be unfit for military service. This shows that the Caste System does not embody the eugenics of modern scientists. It is a social system which embodies the arrogance and selfishness of a perverse section of the Hindus who were superior enough in social status to set it in fashion and who had authority to force it on their inferiors.

Such a statement might seem crude and reductionist. But if an entire population was forced to breed for some 2,000 years within extremely restrictive patriarchal sub-caste specificities, the theoretical possibility of choosing mates is drastically reduced, and there is extensive sub-caste inbreeding. And we are talking about a situation where, even today, a Tamil Brahmin, more specifically a *vadakalai-iyyengar* of a particular *gotra* (now figure that out!), does not look for a mate in an equivalent sub-caste grouping in neighbouring Andhra Pradesh or Karnataka. In fact, the socially mobile Tamil Brahmin, whether s/he is in Delhi/Bombay or Detroit, seeks an alliance only in the sub-caste and sub-group, sub-region-wise suitable sub-community.

Since the category of caste has been abandoned in censuses regarding caste Hindus, we have data only on the Scheduled Castes and Scheduled Tribes (Dalits and Adivasis) who officially account for 4,685 communities. With this figure, we can imagine how many sub-castes and sub-communities there might be among the rest of the 77.5 per cent of the population. Even if we do not take into consideration Adivasis, in a country where couples marrying outside caste are forced to commit suicide (as in many much-highlighted cases in Uttar Pradesh and Haryana), there are strictures against inter-caste marriage in all caste-bound communities. To suggest that such massive forced inbreeding is likely to produce weak bodies—in Ambedkar words, 'a nation 9/10ths of which is declared to be unfit for military service'—is not too wild, I hope.

It is such a context—where a billion bodies cannot yield a single Olympic gold—that results in a much-unplayed game like cricket becoming the pre-occupation of a caste-ridden country. In the parent country, England, cricket is hardly the most popular game, football being the game that matters. However, English cricket today, led by a Madras-born Muslim, is more ethnically represen-tative and balanced than perhaps any other, though there are fewer blacks and more Asians now. While Indian cricket is dogged by casteism, in South Africa cricket practises racism by omission: some 15 years after the country formally gave up Apartheid, there have been few black players. Ditto for Zimbabwe. In both of these African countries, football remains the basic male sporting passtime. In Australia (or New Zealand), the game does enjoy popularity, but this country equally keenly follows other sports, and has even yielded an aborigi-nal Olympic gold medallist in Cathy Freeman. It is in the Subcontinent that we seem so fixated on cricket. And caste.

India/Bollywood produces films such as *Lagaan* because it patronises a game like cricket. And cricket rules because the Brahminical caste system, with its bedrock of inequality, continues to grip India. Much of the obsession with cricket can be understood if we understand the popularity of cinema in India, which produces a phenomenal 1,000-odd movies a year. (India also plays more one-day matches than any other country.) Popular cinema in India, be it from Bollywood or Kollywood (as Tamil filmdom is called), which began its career by retelling Brahminic Hindu mythologies, continues to be a major site that sustains and nurtures the caste system and the Brahminical social order. While Valentine's Day comes to be celebrated in select urban pockets, only post-Hindutva—and it is repressive Hindutva that finds this unacceptable—not many question the consensus over the continuing ban on kissing in Indian cinema.

Cultural-studies scholars have extensively deliberated on why kissing and sex scenes are almost self-censored in India. They would benefit by looking for answers in caste taboos. Caste-conscious Hindus are extremely touchy about *jootha* (contact through saliva, *yechchal* in Tamil), and kissing can be the most despicable jootha act. And you certainly cannot indulge in it publicly. While

Hindi films celebrate the act of the wife eating the leftovers on the husband's plate, even married couples cannot kiss on screen. Before saying 'Ah, this in the land of Khajuraho and the Kama Sutra,' we must remember that more than these two Ks, it is the strictures in Brahma Purana and Shiva Purana—which encourage only coital/reproductive sex, quite like the older Gandhi did—that caste Hindus take seriously.

If even kissing and making love have to be seen as subversive in popular cinema, one can well understand why nothing really subversive is possible in this genre. Yet, cinema has emerged as the most popular cultural form in post-British India, as much as cricket has emerged as the most popular sport. Both cinema and cricket, in their banyan-like existences, have prevented the growth of anything under their unhealthy shadows. Fluff such as *Lagaan* and false icons such as Sachin are the best that these institutions can throw up; their worst—match-fixing and *Gadar*.

Chapter 9

The dark white shroud

Himal, March 2003

Shruti Debi

In the winter of 2002–03, a protracted fog hugged the ground of the Indus and Ganga plains in the north and east of the Subcontinent for approximately 45 days. The resultant *seet lahar* (translated as 'cold wave') of December and January condemned 500 million people, living in a swathe of territory from Rawalpindi to Rangpur, to a sun-starved and frigid existence. The fog disrupted life, beyond just upsetting local airline schedules and delaying trains. In this, one of the most fertile belts of the world—the tropical and semi-tropical northern half of Southasia—lives a large section of the world's humanity, mostly in poverty. And it was exposed—under-clothed, undernourished—in its millions, to temperatures in the low single digits. Together, the fog and accompanying cold of winter struck a bitter blow.

The effects of this winter fog are compounded every year, as its growing incidence coincides with the growing numbers of those it shrouds. Yet, as *Himal*'s investigation over the last two months has confirmed, the Indus–Ganga fog is a grossly understudied meteorological phenomenon. This shortcoming is evident when one begins to examine available literature. Meteorological data confirm anecdotal information that the duration and thickness of fog in the Indus–Ganga *maidaan* has been on the rise over the last half-century, yet there is a singular lack of academic concern over its socio-economic impact, and not enough scientific interest in investigating comprehensively the factors behind this increase. While the changing air quality, which appears to have a significant impact, and the inversion layer that now persists for long periods of time preserving cold air at the surface, have received some attention, the rise in ambient moisture—more significant for the plains than in deltaic Bangladesh—as a potential major cause has been neglected.

The familiar term 'cold wave' does great disservice in this, implying that the cold comes from elsewhere. Even experienced meteorologists will fob off enquiries by invoking the 'northwesterlies' to explain away the cold as something about which nothing can be done. True, the northwesterlies that blow over the land in the winter are cold moist winds that come from elsewhere (as all winds must); but they have always been coming down from the same direction, and therefore are a constant factor. In fact, the cause for the cold, in the sedentary fog that sits on the Indus and Ganga plains keeping the sun from warming the land and its people, might just be homegrown.

Engineering in this region, from Pakistan's Indus basin to the Nepal Tarai, has interfered substantially in the last 50 years with the natural hydrological cycle of the plains. The result is that there is a lot of unseasonable water on the ground's surface in the winter due to irrigation canals, the pumping of ground-water and the building of embankments and other structures that cause water-logging. The impact of this ecological modification on the weather has gone entirely neglected by the Subcontinent's scientific community.

There is also a distinct lack of caring when it comes to the impact the fog has on those living in abject poverty, who number in the hundreds of millions. Living in a region that is warm or hot most of the time, even under normal cir-cumstances the poor do not have the clothing, diet, shelter or services to cope well with the cold. Given that historically the seet lahar lasted no more than a few days, it was possible to overcome the brief misery. But with the number of foggy days extending up to a month or more now, misery levels have risen and continue to rise. An index for this misery has not been proposed, let alone configured—not by physical scientists, nor by social scientists. While the media reports separately on the fog and the cold, there is no attempt to link the two and analyse the inescapable trend.

The fog has caught the metropolitan media's attention mainly because of poor visibility—flights and trains are often cancelled or delayed. Occasionally, when the numbers are sufficiently impressive, there is disconcerting news of so many 'cold-wave deaths' and the plight of the urban homeless. But the

161

loss to the economy has not yet been calculated: the destruction of winter crops, the standstill in the brick-making industry, the slump for builders and masons, the impact on *dhobi*s across the land (whose clotheslines remain soggy in the absence of sunshine), and a hundred other professions and industries that are affected by the fog and suffer without registering on the public's radar.

Sociologists have not thought it necessary to look into the number of people affected by the extended presence of the winter fog, and no public-health expert has considered its impact on them in terms of problems from the exposure. No observer or analyst has considered the fact that the duration of the seet lahar (though getting longer, yet short when compared to the hot months) makes it unviable for the poor and very poor to even aspire to add a winter wardrobe, or to buy quilts, or build a heat-conserving space in which to live. In the Indus and Ganga plains, which register among the lowest on human-development indices anywhere in the planet, it just does not do to say, 'Let them wear sweaters,' for people have only ever had to plan for thin cottons.

Flying blind

In his novel *Blindness*, the Portuguese novelist José Saramago describes the progressive blindness of an entire city and the consequent breakdown of social order. Social order might not be under threat in this case, at least not yet, but the Subcontinental fog, in its engulfing whiteness and in its neglect at various levels of investigation, draws a parallel to Saramago's tale. While the intuitive conclusion that the incidence of fog is on the rise finds numerical validation, most meteorologists still hide behind the 'need to study data' before pronouncing a trend. Rather than concede to this insensitivity, *Himal* extrapolated from its collated findings the undeniable fact that the northern half of Southasia is indeed a foggier and more miserable place now than it was even in the 1970s.

As per the definition used by the Indian Meteorology Department (IMD), fog is the condition in which horizontal visibility on the surface is less than 1,000 m while relative humidity is above 75 per cent. There is nothing new about the science of fog, and it is known that fog develops when there is the standard mix of atmospheric moisture, aerosols around which this moisture can condense, and appropriately low temperatures for the condensation to occur. The science of fog has not changed. What has changed is the increasing severity of the fog (and, correspondingly, the cold), in terms of both how long it lasts and how thick it is.

Weather data are at the core of meteorology, and the best place to seek continuous data on the fog is the airport, where meteorologists are more exercised than others about its incidence. Reduced visibility disrupts flights and inconveniences the privileged of an underprivileged Subcontinent. Data from Safdarjang, now an under-used airstrip at the heart of New Delhi, reveal that of the last six Decembers, four have had over 20 foggy days. Compare this to the average of 6.2 days of fog for the month of December between 1951 and 1980. During the same period, the average for January at Safdarjang was 6.8 foggy days. However, only in one year between 1996 and 2003 did New Delhi have less than 20 foggy days in January. This dramatic rise in foggy days in Delhi is repeated again and again in airport weather stations across the plains of North India, whereas data from the south or from the Himalayan region do not show such a trend.

A study was published in October 2001 on visibility at 25 Indian airports across the country, conducted by a team that included the former assistant director-general at the IMD. It shows that, at 21 northern stations, the number of days with visibility of less than 2,000 m (the benchmark commonly used as the 'runway visual range') in the winter months (December–February) is on the rise. Tracking trends through the 1970s, 1980s and 1990s, the graphs for Allahabad, Amritsar, Benaras, Delhi, Lucknow and Patna are particularly steep.

In Amritsar, the number of poor-visibility days has shot up from two out of 90 in the 1970s to 72 out of 90 in the 1990s. Benaras registered an increase from nine foggy days to 72, Lucknow and Allahabad, from nine to 63, and Patna from 12 to around 75. The meteorologists, writing in the journal *Mausam*, say that 'in the north Indian stations viz., Amritsar, New Delhi, Varanasi, Patna, Lucknow and Allahabad ... the visibility deteriorated significantly with poor visibility days increasing to 70 to 80 per cent in the winter season.'

Learning from recent experience that the fog has begun playing havoc with domestic and international flights, the airport at Palam in Delhi upgraded its landing instrumentation system this year to enable aircraft arrivals at even 500 m runway visual range. But the fog beat the technology, with visibility keeping well below that mark except for a small window during the day, when the rush to clear flights often overwhelmed the system. Irate passengers make for chaos at airports and may give airlines a bad name, but at worst they are only inconvenienced.

The fog and the cold made obvious yet again the startling income inequality in the fertile plains of the Subcontinent. On the one extreme, in Lahore and Delhi, the two major international airports in the affected area, the hotel business picked up, with five-star establishments gaining substantively from disrupted air traffic in the first three weeks of January. At the other extreme, in Bihar, where the government distributed blankets in the last week of January, almost four weeks into the fog, only those who could prove that they were below the poverty line (BPL) could take refuge in state largesse. Never mind that BPL computation is so flawed that it is not a realistic reckoning of poverty at all; the Bihar government linked blanket distribution to BPL schemes that require the applicant to furnish an address. As a result, not only were the not-poor-enough bereft of state protection, but the 'too poor' were left at the mercy of the weather as well. Meanwhile, it was reported that room heaters, blankets and hosiery saw brisk sales this winter.

Command areas

The Indian airport data provide convincing proof to support accounts that the Ganga plains have seen a dramatic increase in the incidence of fog and extended cold periods during December and January. The same seems to hold true across the western frontier, in Pakistan, whose national meteorological department reported that, in January 2003, 'The mean daily bright sunshine duration remained below normal all over the country due to persistent fog.' Specifically, 'thick fog persisted over the agricultural plains of Punjab and NWFP.'

The conditions in the 800 km stretch of Nepal's southern plains are mirrored in the adjacent areas of Uttar Pradesh, Bihar and north Bengal. In its preliminary weather summary for January 2003, the Department of Hydrology and Meteorology in Kathmandu dwells at length on the abnormally severe fog in the Tarai. This year, the Tarai region reported 'dense foggy weather resulting in severe cold condition for the long period from the last week of December 2002 till 24 January 2003 … The sun was completely obstructed by the dense fog, preventing the sun's ray from reaching the ground.'

The department's figures for December and January over the last two decades suggest that the Tarai—from Dhangadi in the far west near Pilibhit in India to Biratnagar in the east, close to Siliguri—is becoming progressively colder during the day but rarely registers negative variations from the normal at night. (Cold days and warm nights, as the meteorologist will confirm, usually indicate fog or cloudiness.) In January 1983, Dhangadi's mean maximum was 20.2 degrees C, 1.5 degrees below average. In 1993, the variation was −2.6 degrees; in 1998, −4.1; and finally this year, −6.1 degrees below average.

Right across the stretch of the Tarai, Nepalganj, Bhairahawa, Simara and Biratnagar are on a similar trajectory as Dhangadi while, interestingly, the Kathmandu Valley and other hill towns seem headed in the other direction. There are ample narrative accounts in the Tarai about the increased incidence of the fog. To begin with, conditions are such now that the plainsfolk, incongruously, have started heading up the hills to find sunshine and warmth. Since the ground-hugging fog does not extend beyond a couple of hundred feet, sunshine is often less than an hour's drive away. Says an anthropologist who grew up in the Tarai town of Butwal, 'I never remember fog in Butwal. But now to escape it and the cold, people go up to Palpa for warmth.' Tulsi Basnet, a Butwal businessman, closed his shop and undertook the 90-minutes bus ride to Palpa to reach the sun's warmth. He says, 'We heard it was sunny in the hills; we had to go there to give my father some relief from his asthma.'

For at least the period of the seet lahar, the remote Himalayan districts of Nepal are actually warmer than places in the plains. Nepalganj is known to schoolchildren through their primers as the hottest town in Nepal. But these are abnormal times, and this year, for days on end, fog-stricken Nepalganj was colder than the remote mountain-district headquarters of Jumla, directly to the north. At 2,340 m elevation, Jumla had bright sunshine, while in Nepalganj underclad rickshaw-pullers shivered in the fog. On 19 January, for instance, Jumla recorded a daytime high of 21.3 degrees, while Nepalganj had a maximum of 10.4. Two days earlier, Kanpur in Uttar Pradesh, among the hottest places in the region in summer, recorded an 'unverified' minimum of −0.6 on a night when even Srinagar was warmer.

Says one Kathmandu-based editor, 'We used to hear of people dying of the *loohoo*, or heat wave, in the Tarai. Now more people are suffering and dying in the winter, and in a shorter period of time. And it is the same people affected in both summer and winter, without air conditioning and without heating.'

Globally, the weather might have changed incrementally over the past few decades, but climatic factors such as prevailing winds have remained relatively constant over the period. Although the moisture-bearing low-pressure northwesterly winds are ascribed more than their fair share of the blame, they cannot be the explanation for the steady rise in winter relative humidity and Indus–Ganga fog over the last few decades. Instead, three key variables in the increasing fog are moisture, pollution and temperature inversion. The inversion layer, when normal atmospheric temperature 'inverts' so that it is coldest near the surface and gets warmer with altitude, results in a cap where cold (in this case, polluted, foggy) air is trapped at the bottom. In the Indus–Ganga winter, a strong inversion layer forms at a low level, which increases the longevity of the fog.

The other two factors relate to human intervention in the Indus–Ganga belt: greater air pollution in the lower atmosphere, and the increased presence of water and moisture on the surface during the winter months. There is now an unprecedented amount of surface moisture in the Indus–Ganga belt in the cold months, when historically the land would have been dry other than during the brief spells of winter rain. This appreciable increase in the presence of surface water is explained by three factors.

First: the building of a network of canals all over the plains during the last half-century, particularly in India and Pakistan. In these places, post-Independence, irrigation gained credence as the panacea for illnesses that ranged from rural poverty to agricultural production shortfall to the 'burden of backwardness'. So, from just a few hundred kilometres in 1950, there is now a network of thousands of kilometres of canals carrying water year-round to the 'command areas' that cover the length and breadth of the Pakistani and Indian Punjab, Haryana, UP and Bihar. Today, in the Indian Punjab, more than 1.5 million hectares are under irrigation. Next door, the Indus Basin Irrigation System, the world's largest irrigation network, comprising 45 main canals, diverts almost 75 per cent of the average annual river flow into the Indus basin, irrigating 17 million hectares of contiguous land. In UP, total canal length grew by 3100 km in the 14 years between 1972 and 1986 alone.

Second: the revolution in the exploitation of groundwater for irrigation, powered by diesel pumps and electricity subsidies, now brings to the surface water that used to stay underground. Today, deep boring brings up 'sweet' water to irrigate vast swathes of land, thus bringing unprecedented prosperity to some areas but also helping in the creation of conditions for fog, which in the end adversely affect the very crops being irrigated.

Third and finally: the building of concrete embankments to control the waters of the Indus and the Ganga, which has been a 'growth industry' over the last five decades, takes its toll. Pushed by the perceived need to protect the people from floods, the construction of embankments (*tatbandhs*) has become a populist measure used by political parties, with the active collusion of private contractors, to show their concern for the people. Over time, this activity has generated a momentum of its own, and the cumulative length of rivers roped in behind embankments has increased from almost nil in the early decades of the 1900s to thousands of kilometres today. In Bihar, where the tatbandh mafia is particularly influential, the total length of embankments grew from 154 km in 1954 to 3500 km in 1997.

The effect of both canals and the embankments is the same, increasing the moisture content of the soil or allowing bodies of water to exist outside of the natural watercourses. Canals, by definition, divert water to areas where there is naturally none. And embankments, while they block floodwaters in the monsoon, play a significant role in ensuring that water does not properly run into the rivers. As a result, there are large, year-round pools that do not drain. Flawed engineering in both cases ensures seepages that result in waterlogged fields. Thus, an estimated 182,000 hectares of 'protected land' are waterlogged outside the eastern Kosi embankment, and another 94,000 hectares on the western side, apart from the 34,400 hectares waterlogged above the contour line.

The other variable, pollutants, plays an undeniably active part in the intensification of the fog. Particulate matter in the air act as nuclei on which water vapour can condense; over the years, the increased activity of a rapidly growing population in transport, agriculture and other sectors has dispelled into the air a variety of pollutants. The effects of winter cropping, vehicular emissions, the smoke output of tens of thousands of brick kilns and other more modern smokestack industries are only now being studied in some scientific depth. The effects of the greater availability of surface moisture from irrigation and embankments, meanwhile, have yet to ignite even a spark of interest in the scientific community.

Seet lahar

The most graphic visualisation of the fog is to be had from satellite imagery. Hour after hour, day after day, an enormous white sheet wraps itself over the super-hydrated plains, staying stubbornly in place, only its edges fraying or consolidating. The term *seet lahar* captures most evocatively the condition of the Subcontinental cold wave. *Seet*, which can convey both 'cold' and 'dew', loses some of its connotations of dampness in English, however, breaking the connection between water and the winter for the influential English-educated in the Subcontinent. Indeed, as noted previously, because the term is translated into 'cold wave', the impression is of a chill blowing in from some distant trans-Himalayan region. Whereas the reality is that the long periods of cold of the last few years are linked to the increasingly longer periods of fog, which is actually predicated on the absence of winds any stronger than 8 km per hour. Of course, not all cold days have to be foggy. 'Western disturbances' are known to bring gusty winds and rain, which bring the temperature down. But these conditions prevail over a period that is accurately described as a 'cold snap'—intense but brief. The protracted cold-wave periods, in contrast, are about days on end of fog-induced misery.

Turning to the science of the fog, consider this. For two samples of air at a certain temperature, the one with more water molecules will have a higher dew point, the temperature at which water vapour condenses to form water droplets or fog. As such, even 'normal' semi-tropical temperatures (such as in the Ganga plain) that do not dip very low are conducive to fog formation because of the high atmospheric water-vapour content. Then, because water droplets or fog are an even more effective absorber of radiation than water vapour, not only does the fog prevent the sun's rays from reaching the huddled masses of the Indus–Ganga plains, but it actually sucks up what heat is available in the atmosphere and soil. However, perhaps by force of habit, meteorologists continue to attribute winter humidity to the moisture-bearing northwesterlies, failing to explain the recorded rise in relative humidity at northern stations, or to connect it with the rising incidence of the fog.

The hundreds of millions of penurious or near-penurious, who are the worst hit, might know intuitively that the fog's incidence is on the rise. But as with every water-related contention, they will yet again not determine what must be done about it. Instead, it is the influential pockets of urban Southasia, where live those with access to woollens, electrically wired homes and heated vehicles, only briefly exposed to the cold between the house and the car, that will persuade studies, legislation, even activist judges to consider the problem. They have heard that the fog has to do with the unacceptably high air pollution and, consequently, air pollution now occupies inordinate space in the 'national' consciousness. So, evening news features include minutiae on daily decimal variations of CO, NO_x and SO_2 emissions, and the study and resultant activism with regard to air pollution in New Delhi inspires even the lofty Supreme Court of India to plunge its gavel into the matter.

The apex court's exertions seem to have borne fruit, with pollution levels having palpably altered in Delhi. But this has not had the expected corresponding effect on the fog, which continues to intensify even though pollution levels have fallen. This seemingly incongruous eventuality has prompted perhaps the only investigative study of the fog in India—where, expectedly, the link being probed is that between the fog and pollution.

The National Physical Laboratory (NPL) in Delhi, in partnership with the IMD and the Central Pollution Control Board, is currently perhaps the only organisation studying the Ganga fog. Still in its nascent stages, the two-year-old study has focused on the effect of air pollution on the formation of fog, and has found that the two are not as simply linked as first thought. The NPL says that the particular interactions of individual pollutants—hygroscopic emission gases such as NO_x, SO_2 and CO, greenhouse gases and the secondary pollutant, surface ozone—warrant special attention. The NPL study has discovered two things: that the concentration of aerosols influences the size and distribution of activated fog nuclei, affecting the fog's liquid content and visibility. Second, that the activation of fog nuclei occurs at different levels of supersaturation for different aerosols. Working on the hypothesis that fog density, frequency and longevity must depend on aerosol properties, the NPL team is investigating the particular ways in which different pollutants influence fog.

Pollutants affect the development of fog because exposure to aqueous air promotes chemical growth, resulting in the evolution of aerosols, which become the nuclei on which water vapour can condense. While the formation of fog is predicated on low wind speed, clear nights, high humidity (above 80 per cent, but especially between 90 and 100 per cent), appropriately low temperatures and the presence of pollutants, according to M K Tiwari of the NPL's Department of Radio and Atmospheric Sciences, the strength (density and longevity) of the fog depends on the concentration of pollutants and the low-height tempera-ture-inversion layer.

In the Subcontinent, low-height inversion in particular fosters the lon-gevity of the fog. Land being a better radiator of heat than air, after sundown it and the air close to it cool expeditiously as compared to the air above, thus 'inverting' the normal state where air gets cooler with height. While, as the night wears on, the air at ground level cools to its dew point, promoting fog forma-tion, the cap formed by the inversion layer stifles wind movement, discour-ages cloud formation and keeps the pollutants, including water vapour, trapped. Temperature inversion should be strongest over those soil types that absorb, and subsequently release, heat most easily—i.e., sandy surfaces. But the truly arid regions in west Southasia are spared the phenomenon because of strong convection, typical of desert environments. In semi-tropical UP, Bihar and the Nepal Tarai, where the inversion layer does not persist, there is enough moisture available from the irrigated surface and low-pressure northwesterlies, and tem-perature and pollution conditions are aggravated enough, for thick fog to linger for long periods into the day.

Coming back to the legalities, having taken care of urban air pollution, the court in India has since shifted its attention outside the city. It has directed the Indian government on a grand, multi-crore 'garland canal' scheme that will purportedly connect parched areas of India to 'water surplus' areas. The effects of this are inconceivable in their entirety, not least because the matrix of the climate has yet to be comprehensively mapped. The immediate consequences are apparent, though: massive rural dislocation, and the magnification of the already well-documented problems with canal irrigation.

Nowhere among these well-documented problems, however, is the one of fog. Indeed, there has been considerable study and activism related to other aspects of the hydrological cycle in the Indus–Ganga region. Organisations as diverse in approach and focus as the Centre for Science and Environment in New Delhi and the Bihar-based activist river-focused movement known as the Barh Mukti Abhiyan have fought political, bureaucratic and engineering obtuseness related to flood-control and waterlogging for years. However, even they have not yet made the link between canals, embankments, groundwater exploitation, and the fog and the misery they bring. While this investigation by *Himal* suggests a causal link between faulty water engineering and the fog, the hypothesis needs to be scientifically investigated. A serious study must be followed by a sensitisation of those who matter, and (to the extent possible) mitigation measures to reduce the bitterness of the winter for those inadequately clothed or housed.

Vegetable crop

The exceptional situation of the Indus and Ganga plains is that, for most of the year, it is a hot and humid home for its overwhelmingly large population, where the poor expectedly have not evolved mechanisms to cope with cold. In the cold higher latitudes of, for instance, the Chinese heartland, which also has a large population of the poor, and where too the fog may be intensifying, people are prepared by historical experience to deal with the harshness of winter. In Sub-Saharan Africa, where a large number of the world's extremely poor live, it will never be cold or foggy. In the Indus and Ganga plains, however, the relative brevity of the bitter fog and cold renders unviable the building of new structures and the procuring of warm clothing—moreover, many would not even have the place to store such new clothes. So north Southasia, uniquely, is a site where people in the millions suffer from not having insulation through clothing or construction, a deprivation that is as primal as not having food.

Whether in terms of construction techniques, purchasing power or agricultural practice, the sub-tropical north of the Subcontinent is fundamentally unequipped to deal with either the fog or the cold. Winter is still remembered as the season of relief between harsh summers and the long monsoons. But now, winter has become a dank cold season with endless days of physical and fiscal distress. For those with material means, it is distress over the crop or business, or medical bills and delayed travelling. And for those who have nothing, such as the millions of urban homeless, it has become the season for worrying about survival.

While the loss of human lives to the cold has been computed (at 1,500 for this winter), a material cost-evaluation exercise has not been carried out at the governmental level in Bangladesh, India, Nepal or Pakistan. That verified figures are not forthcoming on this issue is not, for once, due to official unwillingness to share data but rather to a complete lack of imagination. R P Singh, head of the Department of Agricultural Economics at the Indian Agriculture Research Institute (IARI), concedes that putting a figure to the agricultural losses would be 'socially relevant'. And yet, a researcher at the institute shrugs off the suggestion, saying such an exercise 'would not be economically viable in a developing country such as India'. It is through cracks such as these, in the disconnect between politicians and scientists and the 'constituency', that the common person falls.

Take the case of Prakash Yadav, who is chief whip at a taxi stand in Gurgaon. The area straddles Delhi's urban conglomeration and Haryana, and many like Yadav travel the short distance from their fields in the latter to the bustling urban economy. Like so many others he knows, Yadav too has suffered the ills of the last few winters. While almost 40 per cent of his mustard crop was laid waste by white rust, a fog-related disease, he calculated a 50 per cent dip in his earnings from the taxi service for December and January.

Even if the scientists and administrators have not yet made the connection, the peasants and small-scale farmers know well that the intensity of the winter fog is on the rise. In the Subcontinental belt under consideration, the major winter crops are wheat, mustard, potato and pulses. In India, owing to government policy fashioned in response to food grain surplus, vegetable cropping has for some years been replacing wheat cultivation. The policy calculation obviously factored in import, export, storage costs, supply and demand; but it neglected, not atypically, to look at the data on the ground. Wheat is a hardy crop as compared to the 'short-duration young crops' of winter vegetables that farmers have been encouraged to adopt, which cannot withstand sustained exposure of even four or five hours to relative humidity above 80 per cent in combination with temperatures as low as 7 to 12 degrees C. Relative humidity above 80 per cent promotes bacterial development and, this winter, when relative humidity stayed as high as 90 to 100 per cent for as long as 10 hours a day, the conditions were devastating. White rust and a blight known as alternaria struck the mustard this winter, and blight also affected other common winter crops including potato, tomato and brinjal.

N V K Chakravarty, principal agricultural meteorologist at IARI, explains that the late-sown varieties of the vegetables are particularly vulnerable to the cold and fog. They are late-sown because timetables for multi-cropping, an irrigation-enabled practice, are not quite synchronised yet. Thus, the plants are still in the early stages of development when the fog develops its intensity, and a high level of humidity promotes bacterial growth. Additionally, the fog also affects photosensitive growth activity in the plant, and low temperatures retard its development.

The narrative of human ambition vis-à-vis nature that frames the story of the fog is sublimated in the potato. The potato is not indigenous to the Subcontinent, but almost all major viral, fungal and bacterial diseases that it is vulnerable to are endemic here. An input-intensive crop requiring fertilisers, irrigation and expensive hybrid seeds, the potato never caught on in the Indus–Ganga plains till rapid canal proliferation post-Independence, coupled with state inducements, made it possible. This winter, potato farmers from North West Frontier Province (NWFP) to north Bengal suffered crushing losses, possibly because of the same irrigation network that enabled this unnatural cultivation in the first place.

This winter was perhaps the worst for potato and mustard, but numbers are hard to come by. In January, IARI estimates for Punjab's losses (which contributes almost five percent of the national yield) varied wildly between 15 per cent and 40 percent. In West Bengal, where 32,000 hectares are under potato cultivation, farmers were told to use pesticides when it became apparent that the fog would linger long enough to ruin the crop. Says S Mishra, an agricultural meteorologist with the West Bengal government, 'There is definitely an increased incidence and duration of fog during the winter months in this region. This is based on observation; we have not done any study on the phenomenon.'

The absence of econometric application to fog by those whose job it is to engage in such study is glaring. An aggregation that takes into account aviation, railways and road transport, commerce, agriculture and industry, vehicular accidents, costs of delays, public health expenses, among others, has not been done and is not on the cards. Only if such an investigation is undertaken will ironies such as the plight of the potato farmers of the plains find a narrative framework. As things stand now, Prakash Yadav's woes continue to be blamed vacuously on the 'cold wave and unusual fog', while meteorologists debate endlessly whether the conditions are a regional manifestation of global climatic changes—and the establishment as a whole prefers not to involve itself too deeply in this complicated, potentially controversial subject.

Cold threshold

Over the last few decades, the ground fog has grown from localised patches into an enormous blanket. While satellite images from the early- and mid-morning currently show it covering a stretch from the Northeast to Pakistan, more often the concentration falls somewhere between these two extremes. In that region where dense fog has recurred year after year, growing towards its present spread and intensity, live at least 400 million people. Of these, as per calculations from the most conservative government estimates, the poorest of the poor, those who are denied the basic opportunities of life to procure even adequate nutrition, number no less than 150 million. An additional 200 million, while perhaps not 'the poorest', are still too poor to afford a severe winter, and would need substantial state assistance to weather it.

Among this aggregate 350 million who were most profoundly affected by the fog and cold of the recent winters are groups such as the *kamaiya*s of the Nepal Tarai, a traditionally disadvantaged community of former bonded labourers that has received little state support after being 'freed' by it. At least 46 Kamaiyas, mostly infants and the elderly, died in camps for former Kamaiyas this winter from pneumonia and upper-respiratory-tract diseases. These deaths were not caused by sheer cold—temperatures have to be much lower than those in the region to induce hypothermia—but were contributed to by the fog. The cold and damp of the fog simultaneously weakens natural defence mechanisms, especially pulmonary resistance; further, since high relative humidity promotes the formation of acid aerosols, it also increases toxicity in the atmosphere.

Though the Kamaiya system has been abolished, it will be a long time before the thousands who were yoked to it will be able to afford special provisions for the foggy days of winter. Whether in UP or Bihar, in the Nepal Tarai or the Duars of West Bengal, in Punjab or NWFP, the majority does not have the wherewithal to materially bolster themselves for two extreme seasons, especially when the winter season lasts only for a few weeks.

Indeed, one is struck by the oddness of it all. The same steaming plains that once repelled the first Mughal, Babar, making him homesick for the cool climes of Kabul, were this year the site for three times as many deaths in the five weeks of foggy winter than in the four months of summer last year— 400–500 people succumbed to the heat, while some 1,500 died in the fog. This year's experience will likely be a variant, a spike like was seen in 1997, a particularly severe instance, but still within a larger trend. The next winter will be judged against this one, and if not cold or foggy 'enough', which it will likely not be, the recent season will be remembered merely as an aberration. But going by the data, the trend is a reality; only its causes might be open to discussion.

There is no doubt that climate is a complex rubric, and we are yet to figure out how exactly all the pieces fit together. Perhaps it is not even possible to conclusively answer questions of such proportions. But the Subcontinental fog, which might not even be caused by macroclimatic changes, should not be neglected simply because grander, potentially impossible questions might be attached. There is enough indication that the Indus–Ganga plains show a growing incidence of fog for it to warrant scientific investigation from every possible angle, going beyond what this journalistic investigation has laid out. Probing the proximate link with pollution is clearly one facet. Another must be the rapid and relatively recent introduction of growth in surface moisture from groundwater extraction and the agglomeration of canals and embankments.

Regardless of whether the intensification of the Indus–Ganga fog has a causal relationship with the proliferation of canals, embankments and tube-wells, assuming it will recur at its current rate if not worse, a comprehensive loss-calculation exercise must be undertaken. Only a quantified account of the gloom will enable the building of a model to try and reduce avoidable losses, and for streamlining costs that, as is the nature of losses, will mount if neglected. Also, to the extent that the fog can be minimised, such an analysis is indispensable for calculating whether the investment required yields a justifiably substantial drop in losses. Until figures can be ascribed to it, the fog will continue to be a shroud over the Indus–Ganga plains.

Even if the fog were not more prevalent now than before, it would still be time for sensitive scholars and administrators to consider the difficulties faced by the population due to it. Now that it looks as though the duration of the fog has risen dramatically, it is the duty of those in positions of responsibility, direct or indirect, to delve deeper into the phenomenon. It is simply not fair to say, as so many did to this reporter over the course of researching for this article, 'We do not know; no one has studied it.'

Chapter 10

Between despair and hope
Interrogating 'terrorism'
Himal, September–October 2005

Dilip Simeon

> *The practice of violence, like all action, changes the world, but the most probable change is a more violent world.*
>
> — Hannah Arendt

The words *terror* (meaning intense fear and dread), and *terrorism* (the systematic employment of violence and intimidation to coerce a government or community into acceding to specific political demands) are steeped in controversy. From the time of the French Revolution, terrorism has been used to describe a range of violent political activism, including certain forms of Russian populism; Italian, Serbian and Irish nationalism; anarchism; and the actions of the Ku Klux Klan. Nowadays, 'terror' is what the 'civilised world', led by the United States, is combating. It is identified with Islamist fundamentalism, the Taliban, suicide bombers, Palestinian resistance and Maoist revolutionaries. Even though

This article includes material extracted from the author's earlier publications, including a lecture in Patna delivered in 2000 entitled, 'The End of History or the Beginning of Transformation?'; a seminar paper, 'The Brains of the Living: A discussion on political violence' (Patna, April 2003); and articles, 'The enemy system' (*Hindustan Times*, 6 December 2002), 'The threads of conscience' (*Biblio*, March–April 2002), and 'Out of the shadow' (*Communalism Combat*, February 2003).

terrorism is quite clearly a form of political violence, mainstream journalism today does not associate it with aerial bombardment (although Adolf Hitler's use of the Luftwaffe against the Spanish town of Guernica in 1936 was considered an act of terror); nor with armed actions by the American and Israeli defence and special forces against their real or perceived enemies; nor with kidnapping, collective punishment, and encounter killings by the apparatus of various Southasian states.

In India, 'terrorism' is also not generally used to describe the activities of the Bajrang Dal, Vishva Hindu Parishad (VHP), Rashtriya Swayamsevak Sangh (RSS), the Ranvir Sena or the Shiv Sena, even though some of their activities would qualify them as terrorists within the dictionary meaning of the word. Yes, the usage of *terror* is heavily politicised.

Stark examples of these differentiated standards of judgement confront us when we consider the boundaries that religion shares with the world of terror. Contemporary common sense does not associate Buddhism, Judaism, Christianity or Hinduism with terror and terrorism. However, Sinhalese Buddhist monks have been known to participate in anti-Tamil violence in Sri Lanka. The Zionist Stern Gang and Irgun indulged in 'communal killings' of Palestinian villagers to enforce the evacuation of territory. Irish nationalists and loyalists alike (Catholics and Protestants) used terror for decades as an integral part of their politics. And it was the Hindu Tamil Tigers who began the latest use of suicide bombers—Rajiv Gandhi was killed by one in 1991. Let us not fool ourselves. Every major religious tradition has produced theological justifications for murder and mass killing in the name of sacred causes. And it is clear that terror is and has been employed by states and anti-state activists alike.

Historically, national liberation movements and democratic movements have often taken for granted that violent means would be necessary for the attainment of their ends. The French Revolution of 1789 was the first major instance of the marriage of terror with modern democracy. 'There is nothing which so much resembles virtue as a great crime,' said Maximilien Robespierre's comrade, St Just, one of the architects of the Reign of Terror in 1794 France. Mid-19th-century Italian nationalism was an inspiration for military-style patriotism in the early 20th century, such as the Serbian, Irish and Indian. Russian populism, which later emerged as the Left Socialist Revolutionary tendency, used terrorist methods in varying degrees, as did Anarchists and Bolsheviks. Trotsky wrote a lengthy pamphlet, 'Terrorism and Communism', justifying such acts as hostage-taking as a means of ensuring good behaviour by 'class enemies'.

Terrorism is the quintessentially ambivalent political deed, the place where good and evil are mixed to the point where its proponents need to invoke god, or a secular metaphysic such as History or Revolutionary Destiny, as justification. Apparently, transcendental dogma can transform great crimes into virtuous deeds. In a situation where terror has become normalised (virtually the entire span of the past century), it is to be expected that rational debate aimed at understanding political crises becomes next to impossible. For example, in the international context following the attacks of 11 September 2001, anyone putting forward a historical analysis of the emergence of Islamist fundamentalism against a background of Western imperialist policies in West Asia, Arabia, Palestine, Iran and Afghanistan would draw suspicion in establishment circles as an apologist for terrorists—even if he or she vehemently denies such sentiments. Someone who adduces the reparations imposed upon Germany in 1918 as a factor contributing to the rise of Nazism is not necessarily a sympathiser of Hitler. In considering the history of Zionism, we would have to remember that Christian anti-Semitism provided fertile ground for Nazi ideology and the genocide of European Jews, which in turn fuelled the demand for a Jewish homeland. Such an analysis would not imply an approval of Israeli expansionism and oppression of Palestinians.

It is the historian's job to suggest explanations of major events by weighing context with cause, structure, popular moods and ideological developments. In today's world, however, history is rapidly being replaced by propaganda. Speaking about terrorism in 1998, the late Eqbal Ahmad described the official approach to it as one that eschews causation and avoids definition, because such concepts involve 'analysis, comprehension and adherence to some norms of consistency'. He cited a query about the causes of Palestinian terrorism, addressed in the mid-1980s by the Yugoslavian foreign minister to US Secretary of State George Shultz. According to a newspaper report, the latter 'went a bit red in the face. He pounded the table and told the visiting foreign minister, there is no connection with any cause. Period.' Former Prime Minister Atal Behari Vajpayee told the United Nations General Assembly that all talk of 'root causes' served only to justify terrorism. However, his RSS soulmates routinely talk of 'root causes' when they need to defend the demolition of the Babri mosque in 1992. Terrorism has a 'root cause' when we identify with it, but becomes a monstrous violation of human rights when we do not. Such ethical contortions are as common in the ranks of leftwing intellectuals as they are among religious fundamentalists and the ultra-right.

The decline of conversation

The dynamic nature of social reality implies the need for constant theoretical reflection. Without this, the radical imagination loses itself in the dominant discourses of capitalism, nationalism and identity. This is what is happening today, even within the so-called extreme left. Unfortunately, this trend is buttressed by a habit of denigrating critical thought to a level inferior to so-called 'activism'.

A further complication is that nationalist ideology and capitalist media have perverted the concept of truth. In the first case, God or Truth (sometimes named History) is always with Us. In the second case, truth is substituted by credibility. This is demonstrated by the phenomenon of advertising. The 'truth content' of a message is of no importance; rather, what matters is whether it is credible or incredible. This is why the concept of 'image' dominates modern political vocabulary, despite the obvious distinction between image and reality. The war of images goes on in the political realm as well, and affects the question of terror. As they say, one man's terrorist is another's freedom fighter. We owe it to ourselves and to the coming generations to pierce the imagery and arrive at a well-considered understanding of terror and political violence.

In India, the dogmatism surrounding political theory has reduced radical politics to a moribund condition. Both the Leninist concept of 'the outside' and the Stalinist convention that 'the party is always right' imply an authoritarian notion of truth. The comrades' habit of claiming possession of Absolute Truth (party line = *param satya*) is similar to the religious belief in divine revelation (*ilhaam*). Such approaches to knowledge are shared by organisations as far apart as the Vatican (with its notion of papal infallibility), the RSS, the Taliban (and its variants), and various Leninist groups and parties.

This attitude is an important causative factor for the fractious nature of Southasian leftism. An absolutist mentality finds ambivalence intolerable; faced with historical complexity, it finds refuge in black-and-white ideas about the social universe. The resulting theoretical vacuum has left certain questions, such as the value of democracy and the nature of violence, to be treated as 'tactical' matters rather than as aspects of social relations. The political ideologies dominant in our time attach a pragmatic or positive value to violence and to the nation. The word *foreign* is too easily used as a term of abuse. Many radical political currents treat democracy as something to be used rather than preserved. Where it is yet to be achieved, its protagonists preach but do not practice democracy within the movement—they believe authoritarian methods can achieve democratic goals.

Such issues need to be addressed. Unfortunately, it has become a habit among radical activists and intellectuals to attribute base motives to those who criticise established doctrine. Polemic is what passes for debate and discussion in the Indian socialist tradition. (*Polemos* in Greek means strife.) Our mode of debate is often coloured by personal remarks, sarcasm and pointless rhetoric. Indeed, there will be moments when nasty verbal contests become unavoidable, but the replacement of all political conversation by polemic is symptomatic of an authoritarian attitude to ideas. Polemic reinforces factionalism, causes useless distraction and is a waste of time. It also signifies mental laziness. Instead of a careful and rigorous consideration and/or refutation of critical ideas, we prefer to dismiss them with contempt. Firm adherence to dogma might be psychologically comfortable, but it can only ensure political marginalisation.

Militarisation of social democracy

The word *terror* is used to distinguish between forms of violence. In commonplace conversation, it conveys the meaning of something other than war, mass resistance, police action and so on. Closer attention will reveal that political terror is a manifestation of militarism in the domain of civil society—whether expressed by left- or rightwing terrorists.

Actually the very norms by which we define left and right need redefinition. Rightwing neo-liberals often speak of the need for far-reaching economic and political reform, whereas leftists seem to be taking a conservative position. Multinational corporations advocate a capitalist version of internationalism, whereas leftists appear to have become nationalists, paying lip-service to international working-class solidarity. Rightists fabricate history one way, leftists do it another way. Nobody can say whether the terms *left* and *right* carry any definitional meaning for ethnic identity movements—support for or opposition to Lankan Tamil, Kurdish, Baloch, Kashmiri, Naga or Tibetan self-determination depends upon political convenience or pure whim rather than consistent principle.

When it comes to positions regarding war, militarism, nuclearism, violence, patriarchy, democratic freedoms, human rights or ecological degradation, it is difficult to discern a systematic difference between left and right. The Communist Party of China has become (effectively) the Capitalist Party of China. It supported Yahya Khan in 1971, and even launched a war against Vietnam in 1979. As George Orwell once said, there is no enormity that we condemn in the conduct of our enemies that we would not commit ourselves. Is there a way out of this labyrinth? There is, but only if we embark once more upon fearless critique.

Leftwing terrorists, including certain left-nationalists and communists, display a self-conscious attempt to convert social-democratic protest and struggle into a form of warfare. ('Social democracy' is used here in its broadest and pristine meaning, as the original name of the socialist movement.) The capitulation of Europe's major social-democratic parties to war hysteria and patriotism in August 1914 was arguably the greatest political disaster in the history of international socialism. It is a complex and tragic tale, but the nature of 20th-century communism was unalterably coloured by warfare and the warrior cult. In fact, the century gone by has been one of the bloodiest periods ever. One result has been the appearance of Bonapartism, the domination of the communist movement by men of military stature—warlords like Stalin and Mao. Another has been the erosion of any respect for human life, as mass slaughter has come to be accepted as the natural price to pay for 'victory'.

This mixture of socialism, nationalism and militarism has produced many political hybrids. Subhas Chandra Bose was one of them. In India today it is not a good idea to criticise Subhas, a popular icon for many leftists, even though he allied himself with Hitler's imperial war aims and bemoaned the defeat of the Axis forces. Although it takes off from a conservative standpoint, fascism too is another such hybrid—and religion-based communalism is Southasia's brand of fascism. In summary definition, communal politics are projects for the militarisation of civil society. The ultra-left programme of 'people's war' feeds upon the same mentality. The utilitarian morality expressed by the phrase 'The end justifies the means' has cast its effect on left and right alike. Quite apart from the matter of political ethics, it is remarkable that the Maoist worldview finds 'people's war' as relevant in India as it does in Nepal, despite the obvious differences in the constitutions of the two countries.

Among some comrades, it would appear that strategies are decided upon first, and doctrinal justifications invented later. It is also significant that, on the whole, the ultra-left and the ultra-right avoid confrontation with one another. Thus, in its declaration of October 2004, the newly formed Communist Party of India (Maoist) stated that armed struggle would 'remain the highest and main form of struggle and the army the main form of organisation of this revolution', and the main purpose of mass organisations would be 'to serve the war'. The declaration includes a passing reference to 'Hindu fascist forces', but makes it clear that it would keep 'the edge of the people's struggles directed against the new Congress rulers in Delhi along with the CPI/CPM and their imperialist chieftains'.

On 15 August, the CPI (Maoist) allegedly carried out an armed action in Andhra Pradesh, gunning down an MLA, his son, driver, some local Congress activists and a municipal employee. An ideology that can cast such ordinary people in the role of 'class enemies', deserving extrajudicial execution, reflects a mentality closer to fascism than to socialism. These 'revolutionaries' have not even publicly challenged the mass murderers responsible for pogroms in India during 1984 (Delhi) and 2002 (Gujarat), let alone called them to account. Yet they constantly direct scornful polemic at all kinds of moderate democratic politics. Apparently, radical rhetoric establishes one's commitment to the public good, and proposing violent solutions provides proof of one's admirable character.

A callous disregard for human life is apparent among 'revolutionary' groups in Southasia. In August 2004, 13 people were killed (including nine children) and 20 injured due to a bomb planted by the United Liberation Front of Asom (ULFA) at an Independence Day function in upper Assam. In June 2005, 40 or more bus passengers, mostly peasants and working people, were killed in a landmine set off by Maoists in the Chitwan district of Nepal. The ULFA call themselves Marxists, as do the Nepali comrades. Marxist revolutionaries perceive themselves as guardians of human rights, democracy and justice. But we need to ask them: What are the grounds for your claim to represent the poor? Who gave you the authority to be judge and executioner, to kill people without even the pretence of a consensual procedure to decide guilt and award punishment? Why do you complain about extrajudicial killings by the state when you have no qualms about carrying out such killings yourselves? Is there any human-rights body that the victims of your cruelty (or your bloody 'mistakes') can approach for justice? Why do you talk about the 'murder of democracy' (this is how the Indian Maoist party described the ban imposed upon it after their 'action' on 15 August) when you have no respect for the lives of children and poor people, let alone for democratic values and norms?

With honourable exceptions, human-rights activists remain silent or defensive about atrocities committed by proponents of revolution and self-determination. This strengthens the impression among the general public that 'preferred' victims qualify as human beings—but if they happen to belong to the wrong caste or religion or profession, or simply be in the wrong place at the wrong time, their lives are dispensable. Sensitive observers the world over have rightly protested the atrocious principle of 'collateral damage' invoked by the US Department of Defence when its soldiers and pilots kill people they say were not targeted. It is equally infuriating when successive US presidents talk about 'American lives' as if Arabs and Rwandans and Vietnamese belonged to an insect species.

At the same time, is it not apparent that revolutionaries of various kinds function with their own version of 'collateral damage'? And what of situations where civilians are deliberately targeted? World War II abolished the distinction between combatants and civilians. We, who dreamt of a better life for humanity, have descended to the point where the deliberate slaughter of bystanders and bus passengers by 'our' side barely causes us to raise an eyebrow. Even to point to this selective and self-righteous morality causes intense irritation among the ranks of the politically correct. For socialists to 'normalise' the commission of mass murder is nothing short of an ethical–political catastrophe. And it lends a poignantly different meaning to Marx's warning that the choice before humanity is either socialism or barbarism.

Autumn of the patriarchs

After the overthrow of the doctrine of the Divine Right of Kings and the rise of democratic politics, the process of governing became impossible without some degree of popular legitimisation. That is why even empires and dictators talk of freedom and the will of the people. But these developments, associated with modern capitalism, cannot occlude the fact that the state is the institution-alised crystal of centuries of warfare. At its core are the armies that (during 19th-century Europe), countered universal adult suffrage with universal male conscription, and the ideals of equality, reason and compassion with hierarchy, faith and the glory of war. We can judge for ourselves which set of values con-quered the 20th century.

The Great War of 1914–18 ended with the overthrow of four medieval autocracies. But alongside the establishment of Weimar democracy, the defeated German army of 1918 set in motion a political process that culminated in the conquest of the state by Nazism. It is the greatest historical irony that it was democracy that enabled ex-corporal Hitler to become Reich Chancellor, and that his actions led not only to the overthrow of democracy but to the complete destruction of the German Army. Fifty-five million people paid the ultimate price. Hitler's regime was the historical acme of state terrorism—those who use these words frequently ought to study this period—and the most glaring feature of the political mobilisation that preceded it was the binary dynamic of fear and revenge.

Contrary to their self-understanding, the political paramilitaries and revolutionary warriors of all kinds are the loyal opposition of capitalist modernity. They share its fascination and structural use of revenge, martyrdom, heroism and patriarchal codes of honour, which invariably imply misogyny. Hence they are the last refuge of patriarchy. Each of their 'heroic' actions strengthen the state, as each side counters war with more war, terror with counter-terror, revolutionary militarism with statist militarism. The link between state violence and the violence of left-right radicalism has become seamless—each feeds upon the other.

This process is unfolding before our eyes. With 9/11 and, indeed, with every act of murderous resistance, hard-won democratic rights are further eroded, and the state gathers legitimacy to impose draconian laws. With the growth of a universal climate of fear, the bonds between governments and the ordinary public are strengthened, rather than dissipated. This takes place not on the basis of class interests, but on account of the dreadful fear of the murder of innocent people. What happens then is an unending spiral of violence, driven by the lust for revenge and very difficult to control. As Hannah Arendt said, all this bloodshed will indeed change the world, probably for the worse.

It is impossible to achieve democracy by authoritarian means. A new dispensation might be realised by such methods, but it will carry with it the whiff of tyranny. Those who survive such a revolution will be a brutalised and damaged people. Undoubtedly, the Nepali establishment, an outdated remnant of arrangements made between Nepali feudal potentates and the British during the heyday of imperialism, has managed to survive by maintaining the sheer poverty and educational backwardness of the population. (Its members' decision to impose customs duty on educational books is only the latest example of their investment in ignorance.) The government has also been assisted by cynical neighbours. The monarchy is not a 'pillar of stability', as its Indian well-wishers like to portray it, but the reverse. The Nepali state's brutal aversion to democratic governance perpetuates instability. But the sad state of affairs has been worsened by the ruthless and destructive policies of the revolutionaries (including the recruitment of children and disruption of education); and the bankruptcy of the moderate democratic opposition, which found it impossible,

especially during the troubled decade of the 1990s, to construct a responsible united front. Constant factional fighting and egotism are also symptoms
of authoritarianism.

The politics and practice of revolutionary terror are detrimental to
socialist ideals. They represent and reproduce desperation, cynicism, organisational autocracy and doctrinal dogma. As such, they generate fear and paranoia
in the ranks of the revolutionary cadre themselves, as well as among the very
people they seek to liberate. Most individuals drawn towards terrorist politics
are undoubtedly sincere in their vision and aspiration for a humane socio-
economic order. But how easy it is to commit atrocities for the sake of kind-
ness! To interpret our primeval lust for revenge as a source of 'modernisation'
and 'progress'!

Some three decades ago, in 1976, this writer had the privilege of participating in a conversation with the great Marxist historian and peace activist
E P Thompson. It was the year of the Emergency imposed by Indira Gandhi,
a development that had forced us to think seriously about the value of democratic rights. Thompson made the acute observation that the use of the prefix
'bourgeois' before 'democracy' was the most self-defeating practice of communists the world over. Democracy, he said, was a hard-won institutional gain
of the international labour movement and, in the Indian case, of the struggle
for independence. Rather than dismiss it as 'bourgeois', we ought to work for its
preservation and extension into social life—that was what was meant by social
democracy.

Many of us in India have realised the truth of this approach as we have
traversed the difficult and painful quarter-century from the 1980s till today—a
period that has seen the rampage of communalism and the politics of mass
murder. It is significant that the Indian left took a very long time to recognise
the fascist nature of communalism. Even today, the relative weakness of our
democracy is reflected in the fact that no party dares to place a resolution in
Parliament condoling the death of thousands of victims of communal violence.
Nonetheless, despite its terrible flaws, certain democratic norms, institutions
and practices remain alive in the Indian polity. Groups that support the politics
of secession or armed revolution still manage openly to propagate their ideas.
Would it be possible, say, for a Tibetan version of the Hurriyat Conference
to function in China, before or after Mao's death? Or for Baloch or Sindhi
secessionists to advocate separation from Pakistan, and conduct meetings with
a visiting Indian dignitary? How much democratic freedom of expression
and organisation could political opponents expect under a People's War regime?

An urgent political issue confronts those of us who identify with the civil-liberties movement of the 1970s. The revolutionary movement of that time aimed at the violent overthrow of the constitutional polity, and the Indian ruling elite took refuge behind the rule of law. A quarter of a century later, significant sections of the radical left and its well-wishers became staunch defenders of the democratic rights and liberties enshrined in the Constitution, while the Indian establishment repeatedly showed its discomfort with consti-tutional proprieties. In fact, the most massive violations of law (witness the carnages of 1984 and 2002), have been practiced by establishment parties and politicians. This should make leftists think about their attitude to democracy: Is it merely a tactic, or do democratic norms and institutions deserve a deeper philosophical commitment?

Satyagraha

The left could begin to rejuvenate itself if it gave up its revelatory approach to truth, its dogmatic approach to knowledge, its metaphysical attitude to pol-itics, and its addiction to the warrior cult—society's oldest and most powerful preserve of authoritarianism. The comrades should examine their conscience and consider the social consequences of children being denied an education and made accustomed to bloodshed and cruelty, and of armed groups and individuals functioning with the same kind of impunity that the army and police display. A mature course of action would be to agitate non-violently for a programme of political and social democracy and demilitarisation, and engage in constructive work to better the lot of the people. This would gain them wider credibility and respect than they will ever get via armed struggle. It would also gain them the gratitude of people whose lives are too full of violence and uncertainty.

A close friend took a photograph of a slogan on the wall of a building in the village of Ghandruk, in central Nepal, after an armed clash between the army and the Maoists: 'Maobadi + shahi sena suniyojit daman banda gara.' Addressing both the Maoists and 'royal army', the graffiti asked them to desist from blood-shed and 'deliberate suppression'. Whatever the support base of the Nepali comrades, there are also those who are tired and fearful of the bloodletting. Whatever the romance of extremism might once have been, freedom from fear has become a major political aspiration. Terror is no longer a means to an end; it has become an end in itself, autonomous of social and political control. It is no longer merely a symptom but the disease par excellence of capitalist modernity.

Socialists should remember that respect for life and liberation from fear must be the foremost ideal and goal of socialism. Otherwise, they will make themselves instruments of the system they claim to be combating.

The recruitment of women cadre and soldiers by paramilitaries is hailed by some comrades as a symbol of female 'empowerment'. Actually, this should be characterised as yet another manifestation of the oppression of women by entrenched patriarchy. Would it not seem ridiculous to view child-soldiers as liberated children? Warfare empowers neither men nor women; it imprisons all of humanity in an endless spiral. Since 1914, we have never had peace—more than 200 million people were violently done to death during the 20th century—and it is clear that 'modern civilisation' is structurally dependent upon war. That it is now recruiting women and children in the name of 'empowerment' is a travesty. The struggle for the complete equality of the sexes continues to be opposed bitterly by patriarchal structures and politicians. (The fate of India's Women's Reservation Bill is proof of this fact.) Subjugation by fear is a common experience for women from all classes across the globe. Feminism is hence implicitly a struggle against militarism and terror.

The abolition of state terror and its twin brother requires the collaboration of all groups and movements working to end the grip of caste oppression, patriarchy, racism and the exploitation of labour. Wide-ranging campaigns are necessary against all forms of oppressive institutions, including militarist ones, in order to defang the enemy-producing killing-machine that the 'West' has become. But ambivalence about brutality as a means of resistance must cease. Millions of Europeans and Americans are opposed to war. The imperial system can only be encouraged to implode, as did the USSR. It cannot be destroyed by military means without exacting a merciless price that no revolutionary can wish on the common people. Terrorist attacks will only increase fear and feed conservative ideologies, which is the aim of the rulers.

Is it possible to combine a radical programme with non-violence? Indeed it is. Undermining the British Empire was the most radical programme in Southasia during the first half of the last century. In a time that identifies Pathans with religious fundamentalism, we may yet learn something from the work of Khan Abdul Gaffar Khan, aka Badshah Khan and the Frontier Gandhi, and the Khudai Khidmatgar ('servants of god') movement of the 1930s, whose commitment to non-violence was based on Pukhtunwali culture and Islam. The Khudai Khidmatgar's alliance with the national movement as a whole, its popular constructive projects and openness to non-Pathans and non-Muslims alarmed the colonial rulers, who subsidised the clergy to denounce its members (popularly known as the Red Shirts) as Bolsheviks and enemies of Islam. Confronting massacres, torture and repression, the Khudai Khidmatgar emerged as one of the staunchest Gandhian movements in the history of Southasian nationalism.

The Frontier Gandhi instructed his followers: 'Abstain from violence and do not defame your nation, because the world will say how could such a barbarous nation observe patience.' Even as the 'civilising' Englishmen behaved like mad dogs, the 'volatile' Pathans were teaching their rulers a lesson in restraint. A Turkish scholar who visited the NWFP during the 1930s suggested that the Pathans had developed a new interpretation of force. In her words, 'Non-violence is the only form of force which can have a lasting effect on the life of society ... And this, coming from strong and fearless men, is worthy of study.' Badshah Khan was the last of those Gandhian stalwarts who could walk across four international boundaries in post-1947 Southasia and be treated by the citizens of each country as one of their own. His life's work exemplified the compassionate spirit that stayed alive during the bleakest period of the 20th century, proof that the self-assertion of the oppressed need not always be strident and narrow-minded. That he was an Indian national leader even after he became a Pakistani citizen ought to give chauvinists of all colours some food for thought. Not for nothing was it written of him that 'people brought him food and sat him down in the shade of trees.'

Let us also spare a thought for Chander Singh Garhwali, a platoon commander in the Garhwal Rifles. When Hindu soldiers were facing a Muslim crowd in Peshawar in 1930, he was court-martialled for refusing to order firing on his fellow-countrymen. Somewhere, somehow, Chander Singh and his troops too had been affected by the spirit of ahimsa. Decades before, so had the ordinary Russian soldiers who refused to shoot women demonstrators on International Women's Day in St Petersburg in 1917, thus heralding the overthrow of tsarism and the advent of the Russian Revolution. Would it not be truly radical for the revolutionaries to prevail over the soldiers and policemen via their conscience rather than through fear? Did not M K Gandhi speak profoundly when he said that what is obtained by fear can be retained only as long as the fear lasts? The radicalism of Satyagraha consists in this: that it (potentially) abolishes the distinction between method and goal. 'Overcoming' ceases to be a military concept, and social democracy transcends its hysterical tension over ends and means.

Today, when Southasia is engulfed in civil strife and civil war, it is time to consider again whether the pursuit of truth and non-violent resistance are not the only radical social procedures left for the survival of the biosphere. The movement must be the germ of its goal. Social democracy's associative principles and active ethos must prefigure those of the society it wishes to create. Ahimsa is not a tactic but the ethos of respect for life. That which claims to be new must stand on its own feet.

Speak the truth
Stop the killing

Chapter 11

SAARC and the sovereignty bargain

Himal, November–December 2005

Pratap Bhanu Mehta

Where exactly did the earthquake of October 2005 occur? The short answer is easy: Kashmir. But even the naming of 'Kashmir' cannot be done without problems arising; the area cannot be identified in its wholeness, without various qualifiers. How does one most efficiently organise relief? Clearly, India and Pakistan had to use each other's territories and resources. Fortunately, in this instance the leaders did take recourse to history to address the demands of humanitarianism; borders temporarily melted faster that anyone could have dared to hope. But can this experience be a catalyst to help with the recognition that, if the countries of Southasia fight regional interdependence, they are fighting against their own interests? Can we recognise that our borders and restrictions, our mutual mistrusts and fears, harm no one but the people in the states of the Subcontinent? Does greater regional integration have a future in the Subcontinent?

In examining the future prospects for the SAARC organisation, it is worth considering the conditions under which successful regional integration can take place in Southasia. If the SAARC process is to be successful, it will have to be based on hard-headed economic and political logic—not sentimentalism and rhetoric. What are the conditions that promote regional integration? Do these conditions exist here?

We must distinguish between regional cooperation and regional integration. The former refers simply to a type of cooperation between governments. Regional integration, on the other hand, is the unleashing of a process that binds the societies and economies of neighbouring countries much more closely together. On one level, any project of greater regional integration involves what are called 'sovereignty tradeoffs'. Integration often requires the establishment and maintenance of structures of authority and institutions that surpass national boundaries. The European Union is a prominent example of an entity that possesses wide-ranging, supranational prerogatives. What are the reasons justifying sovereignty tradeoffs? Under what conditions can we expect these tradeoffs to take place?

Sovereignty obsession

The first condition that will make Southasian integration possible is a revolution in the understanding of 'sovereignty' itself. Although nationalists wave the flag of sovereignty as if it was a mystical, indivisible whole, in truth it is no such thing. Sovereignty actually has at least four separate components that pull in different directions: autonomy, control, legitimacy and identity. *Autonomy* refers to the independence a state has in making policy. *Control* refers to the actual ability of the state to produce the outcomes it desires. *Legitimacy* refers to its right to make rules in ways that are widely accepted and recognised internally and externally. *Identity* refers to the capacity of the state to endow people with an overriding sense of who they are as a collective group.

The difficulty is that these components of sovereignty do not hang together particularly well. A state might be autonomous, but might still be quite ineffective in bringing about the results it desires. Meanwhile, we in Southasia tend to confuse sovereignty with just one of its components—autonomy. Arguably, the postcolonial opposition to free trade that still marks most countries in the region (with the exception of Sri Lanka and now, increasingly, India) is rooted in just such a confusion. Bangladesh might nominally assert its autonomy regarding India by refusing to sell it natural gas, but by doing so it is diminishing its own power. Paradoxical as it might sound, sacrificing autonomy can sometimes enhance power. The crucial starting point for regional integration is when states begin to realise that autonomy does not necessarily create either control or power; that committing to forms of interdependence can enhance power, even though it might at first seem to diminish autonomy.

Almost all of Southasia was thus caught in a postcolonial syndrome, wherein that particular, narrow understanding of sovereignty became a mark of self-respect and identity. After all, colonialism was seen to have violated just this most-cherished aspect of political identity. An obsession with sovereignty, initially the result of the colonial experience, evolved on the part of the neighbouring states into a defensive claim against possible Indian domination of the region. India's political difficulties in the region have stemmed mainly from its relative size and power. In the interests of regional integration or the creation of free-trade zones, one of two conditions must be met. Either most of the countries have to be of comparable size, or the economy of a dominant country has to be so attractive that others cannot resist the allure of integration. Neither condition currently exists in our region. With India's economy currently in the process of acquiring a new standing, however, this could eventually offer a dynamic to pull the region together.

Even if New Delhi does not act threateningly, however, the mere possibility of its regional domination elicits a defensive response from the neighbours. Arguably, if India sins against its neighbours, it is more a sin of condescension than a naked desire for domination. But for fragile states with insecure identities struggling to establish themselves, condescension might appear to be even worse that overt hostility. The result is that India finds it very difficult to overcome the fears and anxieties of countries such as Bangladesh and Nepal, which is necessary in order to stabilise relations. As a whole, the region's countries have never felt secure enough, as states, to engage in sovereignty bargains that would be in their interest. Perhaps regional integration depends upon individual countries coming into their own as classic, full-fledged states that feel confident enough to consider transcending their own limitations. But with many not yet having achieved that status, the ruling establishments tend to become defensive at the mention of regional cooperation or integration.

Liberal economy

The second prerequisite for regional integration is a commitment by states of the region to liberal economic policies—'liberal' in this case not in its strongly theoretical sense, but simply implying the promotion of free trade, greater mobility of citizens and so on. Will the Southasian states recognise the benefits of an integrated common market? Certainly, all would see the benefits in the long run. In the short term, however, entrenched interests fear the consequences of opening up their economies; as such, they artfully disguise their immediate interests as the long-term welfare of their larger societies. The commitment to economic liberalism is still very thin in Southasia, and there is simply no example of successful regional integration among sovereign states that is not founded on a commitment to economic liberalism.

Here, two factors might turn out to be crucial. First, India has now clearly emerged as a dynamic economy—one that has sufficient power to carry the region with it. Sri Lanka, always a pioneer in this respect, has realised that it can piggyback on India's economic success. Not only has Colombo signed a free-trade agreement and relaxed its visa regime for all arrivals; it is also negotiating a comprehensive economic agreement with New Delhi and openly discussing the possibility of a currency union.

The second factor is, in some ways, the opposite of the first. It could be argued that, precisely because India is becoming a powerful economy, its smaller neighbours will fear it even more and become more defensive. But while this fear is often exaggerated (if the Pakistani market were to open to Bollywood, the allure of 100 million-strong consumers would transform Bollywood cinema more than it would impact Pakistan!), India will still need to prepare to make unilateral concessions in order to avert those fears. When it comes to economic integration with its neighbours, India must move away from a paradigm of cyclical bilateral diplomacy, where each tariff concession depends on some reciprocal gesture from the other side. New Delhi can now easily afford to give preferential treatment to goods and services produced in the neighbourhood. This would create a long-term constituency for regional cooperation and defuse much of this fear.

If one looks beyond strictly Southasia, regional economic integration is already on the move, and the momentum is substantial. In some ways, India's strategy to look beyond SAARC and negotiate free-trade agreements with ASEAN, Thailand and Singapore, and possibly the BIMSTEC grouping that brings together some South and Southeast Asian states was a clever move. As far as India is concerned, the possible free-trade zone now stretches from Kabul to Manila, in which only Pakistan and Bangladesh would be left out if they did not come on board. In the long run, they will have to join the party or pay a heavy economic price. But there is also this: politically, Dhaka and Islamabad might find it convenient to join a larger grouping than SAARC, which always carries the taint of being dominated by India.

Empowering the hinterlands

The third condition for the emergence of greater regional integration would be the acceptance by regional states of what might be called a 'simultaneous dialectic' of greater regional integration and subregional power. Imagine if there was a free flow of goods and services throughout Southasia. Sri Lanka would likely develop extensive links with Tamil Nadu. The two Punjabs would come to a greater interdependence, as might West Bengal and Bangladesh or parts of Rajasthan and Sindh. It would also mean the greater development of the border regions of current states, where growth has been deliberately slowed.

Would the region's states look upon this kind of subregional integration without suspicion? On the ground, regional cooperation can gather momentum only when it is based on organic links between different subregions of the Subcontinent—not on links enforced from the centre of each country. None of these subregional linkages is likely to create any serious problem of secession from existing political units—though they will lead to a rediscovery of some old cultural identities. The allure of 'Punjabiyat', which has marked the recent thaw in relations between India and Pakistan, is one such instance. Regional integration will require future Southasian states to have strong centres but weak 'circumferences'. The fears that regional integration would somehow swallow existing states are exaggerated; these states would emerge even stronger, just with different definitions.

In a curious way, as has been shown by the experience of the European Union, regional integration can also help to solve identity conflicts. First, when states get habituated to unbundling sovereignty into its different components, they are less susceptible to seeing that sovereignty as an all-or-nothing affair—the outcome should not be seen as a zero-sum game. States used to sovereignty tradeoffs have a structure of domestic politics in which such arguments and bargains are more acceptable. These are states that have begun to understand that, just as in areas of trade, sovereignty tradeoffs can bring benefits; they can, in principle, do so in other areas as well.

Second, regional integration can help in identity conflicts because subregional devolutions undertaken in the context of wider regional settlements are generally easier to sell politically. As part of a larger process of restructuring, they are not seen as concessions to a demanding party, but rather as an innovation. Third, the parent state itself can begin to redefine its own core stakes in the subregional conflict. If, for instance, its interests in trade, free movement, human rights or rights of minorities can be secured, then it might be more willing to concede some of its other powers. In fact, because both the subregional units and the parent state are encased in a larger, international set of institutions, both have credible assurances that their interests in these areas will not be undermined.

Fourth, as regions come together, the major laws of all countries, together with the values that they protect, begin to look more and more alike. Thus, the state itself is no longer the site where national differences need to be articulated and defended. Fifth, in cases of subregional issues that involve interstate conflict, the two states in question can acquire greater experience of working together within interlocking institutions. Sixth, states are also more attuned to accepting outside mediation.

Ideological convergence

Whether or not any one of the mechanisms described above will lead to desired outcomes will depend on a variety of other factors; it would be unwise to believe in economic or political over-determination. But if the experience of the European Union is any guide, regional integration in Southasia under these mechanisms is certainly plausible. In fact, the one case that particularly bears this out is Great Britain—in reference to Scotland and Wales, but more importantly, Northern Ireland. It is noteworthy that the devolution to Scotland and Wales that took place was facilitated by Britain's integration into the European Union. That process provided assurances to the core British interests: a local assembly could not expropriate the English or pass legislation that discriminated against outsiders.

One of the fears of greater devolution in places like Kashmir—and one of the arguments against it—is that it is not clear what a new power structure might look like. But if power is devolved to regions within the context of a broader regional framework—where the larger region as a whole is committed to certain, specific values—these anxieties can become less pressing.

But the most crucial aspect of regional integration is ideological convergence across the member states. This does not mean that all politics would begin to look alike, but it would necessitate a set of commitments that all states would abide by and incorporate into their own laws. These requirements would include a commitment to basic liberal values, a respect for minority rights, a commitment to the rule of law and so forth. Unfortunately, for the moment, the domestic politics throughout most of Southasia often disallow pledges on these core values.

On the face of it, the prospects for SAARC would look very grim. There is no ideological convergence on the Subcontinent; no deep commitment to trade as an engine of growth; and none of the states are willing to acknowledge that any solution to their problems might be found regionally, outside of their own national boundaries. On the other hand, insecurities abound in our individual states. Rather than transcending identities, the region's governments use identity politics to keep their populations hostage and to bait their neighbours. No country is serious enough or willing enough to make a definitive break from the historical agreements and compromises that, in the final analysis, are to blame for the current impasse. Thus, we have absurd situations where SAARC's countries do not collaborate on energy and hesitate from facilitating bilateral trade, even when their own populations would benefit. Meanwhile, every possible economic, geographical or cultural link is reduced. The result is that Southasia is one of the world's most militarised areas, with states needing to protect themselves against their own region.

Lankan paradox

At the end of it all, is there hope for SAARC? This question is best answered indirectly, by asking why one country in the region, Sri Lanka, is less afraid of regional cooperation and integration than are others, including big India. Modern Sri Lanka has always been something of a paradox. On one level, Sri Lanka has been an extraordinarily vibrant and cosmopolitan country—the first true democracy in Southasia. Of all of the region's nation states, for much of the 20th century it was the most open. Even at modest levels of economic growth, Sri Lanka's human-development indicators put the rest of Southasia to shame. At the same time, this country, like so many others in the region, has also borne the deepest scars of modernity: a potent combination of Sinhalese and Tamil nationalisms have fed off of one another to produce one of the century's most brutal and stubborn ethnic conflicts. The civil war diminished the lustre of Sri Lanka's other achievements and cast a long shadow on its economy.

Yet even today, the country remains the source of immense hope. Anyone following Sri Lankan politics and economic policy is struck by how it is positioning itself to take advantage of the process of economic globalisation. Of all of the region's countries, it has found it easiest to overcome the legacy of strained relations with its neighbours. After India's controversial late-1980s intervention in Sri Lanka with the Indian Peace-Keeping Force (IPKF), the Colombo–New Delhi relationship hit a low point from which few thought it would ever emerge.

Yet within a decade, relations between these two countries acquired an extra-ordinary momentum. Today, not only do they have a free-trade agreement and allow unhindered movement of nationals; as stated earlier, there is also discussion in Colombo of a currency union with India. Sri Lanka already has a free-trade agreement with Pakistan. In short, it has emerged as the one country that is determined to integrate its economy as quickly as possible with the rest of Southasia.

There is a good deal of farsighted prudence behind Sri Lanka's drive towards regional economic integration. First, Colombo has realised that the country can benefit from the general dynamism of the region. Indeed, growth all across the world seems to follow regional rather than national patterns; regions often sink or swim together. Sri Lanka has therefore had few second thoughts in aligning itself with the region's larger economies. Second, Lankan leaders have realised that national strength comes from creating economic interdependence, not by standing aloof. If a significant constituency in the large country comes to depend upon trade with a smaller country, that constituency then becomes a champion of the interests of the latter. To repeat: interdependence enhances power rather than curtails it. This is perhaps understood better in Colombo than in any other Southasian capital, including New Delhi.

Third, opening up has also been a partial solution to some of Sri Lanka's domestic challenges. The government is under serious fiscal pressure and the country needs all the investment it can muster. The process of capital formation will only be bolstered through trade and openness, something that government intervention can never achieve. Although they will not openly admit it, many Colombo politicians are of the view that greater regional integration will help to ease the brutal internal conflict.

Here the Sri Lankans take the cue from the experience of the European Union. Once a country gets used to making beneficial sovereignty bargains in areas like trade and currency, it opens up the path to sharing sovereignty in many other areas. Sovereignty was supposed to be a means to stability, peace and prosperity. Instead, our states have turned a narrow conception of sovereignty into an end in itself. Instead of an instrument of well-being, obsessive concern with sovereignty and boundaries becomes a shackle on peace and prosperity. From the European Union to ASEAN, those countries that have chosen the path of credible regional integration have not given up on sovereignty. But they have put its claims into proper perspective.

The requirements for integration into a wider region and global economy also necessitate a different kind of politics and conception of the state in

Southasia. Contrary to the fears of so many, regional interdependence does not swallow up the identities of nations. Instead, the process provides opportunities to shape the new identities of the future. Consider what might happen to Tamil identity in both India and Sri Lanka if the economies of South India and Sri Lanka were to be integrated. By itself, regional integration will not solve the violence that has become entrenched in Sri Lanka; but imperceptibly, it could help to reduce the allure of entrenched identities. Somewhere in the rapid steps being taken by Sri Lanka towards regional integration is a powerful understanding: that economic integration is an opportunity to create new prosperity, to define new identities. Above all, it is not in the least a threat.

Chapter 12

Relevance of the middle path
*Rediscovering Gandhi
for all Southasia*
Himal, January–February 2006

C K Lal

Attribute it to the power of the Empire, but Southasians have no hesitation in embracing Adam Smith, Ayn Rand, Marx or Mao as their own. In one country where the Turkish Ataturk is a role model of 'enlightened moderation', the proponent of real enlightened moderation is an 'Indian'. In the countryside of another Southasian country where the guns rule, the epitome of courage with conscience is seldom remembered. Is it a deep-seated inferiority complex that makes Southasians oblivious of the legacy of Mohandas Karamchand Gandhi?

From South Africa to the United States, proponents of peaceful protests draw their inspiration from the pioneer of *ahimsa*. But most Southasians look at him through the tinted glasses of bigoted nationalism and see a nationalist 'Indian'. Within India itself, Gandhi is consigned to history textbooks, his values dismissed as romanticism in the power corridors of Delhi and state capitals. However, more than a concerted effort to rehabilitate his memory, it is the needs of the time that will eventually establish the primacy of Gandhi: as a Southasian ideal who foresaw the complexities of the region and devised a middle path with which to face the challenges of the future. His legacy is a shared

Southasian heritage, and the region will discover his relevance as it enters into yet another turbulent phase in its history.

These are sanguine times for some Southasians. Unocal alumnus Hamid Karzai has declared the dethroned King Zahir Shah, the Father of the Afghanistan nation, once destroyed and then rebuilt to the specifications of the US Pacific Command. Bangladesh is happy being at the centre of SAARC and BIMSTEC, two sets of idiosyncratic alphabet mixes that stand for largely ceremonial organisations. Bhutan is enthralled by the prospect of democracy that King Jigme Singye Wangchuk has promised to introduce by 2008. The Burmese junta has just shifted its capital to correct the feng shui and entrench itself further. India is not exactly shining, though some Indians are certainly gloating over the prospect of becoming the back office of the world in the next one, two or three decades, depending on whether you are talking to a free-market fundamentalist, a socialist planner or a self-proclaimed pragmatist. Either way, they all seem to share the same brahminical dream of making it big without getting their hands dirty.

Pakistan is content with a general-in-sherwani espousing enlightened moderation on the strength of a couple of F16s with nuclear capabilities. Nepal is rediscovering its golden days of 'monarchical democracy' by importing Chinese arms. President Mahinda Rajapakse is proud to have ridden the wave of anti-LTTE sentiments in Sri Lanka's south even though his victory has put the peace process of Serendib in peril. All in all, the power elite of Southasia is happy and content. Very few, too few it seems, have the time or inclination to remember the frail old man in *dhoti* striding the length and breadth of the Subcontinent with a toothless smile on his face. But just as these are the best of times for some, there are many others for whom these are the worst of times. In a region where paradoxes are the rule rather than the exception, the Dickensian metaphor of two cities is the most accurate description of everyday reality. Just below the shine of the thin silver lining, there is the reality of an unpredictable dark cloud hovering over Southasia.

The al-Qaeda organisation recently claimed, with some justification it seems, that it still holds large swaths of Afghan territory. An Islamist upsurge threatens Bangladesh, a country that grew out of violent conflicts, first for religious homogeneity and then for independent cultural identity. The racial regime of the Drukpa in Bhutan has refused to mend fences with the Nepali-speaking Lhotshampa it forced to flee. The deepening grip of the Burmese junta is enticing its neighbouring countries into dealing with an abhorrent regime. The democratic decay in the largest democracy of the world has become quite alarming: members of Parliament guzzle local development funds and accept bribes in order to raise questions in the Lower House. The royal-military rule in Nepal is digging in its heels. The unity of Sri Lanka's people stands threatened. The dilution of Tibetan culture will be a great loss for human heritage generally, but most Southasians appear blissfully unaware of the processes that have been unleashed by Beijing upon the roof of the world.

This is the time, then, when the modern apostle of peaceful resistance needs to be rediscovered. M K Gandhi's ideas were extremely powerful during the independence struggles of Southasia. His beliefs and methods are even more important today in a region passing through the pangs of adulthood. Decomposing democracy, arrogant autocracy, insecure intelligentsia, boastful business and violent conflicts are actually symptoms of the coming-of-age of a region that had remained mired in orthodoxy and hopelessness for centuries. When the status quo is too oppressive and change threatens to tear the place apart, Gandhi's vision beckons like the proverbial light at the end of a very long and dark tunnel.

But first, a powerful myth must be broken to reclaim Gandhi for the entire Southasia. Indians have done a great disservice to the Mahatma by appropriating his legacy for a truncated Bharat that is India. Gandhi was an apostle of a non-brahminical tradition whose teachings and practices are the common heritage of humanity. Every Southasian has as much right to stake a claim upon his teachings as any flag-waving Bharatiya.

Misunderstood messiah

Any attempt to depict the teachings of the Mahatma in a hurry would be inherently preposterous. After all, his own writings span 100 collected volumes, and there are numerous other works that delve into his work and thought. Unable to access the true depth of his life and message, his legions of admirers do the next best thing—they portray him through epigrammatic quotations often lifted and quoted out of context. From the mischievous ('I believe in equality for everyone, except reporters and photographers') to the rhetorical ('What difference does it make to the dead, the orphans, and the homeless, whether the mad destruction is wrought under the name of totalitarianism or the holy name of liberty and democracy?'), and from the banal ('It is unwise to be too sure of one's wisdom') to the profound ('Whatever you do will be insignificant, but it's very important that you do it')—all kinds of quotable quotes have been picked up and paraded according to the bias of the presenter.

Indeed, this has happened so much that Gandhi has become some kind of an emblem of the high-end alternative lifestyle, where laptops are Macs, *khadi* serves for silk, watches are handcrafted only in Zurich, and there is no taboo on sipping wine from paper cups. These 'Page 3 Gandhians' of jet-set Hindustan have done more harm to the memory of the Mahatma than the armies of RSS *swayamsevaks* doing callisthenics in khaki shorts. Caricature too is a form of tribute, but not when the object of spoof is too complex to be understood through inexpert simplification.

Presenting Gandhi as the 'Father of the Nation' of India was one of the grossest simplifications made by the otherwise erudite Jawaharlal Nehru, with his own visions of Indian grandeur. In fact, that appellation rightfully belonged to Chacha Nehru himself, more than to anyone else. Along with Sardar Vallabhbhai Patel, it was Nehru who wanted an independent India, even at the cost of its division. Nehru probably thought that he was paying his mentor tribute by having him declared the father of the independent but truncated territory that became present-day India. In fact, that title downgraded the contributions of an outstanding Southasian of Gandhi's stature.

Unlike Quaid-i-Azam Muhammad Ali Jinnah, Banglabandhu Sheikh Mujibur Rahman, Don Stephen Senanayake or Bishweswor Prasad Koirala, Gandhi did not set out to form a state in the Westphalian sense, or be the ruler of a pre-nationhood tribal homeland. The Mahatma consistently aimed higher. In a region wracked by centuries of colonialism, the Mahatma wanted to build nothing less than a whole new civilisation. If building a state through conquest, compromise or consensus was his sole aim, he would not have died a broken man, deeply disappointed by the Partition that created countries that most political leaders of his time wanted. Keep in mind that Gandhi was nowhere near the Red Fort celebrations when the 'tryst with destiny' was heralded by Jawaharlal.

In many ways, Gandhi was an inheritor of the non-brahminical tradition of Hindu philosophy. It is not just a coincidence that the Gandhian ideology began to take shape after Gandhi visited Champaran in the backwaters of Bihar in 1917, an area that has been the natural refuge of non-Vedic scholars throughout history. Bihar, and parts of the Ganga plains that now fall in modern Nepal, has always been home to non-brahminical paths of salvation. Householder King Janak refined his beliefs in participation without attachment in Mithila. Mahavir and Buddha, born into Vaishya and Kshatriya clans respectively, began their movements against entrenched brahminism from this region. Gandhi led the movement against indigo planters in Champaran. In the decayed remnants of historic Vaishali, he probably began something even bigger—a quest for self-definition. There, in the cradle of the Lichchhavi civilisation, he initiated a movement to restore the dignity of every individual, irrespective of race, caste, class, gender or age. For a society steeped in the tradition of codified hierarchy, this was nothing less than a 'total revolution', an expression that a disillusioned Marxist Jaiprakash Narayan appropriated once he embraced Gandhianism in the early 1970s.

Gandhi surmised with uncanny intuition that there was not much material surplus left in India to redistribute among its 350 million people. Theories of Marx had little resonance in an area of agricultural decline and industrial darkness. Centuries of plunder by waves of raiders had killed the entrepreneurial spirit of the people of the Jamuna–Ganga plain, where 'commerce' had become a dirty term associated more with deceit than fair trade. The mythic duo of baker and butcher trading with each other in self-interest, as immortalised by Adam Smith, had no use for subsistence farmers residing in villages with almost no connection to each other. There had to be a third way, thought Gandhi, as he saw the depth of physical and moral poverty of fellow human beings on his way to and in Champaran. He saw the alternative in the dream of Gram Swaraj, where individuals did trade with each other—though not for profit, but to ensure collective survival through self-help and self-sufficiency. The British Empire, founded on the principle of trade and rooted in the traditions of the East India Company, found it hard to understand a logic in which profit did not deserve even to be denounced. Ergo, the British had to go and let India find her way.

Goal established, Gandhi searched for the right mix to advance his cause. He had seen the efficacy of non-violent protests in South Africa. He refined it further by adding the element of self-inflicted suffering, probably derived from the Buddha's teachings—the same Sakyamuni who had walked these mid-Ganga plains two and a half millennia earlier. The importance of prayers might have been inspired by Mahavir's mediations. Was the spinning wheel an indirect homage to Kabir, the weaver-prophet of Banaras, who had sung the songs of salvation through faith in the self and bread-labour?

The potency of Gandhi's terms is often lost in translation. For example, *ahimsa* is much more than a passive strategy of non-violence; it is an active seeking of the absence of violence. The literal meaning of *satyagraha* suggests an insistence on truth, but it is much more than a tool of protest; it proposes a whole new way of life centred on the power of belief in one's own convictions. *Bramcharya* is not just celibacy, but an adoption of the righteous path.

Going beyond non-attachment and goal-seeking, *aparigraha* is a total commitment to truth in every aspect of a seeker's life. *Ashahayog* is often translated as 'non-cooperation', but there is no negativity here; rather, ashahayog
suggests an insistence on proactive cooperation. If ethics are to a society what
morals are to an individual, Gandhi sought to establish certain principles of *ram
rajya* derived more from the Buddha and Mahavir than from Balmiki or Tulsi
Das, two popular bards believed to have penned the epic *Ramayana* in Sanskrit
and Awadhi, respectively.

To the band of ambitious Westernised oriental gentlemen around
him—M A Jinnah in his Saville Row suit, the Etonian Nehru or the upwardly
mobile middle-class geniuses such as Rajendra Prasad and B R Ambedkar—these
principles were blasphemous to the ideals of freedom set out by the French
Revolution, the American War of Independence and the Russian October
Revolution. Gandhi's teachings questioned everything they thought they knew.
It was heresy they had to accept only because it seemed to work: Gandhi's
appeal galvanised the masses. No other apostle since the Prince of Peace in
500 BC has been accepted by the ruler and the ruled alike. Gandhianism had
acquired the potency of a new religion, a way of life that had to be resisted by
those who wanted to build India or Pakistan in the image of Britain, France
or the United States of America. Gandhi's most trusted lieutenants—Jinnah,
Nehru and Vallabhbhai Patel—followed his strategy faithfully, but without the
conviction that the means propounded were the ends in themselves.

Nehru wanted to build an India that would be a hybrid of Mauryan glory
and Mughal splendour. Fearful of his fate in such an entity dominated by the
personality of a self-assured Kashmiri Pandit, Jinnah, a non-believing Shia within a Sunni-majority Muslim community, sought an alternative vision of a secular
polity governing over a homogeneous population of the faithful—an Islamic
ram rajya. He found it in the aspirations of the United Provinces' landed gentry
longing for an Awadh renaissance patterned after the court of the last nawab of
Lucknow, Wazid Ali Shah.

That Nehru could never replicate the Mauryan glory in a pauperised India
was a foregone conclusion. His 'tryst with destiny' speech was in fact the swan
song of a disillusioned Emperor Ashok, who suddenly found that the India he
was about to rule held no resemblance to the India he had bargained for. Like
all images of an idealised past, the secularism of the Awadh court was only partially true: Hindu subjects of the nawab had accepted a second-class status long
before Wajid Ali Shah had begun to sing and dance like Radha. Jinnah's
oft-quoted speech before the Pakistan Constituent Assembly on 11 August

1947—'You are free to go to your temples...'—was thus fundamentally flawed: in any *ram rajya*, rule of the enlightened is based on the principle of its complete acceptance by all the rest.

Gandhi had therefore already died the day India and Pakistan became independent. Like most visionaries, the Mahatma had been way ahead of his time. Colonial India was not ready for his revolution. It accepted his politics but with strong reservations, and then only because his methods seem to work—to the amazement of his sophisticated contemporaries. Gandhi's famous retort, that he was a politician trying to be a saint, was perhaps an acceptance of defeat of his life's mission. In 1947, he was ready for the parody that independent India would make of his life and teachings.

Nehru consigned him to the pantheon of gods no sooner had the Hindu zealot killed him and his ashes were consigned to the Jamuna. More zealots kill him every time they garland his statue, parade him through the streets in religious processions and ridicule him as the 'father' of the Indian nation, which bears no resemblance to his formulations. Pakistanis kill him every time they denounce the man who first sought to establish Muslim pride through his Khilafat movement (the Quaid had thought, with remarkable foresight, that it was madness to rekindle Islamic passions) and worked for the interests of Pakistan even after Partition.

Method in madness

Sincerity was the source of Gandhi's power. He believed in the purpose of his mission and worked to achieve a unity between his thought, speech and actions. His modus operandi was based upon mobilisation of the people rather than the political parties. Once these noble goals were established, he had no hesitation in using the nascent media of his time to advance his cause. Whether it was his fast unto death, or the long walk to defy the Salt Law, theatrics were built into the Mahatma's every protest. The media loved it, and its power shamed the rulers every time a reporter sent a dispatch from the boondocks of the far-flung empire. With a mischievous twist, Gandhi used the very instruments of empire to undermine it from within. Various leftist groups have since tried to replicate this technique, but since they ignore the fundamental feature of this moral method of political arm-twisting—non-violence—they fail to create a favourable impact and cannot move the masses.

Gandhi improvised on the anarchic impulses of Marx, and established that any action meant honestly to recreate cannot be called 'destruction'. Jinnah and

Nehru, the other two outstanding lawyers from the Temple Inn, could never appreciate the ancient Hindu logic of dying to be reborn. Like other god-fearing and law-abiding English gentlemen, wogs at the fag end of the empire loved order and feared anarchy. They could not recognise the method in the madness of Gandhi, who had experienced firsthand the tyranny of 'order' that then existed in Indian society—caste, untouchability, gender discrimination and an utter disregard for health and sanitation. These issues could not wait for either Jinnah's homeland or Nehru's utopia. A revolution was needed to reform the Indian mindset, and revolutions are by definition anarchic. Order implies continuation of the status quo. Fear of anarchy has to be overcome in order to initiate long-needed changes in the existing order that had institutionalised inequality for millennia.

All the societies within Southasia are passing through a dangerous phase of disillusionment and hopelessness. In some parts, as in Nepal, Telangana, Jharkhand and Marathwada, political entrepreneurs are seeking solutions by reinventing Maoism. In West Punjab, East Bengal and Saurashtra, experiments in militant Islam and Hindutva are vitiating the environment of peaceful coexistence. East of the Brahmaputra, a fascist upsurge plagues separatist movements and racist rulers alike. Elsewhere in the region, there is a dangerous drift and listlessness. Rediscovering Gandhi in these times is essential if one seeks the play of sanity in Southasia.

The challenges have multiplied since Gandhi died in 1948. Commercialised newspapers, instantaneous television images, impromptu SMSes and mindless blogs have made the task of creating a unified answer to the empire of market fundamentalism extremely difficult. But responses are being crafted that raise hope. The human-rights movement in Pakistan, the agitation by the Narmada evacuees, the voices of dissent in Bangladesh that speak for its Hindu and Buddhist minorities, the modest Sarvodaya experiment of Sri Lanka, the people's movement in Nepal and the transformation of erstwhile socialists in the Jamuna–Ganga plain—all are indications of churning of a society on the threshold of change.

Like most philosophies, Gandhianism too needs to be rediscovered by every generation to suit the needs and aspirations of its time. That Gandhi has endured and thrived in the dreams of Martin Luther King, Jr, and Nelson Mandela alike is ample tribute to his memory. He has become even more important after the end of the Cold War and the consequent declaration of the Clash of Civilisations in the wake of the attacks of 11 September 2001. Mull over the ancient Christian aphorism about 'turning the other cheek' in its transformed Gandhian version—'an eye for an eye will make the whole world blind'—and there is no way you can ignore the force of his ideas and their relevance in our times.

'Generations to come will scarce believe that such a one as this ever in flesh and blood walked upon this earth,' wrote Albert Einstein. Hindus and Muslims schooled in the belief of the birth of a redeemer in every epoch might find it unbelievable that a scientist of Einstein's stature failed to see that there was no way Gandhi could not have emerged in a region virtually at the edge of collapse in the early 20th century. Passing through almost a similar phase once more at the start of the 21st century, Southasia will have to rediscover Gandhi because redeemers are not born whenever they are needed. They have to be found in their philosophies.

Chapter 13

Two chairmen and a people

Himal, March–April 2006

Kanak Mani Dixit

It has not rained in Nepal for five months and the ground this spring is parched, the haze thicker for the dryness all around. Electricity production is so low that even the privileged of Kathmandu Valley are seeing 17 hours of load-shedding per week, and this has also affected drinking-water distribution. The tourists have disappeared with the Maoist blockades and government curfews, and the five casinos of Kathmandu meant to trap them are filled instead with Nepalis betting their fortunes. Petroleum prices are suddenly up, and double-digit inflation is on its way. The political confusion on several fronts, however, is as yet preventing the accumulated frustrations from boiling over in a rash of spontaneous violence.

Everywhere in Nepal today there is listlessness, a waiting for something to happen. Potholes are not repaired, nor are buildings painted; and in the districts, the people have nearly forgotten the ubiquitous term of four decades' standing, 'development project'. There is a hope that the vortex of violence that has Nepal in its grip will be broken by the end of spring, before the monsoon sets in. Spring is historically the season of political change in Kathmandu, and something must give, or so people hope. That 'give' must come from the direction of the Narayanhiti royal palace, stuck in its militarist, undemocratic ways. As for the Maoist rebels in the jungle, they have already indicated in a variety of ways their desire—indeed, their desperation—for a way to open, aboveground politics.

The polity is today at a stalemate awaiting release, either planned or forced, so that the 26 million people of this sizeable country can once again breathe the air of peace and freedom. That peace was wrested by the violence of the Maoist insurgency of ten years' standing and the state security's response, which has placed the country towards the top of the charts in numbers of tortured and 'disappeared'. The freedom was first stolen in the villages by the gun-toting rebels, who even today like to claim they have public support; and in the last three years by a newly crowned king-turned-despot, who shows contempt for the people at every turn and speaks in Orwellian doublespeak of democracy and constitutionalism while proceeding to demolish both.

Both of the chairmen—the Maoists' Pushpa Kamal Dahal and the royalty of Gyanendra Bir Bikram Shah Dev—hold the belief that the Nepali public is a peasantry more than willing to submit to their individual feudal diktats. They do not seem to recognise, or care to concede, that the citizens have developed a taste for democracy, and for what a modern-day pluralistic state can deliver in social and economic progress. They know that that future lies neither with king nor rebel—neither in rightwing dictatorship, nor with ultra-left totalitarianism.

Over the autumn and winter, the insurgents have given ample indication of their desire to submit to the people's will. The Maoists must perforce be tested in their announced willingness to join multiparty politics, but today it is the royal chairman who is the stumbling block to peace and democracy: by not responding to the Maoist ceasefire of four months' standing last autumn, by continuing to snub the very parliament-abiding political parties who could save his throne and his dynasty, and—the unkindest cut of all—by militarising the Nepali state.

The entire national superstructure is crumbling around Chairman Gyanendra, and yet there is no indication that he understands the gravity of the situation. The destruction of the state structure and economy over a single year leads to the inescapable conclusion that Chairman Gyanendra has neither the aptitude nor acumen to be a head of government, which he has been since he appointed himself chairman of the Council of Ministers following the royal coup d'etat of 1 February 2005. It could even be that, having gotten himself into a jam, the chairman's arrogance does allow him to extricate himself. He has not reached for the lines that have been thrown to him in the past year.

The frustration with the head of government is exemplified by the anger of a soldier shouting into a phone at a public call booth in Nawalparasi district last month, after a devastating attack on an army convoy. Here is how he was overheard: 'Sir, how many more of my boys have to die because of the arrogance [*hath*] of one man?' There is disillusionment in the police force with a king who insists on moving about in army combat attire, and increasing disquiet among the army officer corps who are unable to pass the message up the ranks. The police these days surrender at the first instance of attack, and the soldiers are fatigued without having really taken on the rebels—socially isolated and without inspiring leadership. They might well have put up a good fight for the sake of the citizenry, but not for the 'supreme commander-in-chief'.

A time for sanctions

If the knot lies in the obduracy of Chairman Gyanendra, then the question would be how to force his hand. International condemnation has not worked for someone who seems willing to operate under the isolationist junta model perfected by the generals of Rangoon. Neither is the chairman bothered that his failures are paraded before the people, with fiascos in governance, diplomacy, development, economic management, administration and warfare. The public, finally, got a flavour of what some diplomats had known earlier about the royal ability to misrepresent, with the televised address on the anniversary of the takeover. Looking straight to the camera, on the morning of 1 February 2006, Chairman Gyanendra claimed that the Maobaadi were reduced to indulging in 'isolated incidents of petty crime', even while, at the moment of the taping, the guerrillas were destroying the Rana-era administrative centre of Palpa. He proposed that the national image and pride had been restored, when in fact the chairman cannot extract a single invitation for a state visit overseas, and foreign dignitaries shun the country like the bird flu. Chairman Gyanendra also, with a straight face, claimed that democracy had been strengthened during his year of royal rule.

Nor was that it. Having squandered numerous opportunities to build bridges to the political parties, in a Democracy Day message on 19 February, Chairman Gyanendra called on those 'interested' parties to approach the royal person for discussions. He did this while scores of political leaders—including the topmost, such as Madhav Kumar Nepal of the Communist Party of Nepal

(Unified Marxist–Leninist) and Ram Chandra Poudel of the Nepali Congress—
were in detention at his command. This was yet another exhibition, by now
too numerous to list, of the chairman's contempt for the Nepali public. It
is part and parcel of a mindset that thinks the international community will
believe his democratic credentials if he repeats the term *democracy* several times
in a speech.

Given the recalcitrance of Chairman Gyanendra and his royalist cohort,
and the unwillingness of the Royal Nepal Army (RNA) leadership to caution
the chairman from this destructive path, the time has come for targeted international sanctions to check the anti-democratic, militarist royal agenda for the
sake of the people of Nepal. As called for by several international human-
rights organisations, and increasingly by bold activists speaking out within
Nepal, the sanctions would apply to the individuals of the royal regime—
freezing the international bank accounts of members of the royal family, including a nefarious son-in-law, and denial of visas for international travel by both
that family and by the topmost handful of military generals and all members of
the royal Council of Ministers. The international community must also demand
information from the RNA on officers implicated in violations of international humanitarian law, so that they can be prevented from going on the highly
regarded United Nations peacekeeping assignments. If the army does not
supply those names to the United Nations High Commissioner for Human
Rights, as it is currently refusing to do, then the individual battalions implicated
must be refused peacekeeping stints.

It is important to go for targeted, individualised sanctions because the
Narayanhiti regime does not respond—as even minimally democratic governments would—to the kind of sanctions that directly and indirectly hurt the
people at large, such as reduced or cancelled foreign assistance to development
projects and the government budget. A personal targeting and shaming, on
the other hand, might yield results. It would spread immediate panic among
the royalist ranks, and serve as a potent 'feudalist' pressure on the chairman to
back down.

Chairman in fatigues

The deadlock of the moment is not of the Maobaadi's making, but of Chairman
Gyanendra's, and of an army brass that was a willing accessory to the coup
d'etat. Narayanhiti has rapidly converted Nepal into a militarised state, where

military officers have sidelined the civilian administrators and police throughout the 75 districts. Every one of Chairman Gyanendra's actions over the past
year of absolute rule must be overturned if Nepal is to return to a pluralistic
state, including prejudicial appointments, illegal ordinances and numerous royal
fiats. But most urgent is to undo the damage done to society by the politicisa-
tion and deployment of the RNA as de facto administrators. This illegitimate,
unworkable diversion must be abandoned if social progress and economic
advancement are to be guaranteed through an inclusive, democratic society. The
people's future must not be compromised because one man, who happened to
get to sit on the throne at age 56, did not care enough about what 'militarisation'
could do to society.

The RNA must return to its professional position as a national army,
rather than serve as the master-monarch's bodyguard; the professional officers
who value their profession must make themselves heard by the generals currently locked in a feudal embrace with the royal palace. For now, the haughty
generals have no humility to show for their force's lack of fighting spirit since
it was deployed four full years ago, even though the number of soldiers has
nearly doubled in that period. Are they proud to be part of an army that refuses
to go on the offensive, which today mostly guards only the barrack's perimeter
fence even as neighbouring police posts or district headquarters are razed to
the ground? Can they take satisfaction in a force that carries out 'air offensives'
by throwing mortar shells out of helicopter windows onto populated terrain?
What will happen when human-rights organisations investigate the reported
large-scale executions at the Bhairabnath Battalion in downtown Kathmandu?
And how is it that the officers guilty of the 2003 point-blank massacre of 19
people—17 unarmed Maoist activists, and two innocent civilians—at Doramba
village in Ramechhap district, during a ceasefire period, did not receive their
deserved punishment?

And how does one defend an army that has so little self-respect that, when
challenged about human-rights abuse, its topmost generals invariably reply,
'Why do you not challenge the Maoists when they do the same thing?' This
willingness to be judged at the same level as the renegade insurgents speaks of
the quality of leadership with which the RNA is saddled—the same leadership
that accepted Chairman Gyanendra's call to arms, not to fight the Maoists in the
jungles but to battle politicians, lawyers, journalists and human-rights activists.

The supreme commander-in-chief is bent on destroying the Maoists
militarily, even though the RNA has shown itself incapable of going on the
offensive, which had been the hope of many at the time of the royal takeover.

There is also every reason to believe that Narayanhiti seeks a continuation of the conflict. It provides the chairman with the excuse to continue to rule, and to distort the political process in such a manner over the next year or two that he will have created an irreversible process through a sham parliamentary election—a constitutional coup on the shoulders of a military coup—that leaves him with a quantum of power with which he would be satisfied, but which was not sanctioned for the constitutional monarch by the 1990 Constitution of Nepal.

It is difficult today to imagine Chairman Gyanendra reverting to being a 'constitutional' or 'ceremonial' king, so prejudiced are his views on pluralism and democracy, so public his contempt for the politicians and political parties, and so blatant and self-serving his agenda. It is not just the political activist that is reacting negatively—Narayanhiti would perhaps be taken aback by how the royalty has fallen in the public esteem. It is a surprise to find village elders scornful of Chairman Gyanendra, and the ability of the mainstream press to print 'full frontal' cartoons of the chairman is another indication of what has become acceptable. There is even a stirring of discontent palpable among Kathmandu Valley's urban middle class, who have given Narayanhiti the benefit of the doubt for this long. The destruction of the monarchy's image is not the Maoist's doing; it is the chairman's own.

And yet, it will not do to simply wish away monarchy in the arena of one's mind. Responsible politicians are required to seek out ways in which to pressure Narayanhiti to backtrack. They also need to consider that the Maoists are not disarmed, even if their call has suddenly turned syrupy. Indeed, the need of the hour in Nepal is to find ways to force the chairman-king to back down, and to take it from there if he does not. While there are things that the international community can do (condemning the royal takeover, suspending arms assistance and contemplating 'smart sanctions'), the pressure on the palace must come from the Nepali people and their representatives—whatever it takes to get the palace with its back to the wall, and preferably in the form of an effective, well-organised, mass-based people's movement. On the other hand, nobody need ever plan an anarchical revolution, after which it would be a question of picking up the pieces.

Even at this precarious and penultimate hour, it would be possible for Chairman Gyanendra to backtrack. He could still rescue his dynasty, if not his own rule, by surrendering to the public. This would happen through direct admission that sovereignty lies with the people and not in the crown, and in accordance with the Constitution of 1990. Following the royal climb-down, there must be guarantees of unquestioned control of the RNA by the civilian government; a rollback on all ordinances, orders and appointments from at least the last one year; an all-party government either by reinstatement of the Third Parliament (disbanded in 2002) or through an understanding among the political players; and the all-party government calling for a constituent assembly to draft a new constitution. This last is required to bring the Maoists in from the cold, given their process of reformation and given the past year's proof of Chairman Gyanendra's naked ambitions. Even to do away with the monarchy, the citizenry would have to be given a choice through a constituent assembly.

To believe or not

And the Maoists do, very much, want to come in from the cold. The rebel change of heart is based on cool pragmatism or sheer desperation, depending on how you read it, but their recent pronouncements are credible enough to take them up on their offer. As the country is already at war, there is really nothing to lose in doing this. If the rebels are being manipulative and are found out, the state would simply be expected to return to war. To the plaintive question, 'But can we believe the Maobaadi?', the answer is simple—there are reasons to believe that their resolve is genuine, and not because they are 'nice' people.

In August 2005, the Maoists held a plenum in their 'home district' of Rolpa, and debated a resolution that was finally passed unanimously: the rebels would take a 180-degree turn (not announced as such), turn their ideology on its head and enter 'competitive multiparty politics'. This was the untying of the most important and troublesome knot, for in one stroke the Maoists put behind them the rhetoric and agenda of 'people's war', on the basis of which, for ten long years, they have motivated their fighters and propagandised them on the takeover of Kathmandu Valley. There remains the challenge of how to tackle the rebels' gun-in-hand, which no longer has even the sanction of a 'people's war'. The violent inertia among the Maobaadi must be allowed to dissipate without further violence, which is why responsible politicians, society leaders and foreign diplomats should promote an engagement with the rebels, rather than go into naïve or self-serving denial.

It was after the Maoist plenum, on the basis of their willingness to move towards non-violent politics and on the rebound from Chairman Gyanendra's constant rebuffs, that the mainstream political parties decided to engage with the rebel chairman, Pushpa Kamal Dahal ('Prachanda'). The leaders of the alliance of the seven parliamentary parties agitating against 'royal regression' flew to Delhi and met with Dahal and his ideologue-in-chief, Baburam Bhattarai. They emerged on 22 November with a 12-point understanding, the goal of which was to challenge the royal move and prepare for a constituent assembly as a way to address the Maoist bottom line. In early February, the Maoist leadership suddenly unleashed their leader, Chairman Dahal, on the national and international media with unrehearsed on-camera interviews.

In the interviews, the Maoists supremo was playing to diverse national, Subcontinental and world audiences, as well as to his own cadre; and so, while disarming, his statements contained their share of contradictions. At times full of uncompromising bluster, at other times sounding conciliatory, Chairman Dahal sought to convince about the Maoist decision to come into multiparty politics, laying it out as a magnanimous act of great proletarian wisdom. The chairman presented several scenarios of possible resolutions on a 'pick one' basis; but most importantly, he conceded that the Maoists' descent to 'multiparty politics' was dictated by regional geopolitics, and the US and Indian support for the RNA that had made the fight difficult. The Maoist conclusion, he said, was that adjustments were required to Mao-Lenin's 20th-century communism for implementation in the 21st century. The Maoists of Nepal were the vanguard for this, from whom even the Indian Naxalites could take a lesson or two, he said—such as the importance of parliamentary politics!

Sitting in a New Delhi safe-house during the interviews, the Maoist chieftain then proposed, with his chief ideologue and one-time rival, Bhattarai, by his side, the specific 'nikas' or way out of the quagmire. He suggested that the Maoists should stay out of the fight for democracy in the beginning, recognising perhaps the domestic and international difficulties if armed rebels were part of a democratic movement. At one point, Chairman Dahal suggested that the most practical nikas is a revival of the Third Parliament. This reinstatement was not to be through royal initiative, but something to be wrested from Narayanhiti through an energetic movement that would unilaterally announce the revival. The Parliament would garner international recognition, and appoint an all-party government that would negotiate with the Maoists and pave the way for a constituent assembly.

At several points in the interviews, given to Nepali and Indian dailies and the BBC World Service, the Maoist chief even indicated his willingness to accept a 'ceremonial' kingship if the outcome of the constituent assembly so warranted. In the run-up to the assembly elections, the rebels would need international supervision of the RNA and the rebel fighters. This is seen by their leadership both as a means to protect the cadre in the process of weapons decommissioning, as well as a sop to prove 'international recognition'. The greatest difficulty for the rebel commandants will be to convince battle-hardened fighters that the ten-year fight has been worth it. Besides the fact that Chairman Gyanendra will not hear of UN involvement, there is a problem in the Maoist projection here: all-powerful New Delhi too rejects the suggestion, for reasons of geopolitics quite different from the chairman's.

How does one believe the Maobaadi leadership, given their history of manipulative manoeuvring? Would they not take the political parties for a ride? Fortunately, the credibility of the insurgents' desire to jettison the 'people's war' and enter the world of competitive parliamentary politics does not depend on the 'Prachanda interviews', which are but attempts to make the act of climbdown convincing to the Kathmandu middle class, the Indian intelligentsia and the world at large—not to forget their own cadre, who are all listening in on their FM and short-wave receivers.

There are several reasons why Dahal and Bhattarai are convincing on this one, this time around. To begin with, the change of policy was the result of a unanimous decision of the rebels' expanded central-committee meeting—called a plenum—which makes this reversal more than what is contained in polemical press releases that get faxed and e-mailed to Kathmandu. The fact that Chairman Dahal was openly on television and allowed himself to be photographed for the press indicates a desire to end underground life at age 52. Also significant is the fact that the chairman was committing himself before the Indian government and public opinion, which would have New Delhi breathing down his neck if there were any blatant backtracking.

Non-Maoist Maoists

Why did the August plenum take the decision it did? Obviously the Maoists had grown too big too quickly and were having to make adjustments to save their 'revolution' from internal corruption, this last being something Chairman Dahal has admitted. Having gotten to within fighting reach of political power-sharing in Kathmandu—which was never, perhaps, really expected—the leadership realised the need for a change in strategy. This is because no government in the world, including India's, would recognise Maoists as 'Maoists' in the seat of power in Kathmandu. There was only one way out: renounce the 'people's war', even if one did not say it out loud, and put your best face forward.

The violent politics of the Maobaadi had properly incensed the international community, and the post-9/11 'war on terror' was a setback for a group that has used terrorist methods. American, British and Indian assistance began to flow in large volume to the RNA, and was suspended only as a result of Chairman Gyanendra's coup. But it was when India began to sense a danger to its own internal security from copycat insurgencies in its hinterland—due to the high-profile Nepali Maobaadi—that the ground shifted for the insurgents. It did not help that, during their rise and spread, the Maoists had made liberal use of anti-Indian rhetoric, based on an ultra-nationalist ideology actually devised by Gyanendra's father, Mahendra, back in the Panchayat era.

The Maoist vitriol against India, the bans on Indian vehicles and cinema, the targeting of Indian multinational property in the Nepal Tarai and, in the last instance, the whimsical preparation for an Indian attack through a widespread campaign of digging trenches—none of this endeared the Maobaadi to the Indian state. When India decided it had had enough—and its foreign minister had termed them 'terrorists' even before Kathmandu did—it deployed its SSB paramilitary force along the open Nepal-India border to monitor movement. It nabbed two central Maoist leaders in Madras and Guwahati and put them on trial, and it prevented wounded Maoist fighters from being treated in nursing homes in towns like Lucknow or Gorakhpur. Proactive Indian displeasure, as well as the realisation that New Delhi would never 'allow' a Maoist government in place in Kathmandu, have been possibly the most important factors for the rebels to want to come aboveground—it is a requirement of their very success that they abandon the 'people's war' that has brought them thus far. In addition, the role of the Indian left parties, particularly the Communist Party of India (Marxist), seems to have been important in influencing the Nepali Maoists to see sense.

No less important, perhaps, is the domestic challenge faced by the Maoists. Here, too, the rebels realised that they could spread thus far and no further in their goal of state takeover. While they have been able to make spectacular hit-and-run attacks in the hinterland, they never came close to taking over any of the 75 district headquarters, let alone Kathmandu Valley. The militia and guerrillas were thus confronted with the prospects of a never-ending fight, whereas joining aboveground politics would require laying down the gun and joining multiparty politics. In the early years, the rebels were able to motivate fighters with their run of assaults on police and army posts, and the promise of the prize of Kathmandu. Successful mass attacks on barracks and the looting of weapons also served to keep up morale. As the army acquired Belgian Minimi belt-driven guns and more-efficient American M-16s in place of aging India-donated SLR rifles, and with the RNA learning to defend its barracks with mines and concertina wire, the insurgents had to turn to the 'lowly' task of destroying administrative offices, government infrastructure and poorly armed police *chowkis*.

With the army refusing to engage them in the field, the Maoists could not hope for firefights and battles to show their fighting mettle. All in all, for the last few years the rebel fighters have been reduced to clandestine ambushes of security forces, laying down improvised explosive devices on public roads, as well as blockades and highway closures. Even as it was getting harder to motivate the cadre, the instances of banditry and wayward violence not sanctioned by the high command indicated disintegration of the fighting spirit. A sudden, deep and open ideological split between Chairman Dahal and Bhattarai in the spring of 2005 divided the rank-and-file all the way down to the district level. It is not yet clear how that rift was patched up, but the leadership seems to have decided to seek a *surakshit abataran* (safe landing) while the movement was still united. The Maoists could continue to make the country ungovernable, and that was even easier with Chairman Gyanendra leading an unmotivated security force, but the goal of capturing Kathmandu was receding.

Due to domestic, regional and international considerations, therefore, the Maoist decision to come to a 'safe landing' is convincing to all players. All players, that is, other than some diehard members of Kathmandu's royalist elite and the American ambassador, who in mid-February conducted a frenzy of meetings, speeches and letters to the editor, trying to convince whoever would listen of an impending Maoist takeover of Kathmandu, and of the need to reject the Maoist siren calls that the 12-point understanding and the Maoist interviews represented. Lacking a nuanced understanding of the fast-changing Nepali political discourse, and obviously running to the diktats of his own administration's 'war on terror', the ambassador managed—it is hoped, momentarily—to deflect the debate and the search for peace. Whereas a civil cautionary note to alert the political class of the dangers of Maoist doubletalk would not have been untoward, the ambassador was acting very much the American cowboy in a Nepali china shop. As the royal regime's detainee, civil-society leader Devendra Raj Pandey, said from jail on a mobile phone, 'The ambassador's statements are designed to take the country back to civil war, more bloodshed and away from a political solution.'

Closure of the 'People's War'

If the Maobaadi are to be believed in their desire to bring the 'people's war' to a close, then it is Chairman Gyanendra, leading the RNA by the nose-ring, who is the obstacle for a return to both peace and democracy. And so, once again the question: How to bring Narayanhiti to heel?

Today the regime seems to stand tall, but its bones are brittle. The king has with him no supporters, other than the quislings and opportunists who have joined the cabinet and leaders of mini-parties who want to make good under royal patronage. His plan is to ride it out through the spring of 2006 in the hope that the monsoon will defuse the political agitation, and a year from now he can organise a sham parliamentary election to gain sham legitimacy. But this is a plan concocted in a royal vacuum, by a man who believes in his ability to stay in power with the help of a dispirited RNA. In the towns and villages, there are very few opinion-makers today who feel for the monarchy, especially for the current incumbent. Internationally, it is not likely that the players important to Nepal—India, the UK, China, Japan, the European Union, the UN secretary-general or the US (despite one odd plenipotentiary)—will come around to seeing things the way Chairman Gyanendra would like them to do.

But while the international community should stand ready to provide support in addition to what it has already done, peace and democracy are goals for which Nepalis themselves must fight. With the plethora of 'donors' willing to invest money in all kinds of conflict-resolution exercises, it will be the death of the 'fight for freedom' if the politicians too start accepting foreign assistance under the line-item 'restoration of peace and democracy'. There is no doubt, however, of the need for the politicians to ratchet up the battle, and their lethargy thus far is no proof of the lack of urgency in the situation. It is just that the rage against the royal takeover has not been translated into effective mass action.

Obviously, there are detrimental contradictions afoot. The contradictions that exist between the political parties, the power centralisation within the parties—particularly around the person of Girija Prasad Koirala of the Nepali Congress—and the copious lack of imagination and planning in the leadership ranks generally, have all been contributing factors to the inability to defeat the royal action more than a year after the takeover, even though the militarisation underway should have energised the political class. But it is also important to note that politicians better understand the challenges, particularly those who have held national office. This is something the firebrand members of civil society or impatient diplomats do not appreciate enough.

To take one example, the seniormost politicians are circumspect when it comes to the slogan for the creation of a 'democratic republic', even though sections of civil society have already run with it. The goal of a democratic republic is not only compatible, but goes to the heart of the demand for a pluralistic state; but until recently, it was the battle cry of the Maoist rebels. Indeed, 'democratic republic' as a slogan to fight the royal agenda is compromised unless simultaneously the matter of the Maoist gun is addressed. The political parties have today come around to accepting the constituent assembly as the departure point for the post-Gyanendra evolution of Nepali democracy, and they did this only after the Maobaadi were able to convincingly project their about-turn on the 'people's war'. But the Maobaadi still hold arms, whereas the political parties never have.

It must be added that just as Chairman Gyanendra over the past few years has done more than the Maobaadi to destroy the image of monarchy, likewise he has done more to give energy to the 'democratic republic' than the rebels in the jungle. It has become difficult to conceive of the man with the crown functioning as a constitutional monarch, bound to a ceremonial throne, without residuary powers.

Building democratic steam

It is already very late in the day to wrest democracy back from the grip of Narayanhiti. And it is the political parties—assisted by various branches of civil society, including the bar, the journalists, academia, human-rights activists and independent citizens—who must rise to the occasion. What are they to do? Why, they must build steam in the movement to force the regime against the wall, for the sake of democracy and for peace through dialogue with the Maobaadi.

But what to do if Chairman Gyanendra refuses to budge? Many political players are reduced to waiting for a spark, some accident, which would act to release all the public's pent-up anger in a flood that would wash away the monarchy. But that would be to invite anarchy, which in Nepal could be savage, and the political actors as yet have no mechanism in place to manage such a destructive bout. A planned roadmap would have to be a mix of what is practical and desirable, given that the situation is complicated by the three-way tussle between the rebels, the royal regime and the political parties/civil society. The goal is a return to representative government, for which the rebels have to be brought to a safe landing, while the monarchy has at the very least to be constitutionally neutered.

The great advance of the last half-year has been the convincing presentation of the Maoists that they do indeed want to come to a landing. The four-month-long ceasefire allowed the Maoists to recoup a large measure of their political capital, which had been lost in their heightened militarism of the past few years. The Maoists took back their ceasefire when it became difficult to sustain under the RNA's 'non-cooperation', and now they have gone back to attacking state security and destroying government property, and have announced an onerous period of nationwide closures in the coming two months. The rebel leadership must have its compulsions, but its members surely realise that their return to violence weakens the very political parties whose help they need to come aboveground. Their continuing violence strengthens no one but Narayanhiti and the RNA, and makes the already-sceptical international community nervous.

The Maobaadi must unilaterally call for a cessation of hostility and do their bit, even if the state security fails to respond as before. They must do this to allow politics to revive in a country where it has almost died, and to give peace a chance. Meanwhile, the political parties do not have a choice in the building of a people's movement. At the moment, they are waiting for international pressure, the public shaming, and desires for continuity of dynasty to force Chairman Gyanendra to backtrack. His record thus far points against such a possibility. There is no alternative to an energetic political movement.

The mainstream political parties are united today on the political fight for a constituent assembly, which would also carry along those who seek a democratic republic. The constituent assembly is thus a widely recognised roadmap to peace in Nepal today—it has the intelligentsia and the political class united, the international community on board. Ironically, in one of his interviews, Chairman Dahal has even spelled out how this is to be done: as mentioned previously, it would take place through the revival of the Third Parliament, followed by the formation of an all-party government, which would hold dialogue with the rebels and organise the elections for the assembly.

The brave new world that would suddenly unfold with the revival of Parliament—or another way in which an all-party government could be formed, if that were possible—is tantalising for anyone with some political imagination. The all-party government would start a dialogue with the Maoists.

Simultaneously, the army would come under the Parliament and the all-party government of the day, for which the existing National Security Council, which ensures civilian control of the military, would be activated. The nature of the constituent assembly would have to be worked out.

This is how the ground has shifted in Nepal. Before the August plenum, it would have been premature to propose the constituent assembly as the road-map, because the Maoists were steadfast in their violence agenda and 'people's war'. With the rebels having made a credible departure, the constituent assembly, as a means of giving the people their ultimate right to choose their system of government, suddenly comes onto centre stage. This, then, would be the slogan with which to challenge Narayanhiti. Chairman Gyanendra is by now the only powerful player opposed to the constituent assembly, and he would certainly try and sabotage every move to restore democracy through a revived Parliament.

It would be a welcome thing if Parliament were to be revived through a Supreme Court verdict on a long-pending case, as some politicians seem to be hoping for, so they can be saved the trouble of organising a movement. It is even possible that the concerted show of national and international solidarity might shake the moorings of Narayanhiti, its cohort and the military leadership, forcing them to capitulate without further fight. That seems unlikely to happen, however. Besides, almost by definition, a democracy that has not been fought for is bound to have within it elements of anti-people compromise. There is no way around it: a people's agitation is required to push back the autocratic agenda of Narayanhiti, supported by an international community willing to place individualised sanctions against royalty, the military top brass and the ministers.

It is just possible that the Spring of 2006 will bring such a political tsunami of sheer people power. But it is also possible that the chairman-king will continue to bleed the people, making it into the monsoon period and getting himself a respite. If that happens, there are no alternatives but to continue the non-violent fight for peace and democracy—through the next monsoon, and the next and the next.

But the best will be if the Spring of 2006 yields a people's movement that vanquishes Chairman Gyanendra. At that point, Nepal could start on the long-delayed process of reconstruction and rehabilitation, and the revival of a democracy better than that experienced between 1990 and 2002. There are too many young widows, too many orphans, too many displaced, too many young fighters in the land. The long haul will begin once Chairman Gyanendra's agenda is defeated and the Maoists are taken along on the march of peaceful, aboveground, multiparty parliamentary politics. The last time democracy was ushered in was the people's movement in the Spring of 1990—the *jana andolan* 2046, according to the Nepali calendar year. What the people await this spring is Jana Andolan 2062, not expecting the chairman-king to give up without a fight.

Chapter 14

Gujarat as another country
The making and reality of a fascist realm
Himal, October 2006

Prashant Jha

Ahmedabad is a divided city. On one side reside fear and anxiety, helplessness and anger. Walk across Jamalpur, Mirzapur, Dani Limda, Kalopur, Lal Darwaza and other parts of the Walled City. Go to Juhapura—one of the largest Muslim ghettos in India. Scratch a little, and people want to talk. An entire community feels under attack, with many resigned to their newfound fate of being second-class citizens. Rights are negligible, and the sense of representation non-existent. What remains strong is the cry for justice, and the knowledge they will not get it—not in Gujarat. Why? 'Because,' explains one elder in Shah Alam, 'we pray to Allah. That is our transgression.'

There are the borders everywhere. A patch of road, a wall, a turn across a street corner, a divider in the middle of a road—this is all it takes to polarise and segregate communities throughout Gujarat. Each town and city now has countless borders, forcibly making people conscious of their religious identity. *Me Hindu, you Muslim.* Or one could look at it differently: the borders on the ground merely reflect and reinforce the polarisation that has already taken place in the minds of ordinary Gujaratis.

Yet nothing prepares you for the certitude on the streets of the other Ahmedabad—in Navrangpura, Vastrapur, M G Road, Judge's Bungalow Road, Satellite, Vejalpur. Many Gujarati Hindus think they have the answers to some of the most troubling questions of our times. The subtler would say there is a problem 'among' Muslims. Others argue that Muslims themselves are the problem. They look back fondly at the '*Toofan*', the 2002 riots, and their reminiscences have a striking thematic unity. *The Muslims deserved it. They are all bloody Pakistanis and criminals. If we had more time, we would have wiped them out. See, they are crushed and scared. We taught them a lesson. And now, the world should learn from Gujarat about how to deal with the miyas.* The one sentiment that is almost wholly absent is remorse. What remains, 54 months after the pogrom, is an all-pervading sense of arrogance among Hindus in the public sphere. Those who think differently possibly keep silent.

The story of Gujarat as a whole, then, is a tale of pride and prejudice on the one side, victimhood and alienation on the other. In control of this divisive agenda is the fascist government of Narendra Modi, who happily builds on this evolving social reality, and reinforces it. The everyday tragedy of Gujarat, often invisible, is in many ways more telling than the state-sponsored pogroms of 2002. The high degree of alienation among Muslims, the stereotypes and discrimination they face, the fact that a substantial section of society is committed to the Hindutva agenda, the absence of justice and accountability, and the continued secession of the state from its basic constitutional obligations—these are all elements that go into making Gujarat, in the very words of the Hindu right, its laboratory.

This is happening even as Chief Minister Modi, the principal architect of the 2002 killings, seeks to carve an image for himself as a development leader, and the chaperon of India's best-governed state. While the former is true—that Modi guided the horrors of 2002 and the subjugation of Muslims in the aftermath—the latter is far from proven. Despite the loud applause that is beginning to be heard in New Delhi and elsewhere, the facts on the ground reveal that Gujarat is neither the embodiment of progress nor of good governance.

Babu's bomb

If 2002 was an experiment in the Hindutva laboratory, men like Babubhai Rajabhai Patel of the Hindutva outfit Bajrang Dal were at the forefront of conducting it. The short, stocky Babu Bajrangi, as he is popularly known, would pass off as an average middle-class trader. He claims to be a social worker.

Sitting in his second-floor office in the Ahmedabad suburb of Naroda, Bajrangi talks about his NGO, Navchetan, which 'rescues' Hindu women who have been 'lured' into relationships with Muslim men. 'In every house today there is a bomb, and that bomb is the woman, who forms the basis of Hindu culture and tradition,' Bajrangi begins. 'Parents allow her [sic] to go to college, and they start having love affairs, often with Muslims. Women should just be kept at home to save them from the terrible fate of Hindu-Muslim marriages.'

Bajrangi's Navchetan works to prevent inter-religion love marriages, and if such a wedding has already taken place, it works to break the union. When a marriage between a Hindu woman and Muslim man gets registered in a court, within a few days the marriage documents generally end up on Bajrangi's desk, ferreted out by functionaries in the lower judiciary. The girl is subsequently kidnapped and sent back home; the boy is taught a lesson. 'We beat him in a way that no Muslim will dare to look at Hindu women again. Only last week, we made a Muslim eat his own waste—thrice, in a spoon,' he reveals with barely concealed pride. All this is illegal, Bajrangi concedes, but it is moral. 'And anyway, the government is ours,' he continues, turning to look at the clock. 'See, I am meeting Modi in a while today.'

One might dismiss Babu Bajrangi as a bombast when he claims proximity to the chief minister, or describes the beating of Muslim boys. But for a man of obvious stature in society he is also accused of burning Muslims alive. As the chief accused in the infamous Naroda Patiya case, one of the worst instances of brutality during the 2002 violence, he is alleged to have led the mob that killed 89 people in the area. It is a burden that rests lightly on Bajrangi's shoulders. 'People say I killed 123 people,' he says. *Did you?* Bajrangi laughs, 'How does it matter? They were Muslims. They had to die. They are dead.'

Evidence of Bajrangi's complicity was so overwhelming that even a pliable state administration could not save him from an eight-month stint in prison. 'They cannot reduce my hatred for Muslims with that, can they? While in jail, I demolished a small mosque that was located in there,' he says with a sly, childlike grin. Bajrangi's views on what is wrong with Muslims are unabashedly straightforward. 'They are all terrorists. Refuse to sing even the national song. Why don't they just go to Pakistan? Now, our aim is to create a society where we have as little to do with them as possible.'

Bajrangi is now out on bail. But what has allowed a man accused of such a heinous crime to walk and operate freely? Perhaps it is the manner in which the Gujarat government has, since 2002, consistently violated its constitutional obligations to safeguard life and liberty and provide justice.

After there was fire in a train compartment carrying Hindutva activists on the morning of 27 February 2002 at the Godhra railway station, killing 59 people, Narendra Modi decided to unleash a reign of terror against the state's Muslims as a 'reaction'. The cause of the fire is still not certain, though a central government enquiry committee has reported that it was accidental, and not the result of a conspiracy. In a vulnerable political position, and unsure of future electoral prospects, Modi felt this was the right spark to ignite communal passions through the state, and blamed the incident on 'Muslims'. He instructed senior officers to let the Hindus express their anger—he was essentially asking for the rioters to be allowed a free hand. Modi's state machinery and the Vishwa Hindu Parishad (VHP) jointly planned the attacks, with the police themselves in many places firing on the victims rather than the rioters.

The state's support to the perpetrators of the pogrom has continued through the four-and-a-half-years since the carnage. Out of the 4,252 cases registered in connection with the violence that gripped Gujarat in February, March and April of 2002, the files for more than 2,100 were closed without the filing of chargesheets. A few senior police officers have revealed the manner in which the state subverted justice at every stage—by distorting and manipulating complaints at the police station, assigning investigations to the very officers accused of assisting in massacres, and allowing the accused free rein to coerce witnesses into changing statements. With several public prosecutors simultaneously in the ranks—or even the leadership—of the Rashtriya Swayamsevak Sangh (RSS) and its affiliates, the prosecution itself silently assisted in getting approval for bail applications. 345 cases have been decided so far, with convictions in only 13 of those cases.

After a severe indictment of the Gandhinagar state government by the National Human Rights Commission, the Supreme Court of India passed a landmark decision in 2004, ordering re-examination by a high-level, state-appointed committee of the decision to close more than 2,000 cases. The court also ordered the transfer of investigation from the state police to the Central Bureau of Investigation in select cases, and moved two cases out of Gujarat entirely. Muslims and secular groups are clinging to these small victories as their last hopes for justice.

And what of the social and economic condition of the victims? The state government's own conservative figures put the total loss of property at INR 6.9 billion. The government has distributed INR 563 million to the affected persons, which makes up about nine percent of the calculated damage. At the peak of the riots, more than 150,000 people were in relief camps, which were summarily shut down by the government after four months. With the state washing its hands of any rehabilitation for the affected, those who could not return home have had to live in resettlement colonies constructed by community organisations. Almost 10,000 families are said to remain internally displaced in Gujarat.

Pathological normalcy

Shakeel Ahmed heads the legal cell of the Islamic Relief Committee, an offshoot of the Jamaat-e-Islami (JeI), a conservative Muslim organisation. A well-read man who can hold forth as easily on Islamic precepts as on Indian sociology, Ahmed stares incredulously when asked about relief and justice. 'It would be so foolish to expect it from the state!' he exclaims. 'This was not a riot; it was a systematically planned pogrom. If the accused get prosecuted and if relief is provided, then their entire political purpose will be defeated.' Ahmed's suggestion is confirmed from a diametrically opposite direction, that of a senior Bharatiya Janata Party (BJP) member of Parliament from Gujarat: 'Compensation, relief, regret—these are meaningless issues. We wanted to crush them, and we crushed them. And most Hindus are with us, as was clear from the subsequent elections. Forget about this now.' For a man of vehement convictions, it was nevertheless interesting that the MP requested anonymity. He must still fear something.

Memory is a convenient, subjective tool. While Hindu extremists tell anyone who raises uncomfortable questions about the killings to 'move on', they do not mind evoking the Toofan of 2002 in the most minute detail in order to get the Muslims to 'behave themselves'. They also evoke the butchery as a 'feel-good' factor among themselves. The continuous discrimination against Muslims is part of the same strategy—and it is not subtle in the least. Explains Ahmedabad-based sociologist Shiv Vishvanathan: 'What happened in Gujarat was a mini Rwanda: your neighbour raped you; people killed between nine and six and went home singing. It was like a football match where the Hindus won. There remains festivity around it, the state denies victimhood, and there is no erasure.' State acquiescence and connivance can only partially explain such an overriding phenomenon of exclusion.

Indeed, in the Gujarat of today, among the Hindus it is considered normal to harbour and exhibit hatred for the Muslims. To those who might ask how is it possible to paint an entire state, of a population of more than 50 million, with such a broad brushstroke, this point is exactly what makes the evolving Gujarat of today different from all other areas where excesses have happened in Southasia. Here, the discrimination against Muslims has the state administration's support without even a fig-leaf of political correctness, as well as broad-based agreement on this matter among large sections of the Hindu masses. Talk to the common Hindu person on the street, from the neighbourhood guard to the autorickshaw-wallah to the shopkeeper, and the refrain is alarmingly deafening: *Muslims are goondas, always doing illegal things. See, they are now bombing people everywhere.* The pathological has become the normal. That is what makes societal evolution in Gujarat unique in India—and exceptionally lethal.

As elsewhere in India and Southasia, polarisation has always existed in Gujarati society. Since time immemorial, Dalits have not dared to stay inside the village core. Muslims and the intermediate and backward castes have been a bit more advantaged, but have still been kept away from the privileges of the Hindu upper castes. But even if the notion of a composite culture is at times over-romanticised, there was at one time an undeniably pluralist culture in Gujarat. In part, this stemmed from its coastal location and trade-based economy, which inevitably forced diverse communities together for mutual economic advantage. Achyut Yagnik, influential author of an authoritative book on modern Gujarat, believes that communal polarisation between Hindus and Muslims began after the 1969 riots in Ahmedabad, and accelerated after the *rath yatras* and political mobilisation by Hindutva forces in the early 1990s.

If some had hoped that the national and international condemnation would make Gujarat's communal rabble-rousers (with Modi as their cheerleader) pull back from their extremist agenda, this has not happened. In fact, the polarisation has intensified across the state in the last four-and-a-half years. If it was difficult before the riots for a Muslim to find a house to rent in Hindu areas, it is now impossible. Sophia Khan would know. A leading women's activist in Ahmedabad, she has had to undergo significant changes in her personal and professional life since 2002. To begin with, the polarised atmosphere in the city led Khan to shift her residence to Juhapura, the city's large Muslim area, although her office remained in the upmarket Hindu locality of Narayanpura.

Sophia's identity had remained a secret in Narayanpura because the office had been rented in the name of a Hindu trustee of the NGO she runs. A month ago, when neighbours in her office complex came to know of Khan's faith, she was asked immediately to pack up and depart. She tried to put up a fight, but gave up in the face of constant harassment. 'Imagine, they were not even willing to let me use the lift,' she says. Khan moved her office to a flat in Juhapura, but with that came a new complication. A Hindu employee who was working with Khan was pressured by her family to resign, for they did not approve of her going to a Muslim area. She is grim as she intones: 'My house is in a Muslim area. My office is here now. My only Hindu employee is resigning, and my work revolves around Muslims. This is exactly how they want to push an entire community into a corner.'

All over, people are beginning to shift to areas in which they are a part of the majority. M T Kazi is a young executive with F D Society, a Muslim trust that runs educational institutions. 'Everyone is insecure,' he says. 'What if a riot breaks out again? Both Hindus and Muslims would prefer to be in areas where they are surrounded by their own kind. That way, the possibility of attack is reduced.' But the ramifications of such a trend can be drastic, says Shakeel Ahmed of JeI: 'Social polarisation inevitably leads to some kind of economic polarisation. And this will have a more pronounced impact on the Muslim minority, because we are too small to create a self-sufficient unit.'

It is not even that the mental and physical dislocation of Muslims is an urban phenomenon, as many think. The rural areas in north and central Gujarat, in particular, are presently seeing a spurt in polarisation. There are 225 *talukas* in Gujarat, the local-level administrative divisions that encompass some 70 to 80 villages each. Before the riots, there was a Muslim majority in five to ten villages per taluka, a smattering of Muslims in another 40 percent, and the rest almost completely non-Muslim. 'Now, those five villages that had a Muslim majority have become concentration camps, especially in villages in the Panchmahal district,' explains Gagan Sethi, who runs Jan Vikas, an NGO working with Muslims. 'Muslims in the surrounding area, who feel insecure or have been pushed out of their own places, come to these villages.' Such rural ghettoisation is also problematic because it allows for the possibility of easy monitoring of Muslims by the state agencies, adding to the tensions within the community.

In the cities and towns, the segregation of residential locations has sharply reduced shared spaces at all levels. A visible example is the decline in the number of schools that have a fair mix of Hindu and Muslim students. Children generally attend schools that are close by, which means that these institutions are increasingly segregated. With the newfound sense of insecurity, parents feel even more strongly about sending their kids to schools with more of 'our people'. Some reports also suggest the existence of discrimination along religious lines in admission to elite schools. This troubles concerned citizens, who are worried that children might graduate from high school without having made a single lasting friendship with someone belonging to another community. The absence of contact since childhood can only accelerate the evolution of

Gujarat as 'another country', where Hindus and Muslims live starkly separate lives and where intolerance becomes the defining characteristic.

Silent underclass

The 2002 riots were a tragic tale of visible violence, under the glare of the national media, which provoked outrage. But Gujarat 2006 is the story of invisible violence—systematic and subtle, at the state and social levels. Prejudice against the Muslims grows by the day.

Salimbhai Musabhai Patel is happy he can introduce himself as S M Patel—at least it gets him an appointment with bankers. 'People think I am Hindu that way,' he says. A young entrepreneur, he runs the Patel Finance Company, with offices in Ahmedabad and Bharuch. 'But that is as far as my initials can get me,' Patel continues with a resigned smile. 'Once they know I am Muslim, they treat me like dirt. Forget about getting a loan.'

It is dusk, and Patel is standing with a group of other Muslim men on 'their side' of Mirzapur in Ahmedabad. Patel's comment unleashes a torrent of similar complaints from the others gathered. *We have no hope of getting a job in Gujarat. Government service is impossible. If we get in, we are relegated to the lowest level. The courts are against us. Muslim vendors are harassed, while Hindus get away with crimes. Even private companies prefer Hindus. The ordinary folk think all of us are Pakistanis. The riots are long over,* goes the common refrain, *and sure we are willing to 'move on'. But what do we do about the daily injustice? They want to create a society in which we just don't matter.*

This perception among Muslims, of being disadvantaged because of their faith, seems based on the hard reality of daily experience. Being Muslim in Gujarat is now a recipe for continuous harassment if you want to be anything but a member of the silent underclass. Activist Sophia Khan had to wage a struggle to get a phone connection from the local Tata branch, because the company had blacklisted certain areas. Banks have similar systems for loan applications. Most Hindu businessmen would rather not employ Muslims, due to a combination of personal prejudice and pressure from the VHP.

For its part, the government ensures that Muslims are deprived of the most basic of amenities. Juhapura has a population of more than 300,000, with a large middle-class base. Yet it does not have a single bank, its former primary health centre was shifted to a Hindu area, and public bus routes now take a detour around the locality. Muslims constitute less than five per cent of the high-level officers in the state's police force, and even those officials who serve are shunted to marginal posts.

Yagnik points to how the two influential centres—the bureaucracy and local power structures—have been saffronised in the recent past. Muslims have been essentially ousted from local Panchayats, cooperatives, agrarian produce markets, government schemes and other services. There are more than 20 sub-communities among Muslims categorised as Other Backward Classes (OBCs) in Gujarat, but they face enormous difficulties in getting the required certificates that would make them eligible for various services. Again and again, it has been revealed how municipal action is deliberately used to communalise an issue so as to hurt and provoke Muslim sentiment, which is then used as a pretext for counter-violence. Recent instances of such provocation include the demolition of a dargah in Baroda in May, and the diversion of a sewage pipe towards a graveyard in Radhanpur in north Gujarat in August.

Schools have become sites for propagating hate, with social-science text-books tailored along 'Hindutva' lines. Even public examinations conducted by the state government are framed not to evaluate a student's competence, but to judge his or her political preferences vis-à-vis the Hindutva worldview. In early August this year, the Gujarat State Public Service Commission conducted an exam to recruit Ayurvedic medical officers. Among the questions asked: '"Christians have a right to convert"—who made such a claim?', 'Which day is observed as "Black Day" by minorities and "Victory Day" by the Sangh Parivar?', and 'Babar, who established the Muslim empire, was a devotee of whom?' (the options for this last were Krishna, Buddha, Shiva and Ram).

Some criticise those who see Gujarat as Armageddon, saying that there are enough traditional linkages among Hindus and Muslims, despite the strains since 2002. Some will point to the fact that a web of economic relationships still binds the two communities, and they will refer to how Muslims and Hindus interact in a variety of sectors, from firecracker-making to *rakhi*-weaving to vehicle repair, all of them monopolised by the Muslims. Muslims also make the kites that dot the Gujarati sky on the Hindu festival of Makar Sankranti in January. Sheikh Mohammed Yusuf, a kite-maker for the last 32 years, says that the communalisation has not turned away his Hindu customers. 'But that's because only Muslims make kites. Where will they go otherwise?' While there may be advantages in the economic necessity that has Hindus and Muslims at least nodding at each other, it is doubtful that the perfunctory transactions can act as a bridge in a society as divided as Gujarat has become.

Why here? Why Gujarat?

These instances of polarisation and discrimination are not mere aberrations, or restricted to pockets. The trend spreads across class and caste lines through the entire state, though it is relatively more intense in Ahmedabad, Panchmahal and Baroda, the core areas that shape Gujarat's political discourse. Certainly, there are Hindus who would prefer a society that is not so mired in conflict and mistrust. But what is important, as this reporter found in his travels through the state in early September, is that this voice is mute. It is the Hindu right that is setting the agenda for Gujarat; and amidst the extremism, the moderate who remains silent becomes irrelevant for his inability to guide events.

What led to such a situation? The Hinduisation of Gujarat has surprised many observers. After all, this is a region that had a pluralist culture; the people are driven largely by a mercantilist ethos; it did not undergo the troubled Partition experience as intensely as did some other states; and, despite being a border state, it does not have any special reason to harbour intense bitterness towards Pakistan, a fact that could have led to animosity towards Muslims within. Instead, the answer perhaps lies in its political evolution and economic competition.

If the state is now considered the lab of Hindutva, a century ago a British ethnographer is said to have termed the state the 'laboratory of Indian casteism'. After Gujarat became a state in 1960, carved out from the then state of Bombay, the Brahmins, Vanias and Patidars held sway over the political structure. This hegemony was broken in 1980 with the Congress's KHAM formula, which encompassed the Kshatriya, Harijan, Adivasi and Muslim. The erstwhile ruling castes retaliated, initially by instigating caste conflict. But they soon realised that the 'lower' castes could not be discarded, and thus began attempting to carve out a broader Hindu coalition where the 'enemy' would not be the Dalit, but the Muslim.

Sections of Dalits and Adivasis were slowly co-opted into the Hindutva-guided system, induced with promises of upward mobility and enhanced status, along with other political and economic dividends. The BJP also seemed like an attractive alternative to these groups because, despite voting for the Congress for five long decades, they had little to show in terms of improvement in livelihood. These developments in Gujarat took place at a time when the Hindutva forces were consolidating themselves at a pan-India level, through the late 1980s and 1990s.

Eventually, the significant organisational work put in by the Sangh Parivar in Gujarat over the previous two decades bore fruit, creating a political base for the BJP that spanned across all sections of society. 'While we were writing op-ed pieces and organising college protests against communalism, they were distributing millions of leaflets all over and building a base on the ground,' says an introspective Shabnam Hashmi, who runs ANHAD, an NGO that works to build communal harmony. The decline of textile mills, especially in Ahmedabad, destroyed common employment spaces shared by working-class Hindus and Muslims. These changes created an unemployed segment of society looking for a cause, and this provided the footsoldiers of the Hindutva movement.

There are some other specificities of Gujarati society that made the polarisation easier there than elsewhere. For example, the fact that Gujarati Hindus are publicly and obsessively vegetarian has helped to create a visible marker of difference between them and the local Muslim communities. This creates a social barrier in and of itself, and makes it possible for Hindutva outfits to capitalise on the matter of cow slaughter by Muslims. '100 percent vegetarian' restaurants crowd the market streets of Hindu Ahmedabad, and the very fact that Hindus and Muslims rarely dine together in restaurants drastically reduces the possibilities of social engagement.

While the chief agent of the polarisation was the Hindu middle class, it found its natural ally in the Non-Resident Gujarati. This group constitutes an extremely prosperous section of the Indian diaspora overseas, and flushes the RSS and its affiliates with enormous sums of money. Supporting this dynamic have been the various religious sects and preachers who crowd the spiritual market in Gujarat, as well as large and influential sections of the Gujarati-language press.

The trading culture of Gujarat might have created a pluralist, inclusive environment in the past, but the economic advantages of social cohesion seem to have been sacrificed at the altar of Hindutva. In fact, the relative affluence and stability of the economy is one reason why—based on Hindutva propaganda—a large section of the middle class veered towards religious chauvinism. The well-off had another reason to join the Hindutva bandwagon. They saw it as an opportunity to push their Muslim economic competitors into a corner with hate propaganda. Economics played a critical role during the pogrom in 2002, when those Hindus on the rampage were keen to destroy the property of some of their rivals.

It did not help that, unlike some others states of India, Gujarat does not have a tradition of left, Dalit or even progressive student movements—which not only provided space to the Hindutva campaign, but also ensured that there was no culture of protest. Muslims constitute around nine percent of the state's population, but have never had an effective political voice, as they do in Uttar Pradesh or Bihar—another reason why the Hindu right could so easily ride roughshod over their basic rights. The Congress party, since the 1970s and through the 1980s, had taken the easy way out to win the Muslim vote, by encouraging conservative elements among them; it also protected certain hardened criminals who happened to be Muslims. The Sangh Parivar cleverly used this as a pretext to convince the Hindus in Gujarat that minorities were being appeased at their cost. While Muslims were and are being targeted elsewhere in India as well, these factors have combined to create a rather unique situation in Gujarat.

One-man state

The critical state support for communal extremism following the rise of Narendra Modi, the fact that a large section of Hindu society harbours extremist notions about Muslims, and the absence of an effective political opposition to this discourse—each of these factors makes Gujarat stand out in the broader Indian context. Fortunately, the particular mix of societal factors that have made Gujarat 'another country', while they may exist in small areas elsewhere, do not come together at a statewide level anywhere else. Gujarat has gone into its extremist cocoon willingly and alone, and there is the hope and expectation that no other part of India will follow where Gujarat has gone.

The elevation of Modi as chief minister in late 2001 has everything to do with what Gujarat has become. He provided the match to the communal powder keg that the state had already become. Political psychologist Ashis Nandy (along with Achyut Yagnik) interviewed Modi in 1992, and Nandy has written about how he was left shaken by the experience. Emerging from the meeting, Nandy told Yagnik that Modi met all the criteria of an authoritarian personality, and was a clinical and classic case of a fascist. A decade later, that assessment proved correct, when Modi systematically engineered the carnage against Gujarat's Muslims.

Faced with the outrage that engulfed India after the Gujarat massacres, rather than take a defensive approach, Narendra Modi has aggressively introduced a potent mixture of Gujarati parochialism and Hindutva to cement his political foundations. His trick has been to construct a four-fold binary: of the insider versus outsider, Gujarat versus Delhi, Gujarati media versus English media, and Hindu versus the 'pseudo-secularist'. By using this matrix, any criticism can be easily deflected.

While manipulation of the mass mindset may have helped Modi turn vilification to advantage, in subsequent elections at the state and local levels the image of the Hindutva ogre is something he has decided he can do without at present. This is because Modi has his vision firmly set on the national BJP leadership, for which he has now to coin a new image for himself—that of a strong, anti-terrorism leader, focused on development and good governance. And this explains the recent brand-building exercise to portray Gujarat as the most developed state in the country. In fact, Gujarat has always been a relatively prosperous state, and for Modi to try to hog credit for the traditional achievements of an entrepreneurial class seems excessive. If anything, Modi can be faulted for not being able to build substantially upon this base.

Economists of varied hues have doubts about the idea of Gujarat as a new economic haven, yet another of Modi's propositions as he tries to reposition his image. Investment in the state is largely restricted to a few large players pumping in huge amounts of money in capital-intensive units, which have little trickle-down effect. Gujarat has missed out on the new economy, with a weak information-technology base and few of the outsourcing units that are all the rage in other successful states. In addition, the state's education system is in a rut, the crucial local co-operatives are riddled with scams and divisions, and the state is quickly slipping in terms of human development.

The idea of Modi as a good administrator, too, is a bogey that has its roots in his image as a strong leader. In interacting directly with the state's far-flung hierarchy, he has been accused of undercutting the authority of ministers and legislators alike. Modi can be ruthlessly efficient, but only when he wants to see results in his pet projects. 'His is the efficiency of the emergency era. This fear-induced work culture is not sustainable, because it is weakening public institutions. Gujarat has become a one-man state,' says Javed Chowdhury, a former bureaucrat of the Gujarat cadre. The 'good management' myth was severely bruised with the late-August floods in Surat, which were entirely due to faulty dam-water management by the state administration.

What Modi's dictatorial style of functioning has done is to create massive dissension within his own party, as well as in the broader Hindutva *parivar*. But while that might somewhat upset Modi's political trajectory, it has had little impact on Gujarat's communalism. The dissidents are more radically 'Hindu'

235

than even Modi. Their differences with him are about power and patronage, not about Hindutva.

One of the reasons the Gujarati political discourse has been so completely captured by the saffron agenda is the abject political and ideological surrender of the Congress party. Flirting with a variety of 'soft Hindutva' itself, the party's Gujarat unit has decided not to take on Modi's fascist state directly. Congress workers, after all, were also part of the marauding mobs in 2002, and even today the party refuses to take up issues of discrimination against Muslims publicly. This has left Muslims despondent, but they have little choice. Usmanbhai Sheikh, a Muslim activist in Ahmedabad, explains: 'Congress treats us like its mistress, knowing we cannot turn elsewhere.'

But the Modi government is not invincible. If the Congress is able to put together a proactive, secular agenda, and consolidate an alliance between Dalits, Adivasis and Muslims, it has a good chance of ousting the chief minister and his party, and of reversing his divisive agenda. At the peak of polarisation during the 2002 assembly elections, after all, more than 50 per cent of the population voted against Modi—a figure that would have to have included a substantial number of Hindus. A change in Gujarat's government would come as some relief, for the state would not be as active in engineering everyday hatred. But even if the state unit of the Congress party was to muster the energy to take on Modi, it is doubtful that this alone would help to restore a social fabric that has been left in tatters. The communalism in Gujarat has not only become deeply entrenched, it has become bolted to the plank of fascism. Politics-as-usual can hardly be the panacea; what is needed is a social movement for Gujarat to cleanse itself.

Modified society

It is early September. Baroda is tense. Its Muslims are scared. It is the last day of the Ganesh festival, when Hindus will take part in large processions before immersing their idols. Trouble is anticipated. Only four months ago, the demolition of a dargah triggered riots here. Security has been beefed up across the city—the state government does not want another blemish on its record, at least not now.

Yusuf Sheikh is sitting in his house in Tandalja, also derisively called 'mini Pakistan' by local Hindus, because of its Muslim majority. Worried about what might happen, he explains the undercurrent of tension: 'If Muslims are out in these areas where processions are being taken out, there is a high possibility that a VHP person will throw a stone at some idol, and blame it on us. Muslims will then be called the instigators and there will be riots.' The city's Muslims have shut their shops, stocked up on supplies and huddled inside their homes.

Sheikh is a ground-level political activist in Baroda. An officer of the central government's Intelligence Bureau, based in Baroda, pays him a visit to get a sense of the Muslim mood. Sheikh's request to him is to keep an eye on the younger elements in the Ganesh processions. The intelligence official is fairly confident that no incident would occur today. 'The state government is determined not to allow violence,' he says. The government's decision could have to do with the fact that, with no elections around the corner, and Modi seeking to forge a new image for himself, allowing a riot would not be politically astute. On the broader communal situation, the officer has a 'realistic' take: 'It is ok. See, in UP, Mulayam Yadav supports Muslims, and so Hindutva-wallahs have no say. Here it is Hindu rule, so it is the Muslims who are down.'

'Afraid' might better capture the sentiment of Muslims, for the Hindus in Baroda do not seem to be merely celebrating a religious festival. Trucks and minivans carry huge idols, followed by hordes of people. Blaring music resonates from all corners, and those gathered dance aggressively to the tunes of hit Bollywood composer Himesh Reshammiya. That in itself would be the nature of a Hindu festival anywhere else in India. But here, the saffron flags seamlessly merge with the Indian tricolour. Harshad, an ecstatic-looking 18-year-old, explains: 'We are Hindus. And Hindus are Indians. In our festivals, you will see the Indian flag also.'

In Baroda in Modi's Gujarat, the Ganesh festival is treated—and exploited—not as a cultural but as a nationalist event. Those excluded accept their status quietly. Silence and deserted streets greet an observer in Muslim areas of the city. Here, there is a curfew-like atmosphere. A few local elders stand outside to ensure that no trouble ensues, while state police guard the city's invisible borders. But while the day of Ganesh might be one when insecurity among Gujarati Muslims comes forth most visibly, they remain fearful, helpless and alienated throughout the year. *We don't have anyone. This is not our government. Who do we turn to?*

But this is not a saga only of victimhood. When a community is pushed into a corner, there are bound to be consequences. Frustrated youngsters will inevitably react one way or the other. The easiest is to leave the state, but that would entail entering as a member of an underclass in an alien society in another Indian state, and few of the poorly skilled, poorly educated Muslim youth would venture forth under such circumstances. Much more likely is that some will take matters into their own hands, to fight the oppression that is an all-pervading reality, or follow the siren call of militant leaders. Where will Narendra Modi be to take the blame when the exclusion of yesterday and today invites the conflagration of tomorrow?

The response of the richer Muslims, who also have nowhere else to turn, has been to try and strike up a deal with the state government. Those belonging to the Bohra and Khoja communities, for example, are trying to see whether they can run their businesses unhindered in return for offering their political support to Modi. But the most positive response would seem to be an emphasis on mainstream, modern education among Muslims as a means to responding to the Modi challenge. Indeed, Muslims across class and sectarian lines have turned to education as a passport to a self-confident future. 'There is a realisation that we must have more skills and make ourselves more useful. That is the only way out,' says M T Kazi of the F D Education Society.

The Gujarati Muslim is realising the importance of education, of learning the language of rights, of asserting his or her presence in the marketplace. But there will remain the question of whether the larger 'Modi-fied' society is willing to accommodate this pool of people when it is ready. And that is why there has been another simultaneous trend in the opposing direction, marked by the increase in the influence of conservative Muslim organisations. 'They are all going into the laps of mullahs. Imagine what will happen if all these people get radicalised,' says Mahesh Langa, an Ahmedabad journalist worried about the end result of what Modi and his ilk have wrought. The continued persecution, direct and indirect, makes it fairly easy for these outfits to expand their influence among Muslims.

When this reporter, with his longish beard, walked into an elite government colony in Ahmedabad to meet a senior official, three children suddenly got off their bicycles. One screamed aloud, 'Terrorist!' *Why?* 'Because you are a Mussalman,' he responded. *So?* 'All Muslims are terrorists. My father is a judge. He will call you terrorist in court.' *Really?* 'Yes. Now get out of here. This is a Hindu area!' Sauyajya is 12 years old and has not met a single Muslim in his life. No one knows how many Sauyajyas are in the making in Gujarat.

Chapter 15

Reframing the 'Burma question'
Himal, February 2007

Thant Myint-U

Over the monsoon of 1946, as the contest between the Congress party and the Muslim League was determining the fate of the Subcontinent, a very different fortune for colonial India's erstwhile province of Burma was also being framed. A little more than four years earlier, the Fifteenth Imperial Army of General Shojiro Iida had driven the British out of Burma, turning the country into a gigantic battlefield in a vicious fight that led to the complete destruction of nearly every city and town. The radical nationalist fighters under Aung San had first collaborated with the Japanese, and then in the spring of 1945 turned against their mentors, Aung San declaring himself an Allied commander and head of a provisional government.

The returning British at first chose to sideline Aung San, planning for a long period of reconstruction, elections and gradual transfer of power. But Aung San upped the pressure, attracting huge crowds of supporters and quietly threatening a mass uprising. Jawaharlal Nehru insisted that the Indian Army would not be available to quell a Burmese revolt; and the British, their hands full with Palestine and India, decided that the prudent thing to do was to quit Burma.

And so they did, in January 1948. But six months beforehand, Aung San, together with most of his cabinet, had been gunned down in a still-mysterious terrorist attack. The most senior Burmese in the Indian Civil Service, U Tin Tut, a King's Commissioned Officer and slated to head the new Burma Army, would soon be killed as well, by unknown assailants. Even worse, the country's leading communists—including many of the brightest and most capable of their generation—had gone underground and were plotting rebellion. By the time the last of the Yorkshire Light Infantry had sailed away from Rangoon harbour to the tune of 'Auld Lang Syne', Burma was already at civil war—a war that has continued without interruption to this very day, the longest-running armed conflict in the world.

For months, the infant Burmese government, under Aung San's friend and colleague U Nu, battled against an array of communist insurgencies, at first depending on the loyalty of ethnic Karen and Kachin battalions, trained by the British and now merged with the Japanese-trained battalions of Aung San's partisan force. Slowly, however, the army began to splinter. New militia and bandit gangs overran the Irrawaddy Valley. Meanwhile, the Karen, seeking their own state within the Commonwealth, split from the Burma Army and raised their own flag of rebellion. In early 1949, the Karens and the communists jointly occupied Mandalay. The soldiers of U Nu's government, led by General Ne Win, fought to hold the frontline just outside Rangoon. Over the next few years, the fighting would only intensify, but with a new inter-ethnic element, adding to the immense destruction already wrought by the Second World War.

Today, sixty years later, there is a belief among many that the 'Burma problem' is something new. The anti-government demonstrations of 1988, crushed with great brutality; the failure of the military government to respect the results of the 1990 elections; the rise of Aung San Suu Kyi as leader of the opposition—all of these frame a seemingly straightforward picture of 'democracy vs tyranny' and 'progressive change vs intransigence'. For many, the problem of Burma is the problem of the present military government and that government's failure to move towards meaningful democratic reform. There is a sense that all would be well if only the military would step aside, and to make this happen many advocate sanctions, boycotts and long-distance condemnation as a way of pressuring the Burmese generals to see the error of their ways. But all this is based on a singularly ahistorical understanding of Burma's present predicament, of the country's poverty, war and dictatorship. To be more mindful of the country's past is the first step in knowing better how to help Burma today.

The old kingdom

There is no doubting that the Burmese military governments are much to blame. That blame runs deep—not just to the past ten or 15 years but to the very beginnings of army rule in 1962, and perhaps even further back to the corrosive role of militant nationalism during the country's emergence from colonial rule in the 1940s. But we must begin at an even earlier date: 1885, the end of the old kingdom.

It was in 1885 that Lord Randolph Churchill, secretary of state for India, decided that the kingdom of Burma would be annexed to the British Indian Empire. His hope was for a speedy colonial victory, one that would bolster chances for his Conservative Party in the general elections that November. The expeditionary force under Sir Harry Prendergast reached Mandalay with little opposition and immediately exiled King Thibaw to Madras, and then to Ratnagiri on the Konkan Coast. But soon, unexpectedly, a determined guerrilla campaign emerged to fight the British occupation. To crush this would require a further 40,000 British and Indian troops, summary executions and the large-scale forced displacement of entire communities. By the end of it all, in the early 1890s, Burmese society had been turned upside down. The old social structure, one that had evolved in the Irrawaddy Valley over centuries, was no more. Burma, more than any other part of the British Empire in Asia, would enter the 20th century with an abrupt, traumatic rupture with the past.

The Burmese were left with other problematic colonial legacies. With the old order destroyed, the British imported nearly wholesale the governing institutions of the rest of British India, entirely alien to the Burmese experience and political culture. A massive flood of people from all parts of the Subcontinent then entered the country in the wake of the occupation. Immigration on a large scale is bound to have its difficulties in any country; but to have this happen under colonial domination led to a bottling up of tensions that, by the 1920s, spilled over into violence. The hill regions of Burma, inhabited by minority peoples and comprising about a third of the country's population, were deliberately kept apart by British policy—something that would have dire consequences for the future. Then the British withdrew almost as quickly as they had come, after only some 60-odd years. Colonialism dismantled Burmese tradition but left behind only the most fragile of institutions for the new, post-independence leadership.

It was into this vacuum that the Burmese army stepped. In the 1940s the army was down to a couple of thousand men, including the Japanese-trained officers of Gen Ne Win's own Fourth Burma Rifles. They fought back the insurgents and reclaimed territory, all the while expanding, purchasing new arms from abroad, learning lessons, becoming more professional and, in many places, forming the de facto administration. There were setbacks, and there was foreign interference. The US, for example, supported remnants of Chiang Kai-Shek's nationalist armies as they retreated into eastern Burma and established opium-producing sanctuaries. Thailand long supported the Karen fighters along its border. And Beijing, in the late 1960s, all but invaded Burma in order to claim a vast swathe of territory for its protégés in the Burma Communist Party. Slowly, however, the Burmese army prevailed, mounting new and ever more brutal counter-insurgency campaigns, and becoming for all purposes a shadow government. In 1962, it was easily able to overthrow U Nu's elected government.

Village Burma

Gen Ne Win and his Revolutionary Council then did three things that would be disastrous for Burma in the modern period. First, like Idi Amin a few years later, he expelled hundreds of thousands of ethnic Indians, including many whose families had lived and worked in Burma for generations. They left with little more than the shirts on their backs. For better or worse, under colonial rule, ethnic Indians had come to dominate nearly all modern and urban occupations, from factory work to the professions to big business. The British had overturned the old royal and aristocratic elites, and then they themselves departed. Now the urban Indian classes were expelled. There would be little left besides village Burma.

Second, Gen Ne Win imposed a pure military dictatorship, which step by step dismantled or undermined all other state capacities. Hundreds of well-trained senior bureaucrats were promptly dismissed, and the Burma Civil Service was undone. Whereas in many other military regimes in Asia army officers preside over other state institutions, in Burma the army became the state. As a result, all else began to wither away.

Third and most disastrously, Gen Ne Win nationalised all major businesses and then isolated the country from the rest of the world. Foreign investment was banned, as was nearly all trade. Tourism was stopped, and for more than a decade no one was allowed to visit the country. Aid programmes were halted and foreign advisors sent home. Burmese citizens were not allowed to travel and few could study abroad. A series of catastrophic economic decisions were made, and Burma's economy quickly entered a downward spiral. Within this cocoon, the Burmese army was able to evolve and grow and to fight insurgencies the way it wanted. Isolation became the army's default and happiest state.

What does all this mean for Burma today? By 1988, when tens of thousands took to the streets to demand an end to army rule, a quarter-century of Ne Win's policies, coming on top of two decades more of war and a peculiarly difficult colonial legacy, had already brought Burmese society to its knees. A whole generation had grown up with little contact with the outside world—Burma had evolved as a strange, parochial society, which knew little other than dictatorship and economic mismanagement. But the people nevertheless knew that things could be better. Even in the army there was a new generation that hoped to join the ranks of Asia's now fast-growing economies, but it did not have a clear idea of how to get there.

In March 1989, there was a dramatic new development in the hills: the Burma Communist Party, in armed revolt since 1948, collapsed as a result of an internal mutiny. The Burmese army quickly agreed to ceasefires with successor militia and then persuaded or pressured many of the other insurgencies to agree to ceasefires as well. For the first time in more than half a century, the guns went silent in many parts of the country.

There seemed to be an opening that allowed for something new. Nearly everyone wanted an end to the complicated, multi-front civil war. Nearly everyone wanted an opening-up to the rest of the world and economic development. In the early 1990s, the government reformed aspects of economic policy and made possible foreign investment and private trade, for the first time since 1962. But the tragedy of recent Burmese history is that this opportunity for a new beginning is being squandered for want of agreement on the country's political future. For the army, an end to the civil war and economic development must precede any political change, which it sees at most as a slow and gradual process that will take place on its own terms. For others, 'regime change' and 'democracy' are paramount and must come first.

In the West, activists have successfully campaigned for trade and investment sanctions and boycotts. But to try to further isolate one of the most isolated countries in the world, whose poverty, repression, ethnic conflict and political violence are in many ways fuelled or made possible by decades of self-imposed seclusion, would be immensely counter-productive. What is needed instead is a fresh approach that takes into account Burma's long history of problems, and seeks not a magic bullet that will transform the country into a prosperous democracy, but some realistic first steps that can break the pernicious cycle of recent years. Progress should be sought across the range of issues—humanitarian, development, political and human rights—ideally in cooperation with the United Nations.

To realistically address Burma's problems, it will not do to place democratic change exclusively at the core of the agenda. Such placement of democratic change at the very centre of focus tends to sideline the necessity for a just and sustainable end to 60 years of armed conflict. It also marginalises the urgent need to get the Burmese economy on track, to invest in basic needs such as health care and education, and to meet the serious humanitarian challenges now emerging. All of these matters, including the building of democratic values and institutions, are linked and should be made to progress together. With development and an end to the civil war, real options for democratic change will rapidly emerge.

It is important that the Burmese authorities be convinced that change is not a zero-sum game, that progress on all fronts is possible and desirable, and that the United Nations will help the country through the transition. This will require patient and creative diplomacy, and not just long-distance censure, from all concerned.

Chapter 16

The beauty of compromise

Himal, February 2008

Ramachandra Guha

> *The fundamental principle that governs—or ought to govern—human affairs, if we wish to avoid misunderstandings, conflicts, or pointless utopias, is negotiation.*
>
> — *Umberto Eco*

Over the past few decades, the nation states of Southasia have been home to some of the most bitter and costly conflicts of the modern world. Subaltern classes have resisted the hegemony of the elite; areas on the periphery have protested exploitation by the centre. To class and geography have been added the fault lines of language, caste, religion and ethnicity.

No region of the world—not even the fabled Balkans—has witnessed a greater variety of conflicts. Southasians are an expressive people, and so they have expressed their myriad resentments in a diversity of ways: through electing legislators of their choosing; through court petitions and other legal mechanisms; through marches, *gheraos*, *dharnas*, hunger strikes and other forms of non-violent protest; through the torching of government buildings; and through outright armed rebellion.

The record of our nation states in dealing with these conflicts is decidedly mixed. Some conflicts, which once threatened to tear nations apart, have been, in the end, resolved. Other conflicts have persisted for decades, with the animosities between the contending parties deepening with every passing year.

From this vast repertoire of experience within Southasia, this essay will foreground some of the more intractable of these conflicts: among others, the Kashmir dispute and the Naga insurgency in India, and the rebellion of the Tamils in Sri Lanka. These conflicts have persisted for so long because of the inflexibility and, dare it be said, the dogmatism of the contending parties. The question to ask is: Would a middle path of accommodation and reconciliation, adopted by either party to a conflict or both, have helped in reducing or mitigating the violence and the suffering?

In search of an answer, let me first turn to some forgotten episodes in the career of a man who might be considered the paradigmatic Southasian, Jayaprakash Narayan, or 'J P'. He was an Indian patriot, but he retained close links with the republican struggle in Nepal, as well as the socialist movement in Sri Lanka. He worked actively for conciliation between India and Pakistan, and was also an early supporter of the Tibetan people and their cause. Thirty years after his death, J P must be remembered for his idealism and activism, which continues to hold meaning for peace and progress in Southasia.

Missed opportunities

Within India, J P is celebrated for his role in two major movements: the Quit India struggle of 1942, and the 'Indira Hatao' movement of 1974–75. During Quit India, J P achieved countrywide renown for his daring escape from Hazaribagh jail, after which he spent more than a year underground, eluding the colonial police. The movement of 1974–75 was, of course, led and directed by him. Starting in his native Bihar, it soon became an all-India struggle against the corrupt and tyrannical regime of Prime Minister Indira Gandhi.

Both the upheavals saw J P in an uncompromising mode. In 1942, he was a charismatic young leftist, who sought to throw the British out and rebuild India on socialist lines. In 1974–75, he was a charismatic old radical, who sought to throw Indira Gandhi out in the process of bringing about a 'Total Revolution' in India. While in India today J P is remembered for his anti-colonial and Total Revolution campaigns of the 1940s and 1970s, what has been quite forgotten is his equally interesting and, in my view, even more noble work during the 1960s, when he tried heroically—if, in the end, unavailingly—to resolve the two civil conflicts that have plagued the Indian nation state since its inception. At either end of the Himalaya, these were the Kashmir and Nagaland conflicts.

Let's begin with Kashmir. Among the politicians and social workers of mainland India, J P spoke out longest and loudest against the illegalities of the Union government in Kashmir. He was a close friend of the popular Kashmiri leader Sheikh Abdullah, who was jailed by the Indian government in 1953. J P called repeatedly for the release of Sheikh Abdullah, and when the sheikh was finally set free, in April 1964, encouraged the idea of sending him over to Pakistan as an emissary for peace. This was originally a proposal of Prime Minister Jawaharlal Nehru, and it was opposed across the political spectrum, from the Jana Sangh on the right to the communists on the left. Even the majority in Nehru's own Congress party thought that the sheikh should not have been released.

Bucking the jingoist trend, two men of conspicuous independence supported Nehru's idea, despite being, on other matters, fierce critics of the prime minister's policies. One was C Rajagopalachari, the first Indian governor-general of India; the other, Jayaprakash Narayan. When some cabinet ministers threatened to put Sheikh Abdullah back in jail, J P wrote, 'it is remarkable how the freedom fighters of yesterday begin so easily to imitate the language of the imperialists.'

Nehru died in May 1964; the peace initiative died with him. The next year, Sheikh Abdullah was put behind bars once again. In June 1966, J P wrote an extraordinary letter to Prime Minister Indira Gandhi, asking that the sheikh be freed in time for the next elections. '[To] hold a general election in Kashmir with Sheikh Abdullah in prison,' remarked J P, 'is like the British ordering an election in India while Jawaharlal Nehru was in prison. No fair-minded person would call it a fair election.' If 'we miss the chance of using the next general election to win the consent of the [Kashmiri] people to their place within the Union,' continued J P,

> I cannot see what other device will be left to India to settle the problem. To think that we will eventually wear down the people and force them to accept at least passively the Union is to delude ourselves. That might conceivably have happened had Kashmir not been geographically located where it is. In its present location, and with seething discontent among the people, it would never be left in peace by Pakistan.

This letter received a brief, non-committal reply from Mrs Gandhi. It took another eight years for her to allow the sheikh to re-enter politics. When Sheikh Abdullah was made chief minister of Jammu & Kashmir, in February 1975, J P welcomed the move—despite being, by then, a bitter opponent of

Mrs Gandhi. But the concession itself was perhaps eight years too late. For by then the sheikh had become reconciled to subservience to New Delhi, and in time was to place the interests of his own family above those of the Kashmiri people. What might have been the fate of Kashmir and the Kashmiris, had Mrs Gandhi listened to J P in June 1966—by releasing Sheikh Abdullah, allowing him to contest a free-and-fair election that he would certainly have won, and then letting him run the administration in the best interests of the people themselves...

The uncompromising west

Let me now move away from India, and J P, to a civil conflict in a Southasian neighbour. In 1966, the rulers in New Delhi were too nervous to allow Sheikh Abdullah to conduct a provincial election in Kashmir. Three years later, the rulers in Islamabad permitted a radical Bengali politician to contest a national election. To their great surprise, and shock, his party won a majority. What were they to do now?

The east of Pakistan had begun to be distanced from the west from the very beginning. On his first visit to Dhaka, the governor-general of Pakistan, Mohammed Ali Jinnah, told his Bengali audience that they would have to take to Urdu sooner rather than later, because 'the state language of Pakistan is going to be Urdu and no other language. Anyone who tries to mislead you is really the enemy of Pakistan.' Jinnah was already dead in 1952, when bloody riots broke out in Dhaka after the police fired on a demonstration of students demanding equal status for the Bengali language. In 1954, this was indeed recognised as one of the state languages of Pakistan, but the feelings of being discriminated against persisted, fuelled by imbalance in the share of government revenue, in the army and civil service, and even the national cricket team.

Pakistan was under military rule between 1958 and 1970. Towards the end of 1970, General Yahya Khan called for elections. Apparently, he had expected the ambitious politician from Sindh, Zulfiqar Ali Bhutto, to become prime minister, allowing him to continue as president. But these calculations went awry. The Awami League, led by Sheikh Mujibur Rahman, won 167 out of 169 seats in the more populous East Pakistan. Playing on the sense of discrimination, Sheikh Mujib's party achieved a majority in the national Parliament.

The Awami League's platform included a federal constitution, in which each wing would manage its social, political and economic affairs, with only defence and foreign relations in the hands of the Centre. Keeping in mind the significant revenue from jute exports, the Awami League also proposed that each wing would get to spend the foreign exchange it earned. The proposals to reform the Constitution were deemed unacceptable by the generals and politicians of West Pakistan. It seemed as though the self-proclaimed martial Punjabi could not abide the thought of conceding power to the allegedly effete Bengali. Another reason for spurning Sheikh Mujib was the large presence of Hindus in the professional classes of East Pakistan. As one general put it, if the Awami League came to power, 'the constitution adopted by them will have Hindu iron hand in it.'

Rather than honour the democratic mandate and invite Sheikh Mujib to take office, Yahya Khan postponed the convening of the National Assembly, and in this he was encouraged and abetted by Bhutto. The response was a general strike in all of East Pakistan, and the Pakistan Army decided to settle the matter by force of arms. But with India choosing to ally with the Bengali dissidents, the task was made much harder than the general had anticipated. Eight months of episodic fighting culminated in an all-out war in December 1971, which led to the defeat and dismemberment of Pakistan.

Would Pakistan have remained a single nation state if Yahya and Bhutto had permitted Mujib to take over as prime minister? In asking this question, I certainly do not mean to turn back the clock, or to suggest that the creation of Bangladesh was a mistake. I mean only to highlight how the techniques of suppression, so often used by a state to settle an outstanding conflict, tend mostly to intensify and deepen it. The ruling elite of Pakistan was both obdurate and deaf: obdurate in hanging on to its privileges, deaf to the justice of the demands of those who asked merely for their rights as citizens. In this respect, the break-up of Pakistan holds lessons for the political elite in other countries of Southasia— not least Bangladesh itself—that are challenged by social and political divisions within their boundaries.

Linguistic anxiety

As it happens, the language problem is one issue that the Republic of India has been able to more or less successfully resolve. Back in the 1920s, Mohandas K Gandhi and the Congress party had promised that, when India became independent, each major linguistic group would have its own province. But, after 1947, the Congress leaders went back on that pledge. India had just been divided on the basis of religion; would not conceding the linguistic demand lead to a further fracturing? However, in 1952, a protest fast by an Andhra Congressman forced New Delhi to agree to the creation of the Telugu-speaking state of Andhra Pradesh. Other linguistic groups then intensified their claims for states of their own. A States Reorganisation Commission was constituted, which in 1956 recommended that the map of India be redrawn to accommodate these demands.

Now, five decades later, it is possible to deem the creation of linguistic states a relative success, despite the occasional hiccup. Once the fear of the eclipse or subjugation of one's language was allayed, the different linguistic groups have been content to live as part of the larger nation called India. There have been periodic manifesations of chauvinism, as in calls for preferential employment for speakers of the local language, but these protests have not in any way threatened the unity of the country.

The experience of Sri Lanka went in the other direction. In 1956, the year the states of India were reorganised on the basis of language, the Parliament of what was then Ceylon introduced an act recognising Sinhala as the sole official language of the country. Sinhala was made the medium of instruction in all government schools and colleges, in public examinations and in the courts. The new act was opposed by the Tamil-speaking minority concentrated in the north of the island. 'When you deny me my language, you deny me everything,' stated one Tamil MP. 'You are hoping for a divided Ceylon,' warned another. An opposition member, himself Sinhala-speaking, predicted that if the government did not change its mind, and insisted on the act being adopted, 'two torn little bleeding states might yet arise out of one little state.'

The protests were disregarded. The insecurity of the Tamils was intensified by the Colombo riots of 1958. In 1972, Sinhala was confirmed as the official language of the state, and for good measure Buddhism was added as the official religion. The interests of non-Sinhala speakers were ignored, and the sentiments of Hindus, Muslims and Christians hurt grievously. The Tamil youth became disenchanted by the incremental, parliamentary methods of their elders. During the 1970s, several paramilitary groups were formed, known by their acronyms—EROS, PLOTE, ERPLF and, not least, LTTE.

Many Tamils still kept their faith in the spirit of compromise. However, two events in the early 1980s decidedly put down hopes of a peaceful, democratic reconciliation of the linguistic question. The first was the burning, by the Sri Lankan Army, of the great Tamil library in Jaffna in 1981; the second, the anti-Tamil Colombo pogrom of 1983, directed by Sinhalese politicians. The Tamils increasingly took to armed struggle to meet their ends. And so unfolded a quarter century of a civil war that cost tens of thousand of lives and deeply undermined the economic and social development of Sri Lanka.

The Northeast's J P

Now we will return from Pakistan and Sri Lanka back to India. During the 1960s, Jayaprakash Narayan was concerned not only with an honourable solution in Kashmir, but with the restoration of peace in Nagaland. This too had been a most troubled part of the Indian Union. In 1946, a Naga National Council (NNC) had been formed, which was undecided as to whether to join the soon-to-be-free India. During the early 1950s, one faction decided to make a compact with New Delhi. The other faction, led by A Z Phizo, held out for an independent Naga state. This was not acceptable to India; as a consequence, an armed conflict broke out in the Naga hills, between the Indian Army and Phizo's guerrillas. As ever, the main casualties in the conflict were the communities caught in the middle.

In 1964, after a long decade of civil war, a ceasefire was declared between the NNC and the Indian government. A three-member 'peace mission' was formed, consisting of the Anglican missionary Michael Scott, the Gandhian nationalist B P Chaliha and Jayaprakash Narayan. Sadly, the mission collapsed within a year, due to inflexibility on both sides, and the rebels returned to the jungle. It was at this time that J P wrote an extraordinary if still little-known booklet in Hindi, based on a speech he delivered in Patna on Martyrs Day, 30 January 1965. The booklet is titled *Nagaland mein shanti ka prayas* (The attempt to forge peace in Nagaland). While ostensibly about a dispute within a single small state of the Union, the document is actually a meditation on the meanings of democracy everywhere.

'In the history of every nation,' began J P, 'there have been disagreements among the servants and leaders of the nation. Where democracy prevails, these disagreements are discussed and resolved by democratic means; but where democracy is absent, they are resolved by the use of violence.' However, history teaches us that violence begets counter-violence and, eventually, violence against one's own comrades. Thus, 'when disputes arise, past alliances and friendships are forgotten, and allegations of betrayal, traitorous behaviour, etc are levied on one's opponents.'

J P proceeded to recount the history of the civil war in Nagaland—the recourse to the gun of one side, the reaction of the other, and the brutalities committed by both. Then, in the spirit of his master, Gandhi, he asked each party to recognise and respect the finest traditions of the other. First, he told the Nagas that, among the nations of Asia, India was unusual in having a democratic and federal Constitution. Were the rebels to abandon the dream of independence and settle for autonomy within the Union, the only control they would have had to give up was over the army, foreign affairs and currency. In all other respects, they would have been free to mould their destinies as they pleased.

Narayan recognised the distinctiveness of Naga cultural traditions. While both East and West Pakistan bore the impress of the Indic civilisation, 'what we call Indian culture has not made an entry into Nagaland.' That said, J P thought that the Nagas could not sustain an independent country, what with China, Pakistan and Burma all close by and casting covetous eyes on their territory. Why not join up, therefore, with a democratic and federal India? When New Delhi could not dominate Bihar or Bengal, J P asked rhetorically, how could it dominate Nagaland? If the rebels were to come aboveground and contest elections, said Narayan, they could give their people the best schools, hospitals, roads and so on.

Towards the end of his lecture, J P turned to educating his Patna audience about the virtues of the Nagas. He was particularly impressed by the vigour of the Naga village councils. Anywhere else in India, he said, to construct an airport the 'government can uproot village upon village,' whereas in Nagaland this could never be done without the consent of the local people. He was even more struck by the dignity of labour, and the absence of caste feeling. In matters of cooperative behaviour, said J P, the Nagas could teach a thing or two to the people of India. He gave the example of a magnificent church that had been recently constructed in a village near the town of Mokokchung: with a seating capacity of five thousand, it had been built entirely with local material and local labour, much of it contributed voluntarily by graduates and post-graduates. J P contrasted this with the contempt for manual work among the educated, upper-caste elite of the Indian heartland.

Pride and prestige

The conflicts of Kashmir and Nagaland had their origins in an inflexible state, but were often exacerbated by recalcitrant rebels. If conflicts are to be successfully resolved, then they require the state to be flexible, as well as the rebels to be more accommodating. That, certainly, is the lesson to be learnt from the most successful peace negotiations of contemporary times, that which led to the demise of apartheid and the birth of a democratic South Africa. Had President F W de Klerk and his National Party not begun a dialogue with the African National Congress, and had Nelson Mandela and his comrades not turned their backs on the gun, there might yet be a civil conflict raging in that country.

One notable aspect of the transition in South Africa was that the reconciliation was racial as well as political. The whites handed over power, but did not relinquish their rights as citizens or professionals. The need for black economic advancement was recognised, but it was not pursued in wanton haste. The comparison with neighbouring Zimbabwe is striking. There, the end of settler colonialism was followed by savage retribution, with the whites forcibly dispossessed of their lands and coerced to leave the country. What was once the breadbasket of Africa has become a basket case.

Looking over to Europe, Southasians can also take instruction from the political transition that took place after the fall of the Berlin Wall. Once run with an iron hand from Moscow, countries such as Poland, Hungary and the Czech Republic have emerged as vigorous democracies. After the hold of the Soviets was loosened—largely through the voluntary abdication initiated by the visionary Mikhail Gorbachev—the different sections of Polish, Hungarian and Czech society eschewed the politics of revenge and retribution. Instead of turning on one another, communists and anti-communists formed political parties of their own and fought elections based on universal adult franchise. Autocrats became democrats, while rebels became governors (most famously, Lech Walesa and Vaclav Havel). Who, in 1960, or even in 1980, would have imagined a transition as painless and productive?

One might also profit from a look at the recent history of Ireland. After the Good Friday agreement of 10 April 1998, the members of the previously militant Sinn Fein put away their guns and entered the democratic process. The two parts of the island remain under separate sovereignties; but the ceasefire has permitted a deeper engagement with the democratic process within the Republic of Ireland as well as Ulster, a free movement of people across the border, and a sharp diminution of sectarian violence. These changes have led to a surge in economic growth, with investments pouring into an island always legendary for its natural beauty, known also for its rule-bound and largely peaceful society. While it took some time to arrive at a compromise, in ultimately forging it the two sides to the Irish conflict gave up pride and prestige, to gain, in exchange, prosperity and peace.

Dam compromise

To return to Southasia, and to move on from political conflicts to social ones, consider the controversy over the Sardar Sarovar dam in central India. The benefits of this project flow wholly to one state, Gujarat, whereas the costs are borne disproportionately by another state, Madhya Pradesh. When it is built to its full height, the dam will displace close to 200,000 people, a majority of them Adivasi. From 1989, the oustees have been organised under the banner of the Narmada Bachao Andolan (NBA), whose leader is the remarkable Medha Patkar.

Between 1989 and 1995, the NBA organised a series of *satyagrahas* to stop construction of the dam. Their struggle won wide appreciation, both for its principled commitment to non-violence and for its ability to mobilise peasants and Adivasis. By now, several scientific studies had been published calling into question the viability of large dams. These studies adduced environmental arguments, such as the submergence of scarce forests and wildlife; economic arguments, such as the fact that sedimentation rates and soil salinity had greatly diminished the financial returns from such projects; and social arguments, namely the utter despair and demoralisation of the communities that the dams render homeless.

The struggle and the science notwithstanding, the construction of the Sardar Sarovar dam proceeded. In 1995, a group of engineers based in Pune advocated a compromise solution. Given that the dam had already come up to a height of about 260 feet, clearly it could not be stopped. But its negative effects could be minimised. The Pune engineers were proposing a model of a dam smaller than that originally envisaged. The reduction in height would greatly reduce the area to be submerged, yet retain much of the benefits that were to accrue in power and irrigation. The drought-prone regions of Kutch and Saurashtra would still get water, while fewer communities would be displaced in the upper catchment.

The compromise formula was rejected both by the Gujarat government and the NBA. The former insisted that the dam had to be built to its originally sanctioned height of 456 feet. The latter insisted that the dam must never be built. The Andolan was continuing with the rallying cry, '*Kohi nahi hatega! Baandh nahin banega!*' (No one will leave their homes! The dam will not be built!), even as the construction and displacement continued. A part of the dam was already complete, thousands of tonnes of concrete had already been poured, and no one really expected a reversal of this. On the part of the state establishment, there was not a hint of its willingness to consider a reduction in the dam height.

In retrospect, it is unfortunate that the NBA did not accept the lowered-height proposal. Had the Andolan advocated this alternative energetically, it is just possible that public opinion would have veered more strongly in their favour. The Supreme Court, before whom an appeal was pending, might have given a more favourable verdict. Confronted with the stark alternative of continuing with dam construction as planned and putting an end to the project, it was expected that the court would be inclined to the former course, for many thousands of crores of public money had already been spent on the project. If the court had been adequately alerted to the compromise solution, which would still bring water to the most deprived parts of Gujarat, while minimising the suffering of the displaced, they might have been persuaded towards reducing the height of the dam. In the event of the NBA's unwillingness to consider compromise, the dam construction now proceeds as planned. In all likelihood the submergence will be complete, and with it the displacement.

Diasporic desires

The case of Sardar Sarovar forcefully brings home the need for social movements to be flexible in their strategies. What seems feasible and plausible at the start may no longer be so during year five or year ten. (As John Maynard Keynes liked to say, 'When the facts change, I change my mind.') Unfortunately, the leaders of the major oppositional movements in Southasia have found it hard, if not impossible, to change their approach and strategy. In Kashmir, in Nagaland, and in northern Sri Lanka, the rebels have refused to abandon their dream of a sovereign homeland in exchange for greater autonomy within the existing nation-state.

It is past time that two of the most enduring oppositional political movements in Southasia change their approaches and strategies. To be more specific: the Naga people stand enormously to gain if their leaders abandon their dream of a sovereign homeland and agree to be part of the Republic of India. So do the Tamils of northern Sri Lanka, if the LTTE settles for an honourable place in a single, united island nation, rather than fighting on for an independent Eelam.

The civil war in Nagaland has gone on, episodically, for 50 years now. The struggle for a Tamil Eelam is almost as old. In the meantime, thousands of lives have been lost, thousands of families have been broken. But the dream of an independent homeland seems as distant as ever. Should not the rebels now sue for peace, peace with dignity and honour?

That last caveat is crucial—'with dignity and honour'. To get the rebels to drop the sovereignty demand will require handsome gestures. As the veteran journalist George Verghese has suggested, the Nagas could have recognition of their distinctive status indicated on their passports—not 'Indian', but 'Naga Indian'. Likewise, Colombo could explicitly disavow the earlier enactment making Buddhism the 'state religion' of Sri Lanka, while at the same time placing the Tamil language on par with Sinhala. Other measures will also be necessary, among them the deepening of federalism to allow true autonomy for the region concerned, special grants to rehabilitate victims and former combatants, and even—why not?—public recognition of the sufferings caused by the state's armed action.

Were gestures like this forthcoming, would the Naga and Tamil rebels give up their arms and, as it were, join the national mainstream? One cannot be so naïve as to think this very likely. There is the issue of pride: having fought so long for a certain goal, it cannot be let go of easily, or at all. There is also the issue of sacrifice: having lost so many lives in the cause, would it be fair to the memory of the martyrs to settle for less than what they gave their lives for? Sentiments such as these are widespread both among the leadership of the National Socialist Council of Nagalim (IM), the leading insurgent group in Nagaland, and of the LTTE, who have for some time now been the main—indeed, unchallenged—representatives of the Sri Lankan Tamil cause.

In both the Naga and the Tamil cases, compromise is also made more difficult by the desires of the diasporic community. Nagas in exile and Tamils in exile are even more emphatic in their demands for complete independence. Since they pay for the guns, their voice carries much weight. This is a depressingly familiar story, the story of the expatriate who is more unyielding than those who live on the ground. Palestine might be a less violent place were it not for the Jewish opinion on the East Coast of the United States. The Good Friday agreement might have come earlier had it not been for Americans of Irish–Catholic extraction. Many fewer lives would have been lost in the Indian Punjab during the 1980s had Sikhs in the United Kingdom, Canada and the United States not decided to support and encourage the struggle for an independent Khalistan.

The Nagas and the Tamils share certain attributes. Both have a very strong sense of identity, and the pride that goes along with it. Both communities have a better-than-average acquaintance with English, the language of professional advancement in the global economy. As compared with other Southasian cultures, they practice less gender discrimination—here (whether in the Indian Northeast, or the Sri Lankan north and east) many women assume leadership roles as teachers, doctors, entrepreneurs and guerrilla fighters. And if one is able to make the last of these professions redundant, there will be much greater scope for the others. Were this generation of Nagas and the Sri Lankan Tamils to put down their weapons, the next generation would reap untold benefits. They would be part of a larger economy in which, due to their communitarian pride and legacy of professionalism, they would enjoy advantages that other Indian or Sri Lankan communities do not.

The leader-in-command

The primary hurdle in the way of a successful resolution of the Naga and Tamil issues is the burden of history. Both sides to both these conflicts have much to complain about. The Jaffna Tamils cannot forget the burning of the great library or the pogrom of 1983; the Sinhalese will remember the assassination of their leaders and the bombs that explode and kill innocents in markets. The Nagas recall the promises made and betrayed by the Indian state down the years; the Indian state remembers only the Nagas seeking Chinese help and the killing of moderates. Looking back to the past, one sees only crimes committed by the other party, crimes real as well as imagined. It is necessary for the contending parties to look to the future instead, to think of the fate of the generations to come. Do today's rebels want the youth of today, too, to live a life of uncertainty and instability, in and by the shadow of the gun? When is enough enough, and a compromise possible?

History is a burden in another way too. In the thick of the rebellion, insurgency leaders are prone to rhetorical excess, to make commitments and promises that make compromise at a later stage difficult. Thus, the LTTE has often said that it will hold out for nothing less than an independent nation, the Tamil Eelam. The NSCN has likewise stood for an independent Nagalim; to consist of the Naga-speaking areas of Manipur, Arunachal Pradesh and Assam as well as Nagaland. When the rebels do come to the negotiating table, these past promises come back to haunt them. If they are not reminded of these claims by their own cadres, then surely rivals within the movement will make certain to draw the public's attention to the 'sell-out'. (In the same manner, Medha Patkar is still constrained by the stirring slogan that captivated her followers when the Narmada movement was at its height: '*Baandh nahin banega! Koi nahin hatega!*')

These constraints and impediments are real and serious. But they must be overcome if the real and substantial benefits that are to flow to the Nagas and Tamils through a successful resolution of the two conflicts are to be arrived at. For the Nagas and Tamils, especially, the potential gains from giving up the gun are massive indeed. The Indian Constitution does allow for a great degree of devolution. If, as Jayaprakash Narayan told the Nagas long ago, they can run their own economy and promote their own culture, then why does it matter that they do not have their nation and their own flag? A deeper federalism can also handily serve the aspirations of the Sri Lankan Tamils. With the attributes that the Nagas and the Tamils share, they stand to gain enormously from the acceptance of an honourable place within the constitutional framework of India and Sri Lanka.

It is, of course, not just the Naga and Tamil peoples who have virtues and traits in common. So do their acknowledged leaders. The main Naga separatist leader, T Muivah, and the Tamil Tiger supremo, Velupillai Prabhakaran, are both men of extraordinary energy and drive. During the course of lives dedicated to the cause, they have nurtured the strengths and talents of count-less cadres and followers. The Naga struggle is inconceivable without Muivah; so, too, the Tamil struggle without Prabhakaran. In the past, their charisma and determination have played a crucial part in the making and deepening of the struggle. Can that same charisma and determination now play their part in forg-ing a compromise? For, if anyone can persuade the Tamils to give up the gun, it is Prabhakaran. If anyone can charm the Nagas into accepting the Indian Constitution, it is Muivah.

These two leaders have a legitimacy and popular appeal denied to their colleagues, and possibly also to their successors. While they are alive and in command, the state in New Delhi and Colombo might consider giving up more than it would otherwise. If a solution is not found within their lifetimes, the state may be tempted to withhold these concessions, in the hope that in their leader's absence the rebel movement will splinter into factions and thus lose its energy and legitimacy. By the same token, the Nagas and the Tamils might, at present, be able to get a better—perhaps even far better—bargain than might be possible ten or twenty years down the line. Speculation on the future of Tamil separatism when its leader dies or disappears might lead to the conclusion that, if Prabhakaran is no more, it will be the beginning of the end of the LTTE. Likewise, it is overwhelmingly likely that a post-Muivah NSCN will be far less influential and credible than it is now. All the more reason, then, for a deal to be struck and implemented while the leader is still living and in command.

As things stand, however, it appears that the claims of passion are winning over the cold logic of reason in both theatres of Northeast India and the north and east of Sri Lanka. Several years of talks have not brought the Indian government and the Naga rebels any closer to a solution. While Muivah is at least talking, Prabhakaran has taken Sri Lanka back into a full-scale civil war.

Back in 1966, when the state was strong and the rebels weak, the Indian government refused to rehabilitate Sheikh Abdullah. What followed has been a continuously violent and unstable Kashmir. The break-up of Pakistan in 1971 was likewise the fault mainly of an arrogant and overbearing state. Looking at the case of the Naga and Tamil rebellions, one is forced to ponder whether the roles have not now been reversed. While the deadlock of the past may be ascribed to the intransigent state establishment, will it be that the window of opportunity in Nagaland and Sri Lanka will be shut principally because of the dogmatism and insecurity of the rebels?

The uncompromised Gandhi

It is entirely likely that the proposals put forward here for a spirit of compromise from the state and the insurgents will be met with scorn and derision, not just from within the Naga and the Tamil fold, but also from scholars and analysts engaged with these issues. But then, as the American critic Lionel Trilling noted long ago, intellectuals have always tended to embrace an 'adversary culture': standing against the state, against the market, against the establishment—in fact, against anything and everything but themselves. Conciliation and compromise does not come naturally to intellectuals, whose armchairs tend to be removed from the zones of conflict and who do not suffer the fallout of continuous, decades-long fighting.

On the other hand, conciliation and compromise were an integral part of the vocabulary and political repertoire of a man to whom I owe the title of this essay, the man whom I can, uncontroversially, refer to as the greatest Southasian of them all, Mohandas Karamchand Gandhi. Gandhi knew when to begin a movement, but also when to call it off; when to challenge an opponent, but also when to talk to and seek to understand the adversary. The only thing he was uncompromising on was the use of non-violence.

In many ways, Gandhi was the arch-reconciler, the builder of bridges—bridges between Hindus and Muslims, between India and Pakistan, between high castes and low castes, between men and women, between the coloniser and the colonised. Independent India has had many failures, but also some successes. The most conspicuous of the latter are owed to Gandhi's political followers having honoured his spirit of compromise. India is not—or, at least, not yet—a 'Hindu Pakistan', because its first prime minister followed Gandhi in promoting religious pluralism. The Indian Constitution provided special privileges for Dalits and Adivasis under the inspiration of Gandhi. In fact, the Dalit leader Dr B R Ambedkar was made both India's first law minister and chairman of the Drafting Committee of the Constitution on the recommendation of Gandhi. It was also Gandhi who first advocated and promoted the idea of linguistic states. All of these initiatives were attempts by Gandhi to reach out to the 'underdog' with a hand of conciliation and unforced magnanimity.

Among the all-pervading but little recognised of Gandhi's successes was the forging of a stable, harmonious and even affectionate relationship between the United Kingdom and independent India. Certainly, nowhere else have Empire and Colony maintained such a friendship after the sundering of the imperial (and essentially inequitable) tie that once bound them. Consider the bitter relations that exist to this day between the French and the Algerians, the Dutch and the Indonesians, the Belgians and Congolese, the Russians and the Poles, the Japanese and the Koreans. That the citizens of India today do not 'hate' the English is owed largely—one might even say entirely—to Gandhi. His closest friend was an Englishman, Charles Freer Andrews. When Andrews died, in 1940, Gandhi wrote that while the numerous misdeeds of the English would be forgotten,

> not one of the heroic deeds of Andrews will be forgotten as long as England and India live. If we really love Andrews' memory, we may not have hate in us for Englishmen, of whom Andrews was among the best and noblest. It is possible, quite possible, for the best Englishmen and the best Indians to meet together and never to separate till they have evolved a formula acceptable to both.

In the six decades since the Raj ended, the 'best Englishmen and the best Indians' have met regularly and amicably, to their mutual advantage. A spirit of conciliation helped England and India to evolve a powerful friendship, which had myriad benefits for both. The economic benefit to India from this friendship alone will have been enormous.

While the India—England rapprochement was admittedly of a different kind, can there be a time when the same can, or will, be said of Nagas and the people of the heartland of India, or Jaffna Tamils and the monks of Kandy? It would take a great deal of give-and-take on both sides, an honest acknowledgement of error, a willingness to compromise and, perhaps above all, the ability to think of a hopefully harmonious future rather than a bitter and bloody past.

The Naga and Tamil struggles are founded on the principle of identity. These two peoples have a strong sense of who they are and what unites them, this defined by a shared territory, religion, culture and language. It is the denial, both perceived and real, of this identity by the nation-state establishment and its policies that explain the origin and persistence of the secessionist movement. The key to a solution lies in converting the currency of identity into the currency of interest. The groups that are currently protesting about threats to their identity must be provided with a stake in power and decision-making. That is how, for example, the Solidarity generation in Poland, or the leaders and cadres of the African National Congress in South Africa, were encouraged to move from being rebels and freedom fighters to becoming administrators and governors. But, for inspiration, one does not necessarily have to look so far overseas. The Dravidian movement in Tamil Nadu and the Mizo National Front once stood out for independence as solidly as do the LTTE and the NSCN today. In the end, however, they dropped the demand of sovereignty, in exchange for a secure place within the federal system.

One can take heart from the history of Tamil Nadu and Mizoram, or study the transformation currently underway in Nepal, where the spirit of compromise evident on the part of the parliamentary parties and the Communist Party of Nepal (Maoist) is holding out the hope of a peaceful, stable and democratic Nepal. It is too early yet to say whether this particular Southasian story will have a happy ending, but it has certainly had a salutary beginning. For Maoist supremo Pushpa Kamal Dahal ('Prachanda') to agree to put down the gun and embrace multi-party democracy was, in ideological terms, just as difficult as it would be for Prabhakaran or Muivah to give up on 'national self-determination'. Credit must also be given to the parliamentary parties, and the elder statesman Girija Prasad Koirala, that they set aside their old animosities and suspicions and welcomed the Maoists into the democratic process by making space in the interim Parliament and interim cabinet.

The examples from Tamil Nadu, Mizoram and Nepal suggest that for there to be peace in Sri Lanka, Velupillai Prabhakaran does not have to become a Mahatma Gandhi. He, his advisers and well-wishers can take their clues instead from leaders and struggles closer to them in history and geography. Mandela's ANC was once just as devoted to the cult of the gun. C N Annadurai was once just as committed to an independent Tamil homeland—this to be carved out of the Republic of India, rather than the Republic of Sri Lanka. And that other rebel in the jungle, Prachanda, also fought on for years in the hope—and belief—that the struggle would ultimately end in a one-party state dominated by his men. The compromises—honourable as well as effective compromises—made by Mandela, Annadurai and Prachanda might also compel the attention of Muivah, although he has an exemplar even closer at hand, in Pu Laldenga of the Mizo National Front.

In a fine essay on the history of political moderation in the Western world, the historian Robert M Calhoon suggests that 'moderates are made not born.' They are 'creatures of the moment, and of circumstance, who move away from antagonistic stances and toward [the] middle ground to achieve a goal or serve a purpose through a wider political advocacy and association.' This definition works well in explaining the moves away from extremism of those great rebels Nelson Mandela and Mahatma Gandhi—or, indeed, of the ending of repression by their respective rivals, the apartheid regime and the British Raj. Calhoon also writes, 'in our own time, moderation rebukes the corrosive partisanship from the Right or the Left.' In our own region, 'Right and Left' might be better represented as Rebel and State. It is the task of the moderate, and of moderation, to find common ground between these two actors, thus to replace a regime of suspicion and violence with one based on trust and cooperation.

That said, those who advocate moderation—including this writer—live more in hope than expectation. Calhoon quotes a passage from Aristotle's *Nicomachean Ethics*, where the Greek sage notes that 'it is no easy task to find the middle.' Closer to home, this sentiment was echoed by C Rajagopalachari, a close follower and associate of Gandhi, when he wrote to a Quaker friend that 'those who are born to reconcile seem to have an unending task in this world.' If not in the whole world, then at least in Southasia, this region that has been so deeply marked by conflict and antagonism between castes, between Hindus and Muslims, between Sinhala-speakers and Tamil-speakers, between the massed armies of its nation states.

It is precisely because our region is such a cauldron of conflict that a special responsibility devolves on the writer and intellectual, who has an obligation to the truth, and additionally to democracy and pluralism. For the signal lesson of the 20th century is that dictatorships of both left and right are equally inimical to human dignity and well-being. Thus, as part of their calling, writers must stand consistently for the right to freely elect one's leaders, the right to seek a place of residence and company of one's choosing, the right to speak the language of one's choice and practice the faith of one's belief (which may be no faith at all).

These responsibilities are onerous enough, but for the Southasian writer and intellectual there are other obligations still. Because our recent history has been so bloody and divisive, the Southasian writer and intellectual must always be in search of paths that might make our future less bloody and less divisive. For this, he or she should seek, always, to moderate social and political conflicts, rather than to intensify or accelerate them. The extreme positions are well represented and passionately articulated in any case. Rather than take sides on behalf of one caste against another, one religion against another, one nation against another, or to throw oneself in alignment with the state or to be always against the state, the writer and intellectual needs to keep away from an identification with one party to a dispute. Rather, he or she must try to interpret and reconcile opposing positions, to make each side see the truth in the other, thus to urge each party to move beyond dogmatism and self-justification, and towards acknowledging and embracing the beauty of compromise.

Chapter 17

**Understanding
the Nepali mandate**

Himal, May 2008

Prashant Jha

Endlessly pestered with requests to arrange an 'exclusive' interview with his boss on the campaign trail, Pratap came up with several ways to evade the media: stop picking up the phone, say the day's schedule was not yet ready, say that there was just no time, or offer ambiguous responses to keep stubborn journalists waiting. The personal secretary of the Maoist supremo Pushpa Kamal Dahal may have hoped to have an easier time after the polls; but, if anything, his workload doubled. As early results made it clear that the Communist Party of Nepal (Maoist) would emerge as the single largest party, a harassed Pratap told restless reporters that the chairman would make a statement once he won the Kathmandu-10 constituency.

The party machinery had turned its attention towards relishing the moment of victory. On 11–12 April, Kathmandu turned red. The Maoist party flag seemed to be everywhere. The cadre was swirling, screaming with joy and aggression, taking out jubilant *bijay julus* and telling anyone who cared to listen that they had won. For their part, the leaders in their victory rallies were celebrating in the same style as politicians would anywhere else in Southasia.

Sitting on a makeshift platform at the counting centre in the Baneshwor area of the capital, Dahal, long known as 'Prachanda', was greeted by the Maoist leaders with garlands. They also smeared him liberally with—what else?—red powder. His face barely visible, the chairman, who wants to be Nepal's first president, made a speech. It was a mix of offering hope ('This is a new chapter; Maoists will lead the path to change'), reaching out ('We recognise new global and regional realities. We want to be friends with our neighbours. Let's all work together to build a *naya* Nepal'), and definitive vindication ('We told you we would win').

The Maoists can rightfully feel vindicated. During the run-up to the polls, conversations inside Kathmandu's Ring Road revolved around how the CPN (Maoist) would probably come in a distant third. At that point, the worry was what the party would do in such a scenario. As it turned out, the Maoists won a staggering 120 out of 240 direct constituency seats, and are expected to win another 100 or so seats out of 335 under the proportional-representation system. In the direct elections, meanwhile, the Nepali Congress was a distant second with 37 seats; the Communist Party of Nepal (Unified Marxist–Leninist, or the UML) won just 33 seats. However, the big national parties made up some lost ground in the proportional system; the Congress might win about 72 seats, while the UML will come in close with 69 seats or so. The Madhesi Janaadhikar Forum (MJF), in the Tarai, won 30 seats, while smaller Madhesi parties won around 13 seats, but did less well under the proportional system than either the Congress or UML. The Madhesi parties can expect to have more than 65 seats in the house, indicating a massive shift in political representation that has been unnoticed due to the focus on the Maoist win countrywide.

The past few months had been characterised by hectic campaigning across the hills, mountains and plains. Polling day was largely peaceful, with a high turnout of 61 per cent. But thereafter, the 'unexpected' results have meant that the entire political class is struggling to grapple with the new balance of power. The Maoists themselves seemed unprepared, and have been 'spending sleepless nights', as the Maoist chief ideologue Baburam Bhattarai put it in a recent interview. Clearly, everyone is thinking about the responsibilities that lie ahead.

Maobaadi lahar

Chairman Dahal may have been elated giving his victory speech. But it was only a few days earlier that nervousness could be seen writ large across his face. Campaigning at Pharping, on the southern outskirts of Kathmandu valley, he was hurrying from one village to another to address modest gatherings. With whispers among locals that the local UML candidate would put up a tough contest, Prachanda was sparing no effort to woo voters. Shaking hands, asking for blessings, picking up children, nodding vigorously as people poured out grievances, smiling, making promises—he was desperate to please everyone around. In his speeches, the chairman talked about how it pained him to see that even the people within the capital's vicinity had not progressed, and promised a *naya* Nepal if voted to power.

At the Gaunle Restaurant in Pharping, the chairman suddenly disappeared into a room upstairs to eat a quiet meal with his family and key aides. Later, speaking to the media, his confidence was back, countering speculation about his party's potential underperformance. 'Mark my words,' he said. 'We will get 140 out of 240 seats.' Asked about the move from war to election politics, he told this reporter, 'It is fantastic, really fantastic. I had never thought we would come so far so soon.'

The same afternoon, the Maoist minister Hisila Yami was busy with internal meetings at her election office in Naya Bazaar, in the heart of Kathmandu. Sitting on a mattress in a closed room, even as her workers outside on the terrace planned the next round of house-to-house canvassing, she said, 'I am an ethnic Newar from Asan, a hardcore local. And this is a Newar constituency. I have a good chance, but the UML candidate is strong as well.' Referring to the electoral prospects of her husband, party ideologue Baburam Bhattarai, who was standing from Gorkha, Yami said with a grin, 'He is better-off than me right now.'

Beneath the self-deprecatory visage, and the acknowledgement of the effort to cash in on the ethnic Newari vote, was clearly a leader who believed that her party was engaged in something historic. She said intensely, 'It has been a difficult struggle. But we know there is a *lahar*, a wave, in our favour. Remember, we have run a parallel state for ten years, built a pan-Nepal organisation, and we have a committed cadre. There is an invisible network that will help us win the polls, and the poor of this country are with us.'

The calculations of Kathmandu analysts did not take into account this invisible network, which was constantly engaging with people on the ground. Neither did it sense the desperate yearning for change, or the 'fear' of the status quo among the country's marginalised, poor and angry population, who proved to be the silent support base of the Maoists. The fact that elections had not taken place for nine years did not make for easy predictions. The past decade had seen an armed insurgency, a royal takeover, rising ethnic consciousness, a generational change, and both massive outward migration and internal displacement.

Wooing victims

Anthropologist Judith Pettigrew spent election day in a village in west-central Kaski district, which has been her area of fieldwork for the last two decades. Pettigrew spoke at a Kathmandu seminar about the way party representatives gathered early in the morning at a polling booth in Kaski, and also about the enthusiasm with which people voted. Strikingly, among the Maoist poll representatives was a man who, during the war, had told Pettigrew how much he disliked the Maoists. 'The People's Liberation Army came and spent two months in the village after the ceasefire,' she said. 'They did not trouble the locals, and instead talked to them constantly about what the Maoists stood for. Fear was slowly forgotten, and people veered towards the former rebels as a ray of hope.'

The relationship between Maoists and former victims sprang up as an issue in other places, as well. At a Maoist rally in the northeastern Khotang district, for example, a woman reportedly asked candidate Pasang Rai why she should vote for him after his cadre had always forced her family to feed them and donate money to their cause. Rai folded his hands and instantly pleaded guilty. 'We made mistakes,' he admitted. 'But please remember that it was because of that struggle and pain that we are seeing a republic, Constituent Assembly and federalism in Nepal. You will now have rights.'

The Maoists used their well-oiled organisational machinery and articulate, well-trained activists to sell themselves as the principal agents of change. They broke the stranglehold of a few local notables over chunks of votes, and reached out directly at the ground. They gave candidate tickets to representatives from marginalised sections, instantly winning them the support of entire communities at the local level, besides sending out a message that the former rebels would walk the talk on inclusion.

At Panchkhal in Kavre district, 40 km from Kathmandu, Tej Bahadur Mijhar, a Maoist Dalit candidate beat his nearest UML rival by more than 6,000 votes, also bagging the upper-caste votes in the constituency. Mijhar, who traversed through several fringe-left outfits before joining the Maoists eight years back, says it is only the CPN (Maoist) that is committed to real social change. 'I faced discrimination when I was a child, and was not allowed to drink water at the community tap,' he said. 'In my job as a teacher in Rasuwa, I was harassed.

I spent many years selling cheap goods on the Kathmandu streets.' He continued: 'The Maoists have changed caste relations. In the party, we remained connected to the ground. We have promised people that we will write the law of the poor into the Constituent Assembly.'

The former rebels were also able to capitalise on the support of large numbers of youth. More than half of the Maoist candidates were below 40. In comparison, the average age of Nepali Congress candidates was 52. This made it easier for the young electorate to relate to the Maoist candidates, besides influencing others in the community to shift allegiance. Bidur Sapkota, a UML leader in Kavre, pointed to age being a significant factor towards the end of the campaign. 'It was in the last three days when the tables turned,' he said. 'Young people, many of them workers from Kathmandu, returned home to vote and supported Maoists.' This reading has been corroborated by Mukta Tamang, an anthropologist who returned to his own village in Kavre for the elections. Tamang says that he was sure that traditional voting patterns in favour of the Congress and UML would continue; but then, a day before the polls, hundreds of workers came back to his village. 'There was a village meeting in the evening to decide whom to support,' he said. 'While the older lot wanted to maintain old loyalties, the younger ones said that the Maoists must be given a chance.'

The Maoists also coined the right campaign pitch. Using a mix of allure and intimidation, they took all of the credit for the peace of the past two years, and cleverly turned the anger and misery of the people against the Congress and UML. The two big parties were portrayed as incumbents, which were solely responsible for the mess in which the country had found itself. It did not take a lot of convincing for this to strike a chord among people, who remembered the irresponsible and constant bickering among these parties during the 1990s—their corrupt ways and the absence of their leaders from the villages right at the time when the people needed them the most. People were sick of the established faces of local elites; and so the opinion-formers, largely with the Congress and UML, no longer controlled the votes.

Capturing mindsets

But that is not the whole story, for the Maoist victory had multiple shades of grey. The party's almost total hegemony over local areas by sheer force, at least until 2006, gave them a dramatic head start to the recent polls. In the run-up to elections, there were constant excesses by the Maoist youth wing, the Young Communist League, with other candidates either beaten up or disallowed from campaigning in many parts—a fact noted by the United Nations Mission in Nepal (UNMIN) and other observer groups. Several Nepali Congress district committees have blamed their poor showing on Maoist violence. At the same time, it is useful to remember that Maoist activists were killed during election violence in Rolpa, Kapilbastu and Dang districts.

The former insurgent leadership had repeatedly stated publicly they would launch a 'struggle' if the poll results were not in their favour—and a return to the jungle was the one thing that the people did not want. Some believe that the Maoists were able to garner the support of the lower middle class because of this fear. Kavre's UML leader Sapkota says, 'This is the people's way of compromising for the sake of peace. The Maoists did not capture booths; they captured the mindset of the people, by playing on their fears that war might be resumed. The state did not provide security; we in other parties did not stand up. The keys were handed over to the thief.'

In addition, on polling day there was a degree of electoral malpractice. A Kathmandu taxi driver told this reporter, as the results were trickling in, 'See, the Maoists are sure to win.' Asked about the basis for his confidence, he smiled, 'Everyone I know has voted for them. I voted five times! The party had already given us a list of people who were outside the country, and said that we could use their names. There was a spray to remove the ink from your fingers, so no one knew you had already voted.'

Discounting the factors related to fear and intimidation would give a flawed picture of the electoral verdict, and limit the overall understanding of what has taken place in Nepal's recent electoral exercise. At the same time, over-emphasising this element would be a mistake, as well. Electoral malpractice is an integral part of Southasian politics, and certainly an art mastered by both the Nepali Congress and UML in the past. In addition, in places such as Kathmandu and other urban centres, where intimidation and malpractice seem to have been limited, the Maoists have likewise scored impressive victories. The nature, scale and margin of the Maoist victory, coupled with its diverse voter base—the Tharu community in the western Tarai, the Rajbanshi in eastern Tarai, Dalits and landless across the country, the petty bourgeoisie in smaller centres, ethnic groups of all hues in the hills—probably means that the thirst for new faces and change was the single most decisive factor in voter motivation.

The other wave

Equally impressive as the Maoist victory has been the turn in the Tarai, with the MJF winning almost as many seats as the big national parties. To sense the anger against the mainstream politicians, visit Bokraha village, off Lauki on the east–west highway in Sunsari district. A bumpy road, small huts housing large families, and a dilapidated school structure may not mark it as being particularly different from anywhere else in Nepal's rural areas. But this has been Prime Minister Girija Prasad Koirala's constituency for years now. His daughter, Sujata, fought elections from the area this time around. Banking on her family name, the support of the sizeable Muslim community and a formidable patronage network, she was confident of her eventual success—until, that is, Madhesi leader Upendra Yadav threw his hat into the ring during the last day of the nomination period.

Addressing village-level meetings in a mix of Hindi and Nepali, Sujata Koirala said during campaigning, 'My family has sacrificed everything for democracy. I will do everything for the women in this area.' But locals were none too impressed. Launching into an angry tirade, a group listed out its grievances: *Look at the road, look at my torn clothes, look at my children who have nothing to do. Why should we vote for her?* Sujata's supporters made a feeble effort to suggest that this was not an election for development but to make up the new law of the land. But the riposte was quick to come: *What will I do with the law when I don't have enough to eat? The Congress must be taught a lesson this time.*

If the lack of any improvement in livelihoods over the past decade was one factor across the country, the rising Madhesi consciousness was another, more potent, ingredient in defeating candidates such as Koirala. Over the past year, Madhesis—plains people who speak Maithili, Awadhi, Bhojpuri, Hindi and share extensive crossborder ties—have been agitating for identity rights and equal representation. This has been particularly intense in the eastern and central plains, which is often referred to as Madhes. In this belt, people such as Sujata and her father were increasingly seen as *pahadi* (hillfolk) outsiders. The Madhes Movement of January 2007, as well as the recent agitations; increasing radicalisation over the past year, buttressed by ethnic militancy of armed groups; a deep anger against the Kathmandu establishment and pahadi politicians—all of these contributed to the creation of a wave in favour of Madhesi candidates. It is now clear that Madhesi identity politics, with its emphasis on respect and representation, is here to stay.

Campaigning in neighbouring Morang district, Upendra Yadav said, 'Slavery to the Koiralas, Acharyas and Aryals must end. That is the only path to Madhesi liberation and self-rule.' Yadav was seen as having led the Madhes movement of the past year and reaped the reward. Brand recognition for the MJF, better organisation, the presence of experienced election 'manipulators' and the widespread support of the Yadavs and Tharu in select eastern Tarai districts all gave the MJF an advantage over other Madhesi parties. Meanwhile, the Mahant Thakur-led Tarai Madhes Loktantrik Party has suffered a major setback with the defeat of Thakur. But, given its nascent organisational set-up, it did as well as it could have hoped, and is set to receive about 18 seats in total in the Constituent Assembly. The results from the Tarai can be interpreted as correcting a historical injustice in Nepal's democratic framework, for it ensures representation and inclusion of Madhesis on an unprecedented scale in the upcoming Assembly.

The poll results in the Tarai also threw up another interesting facet. Contrary to the prognosis in Kathmandu, the Maoists continue to have a base in the plains. The former rebels have suffered an organisational setback over the past year, with the Madhes movement assuming a strong anti-Maoist tilt. But they have won in pahadi pockets of the Tarai that were formerly UML bases, but now see the Maoists as more reliable protectors in case Madhesi politics turns chauvinistic and starts targeting pahadis. The Maoists have also won the support of the Tarai's own landless and Dalits, which brings them into straight contest with Madhesi parties, largely representing 'intermediate' castes, for power at the local level and on issues such as land reform. The support of the western Tharu and eastern Rajbanshi can be read as support to the proposed Maoist federal model of having several states within the plains, which is in stark contrast to the MJF's demand for one Madhes as a single autonomous province. The Maoist–MJF relationship will be tense at many levels, though a tactical alliance could still be possible.

On election day itself, it was feared that Madhesi extremists could drastically escalate violence, leading to a low turnout. They had stepped up intimidation activities in the run-up to the polls, kidnapping a few candidates and killing one. But once the armed outfits realised that elections would go ahead regardless, and that they did not have the capacity to disrupt the process, they seem to have decided to wait out the polls. Some militants even joined in the electoral process, actively campaigning for the candidates of Madhesi parties. Others used the opportunity to make money, by threatening candidates with attacks in case they did not shell out cash. For now, the high turnout in Madhes has marginalised the armed outfits, and exposed their limited mass support. Madhesi people have made it clear that they are not willing to obey orders on mobile phones issued from shady hotels in Bihari towns.

Incumbents no longer

The immediate general reaction in Kathmandu—among politicians, journalists, diplomatic missions—was one of shock and awe at the nature and scale of the Maoist victory and the rout of the established parties. But this surprise inevitably gave way to introspection, in particular a reassessment within the power centres on how to deal with Nepal's new political reality.

The Nepali Congress top brass had been confident that it would emerge as the single largest force in the Constituent Assembly. It had been banking on traditional loyalties, the 'brand' that is Girija Prasad Koirala, a party organisation that usually springs back to life at election time, the support of local elites and established faces, besides the enormous international goodwill it enjoys. The rout upset the Congress's dream of continuing to head the government, but it also exposed internal fault-lines within the party. For the moment, it has also left the party somewhat directionless. Indeed, one Congress leader points out that, more than the electoral defeat, it is the party's complete organisational disarray that is more disconcerting in the long term. 'I could not even get the names and numbers of our 240 constituency committee heads from the party office,' he said. 'The Congress has always relied on informal links and instinctive support because of its history. That faith of the people has collapsed this time. We need to rebuild from scratch.'

But more than serious introspection, the Congress currently seems to be in the midst of a detrimental blame game. Half of the party is pointing fingers at Home Minister Krishna Prasad Sitaula's leniency towards Maoist violence as the reason for defeat. Others believe that nepotistic politics and Sujata Koirala's corrupt image and pro-monarchy statements damaged the party's chances. Meanwhile, Prime Minister Koirala's inability to campaign left the party without a face, even while the Maoists were able to project a notably strong leader, presenting Prachanda as the 'first president of the republic'. The Congress also lost its erstwhile support base in the Tarai due to its arrogant and insensitive handling of the Madhes issue over the past year. The ticket distribution is also being seen as responsible for the disastrous result, with flawed selection of candidates.

With the Congress's acting president, Sushil Koirala, defeated in Banke and his subsequent resignation, there is now a vacuum at the party's topmost level. The Koirala clan has suffered what could perhaps be an irreversible setback, with both daughter Sujata and nephew Shekhar also losing their seats. The former prime minister, Sher Bahadur Deuba, is now expected to become stronger in the party after having won from two constituencies, even though he failed to deliver more wins for the party in his stronghold of the far west.

The UML has been hit with an even greater shock. Party General-Secretary Madhav Nepal had claimed before an international delegation a day before polls that he would soon become the country's prime minister. Instead, defeated in both of his constituencies, Nepal was only one among the pantheon of the party—Pradeep Nepal, K P Oli, Raghuji Pant, Ishwor Pokharel, Bidya Bhandari—who lost their seats in the hills and plains. The party was banking on its moderate centre–left image, a hard-working cadre and dominance over civil-society organisations to bring them a prominent showing. But it is now clear that the UML voters shifted en masse to the Maoists, seeing it as the real left. As for the broader masses, the fact that the Maoists were given the hammer-and-sickle symbol for the ballot (as opposed to the UML's sun symbol) may have been a significant though as yet an un-analysed factor.

Madhav Nepal has resigned from his post. The UML has also withdrawn from the government, saying that it has no moral right to continue in power. There is now a real danger that if the top is adrift, even more UML activists will jump ship and move to the CPN (Maoist). The UML believes it has played a responsible and balancing role between the conservative Congress and the radical Maoists, but the public failed to reward it for doing so. There is bitterness at the moment, even as the party thinks hard about what policy course to adopt.

The Naxalite path

It was not only Nepal's political class that was taken by surprise. India was also caught unawares, with all of its intelligence reports pointing to the Nepali Congress being in the lead, with the UML a close second and the Maoists ranking third. National Security Advisor M K Narayanan even went to the extent of publicly stating that his government had invested a significant amount of faith and hope in the Congress and Girija Koirala, a statement that was interpreted as backing the party during the polls. On election day, the Nepal handlers in

New Delhi were ecstatic, for they saw the event as a policy victory after having consistently pushed for elections over the apprehensions of many, and an un-willingness on the part of key Nepali political actors. But a day later, as results came pouring in, New Delhi's mood changed dramatically, and Indian officials were forced to engage with the emerging new reality.

India has, sensibly, decided to stay the course in supporting the peace process and democracy it has so carefully helped conceive. In private brief-ings to journalists in New Delhi, Ministry of External Affairs officials made it clear that they were willing to work with a Maoist government, and that reports of their panic were inaccurate. Foreign Minister Pranab Mukherjee called up Chairman Dahal to congratulate him, and termed the win as a positive devel-opment. Sitaram Yechury, the Communist Party of India (Marxist) leader who played a central role in the 2005 and 2006 negotiations between the Maobaadi and India, said the vote was anti-monarchy, and urged the Indian Naxalites to emulate the example of the Maoists.

Despite Yechury's exhortations, it is clear that the Naxalites are not plan-ning to do any such thing. Ideologue Varavara Rao said in a recent interview that the Maobaadi and the Naxalites have to chart their own paths, and that it was yet to be seen whether a Maoist government in Kathmandu would maintain its anti-feudal and anti-imperialist character. This rhetoric was notably similar to what Baburam Bhattarai told this reporter, rejecting the idea that there are links between the two ultra-left movements. 'We do not have any comments about what they should or should not do,' he said simply. 'The Naxalites have their own path.'

Meanwhile, the Bharatiya Janata Party (BJP), in a significant policy shift, welcomed Nepal's move from monarchy to democracy, but hoped that a 'secu-lar' Nepal would neither be anti-monarchy nor anti-Hindu. In parsing these two, however, restoring Nepal's Hindu *rashtra* status is more important for the Hindu right than is saving the monarchy. Rightwing pundits in India are now warning of a full-scale Maoist takeover in Nepal, suggesting that the former rebels are merely using this period as a tactical interlude before establishing a dictatorship —and that there would be inevitable spill-over effects for India.

The Maoist victory poses real policy challenges for the American admin-istration, which continues to categorise the CPN (Maoist) as a 'terrorist' outfit. Former US President Jimmy Carter, in Nepal to observe elections, said it was 'embarrassing and frustrating' to see the refusal of his government to talk to the Maoists. But the new US Ambassador Nancy Powell, who joined last year in place of the vituperative James Moriarty, is said to be open to the idea of engaging with the Maoists, and is understood to have met some Maoist leaders secretly last year. In late April, Powell met the interim legislature speaker, Subhas Nembang, to convey to him that the US would continue to support the Nepali government, irrespective of who was in government. There have also been some suggestions in Washington, DC, that the Maoists will soon be taken off the US 'terrorist' list, and that work has already begun on the technicalities required to clear the organisation. But there has been no official government statement to this effect.

Mule-trading

Politics has now returned to Kathmandu. After sweating it out in their constituencies, facing difficult questions from the people, organising activists and resources, and visiting houses and families for votes, the politicians are now slowly getting back to the capital. As such, the power games—the manipulation, deal making, exchange of favours—have begun. In addition, there are some extremely significant challenges, from the formation of a Maoist-led government and the dismantling of the monarchy in the short term, to navigating the relationship between the Maoist fighters and the Nepal Army, dealing with issues of governance, and kick-starting a process of constitution-writing.

Few had prepared for the drastic change in the balance of power that this mandate demands. The Maoists will stake a claim to lead the new government in what is essentially a hung parliament. There was speculation that Baburam Bhattarai would take over as prime minister, while Chairman Dahal would look after the organisation for now, taking care of intra- and inter-party coordination, and assume, as his party had projected, the role of an executive president at a later time. But now there are signs that Dahal himself could head the government as prime minister, given that a position of executive presidency still depends on the model that the Constituent Assembly eventually adopts at least two years from now.

What is more important for now is whether the other parties will join the government. The interim constitution stipulates that the post-poll government would be formed through consultation between all parties. At this point, the Maoists are very keen to have all forces on board, not only because they need their support to form the government and push through any law but also because it would afford their government greater international credibility and allow the other parties to share the criticism for whatever goes wrong. While the UML has already withdrawn from the current government, there are strong voices within the Nepali Congress as well not to join the new government.

These factions within the two parties claim that under parliamentary practice the mandate is clearly in favour of the Maoists, and that their parties must focus on building up their organisational strength after the rout. But a deeper underlying motive also exists. 'Well, we want to expose the Maoists by giving them sole power,' says one Congress leader. 'Even if we join, they will have control, and we will be used as a shield. It is better to stay out.' But others believe that the Congress and UML are acting like bad losers. A Maoist leader says, 'If we had come in third, they would have tried their best to lock us into the government. But they are refusing to do so now.' Political analysts such as Nilamber Acharya, who espouse a national unity government, point out that the polls did not deliver a mandate for Maoist rule—they have received only 240 or so seats in a house of 601. 'The people's mandate is for a government based on consensus of all the major forces,' Acharya says.

It is possible that the current mood is a mere prelude to hard bargaining. The UML's outgoing general-secretary is reported to have asked the Maoists to publicly renounce violence before the party joins the government. What is more likely is that the Congress and UML will try to win some of the more important portfolios before deciding to formally join. The interim constitution requires a two-thirds majority for anyone to be elected or removed as prime minister, leading to some concern within the other parties that the Maoist prime minister, once elected with their support, may never give way. A critical bargaining point may be for the Constituent Assembly to amend the two-thirds requirement to a simple majority, at which point the Congress and UML could relent and join. Others believe that the excessive focus on the government is unnecessary. UML leader Shankar Pokharel told a Kathmandu audience recently, 'Even if we are not a part of the government, we will be an active part of the constitution writing, and push our agenda forcefully.'

What must be noted is that the interim constitution's strictures on consensual government and the two-thirds majority requirement for ousting a prime minister were drafted at a time when the 'democratic' parties thought that the transforming Maoists needed encouragement and guarding. Now that the tables have been turned, there is the argument that the interim constitution must be adhered to in spirit as well. Given that the Maoists do not command a majority, it is likely that a compromise formula will be reached for the formation of a government.

Of kings and armies

The formation of the new government will happen only after the first sitting of the Constituent Assembly, which has a mountain of responsibilities to look toward. As per the interim constitution, the Assembly first has to abolish the monarchy. The electoral verdict has indeed clearly been in favour of a republic, with the royalist parties swept aside. But it is still to be seen whether the Assembly's first sitting—which will also have to look at issues such as oath-taking of members, election of a chair, and adoption of a code of procedures—can even feasibly take a vote on the monarchy.

The Maoists have said it is time for the king to leave the Narayanhiti Palace. However, Kathmandu is abuzz about the back-channel communications rumoured to be taking place between the palace and the Maoists. This has been given further fuel by Chairman Dahal's assertion that he wants a 'graceful' exit for King Gyanendra, that he does not wish to humiliate him, and that he is even willing to meet with the monarch to discuss a dignified way out. Baburam Bhattarai has likewise said that certain 'cultural rights' could be given to the king, who could live on in Nepal as a common citizen. Immediately thereafter, however, the Maoist commander Ram Bahadur Thapa ('Badal') spoke publicly about the unacceptability of any compromise in doing away with the kingship.

It is difficult to discern what kind of space the Maoists could be thinking of giving to the king. But either way, Maoist insiders say that it is too late for any deal. At best, Gyanendra's private property and business interests will not be touched, and he will receive some privileges. At the height of the deadlock between the Maoists and the seven parties last September, India is understood to have sent a feeler to the king. But as an observer who recently met Gyanendra put it, 'He is very clear he will not leave the country.'

Then there is the issue of Nepal's two armies. The Maoists and the Nepal Army have fought a war, and have since differed bitterly on the issue of the potential integration of the former into the latter. UNMIN has been supervising Maoist arms and 20,000 combatants in seven cantonments across the country. The army, especially its politically ambitious chief Rukmangat Katuwal, has been publicly defiant of civilian authority when it comes to the matter of integration. The manner in which the Army–Maoist relationship develops, and how a decision is eventually taken on integration of the former fighters, is critical to the future of Nepal's peace process.

On this, however, the Maoists are clearly trying to reach out. Baburam Bhattarai told this reporter, 'We do not see any problem with the army. Our war was not against the army, but against the monarchy. The monarchy misused the army. The army must listen to the political authority.' For its part, the army is also making the right noises, expressing its commitment to obey the orders of a legitimately elected government. The situation of the two armies will be critical to tackle, as the Maoists are not only a party running the government but continue to have their combatants, in addition to the violence-oriented members of the Young Communist League.

While the issue of the army and monarchy are critical for the idea of Nepal, none is of greater bedrock concern than the economy. As the rebel victory was announced, panic set in among the business community. The stock exchange dropped, and there was speculation of heavy capital flight. The Maoist top leaders immediately went into damage-control mode, and in an extensive meeting with the business community sought to allay fears and apprehensions. Again, they made the right noises. *We are fighting feudalism, not capitalism*, they noted. *We are for public–private partnership and investment in hydropower and tourism. Our economic revolution is the bourgeois democratic revolution. Socialism and communism are a century away right now.*

But it is not only keeping the business elite in a good mood that is important. The Maoists take over the helm of government when the country is reeling under soaring inflation, a huge fuel bill (even as it remains subsidised massively by the government), poor law and order, 42 hours of power cuts every week, and an extremely weak administrative apparatus in large parts, particularly in the Tarai. To top it all off, they have made populist promises during their campaign. A UML leader, barely able to hold back, smirks, 'They have promised to control price rise, generate employment, give land to the tiller, make all workers permanent, provide loan waivers, stop load-shedding and instead give free electricity. With the country already in a difficult situation, let us see how the Maoists deliver on these issues.' The challenge of governance, however, must not be seen solely as a Maoist difficulty: it is a national issue, which is made complicated because it is unclear how the Maoist-bureaucracy relationship will build up.

Writing a new Nepal

Against the backdrop of all of these issues, of course, is the all-important process of constitution writing, for which the Constituent Assembly has been elected. Some elements will be able to be borrowed from the 1990 and interim constitutions, such as fundamental rights and multi-party democracy. But there are other issues on which there could well be deadlock. Some would like to read the mandate as a vote for those parties that have advocated ethnic federalism: the Maoists have proposed 11 provinces based on the 'nationality' that is present in the largest numbers within those territories; the MJF has asked for a single Madhes province, east to west along the Tarai plains. But the Congress and UML have strongly opposed these models of federalism, worried that an ethnic Pandora's Box would be opened, and that different communities—many of which would be minorities in such units—have their own views on how to go about the shape of a federal structure. Between the national and Madhesi parties, there are bound to be serious differences not only on the shape but also the powers to be granted to the federal units.

Another issue where differences will crop up is on the nature of government. On this point, the Maoists are pushing for a division of powers between the president and prime minister; the MJF has emphasised a completely presidential system of government; and the Congress and UML are happy with an executive prime minister and ceremonial head of state. Meanwhile, no party—including the CPN (Maoist)—has the requisite two-thirds majority to unilaterally push its agenda through the Constituent Assembly on such critical issues. The constitution is to be written consensually, in the absence of which a two-thirds majority is required. For all the momentum the Maoists have gained from their formidable showing in the polls, and for all the bluster evident in their government-forming zeal, the fact remains that they are forced to work with the other major forces, particularly the Congress, UML and MJF.

April 2008 has sent out multiple messages to Nepal's political actors. The electorate has endorsed the Maoist transformation, supported the end to insurgency and given the former rebels the responsibility—the opportunity—to run the country with others. It has also forced the traditionally larger parties to introspect, re-organise and keep in tune with changing aspirations on the ground. The centuries-old establishment of the Shah dynasty has been bid adieu. But the common thread of the Nepali mandate for the Constituent Assembly is now to write a democratic, plural, inclusive, social-justice-oriented progressive constitution.

Chapter 18

A people on the run

Himal, February 2009

Rajan Hoole

The capture of Kilinochchi in late December 2008 and the Mullaitivu 'command hub' in late January 2009 by government forces marks another milestone in the unending saga of Tamil refugees. From mid-2007, the bulk of the LTTE was confined to the Vanni, fighting in the last block of land under its control. By now, this war running 30 years, during which the social fabric of the engaged societies has been shredded, has been shown to be futile. The war had nothing to do with honour or the good of the people.

The Colombo government has been conducting the campaign under a blanket of severe censorship, enforced less by regulation than by physical attacks on journalists, in an attempt to hide the figures of troops dead and maimed. But had the government just put forward a political settlement and assured security for Tamils—both those living under its control and those escaping from the LTTE—the rebels' defeat could have been secured politically, rather than through an excess of blood and repression. In the absence of a political vision to win over the minorities and unite the country, the 'war on terror' has become a licence for state terror against them, and for long-term impunity in general. Already, since early 2006, over 1,500 Tamil civilians have been killed by hit squads operating under state intelligence services. Several of these victims had children in the LTTE or gave the rebels food in order to help a young person risking his or her life.

From the time the LTTE forced a large section of civilians living in Jaffna into the Vanni in 1995, it placed severe restrictions on their leaving the area, introducing an elaborate pass system and forcing military training on both schoolchildren and adults. From 2006, it ruled that every family must send at least one fighter to the LTTE forces, a diktat it began to enforce by raiding homes and abducting minors as they reached their 17th birthday. If the victim had already been sent into hiding, they took a proxy. As things became desperate in 2008, the required number of inductees per family was increased depending on its size—two from a family with four children, while one with only a single child was officially exempt. Mostly young, unwilling, barely trained conscripts were being sent into the battlefield. Yet no political means of rescuing these conscripts was ever contemplated by Colombo officialdom.

Even as it pulled back, the LTTE's main hope was to inflict maximum casualties and wear down the government's ability to protract the war. Casualties in recent months have indeed been high. Many of the soldiers being killed are poor, unemployed victims of a mismanaged economy and a massively self-perpetuating defence budget; they had not been told that, after training, they would be sent into a veritable mincing machine. Perhaps inevitably, desertion levels grew significantly. Meanwhile, the LTTE is holding civilians under worsening conditions, their movement restricted and subjected to regular bombing and shelling. Rather than move to government-controlled areas, most of them earlier preferred to either flee to India or remain in the LTTE areas. Of course, the situation in India is little better. Over the years, many refugees have engaged in perilous sea crossings, only to return out of desperation, get beaten again, lose their family members and property, and dissolutely re-make the journey to India. After several such experiences, these individuals inevitably become desperately poor and bereft of will.

In northern Sri Lanka, by the end of January 2009, up to 35 civilians were dying from government bombs and shells every day. A Mullaitivu district government official, Emelda Sukumar, out of sheer desperation perhaps, told Reuters, 'When people occupy particular places, the LTTE sends shells from that area, and then the army also targets the same area.' That dual callousness too is a long-running, unspeakable aspect of the Tamil saga.

The beginning

The refugee issue has its origins back when the government of the day planned the anti-Tamil pogrom in Colombo in July 1983, in which some 2,000 Tamils were killed by state-sponsored mobs. The saga of the Tamil refugees began soon after, in November 1984, when the government threw out the Tamils living in Manal Aru, in the southeast of the Northern Province. This was an ideological project, launched with the expertise of Israeli intelligence, in order to suppress Tamil nationalist aspirations. Minister Lalith Athulathmudali (who was later to earn a dubious reputation as national-security minister) spoke of the government's intention of settling 200,000 Sinhalese, mainly ex-convicts and fisherfolk, among Tamils in the northeast. This undertaking introduced a new viciousness to the brewing conflict, with its intention of building Sinhalese settlements by evicting Tamils from the northeast, thus denying the Tamils physical and cultural spaces in areas where they had for several centuries been the majority. Among the Tamils, these actions created panic. Amidst the militant reaction spawned in response to the July 1983 violence, many Tamils felt that only a military response could safeguard their habitat from aggression.

Events moved quickly from then on. The LTTE massacred about 73 Sinhalese civilians in South Mullaitivu, most of them convicts settled in Manal Aru. The government responded by massacring scores of Tamils in the surrounding area. During February 1985, Tamil peasant families who entered the area to harvest their fields were fired upon by air-force helicopters, killing over a hundred, including women and children. Since then, Manal Aru has remained part of the militarised High Security Zone in which Sinhalese settlements were established, leading to the permanent displacement of at least 2,500 Tamil families. In May 1985, following a series of killings by government forces, LTTE cadres entered the heavily militarised sacred city of Anuradhapura and massacred 120 Sinhalese pilgrims. The government responded with a series of massacres of Tamils, killing 2,200 in 1985 alone. These attacks led to two main developments: first, the rise of the Tigers; and second, the burgeoning phenomenon of Tamil refugees.

The LTTE's ruthless military image appealed to a section of Tamil nationalist sentiment, which saw in it the answer to Sinhalese nationalist violence. Other Tamil militants with Marxist ideas—who wanted to work with like-minded Sinhalese and create a socialist Lanka free of ethno-chauvinism—were weakened by the extreme violence of the times. The LTTE leader, Velupillai Prabhakaran, consolidated his totalitarian control of the organisation, targeting effective leaders in rival groups and, during late 1986, militarily decimating his rivals to become the 'sole representative' of the Tamil people. Thereafter, there were few dissident voices among the Tamils, mainly out of fear. Some students who instinctively reacted against totalitarianism did at first resist the LTTE, but were soon silenced.

Indian hand

The displacement of Tamils from large parts of the east continued through deliberate military action. In the north, too, military reprisals, especially in the coastal areas, led to about 200,000 refugees fleeing to Tamil Nadu by 1987. The eviction of civilians also saw an increasing military presence, the creation of refugee camps and the further displacement of civilians. This may not have led to permanent damage had there been a negotiated settlement enabling refugees to return to their homes. But here, too, the LTTE had become a prisoner of the very violence that led to its sensational rise.

The reality was that once the LTTE had violently eliminated other militant groups, it had also phenomenally weakened the Tamil armed struggle. It was pitted against a state with large population reserves and relatively huge resources. Although the LTTE tried to make up numbers by recruiting children and women, and developing a unit of suicide cadres with which to leverage its human resources, it was not in a position to halt any determined military advance. This meant that Tamil communities were unendingly bombed from the air, shelled, massacred and displaced, with no end to the ordeal in sight.

A chance for peace came when India intervened in 1987, enforcing a ceasefire through the Indian Peace-Keeping Force (IPKF) and pushing through a political settlement under the Indo-Sri Lanka Peace Accord. Although the LTTE agreed to this deal, the result exposed the futility of its brand of politics and its grandiose claims. To the Tamil people, India became the benefactor, while the rebels came to represent a cruel embarrassment. The LTTE resorted to war in an attempt to show India in a bad light, proceeding even to fire at the Indian Army from civilian concentrations and refugee camps.

As the Indian Army advanced into Jaffna in October 1987, two instances in particular stand out. One was when the LTTE fired with small arms at the tanks leading the Indian column from the top floor of Kokuvil Hindu College, which at the time was a refugee camp. One of these tanks subsequently swung its turret and fired into a ground-floor classroom, killing over 30 refugees. The other notable memory from that time was when the rebels directed small-arms fire at the advancing Indian Army column from a Jaffna Hospital balcony; although the LTTE cadres managed to escape, 70 patients and staff were killed when Indian soldiers moved into the hospital. Such strategies became a regular feature of the LTTE's attempt to score political capital in addition to adding to its ranks recruits from disgruntled civilians.

The Indian Army had made excursions into Prabhakaran's jungle hideouts, but had refrained from going in for the kill. It made more sense to Indian policy-makers to negotiate a deal with a weakened LTTE, arriving at some type of political arrangement. Even though in its military actions the Indian Army was guilty of a number of rights violations and reprisal violence, mandarins in New Delhi never lost sight of the political component to the fighting. The North-East Provincial Council was set up, and the Indian Army wanted to ensure that normal economic activities were able to continue. Even as hostilities went forward, there was neither debilitating red tape nor indefinite delays obstructing the free movement of people or goods. Any displacement that took place during the IPKF period was only temporary—a sharp contrast to what happened under the Sri Lankan military, especially from 2006.

To some extent, India's role secured the political rights, economic vitality and habitat of the people of the Sri Lankan northeast. This, of course, would have spelled the LTTE's doom, at least if the Indian Army had managed to bring adequate discipline into its responses to provocations. It was for this reason that the LTTE cut the opportunistic deal with the government of Ranasinghe Premadasa: to get the Indian Army out. The LTTE, which required a total vacuum in the northeast, wanted President Premadasa to dissolve the North-East Provincial Council, to which he gladly agreed. The last Indian Army troops left in March 1990; within 70 days, the LTTE had returned to war. Indeed, this was not even a declared pullout from the peace deal with Colombo but rather a calculated provocation, with the LTTE simply surrounding police stations in the east. Still labouring under the belief that this 'quarrel' could be peacefully resolved, the government instructed the policemen to surrender. The rebels subsequently took hundreds of disarmed Sinhalese and Muslim policemen into the jungle, massacred them and pulled out, leaving the Tamil civilians at the mercy of incensed troops and rampaging government-supported Muslim hoodlums.

The result of this evolution was a swelling of the LTTE's ranks accompanied by the estrangement between the Tamil and Muslim communities in the east. The LTTE followed up with unprovoked massacres in two prominent Muslim villages near Batticaloa that had attempted to keep out of the violence.

In turn, this resulted in a whole new and massive refugee problem, ending the relative respite the people had experienced under the Indian Army. The LTTE had no intention of holding the east or protecting its civilians.

Keeping the Vanni

Once again, refugees from North Trincomalee, who had been resettled when the Indian Army had been present, fled by boat to Mullaitivu in the north or directly to Nagapattinam in India. Then, the LTTE, for the first time raising its own conventional army for offensive operations, attempted to drive the Sri Lanka Army out of the north. This was a desperate gamble. That it succeeded to the extent that it did is surprising, given that the LTTE would ultimately be no match for Colombo. After holding it became untenable, the army eventually withdrew from Jaffna Fort. By the end of 1990, the army was forced to vacate virtually the whole of the Vanni, including Kilinochchi and Mankulam. These were to be the scenes for the battles that took place in 2007 through 2009.

The LTTE's efforts to drive the army out of Elephant Pass in July 1991 failed. The dead included over 500 young children, often 14 and above, thrown into the fray in desperation, at a time when the offensive began to falter. Its attempt to drive the army out of Pooneryn, in 1993, likewise succeeded only partially, leaving nearly 400 dead. All of this meant a huge cost being placed on the civilian population through bombing, shelling and displacement. As society and economic life disintegrated, young recruits, particularly children, were killed in large numbers. Another segment, which used the war prolonged by the incompatibility of LTTE politics and peace, to obtain refugee status in the West, underwent a change of psychology to materially support the LTTE's brand of extremism to the detriment and agony of those in their former homeland.

This period also saw the deliberate displacement of Muslims from the north. Being a totalitarian movement with an ideology—and one that gave its leader quasi-divine status, enjoying the right to the indiscriminate use of humans around him—the LTTE could not get the Muslims, even formally, under its ideological umbrella. This community constituted an indispensable part of the northern society and economy, but maintained a social cohesion and aloofness from the LTTE. Several articulate members of the Christian clergy, on the other hand, long being made comfortable with Tamil nationalism, made opportunistic compromises with the Tigers, which for its part also found their connections with the West useful. In October 1990, the LTTE drove out

80,000 Muslims from the north with just two hours' notice, carrying only the clothes on their back. To this day, most of these forsaken people remain in refugee camps around Puttalam.

In 1991, the army in Jaffna was confined to a small area around Palaly, which was militarily untenable. General Denzil Kobbekaduwa set in motion a plan to retake Jaffna and, as a first step, he extended the area of control around Palaly. This caused a fresh round of displacement from some of the best agricultural land in Jaffna, which has since remained part of the High Security Zone. By 1994, the war had entered a stalemate. The following year, however, the LTTE began another round of war, after aborting seven months of peace talks with the new government of Chandrika Kumaratunga. The rebels also had a new military strategy in place, after having stocked up on anti-aircraft weaponry. The government forces in the Jaffna Peninsula suddenly found themselves under siege, after two military transport planes were brought down and with the Sea Tigers, the LTTE's naval wing, threatening the supply by water.

Colombo was thus forced either to take the whole of Jaffna or lose the north altogether. Once again, the LTTE had underestimated the government's military capacity. The government's first attempt, in July 1995, was aborted after heavy displacement and about 300 civilians killed by missiles. Faced with losing Jaffna, exactly five years after it had forced out the Muslim population, on 30 October 1995, the LTTE forced most of Jaffna's civilian population to move into the Vanni. Recruiting from the displaced population once again, it was able to maintain the Vanni as its main base—at least until government forces began retaking this territory in recent months.

Ideology and extremism

Before coming to the most recent developments, we should pause to explore the links between ideology, displacement, and political and military strategy. First is the Sinhalese nationalist extremist viewpoint that the island belongs to the Sinhalese, and is sacred to Buddhism. Any assertion of the northeast as the homeland of the Tamils had to be confronted by 'Sinhalising' the region—i.e., by planting Sinhalese settlements. As it happened, this was accomplished by violent means and displacement. A direct result of this strategy was to facilitate the LTTE's brand of extremism to take control of the Tamil liberation struggle.

Second, there is the Tamil nationalist extremism. Although having violently marginalised the opposition among the Tamils, the LTTE was no match for the resources of the Sri Lankan state. The rebel force raised the stakes by making Prabhakaran into a demigod, and using its monopoly over propaganda to recruit children and women. Yet its inability to deliver despite several rounds of 'final war' left it politically vulnerable, and unable to survive in a quasi-democratic environment. It had to continue ratcheting up the rhetoric, emphasising that a separate state was the only viable settlement. This meant that negotiations were purely tactical and insincere, leading to the organisation launching an indefinite series of 'final wars' whose only results were displacement, refugees, loss of habitable territory and loss of population, the latter to both death and emigration. The diaspora that resulted from this loss of population also served as the potent mafia arm of the LTTE, able to maintain a phenomenal supply of weapons, thus bringing greater misery to those at home.

An important factor has been the persistent absence of mature political leadership in the Sinhalese south. The LTTE's malicious provocations of the Sinhalese are undoubtedly calculated to weaken the enlightened sections among them. Even though the war continued, Colombo governments until Mahinda Rajapakse's presidency did not formally tamper with the merger of the Northern and Eastern provinces under the 1987 Indo-Lanka Accord. While formally committed to a political settlement, all governments from 1990 kept the North-East Provincial Council dissolved, a disturbing sign that powerful sections in the south continued to harbour the Sinhalisation agenda.

With Chandrika Kumaratunga becoming president in 1994, many among the Sinhalese intelligentsia took the view that a federal settlement was the only way forward, with or without the LTTE's cooperation. The key aim here was winning over the Tamils and defusing the appeal of its extremism. The long-delayed attempt in 2000 to get a settlement through Parliament ultimately failed, however, due to the opportunism of a section of the Colombo elite supporting the United National Party (UNP) opposition and, of course, the Sinhalese extremist parties. The LTTE also assassinated and intimidated Tamil parliamentarians who supported the settlement.

In 2002, the new UNP government signed a ceasefire agreement with Norwegian facilitation, the main inspiration of which was the appeasement of the LTTE. This was supported overwhelmingly by local and foreign peace activists. Predictably, the LTTE used the ceasefire period to build up its military capacity for another round of war. By 2005, the Sinhalese extremists mobilised against the tattered peace agreement, and the peace community was thoroughly discredited. By enforcing a Tamil boycott of the 2005 presidential election, the LTTE played a crucial role in electing, by a whisker, Mahinda Rajapakse, who was backed by Sinhalese extremist groupings. Once more, the LTTE banked on provoking a war in which the president, backed by extremists, would be seen in a bad light. This, the thinking went, would give the rebels a political edge if they could score a few sensational military gains.

Scorched earth

Again, the LTTE miscalculated against a potentially much stronger enemy. Further to the LTTE's misfortune, the West largely blamed it for the failure of the Norwegian-brokered peace process, and several countries, including the EU, banned the LTTE in early 2006. The LTTE's attempt to smuggle in anti-aircraft missiles was intercepted by a US government sting operation. These two events were ultimately crucial in determining the LTTE's military fate. There was now little chance of the LTTE holding onto the areas it controlled in the east, especially after its eastern chief, Colonel 'Karuna', split off from Prabhakaran with many cadres to eventually form a paramilitary outfit under the government's direction. Nonetheless, Prabhakaran's best chance lay in overrunning the Jaffna Peninsula, where 44,000 troops were stationed, and forcing a government with an extremist image into negotiations. This is exactly what he tried, and failed, to do in August 2006. There went the LTTE's last chance.

By this time, the Sinhalese extremists backing President Rajapakse could smell the blood in the water. Just as the LTTE believed that its strategy of negotiations and war would finally push things in its favour, the Sinhalese extremists figured that, given the LTTE's military limitations (particularly following the Karuna split), opposing any political settlement and pushing for a military solution would ultimately work in their favour. The LTTE's provocations and abuse of negotiations helped their cause. Their agenda was Sinhalese hegemony over the minorities, which included their displacement and Sinhalese settlement.

In 2006, President Rajapakse found it expedient to claim that he stood for a political settlement, and thereupon set up the All Party Representative Committee (APRC) to work one out. Although India had been disengaged since the withdrawal of the IPKF in 1990, New Delhi insisted on a political settlement. But in 2006, Colombo began to dismantle the consensus reached under the Indo-Sri Lanka Peace Accord, and moved the Supreme Court to annul the northeast merger, which in principle recognised a Tamil-majority region. Indian policy lacked the focus and vision to counter the government's wiles in these actions and appears to have been caught napping. Two years later, in January

2008, after deliberate delay, President Rajapakse was to go back on his solemn pledges and instead impose his own draft proposals on the APRC chairman. These proposals were a feeble reflection of what was envisaged under the Indo-Lanka Accord, with no pretence at addressing the political aspirations of the minorities. New Delhi announced that the sham proposals were a 'welcome first step', suggesting that it was giving the Colombo government free run in combating the LTTE, without doing anything meaningful to secure the rights and security of the Tamils.

From 2006, the government began to do what would have been unthinkable after 1987. Intense shelling and deliberate displacement of Tamil populations became integral to its military strategy. Starting in August 2006, it drove the Tamils out of Mutur East and Vaharai through massive bombing and shelling, during which 300 civilians were killed. It then declared Sampoor, a culturally important Tamil area, as the location for a thermal power station to be constructed by India. Even while survivors were in refugee camps, the government began to destroy houses and build roads—direct echoes of the mid-1980s plans to establish Sinhalese settlements, which had been shelved after the Indo-Lanka Accord.

During previous rounds of war, precedents had been set in which the army took areas without displacing the civilians, such as by asking civilians by radio to move temporarily into schools and places of worship until the troops arrived. But a distinctly new strategy was clearly at play when the army cleared Mutur, Mutur East and Vaharai, where the military forced civilians to run for their lives under fire. In the Muslim-majority town of Mutur, 50 civilians were killed when indiscriminately fired government shells struck mosques, churches and schools, where civilians had taken shelter after the LTTE occupied the town. Thereafter, Tamil civilians, including children and the elderly, fled south on foot. Wherever they stopped they were bombed and shelled. In Kathiraveli, with no LTTE provocation, the army shelled a school with refugees, killing over 40. Once the civilians reached Vaharai, the LTTE prevented them from moving further south. In December 2006, the army rained shells into Vaharai, and by the middle of that month about 10,000 civilians had placed themselves in and around Vaharai Hospital, as their last hope, until a shell struck the hospital.

Civilians began fleeing, in defiance of the LTTE. At this stage, the LTTE fired at army lines from among the civilians, goading the army into firing back and preventing the civilians from fleeing. A number of witnesses assert that people died due to firing by both sides, and that the LTTE fired at people whose desperation had finally exceeded their fear of the Tigers. Quite a few drowned trying to ford the Vaharai lagoon, or when overloaded boats capsized during attempts to flee by sea. This scorched-earth policy towards Tamil civilians was later to be repeated in the Vanni.

Government control

It was pointed out earlier that Tamil civilians in the east were deliberately displaced and then confined to refugee camps far from their homes. Their resettlement was very slow. In Sampoor and the surrounding environs, the land was converted into the High Security Zone from which civilians are still barred. When troops were withdrawn from their area in 1996, these civilians had no choice but to live under LTTE control. Inevitably, they have children and relatives who had served in the LTTE, mainly under duress. Once displaced and confined to refugee camps, their movements were not restricted; however, several of them were followed by government death squads and either shot on the streets or abducted from their camps. These people are often very poor, and only the few who had relatives elsewhere willing to accommodate them were able to move out and find relative security.

In the Vanni, those who fled the LTTE were confined to detention centres, officially misnamed as 'welfare centres'. One aspect confirming the prison status of these camps is the fact that families are not allowed to seek shelter with host families, hitherto a common arrangement for the displaced in Sri Lanka. People who had made arrangements to go abroad before they were displaced—such as young women whose fiancés were waiting for them—were also not allowed to leave. (After some delay, however, university students have been allowed out.) Such a situation is completely unprecedented. People of all ages are treated as detainees, yet of course there are no criminal charges. The people of the Vanni are now divided into three main groups: those who have escaped to India; those confined to camps south of the Vanni by the government and kept in isolation; and the estimated 250,000 within the shrinking LTTE-controlled area, living without proper care and shelter, and regularly subjected to army bombing and shelling. Recently some have also begun escaping north to the Jaffna Peninsula—an open-air prison.

In Jaffna, the attitude of the government is reflected in the enormous restrictions on movement, such as the arbitrary closure of roads for several hours to allow an army convoy to pass. Long bureaucratic delays, of weeks or months, are required to gain permission to leave the peninsula and fly to Colombo. This has brought the economy to a standstill. By imposing a debilitating security regime on the Tamils, the government is virtually forcing the Tamils to go elsewhere.

In the final analysis, there were ways in which the Colombo government could have won over the Tamil population. All it would have had to do was to acknowledge that irrespective of the LTTE, this long-suffering community has political rights, and the authorities should have used the international machinery to safeguard human rights and maintain humanitarian norms. That would have resulted in minimum loss of life and damage to the economy as a whole. Guided instead by Sinhalese extremists, the Rajapakse regime took the course of inflicting maximum destruction on the northeast, breaking the spirit of the people and using media repression to hide the costs from the Sinhalese masses.

Over the past three decades, the handling of the situation in the east and north has thoroughly alienated the people of these areas. If Sri Lanka is to be put back on its track, there needs to be a political solution that offers genuine devolution. The militarisation of the administration and the arbitrary interference with the people's right to movement must end. So must the pall of xenophobia under which international engagement has been crippled. The people of Sri Lanka need genuine democracy—not the sham democracy that has been put in place in the east, to be managed by killers of the security forces and their armed Tamil proxies masquerading as political parties.

Chapter 19

God and the gospel of globalisation

Himal, March 2010

Meera Nanda

The defeat of the Bharatiya Janata Party (BJP) in India's general elections in 2009 was greeted with relief by secularists and democrats everywhere. Not entirely unreasonably: they read the fact that the BJP lost a solid 3.4 per cent of its previous poll share as evidence that Indian voters had rejected the majoritarian politics of Hindu pride and prejudice, peddled by the BJP and the rest of the Sangh Parivar. The general consensus is that the ideology of Hindu nationalism, or Hindutva, has lost its appeal among the urban youth and middle classes—that secularism has won and 'God has left politics,' to borrow the elegant title of a recent essay by Delhi journalist Hartosh Singh Bal. Market reforms and globalisation emerge as the stars of this saga. Both the friends and critics of the BJP agree that it is the fervour for making money in India's roaring economy that doused the flames of Hindu nationalism from the hearts of the middle classes. But that is not all. The 'free' market, we are told by a section of influential Dalit intellectuals, will not only free India from the menace of communal violence, but will also lift the curse of caste oppression. It is fair to say that the gospel of globalisation is gaining ground in India.

The story about how the markets defeated the BJP goes as follows. Hindutva appealed to the middle classes and youth back in the bad old days of the 1980s and 1990s, when these groups were feeling beleaguered and angry due to the failures of Nehruvian socialism and 'pseudo-secularism', which, in their view, gave undue preference to Muslim and Christian minorities. But in the nearly two decades of economic liberalisation and foreign investments that began in the early 1990s, India has witnessed a great burst of economic growth. As a result, the Hindu middle classes are angry no more. Far from feeling beleaguered and discriminated against, they have become more cosmopolitan, more self-confident, and more willing to take on global challenges and seek out global opportunities. Indeed, so confident is the Great Indian Middle Class that it has claimed the 21st century as India's Century. And so the critics ask: What use can such forward-looking people possibly have for the past glories of Hinduism, about which the stodgy old men in khaki shorts keep harping? This story has found great favour among the self-proclaimed Friends of the BJP, who want the party to drop Hindutva altogether, or at least to make it sound less communal, and emerge as a 'normal' pro-market, pro-defence, anti-'minority-appeasement', right-of-centre party.

A similar story is being told from the opposite end of the political spectrum, made up of Dalit intellectuals, most of whom are no friends of the BJP. Influential members of this circle, notably the journalist-activist Chandra Bhan Prasad and the economist and Planning Commission member Narendra Jadhav, have claimed that economic liberalisation, fostered by globalisation, is improving the living standards of Dalits, liberating them from the caste norms that consigned them to degrading work for generations. They derive their evidence exclusively from two districts of Uttar Pradesh that have access to labour markets for semi-skilled work in Delhi, Lucknow and other cities, while ignoring significant evidence that the incorporation of Dalits in the unorganised sector is taking place only on extremely exploitative terms, without any legal protection to speak of. Yet such thinkers remain convinced of the powers of the market, and are pushing to bring affirmative-action policies into the private sector, which they say will open the doors for Dalits to enter the modern, hi-tech economy. The markets' blow against caste norms in employment is naturally seen as a victory for secularism, because by destroying the material conditions of caste hierarchy the markets are seen as loosening the hold of Brahminical justifications for caste. Thus, at least some friends of Dalits, like the friends of the BJP, have come to embrace the gospel of globalised markets in the name of upward mobility for Dalits.

India is not the only country where markets are supposed to be exorcising the demons of religiously inspired fanaticism, patriarchy and other sources of oppression. Parts of the Islamic world—Dubai, Turkey, Malaysia, and even Egypt and Iran—are cited to support the proposition that 'global capitalism is the single best hope for combating Islamic extremism,' as the American–Iranian author Vali Nasr put it in his new book, *The Forces of Fortune*. Nasr and others refer warmly to Turkey, where the deeply pious and deeply capitalist-minded middle-class entrepreneurs from small towns have been able to moderate the Islamist instincts of the ruling Justice and Development Party. In a reversal of the idea that 'McWorld' breeds jihad, as put forth by the US journalist Benjamin Barber in his well-known 1995 book *Jihad vs McWorld*, the charms of 'McWorld' are now being hailed for aborting jihad by seducing the actual and potential jihadis into shopping malls.

Those who believe in the moderating powers of markets assure us, as the political scientist Alan Wolfe did in a 2008 essay, that 'religion's priority of belief and secularism's commitment to individual rights are not in opposition,' as most religions are adapting to the capitalist world by becoming 'prosperity religions'. The aim of these prosperity religions is not to question the morality of acquiring wealth, but rather to bless the believers into thinking that they can become rich as well by the grace of god. Thus, Wolfe assures us, the rising religious fervour in many parts of the world is nothing to worry about, as this safely feeds into fervour for making money and getting rich.

As such, the new evangelists of prosperity religions cheer the fact that, from China to Russia to Turkey, 'God is back', as the title of a recent book by the British journalists John Micklethwait and Adrian Wooldridge would have it. They suggest that if the entire world were to erect a US-style wall of separation between state and religion, there would be no reason to worry about jihad or fundamentalist religious extremism, because then all religions would learn to embrace both democracy and capitalism and thus metamorphose into prosperity religions, as they apparently have in the United States. Such a celebration of American secularism, of course, fails to account for the fact that this country has an active and very influential Christian-fundamentalist movement.

Others, such as Richard Wright, the author of *The Evolution of God* (2009), go even further, proclaiming that globalisation is carrying out the expansion of moral imagination that was kick-started by the Abrahamic God. Just as Christianity and Islam learned to see other tribes as brothers under the God of Abraham, global economy is setting up 'non-zero-sum games' that allow people to include distant strangers in faraway lands in their circle of moral concern. So, according to this line of thought, when the whole world becomes interlinked through trade, we will all learn to become more tolerant, and a great concord of civilisations will ensue—just as the Abrahamic God intended. Globalisation, in other words, is doing God's work. Again, however, this celebration of global tolerance fails to account for the fact that globalisation is not a non-zero-sum game: it produces very clear winners and losers.

Worship the nation

How believable is this gospel of globalisation? Is globalisation really the antidote to religious nationalism? Can market fundamentalism drive out religious fundamentalism? Are multinational enterprises the unwitting (or witting) vehicles of religious moderation? If so, should not secularists learn to love the corporate world as a friend and ally? Well, it depends. Most importantly, it depends upon what we mean by religious nationalism, which is the form that rightwing religious movements tend to take through much of the postcolonial world, including in this region. If we reduce 'religious nationalism' to street violence or terror in the name of god, then the answer is 'yes' to all the above questions.

Any overt violence is not good for business, and no one knows that better than those who make a living through business. Thus, those upwardly mobile Indians who are benefiting from off-shored information-technology jobs and the expanded consumer choices made possible by foreign investment and trade definitely do not want to create an impression of religious bigotry and political volatility in India. As such, there should be little wonder that the largely Hindu middle classes deserted the BJP in the last election: they do not want to risk bloody riots in Bombay, Ahmedabad, Delhi and other centres of commerce by flogging the dead horse of the Ram temple in Ayodhya, or by getting exercised over a dargah in Karnataka or Christian-versus-Hindu issues elsewhere. That is the reason that even those who admire Gujarat's chief minister, Narendra Modi—which includes captains of Indian industry, well-known journalists and Amitabh Bachchan—advise him to showcase his state's economic development but tone down his anti-Muslim invective. That is also the reason why the business press cheered when the Congress-led United Progressive Alliance (UPA) coalition won in 2009.

If we look at religious nationalism through a wider-angle lens, however, without reducing it to mere communalism, the picture changes entirely. Suddenly, globalisation and its parallel neoliberal economic policies appear as allies, not enemies, of religious nationalism. Indeed, globalisation is turning out to be good for the gods everywhere. This is nowhere more so than in India, where, aided by what can be thought of as the 'state-temple-corporate complex', a new Hindu religiosity is getting more deeply embedded in everyday life, in both the private and public spheres. At least for now, growing economic prosperity seems to have weaned the Indian middle classes from the extremist elements of the Hindu right, who incite animosity against Muslims, Christians and the pub-going Westernised elite. But the rising prosperity has definitely not turned Indians against the more subtle ways in which Hinduism is becoming the de-facto religion of the 'secular' Indian state.

In India, Hinduism, the religion of the majority, is becoming more, not less, entrenched in the routine, everyday conduct of statecraft. Meanwhile, it is also being celebrated in the public sphere as the real fount of spiritual-cum-'scientific' values that are supposed to turn India into the 21st-century superpower. There is a widespread belief, for example, that India's success in information technology comes from the 'Hindu mind', which thinks in abstractions and is good at breaking codes, and that India can be trusted with nuclear weapons because of its culture of non-violence that has Hindu roots. If India were a homogenous Hindu society, such blending of faith and modernity would be problematic only for the tiny (and much neglected) minority of diehard nonbelievers and principled secularists, who want to create a new culture that does not need to invoke supernatural powers and who want the state to have nothing whatsoever to do with any religion. But considering that India is a multi-religious society, home to the second-largest Muslim population in the world and to a considerable number of Christians and Sikhs, the constant conflation of Indian culture with Hindu gods, goddesses and rituals is obviously problematic.

Since there has been an endless debate in India about who really is a Hindu, and what exactly *secularism* means, it is useful to indicate how these terms are being used in this essay. For all practical purposes, this essay assumes that a Hindu is as a Hindu does. That is, all those people around the world who say they are Hindus—including (but not solely) all the men and women who offer *pujas* to Hindu gods and goddesses in their homes, and/or line up outside temples, and/or undertake pilgrimages on days considered auspicious on the Hindu calendar, and all those who observe Hindu rituals at the time of birth, marriage and death—are counted as Hindus. Their rituals, gods and goddesses, and ways of worship do differ along caste, class, gender, age and regional lines, but they are nevertheless unified by a set of metaphysical beliefs about god, nature and human beings that are distinctively Hindu. Insofar as secularism has any meaning in India, it means equal distance between the state and all the various religions of Indian people, just as there is an equal distance between the hub and rim of a wheel. So, in this essay, when the Indian state is held accountable for betraying its secular principles, it means the state has betrayed this principle of equal distance by being partial to the religion of the majority—i.e., Hinduism—over and against the religion of the minorities.

Around the world, the deep embedding of religious faith into the pores of the state and the civil society is what religious nationalism is all about. Communalism is a terrible but still largely accidental feature of religious nationalism, and can wax and wane depending upon the political context. Yet religious nationalism has two far more enduring purposes that go beyond communalism: one, to make the majority religion the basis of the nation's collective identity and the source of its ultimate values and purposes; and two, to allow the institutional space of the majority religion—the networks of temples, ashrams, religious schools or *gurukuls*, charitable hospitals, etc.—to take on the welfare functions of the state, while retaining their distinctive religious nature. The idea is to erase the line between the ritual and political spaces, or to remove any distinction between the worship of gods and the worship of the nation. These features of religious nationalism depend upon the institutional arrangements between the state, religions and other dominant institutions of the society, including of course the amorphous domain of the market. These institutional arrangements are not etched in stone, but rather evolve and change with the changing political and economic context.

In this deeper, more fundamental sense, religious nationalism is able not only to survive but actually to thrive under the current regime of neoliberal globalisation. It would be foolish to try to lay down universal laws of cause and effect for something as history- and culture-dependent as religion and nationalism. But certain trends can be seen to be favourable to a wider role for religion in the public sphere under neo-liberalism, fostered by globalisation. As nation states open up those social functions that used to be performed by public-sector enterprises to so-called public–private partnerships, it becomes easier for religious institutions, often aided by public funds and supported by corporate donations, to establish a greater presence in the public sphere. Indeed, in the US this is exactly how 'faith-based initiatives' were able to punch holes through the much-celebrated 'wall of separation' between the church and the state under the neoliberal presidencies of both Bill Clinton and George W Bush. As US-style capitalism spreads around the world, it is not entirely unreasonable to look at how the changing equation between the state and businesses is affecting the fortunes of religious enterprises.

In a recent book called *The God Market*, I reported on precisely such institutional arrangements between the Indian state, the loose assortment of Hindu temples, ashrams, gurukuls, pilgrimage centres, etc., and the business sector. Using evidence culled from reliable media reports, budgetary data from government documents, reports of state-level temple-management agencies and the websites of prominent temples and ashrams, the book looks at how neoliberal economic policies are affecting the fortunes of Hinduism. It concentrates largely on two domains most relevant to religious affairs: the establishment of 'deemed universities', which specialise in 'Vedic sciences', and religious tourism.

My main theses in that book can be summed up in three simple propositions. First, the demand for religious services in India is currently growing, especially among the urban, educated and largely Hindu middle classes who are benefitting the most from globalisation. Second, the supply of these religious services, which cater to the majority community, is being facilitated by the neoliberal policies of the state. And third, the net result of this is the mindset of Hindu majoritarianism, which accepts the ever-deeper but often invisible (because it is taken for granted) identification of the national culture of India with the religion of the Hindu majority.

This is not to say that neoliberal reforms and globalisation are creating these circuits of demand and supply where none existed before—the process of domesticating and 'Hinduising' modernity did not start with the current phase of globalisation. After all, the very idea of neo-Hinduism has more than 150 years of history. Further, the middle-class religiosity that revels in ritualism, idol-worship, fasting, pilgrimage and other routines of popular theistic Hinduism was not entirely absent from the cultural milieu of the educated middle–upper classes that came of age in the more 'socialist' or secular era.

As such, the new market economy did not create the religious market, as India always had plenty of choices when it came to gods, faiths and modes of worship. Instead, what the new economy has opened up is more spaces in the public sphere into which religion can penetrate. Contemporary Hinduism, both in its more spiritualist and more devotional forms, can thus be seen to have adapted quite well to the new consumer lifestyles, exploiting the new institutional spaces opened up by the public–private partnerships made possible by privatisation drives in higher education.

Four secular myths

One feature that seems to hold true across the world in this age of global capitalism is simply this: The demand for religion is growing all over the world, though, ironically, not in the most religious of all industrially advanced countries, the United States. (There, the number of nonbelievers has doubled over the last decade, to 15 per cent of the population.) In the rest of the world, globalisation seems to have brought about a global Great Awakening in its wake. As Micklethwait and Wooldridge put it in *God Is Back*, 'growth in faith has coincided with a growth in prosperity ... In much of the world, it is exactly the sort of upwardly mobile, educated middle classes that Marx and Weber presumed would shed such superstitions who are driving this expansion of faith.' This phenomenon of the upwardly mobile, urban middle classes turning to faith in increasingly larger numbers has been well recorded in formerly atheistic countries such as China and Russia, which are currently undergoing rapid economic development. The wildfire of Christian evangelicalism, especially Pentecostalism, is spreading all across developing countries in Latin America and Africa. But what is less well known is that a new breed of evangelical Islam is currently spreading in parts of West Asia, which is also learning to package traditional Islamic virtues in a new language of prosperity and individualism.

India is no exception to this worldwide trend, with the population that is prospering simultaneously becoming the most religious. Anyone familiar with India can attest to the growth of popular Hindu devotionalism of *murti-pujas* (idol worship), temples and pilgrimages, and the time-honoured passion for miracle-working god-men and -women, all combined with the growing craze (and market) for *yagnas*, astrology, palmistry and other occult arts. Visible signs of growing religiosity can be found everywhere in modern metropolises, where the statues of popular gods are getting taller, temples are becoming grander, and the lines of well-heeled devotees outside temples and ashrams in posh suburbs are increasing in length.

The rising religiosity in India is demolishing four of the most cherished myths of secularisation theory. Let us look at these myths in the light of Indian evidence: First, *the myth of the prosperous non-believer*. Classic secularisation theory was based on the assumption that growing prosperity and existential security would make people less concerned with god and otherworldly matters. On a macro level, when different countries with different levels of economic prosperity and social welfare are compared, the relationship still holds true. A well-known 2004 study by two Harvard sociologists, Pippa Norris and

Ronald Inglehart, of 19 countries covering most of Europe, North America, Brazil and Japan showed clearly that the level of religiosity declined in those societies, which provided greater 'existential security' through better welfare measures (though some of even these countries, like Brazil and parts of Europe, have also showed resurgence of religiosity in recent years). Within each society, those in higher income levels were found to pray less frequently than those in lower-income brackets. Overall, the poor were found to be twice as religious as the rich, when measured by how often they prayed.

The data from India, as provided by the National Election Survey in 2004 and 2009, turns this picture on its head. In contrast to other countries, the rich, the upper castes and the educated in India are significantly more religious than the poor, the lower castes and those who are less educated. When in 2004 the National Election Survey asked a representative sample of the Indian population how often they prayed, 60 per cent of rich and middle-class Hindus said they offered puja everyday in temples or in family shrines, while only 34 per cent of the very poor and 42 per cent of the poor did so. This trend held up across caste and educational level. The 'twice-born' castes were the most religious, with 58 percent doing puja daily, while Dalits and Adivasis were found to be the least religious, with only 35 per cent of each category reporting the habit of daily pujas. When the data is mapped on educational levels, those with college degrees are more given to daily pujas (at 53 per cent) than those who are illiterate (38 per cent) or with only a primary education (46 per cent).

When measured again after a gap of five years—five years of market growth and 'India Shining'—the trends held up. The rich, the upper castes and the more educated continued to pray more often than other social groups. But there was one surprising result: Dalits and Adivasis seem to be praying more than they used to do. In the 2009 NES survey, 40 per cent of Dalits and 43 per cent of Adivasis said they offered daily pujas, a significant jump from the 2004 survey. (These trends can be compared since the two surveys followed the same methodology and were carried out by the same team of researchers from Lokniti, a research programme of the Centre for the Study of Developing Societies in Delhi.)

It is not entirely clear how this rise in religiosity of the 'subaltern' classes came about. It could be related to rising living standards: there are reports that Dalits who are trying to break out of their caste ghettos and improve their standards of living are beginning to undertake ostentatious religious rituals such as *kathas* and *jagratas* in order to 'pass' as upper castes in their neighbourhoods. If true, this recourse to showy Hindu rituals would be a sad commentary on the prevalence of casteist attitudes in the larger society. Yet however one explains the rising religiosity among Dalits, it belies the expectations that rising economic prosperity of those at the bottom of the heap will break the hold of casteism and secularise Indian society. Even if there is some economic trickle-down in certain places, as the advocates of 'Dalit capitalism' have been claiming, economic betterment is accompanied by a growth of religiosity—rather than a decline, as predicted by secularisation theory.

Second, then, is *the myth of privatisation of faith*. Those who believe in secularisation theory expect that as societies become modern, religion will recede from the public sphere into private lives. But the reality has belied this expectation. In fact, religions all over the world are becoming less private, more visible in the public sphere and more influential on policies on everything from medical research, women's reproductive choices and sexuality to the environment, terrorism and armed conflicts. In India, too, there is sufficient evidence of the growing presence of religion in the public sphere. Many of the rituals and pujas that used to be simpler domestic affairs are now becoming more public and more ostentatious. Indeed, many of these public rituals are becoming full-blown political events, where holy men and political figures join forces. It is common for campaigning politicians to organise 'political darshans', using public money, and representatives of all parties seem to think nothing of using the state machinery for organising large-scale Hindu rituals for political gain. The Congress party's Digvijay Singh's order to hold public prayers and yagnas for his victory in the 2003 elections in Madhya Pradesh was more than a match for the BJP chief minister of Karnataka, B S Yediyurappa, who used up INR 1.1 million in just five months for his pilgrimages to temples. Even the communist government in West Bengal thought nothing of doing a *bhoomi puja* for the land it wanted to gift to the Tatas for the Nano car factory.

Participation in public rituals like *kathas*, *kirtans* and *satsangs* is also growing among ordinary people—or, rather, these events and rituals are moving out of the family and into the public square, while also becoming more ostentatious and expensive affairs. The trends for engagement in public religious activities, again as measured by the National Election Surveys in 2004 and 2009, are following the trends for private pujas, with the wealthy, the upper castes and the educated leading the way. Close to 30 per cent of upper-caste and wealthy respondents were found to have a high level of participation in public rituals, with Dalits and Adivasis generally falling around 16 per cent. In recent years, both the upper castes and Dalits have shown an increase in public religious events, with 18 per cent of Dalits reporting higher participation in 2009, as compared to 16 per cent in 2004.

Third is *the myth of 'de-ritualisation'*. The classical theorists of secularisation, from Karl Marx to Max Weber, believed that modernity would 'melt all that is solid' (in Marx's words), including belief in supernatural powers. The basic idea is that, as the general sense of human powers increase, the scope of 'god's will', or fate, will diminish. To some extent this has happened, with people around the world increasingly accepting naturalistic explanations for natural disasters. But this process seems to have hit its limits already, and religions are learning to use the tools of technology and markets to celebrate god's powers.

India provides a treasure trove of examples of this phenomenon, from the growing trend of 'e-pujas', remote darshans and computer-generated horoscopes, to Disney-like theme parks cropping up inside temples. But even at a more basic level, which may or may not deploy modern technology, the belief in the efficacy of prayer and ritual (like yagna) to change the course of events in the natural world is growing. This belies the hopes of 19th-century neo-Hindu reformers from Ram Mohan Roy of the Brahmo Samaj and Dayananda Saraswati of the Arya Samaj to Swami Vivekananda, who stressed the textual and spiritual elements of the Vedas and Vedanta over the more ritualistic practices.

And fourth, *the myth of rationalism and 'scientific temper'*. The expectation that religions will learn to scale down their claims about the 'truth' in the face of the growth of scientific knowledge has been belied. In fact, the language of science is now used to justify religious beliefs. Modern Hindu gurus have finessed the art of justifying the spirit-centred metaphysics of Brahminical Hinduism in modern, scientific terms. This 'scientistic' Hinduism sells better among those urban sophisticates who make a living in scientific and technological fields.

This growing religiosity of the well-heeled is often dismissed by intellectuals as somehow not authentic enough, as mere 'consumerism' or just one more experience on which the rich can spend their disposable income and feel good doing it. But this disdain is unwarranted. Consuming religion is not like, say, consuming a new brand of beer or buying a new pair of shoes. Rather, consuming religion means participating in its rituals, living by divinely ordained prescriptions and generally sharing the sacredness of the experience—activities that shape people's fundamental orientation of the world, and which give definition both to their view of themselves and that of those who are 'different'. This does not mean that all religious activities lead to narrow-minded identities, or that all those who are more religious end up becoming intolerant—there are obviously many deeply religious Hindus who are not communal and many

302

terribly communal people who are not religious at all. Rather, all this means is that religious activities shape identities, which in certain political contexts can become partisan.

Because it is so foundational for shaping identities and beliefs, widespread religiosity is a necessary precondition for religious nationalism. Only in those societies where old-style religion is sufficiently alive and well can the symbols derived from that religion serve to mobilise believers in the quest for national glory. When a sufficiently large number of people believe in the efficacy of religious rituals—say, the power of a yagna to bring a monsoon or to produce a son instead of a daughter—they do not consider it an illegitimate use of taxpayer money when elected representatives organise political yagnas. When a sufficiently large number of people believe that all that is good and creative about India comes from the country's Vedic 'golden age', they will not complain much when the government gives out land grants and other subsidies to institutions specialising in 'Vedic sciences'; or when preachers and politicians alike link India's success in the global economy to the need to revive *sanatan dharma* (claimed by its adherents to be the original teachings)—as popular Hindu evangelicals such as Swami Ramdev and Sri Sri Ravishankar routinely do.

There is actually an even more direct connection between religiosity and political choices. Up until 2004, there was a clear correlation between religiosity and voting behaviour: those Hindus who participated in public religious activities more frequently tended to vote for the BJP (38 per cent) over the Congress (25 per cent). In the 2009 elections, this relationship broke down, and this category of the highly religious showed the greatest decline (11 per cent) in support for the BJP. According to Sanjay Kumar of Lokniti, who is involved with NES surveys, part of the reason why the more-religious Hindus deserted the BJP was because the party failed to assert strong Hindutva positions. Even more troublesome is the fact that those who are more strongly and more openly religious are also more majoritarian in their thinking. Such individuals believe that Hinduism is not just a religion, but rather a 'way of life' for all Indians—a position that clearly overlaps with that propagated by the Sangh Parivar. It appears that the more ardent Hindus, such as those who pray more often and who participate in religious rituals more often, are twice as likely as others to hold the belief that India is a Hindu country.

Thus, even though Hindu nationalist parties are not always able to win the Hindu vote—or 'harvest the Hindu souls', as one commentator put it after the 2009 elections—a shared ground of understanding does exist between Hindu religiosity and Hindutva politics. Intellectuals and all-purpose commentators (such the Delhi political scientist Ashis Nandy) who confidently proclaim that Hinduism has nothing to do with Hindutva are simply ignoring the available evidence. Popular religiosity is the soil in which religious nationalism strikes its roots. It is for this reason that secularist forces have to pay attention not just to violence in the name of religion, but to popular religiosity itself.

Consumerist mayajaal

Most observers of social trends will grant that popular religiosity is on the rise in societies undergoing rapid economic change under the current conditions of globalisation. But there is very little agreement on what globalisation per se has to do with this phenomenon. The most common connection with global-isation and religiosity is drawn at the social–psychological level. Globalisation and the growing reign of labour flexibility involve layoffs and outsourc-ing to outside contractors, thus heightening the uncertainties and insecurities of the middle classes. The insecurities are percolating into family relations and often challenging the old mores that valued simplicity and frugality as virtues. The nouveau riche are seeking a way to balance their newfound wealth with the 'spirituality' and 'simplicity' they think they are losing by getting caught up in the *mayajaal*, or illusion, of consumerism. This is a socio–psychological explana-tion for the Indian trends that this author has offered in her previous work. In this, India resembles the dynamic described by the authors of *God Is Back* in the Christian context of the US and Britain, where 'many religious people see religion not so much as the enemy of capitalism but as a necessary counterbal-ance to it … Religion provides a way to enjoy the fruits of capitalism while protecting from the thorns.'

At the same time, there is a more direct political–economic link between god and globalisation. As globalisation forces the nation state to privatise more of its social functions, it creates more opportunities for faith-based institu-tions to take over these functions. This link cannot be generalised, as the state-market-religion relations vary in different societies. But there is ample evidence of faith-based institutions benefiting from the cut-the-government-to-size drives in the US, especially under the presidency of George W Bush.

In India, too, the Hindu establishment is benefiting from the recent de-regulatory changes that favour private enterprise, especially in the area of high-er education. (Both the 'secular' Congress-led UPA and the BJP-led National Democratic Alliance support these measures for disinvestment and privatisation of education, health and other social services.) The same privatisation drive that has allowed for-profit 'deemed universities' to crop up all over the county has also opened the door for Hindu gurus and temple endowments to set up their own universities, which either specialise in 'Vedic sciences' such as astrology, *vastu* and *karmakanda*, or offer secular education, mostly in management and engineering, with a traditionalist slant. Once such institutions come into existence—with full credentials to confer degrees, and often with hefty land grants from the state governments—they attract donations and patronage from business houses. Almost all the stars of the guru business in India, from the late Mahesh Yogi to Sri Sri Ravishankar and Swami Ramdev, have enjoyed state largesse in setting up their own universities, as have numerous gurukuls that have cropped up to train young boys to become Hindu priests.

The other sector into which the Indian government is pouring money is the promotion of pilgrimage to countless Hindu holy spots—a cosy relationship within the state-temple-corporate complex. 'Soft' Hindutva, which unabashedly celebrates Hinduism as the national culture of India, is not a monopoly of the BJP and Sangh Parivar; indeed, all the great anti-communal forces routinely indulge in public celebrations of Hinduism for political gains. But more than just public celebrations, they are known to bend state policies to suit Hindu interests, as happened in the construction of the Akshardham temple complex in New Delhi on the banks of the Yamuna, which critics allege is environmentally unsound; and in the dispute over the land grab for the Amarnath yatra in Kashmir recently.

Any purported 'ambivalence' the corporate sector might have toward the BJP extends only to its 'hard' Hindutva politics, which has the potential for unleashing communal violence. But there is not much ambivalence when it comes to the promotion of explicitly religious aspects of Hindu culture as 'Indian culture' more generally. 'Soft' Hindutva has thus become de-facto state policy, regardless of which party is in power, and has the support of the corporate sector as well. Moreover, the concept of the state-temple-corporate complex is not meant to suggest a permanent power grab that has foreclosed all sites of struggle for secularism, but rather to suggest a loose, informal nexus that is using the new enthusiasm for the markets to tilt the balance toward the majority faith in India.

So, what is the answer to the question we started from—namely, can secularists trust globalisation and free markets? It is true that markets might be able to save us from violent religious extremism, and that is part of the reason for why the middle classes deserted the BJP and its allies in 2009. But the markets also deepen the reach of religion into the institutional spaces of society. The only real response to religious nationalism is to actively cultivate a secular culture that can displace the majority faith as the national culture. This would require a purposeful demolition of the truth claims of all faith-based ways of thinking—including the faith in the gospel of globalisation and 'free' markets.

Chapter 20

Why Pakistan is not a nation

Himal, June 2010

Pervez Hoodbhoy

Pakistan has been a state since 1947, but is still not a nation. More precisely, Pakistan is the name of a land and a people inside a certain geographical boundary that is still lacking the crucial components needed for nationhood: a strong common identity, mental make-up, a shared sense of history and common goals. The failure so far to create a cohesive national entity flows from inequalities of wealth and opportunity, absence of effective democracy and a dysfunctional legal system.

While it is true that most Punjabis think of themselves as Pakistani first and Punjabi second, this is not the case with the Baloch or Sindhis. Schools in Balochistan refuse to hoist Pakistan's flag or sing its national anthem. Sindhis, meanwhile, accuse Punjabis of stealing their water, the Muttahida Qaumi Movement (MQM) runs Karachi on strictly ethnic grounds, and in April the Pashtun of NWFP successfully had the province officially renamed Khyber Pakhtunkhwa (against the wishes of other residents). In getting a job, caste and sect matters more than ability, and ethnic student groups wage pitched battles against each other on campuses throughout the country.

The lack of nationhood can be traced to the genesis of Pakistan and the single factor that drove it—religious identity. Carved out of Hindu-majority

India, Pakistan was the culmination of the competition and conflict between natives who had converted to Islam and those who had not. Converts often identified with Arab invaders of the last millennium. Shah Waliullah (1703–62), a 'purifier' of Islam on the Subcontinent who despised local traditions, famously declared 'We [Hindustanis] are an Arab people whose fathers have fallen in exile in the country of Hindustan, and Arabic genealogy and the Arabic language are our pride.'

The founder of Pakistan, Mohamed Ali Jinnah, also echoed the separateness of Muslims and Hindus, basing the struggle for Pakistan on the premise that the two peoples could never live together peacefully within one nation state. But Jinnah was unrecognisably different from Waliullah, a bearded religious scholar. An impeccably dressed Westernised man with Victorian manners, a secular outlook and an appreciation of fine foods and wines, Jinnah nevertheless eloquently articulated the fears and aspirations of an influential section of his co-religionists. Interestingly, he was opposed by a large section of the conservative ulema, such as Maulana Maudoodi of the Jamaat-e-Islami, who said that Islam must not be confined to national borders. But Jinnah and his Muslim League won the day by insisting that Muslims constituted a distinct nation that would be overwhelmed in post-British India by a larger and better-educated Hindu majority.

Thus Pakistan, in essence, was created as the negative of India: it was not India. But what was it, then, beyond being a homeland for Muslims? Decades after the horrific bloodbath of Partition, the idea of Pakistan remains hotly debated. It did not help that Jinnah died in 1948, just a year after Pakistan was born, with his plans still ambiguously stated. He authored no books and wrote no policy paper. He did make many speeches, of which several were driven by political expediency and are frankly contradictory. These are freely cherry-picked today, with some finding in them a liberal and secular voice; others, an embodiment of Islamic values. The confusion is irresolvable.

After Jinnah, the Objectives Resolution of 12 March 1949 was the first major step towards the transformation of Pakistan from a Muslim state into an Islamic state. The Resolution starts with the statement that sovereignty rests with Allah. This obviously limits the legislative power of a representative assembly, since the fundamentals are already defined. Another consequence was the grudging concession that 'Adequate provision shall be made for the minorities to freely profess and practice their religions and develop their cultures'. This created the concept of minorities in the Pakistani polity, and hence negated the right of equality—a basic requirement of modern democracy.

The basis in religious identity soon led to painful paradoxes. An overbearing West Pakistan was to ride roughshod over East Pakistan, and become despised as an external imperial power. Jinnah's 'Two Nation' theory was left in tatters after the separation of East Pakistan in 1971, and the defeat of the Pakistani military. The enthusiasm of Muslim Bengalis for Bangladesh—and their failure to 'repent' even decades after 1971—was a deadly blow against the very basis of Pakistan. Nevertheless, contrary to dire predictions, the Pakistani state survived. Its powerful military easily crushed emerging separatist movements in Balochistan and Sindh.

For a while after 1971, the question of national ideology fell into limbo. Prime Minister Zulfikar Ali Bhutto attempted to create a Pakistani identity around the notion of revenge for the loss of the East Wing. He promised 'war of a thousand years' against India, and started Pakistan's quest for the atomic bomb in 1972. While this served temporarily as a rallying cry, the military coup of 1977 that sent him to the gallows was to revive the identity issue.

Zia's project

Soon after he seized power, General Zia ul-Haq announced his intention to re-make Pakistan, and end the confusion of the country's purpose and identity once and for all. In a sense, he wanted to emulate Napoleon Bonaparte's achievement of creating a nation from a nation state. Eric Hobsbawm, the influential Marxist historian, persuasively argues that the state of France made the French nation, not vice-versa. Similarly, Zia sought to create a nation—albeit one based on religion rather than on secular principles—using the power of the state. The word soon went out that Pakistan was henceforth not to be described as a Muslim state. Instead, it was now an Islamic state, where Islamic law would soon reign supreme. To achieve this re-conceptualisation, Zia knew that future generations of Pakistanis would have to be purged of liberal and secular values.

Thus began a massive, decade-long state-sponsored project. Democracy was demonised and declared un-Islamic, culture was purified of Hindu 'contamination', Urdu was cleansed of Hindi words to the extent possible, capital punishment was freely used, dress codes were introduced, university teachers had their faith examined under a microscope, and religion was introduced into every aspect of public and private life. Education was the key weapon for Zia's strategy. In 1981, he ordered the education authorities to rewrite the history of Pakistan. All new school textbooks would now 'induce pride for the nation's past, enthusiasm for the present, and unshakeable faith in the stability and longevity of Pakistan'. Jinnah and other icons of the Pakistan Movement had to be portrayed as pious fundamentalists, whether or not they carried beards; their lifestyles had to be hidden from public view. To eliminate possible ambiguities of approach, a presidential order was issued to the University Grants Commission that, henceforth, all Pakistan Studies textbooks must:

> Demonstrate that the basis of Pakistan is not to be founded in racial, linguistic, or geographical factors, but, rather, in the shared experience of a common religion. To get students to know and appreciate the Ideology of Pakistan, and to popularise it with slogans. To guide students towards the ultimate goal of Pakistan—the creation of a completely Islamised State.

In a matter of years, Pakistani schoolchildren grew up learning a catchy but linguistically nonsensical jingle about the 'ideology' of Pakistan: 'Pakistan ka matlab kya? La illaha illala!' (What is the meaning of Pakistan? There is no god but Allah!) Although the purported answer has nothing to do with the question, Zia's strategy soon began to show results.

Barely a decade was needed for Pakistan's transformation from a moderate Muslim-majority country into one where the majority of citizens wanted Islam to play a key role in politics. The effects of indoctrination are now clearly visible. Even as members of the Sharia-seeking Taliban were busy blowing up schools in Swat and elsewhere, a survey in 2008 by the online World Public Opinion found that 54 per cent of Pakistanis wanted strict application of Sharia, while 25 per cent wanted it in some more dilute form. Totalling 79 per cent, this was the largest percentage in the four countries surveyed—Morocco, Egypt, Indonesia and Pakistan. A more recent survey, of 1,226 young Pakistanis between 18 and 29, was carried out across Pakistan by the British Council in 2009. It found that 'three-quarters of all young people identify themselves primarily as Muslims. Just 14 per cent chose to define themselves primarily as a citizen of Pakistan.'

Clearly, the country's youth is deeply worried by lack of employment, economic inflation, corruption and violence. In this turbulent sea, it is not surprising that most see religion as their anchor. For some, violent change is the answer to the country's problems. This is precisely what Zaid Hamid, one of Pakistan's fiery new demagogues, advocates. Hamid, a self-proclaimed jihadist who claims to have fought against the Soviets in Afghanistan, builds specifically on the insecurity of the youth, enthralling college students who pack auditoriums to listen to him. Millions more watch him on television, as he lashes out against Pakistan's corrupt rulers and other 'traitors'. Hamid promises that those who betrayed the nation's honour by joining the US-led 'war on terror' will hang from lamp-posts in Islamabad. In his promised Islamic utopia, speedy Taliban-style justice will replace the clumsy and corrupt courts established by the British. Just as Adolf Hitler dwelt on Germany's 'wounded honour' in his famous beer-hall oratory in Munich (where he promised that Germany would conquer the world), Hamid calls for the Pakistan Army to go to war against India and liberate Kashmir, Palestine, Chechnya and Afghanistan. One day, he says, inshallah, Pakistan's flag shall fly from Delhi's Red Fort. The students applaud wildly.

Still no Islamic state?

Notwithstanding the enormous impetus given by Zia, final success still eludes Pakistan's Islamists. The explosion of religiosity did not produce a new Pakistani identity, and a Sharia state is nowhere to be seen. Why? Ethno-nationalism is part of the answer. This natural resistance against melding into some larger entity is the reflexive response of historically constituted groups that seek to preserve their distinctiveness, expressed in terms of dress, food, folklore and shared history. Assimilation of Pakistan's diverse peoples into a homogenised national culture is opposed by this force that, like gravity, always acts in one direction.

Ethno-nationalism is, of course, vulnerable. It can be overcome by integrative forces, which arise from the natural advantage of being part of a larger economy with correspondingly greater opportunities. But for these forces to be effective, it is essential that the state machinery provides effective governance, demonstrates fairness and is indifferent to ethnic origins. Pakistan's ruling elite, unfortunately, is both incompetent and ethnically partisan, drawing its roots from the powerful landed and feudal class. The army leadership and the economic elite had joined forces after Partition to claim authority, but they were transparently self-serving and therefore lacked legitimacy.

Dangling the utopia of an Islamic state raised expectations but did little else. To the chagrin of the political and army establishment, it ultimately backfired and became the cause of infinite division. The post-Zia generation—which believes that every issue would be solved if the country were to go back to the fundamentals of Islam—muddles on in a state of deep confusion and deadly divisiveness. It believes that adherence to 'true Islam' will solve all problems and lead to a conflict-free society. But, in reality, the Quran and Hadith can be interpreted in multiple ways, and 'Islamic fundamentals' can be defined in many contradictory ways. These differences fuel violent political forces, each convinced that they alone understand god's will. Murderous wars between Sunni and Shia militias started during the late 1980s. Today, even those favouring the utopian vision of an ideal Islamic state are frightened by the Pakistani Taliban, which seeks to impose its version of Sharia through the Kalashnikov and suicide bombings.

All this was easily predictable, as sectarian divides are almost as old as religion itself. Basic questions are fundamentally unanswerable: Which interpretation of Islam, for instance, is the 'right' Islam? Of the four schools of Sunni jurisprudence (Hanafi, Shafii, Maaliki, Hanbali), which version of the Sharia should be adopted? Will all, or most, Pakistanis accept any non-elected *amir-ul-momineen* (leader of the pious), or a caliph? And what about the Shia? Democracy is excluded in any theocratic state, which, by definition, is a state governed according to divinely revealed principles wherein the head of state, elected or otherwise, interprets such principles and translates them into practical matters of the state. So, for example, although Abul Ala Maudoodi, in his Islamic Law and Constitution, states that 'Islam vests all the Muslim citizens of an Islamic state with popular vice-regency,' he is quick to point out that all vice-regents need not be of equal consequence. He demands that constitution makers should:

> Evolve such a system of elections as would ensure the appointment of only those who are trustworthy and pious. They should also devise effective measures to defeat the designs and machinations of those who scramble for posts of trust and are consequently hated and cursed by the people in spite of their so-called 'victories' in the elections.

In this 'state without borders', any Muslim anywhere can be a citizen. It will be the best governed not only because its leaders are pious, but also because the only ones who will vote will be the pious themselves.

In fact, religion cannot be the basis of Pakistan, or move it towards integration. This can be said categorically, although religion was undoubtedly the reason for Pakistan's formation. Coming over a half-century after Partition, Pervez Musharraf's call for 'enlightened moderation' was indeed a tacit admission of this fact. He realised that a theocratic Pakistan could not work, even though this conflicted with his other responsibility, that of being chief of the Pakistan Army. Since the days of Zia, the army had arrogated to itself the task of 'defending Pakistan's ideological borders' and, since the end of the 1980s, had consciously nurtured radicalism as an instrument of covert warfare in Kashmir and Afghanistan. Although Musharraf's successor, General Pervez Kayani, also seeks to distance the army from its past, it is unclear as to what extent he or other senior officers actually have control. The Islamists, for their part, hope for, and seek to incite, action by zealous officers to bring back the glory days of the military-mullah alliance led by Zia.

While it is true that religious political parties have yet to receive any sizeable fraction of the popular vote, the secular system of power was never regarded by Pakistan's citizens as just, appropriate or authoritative. So, by default, Islam became accepted as the basis of Pakistan, and any suggestion to the contrary continues to evoke a fierce public reaction. On the other hand, any serious move in the direction of making Pakistan a Sharia state would almost certainly lead to civil war. Why so? This is because while the Sharia is considered a panacea for Pakistan's multiple problems of corruption, inequity and poor governance, its true nature is revealed only once there is an actual move towards its implementation.

In the past, terrible and uncontrollable forces have been released against the people. As in Swat, the Pakistani Taliban's Wahabi-Deobandi-Salafi understanding of Sharia calls for forbidding females from leaving their houses, being educated or holding jobs. Men must have beards, wear shalwars rather than trousers, and never miss prayers. Killing apostates, decapitations, floggings and amputation of limbs are an essential part of the Taliban's penal code. Fortunately, those who defend this notion of Sharia constitute no more than perhaps ten per cent of Pakistan's population. Of course, that still means millions.

Pakistan must remain

In common parlance, the 'state' refers to the government, and an entity in international law. Recognition by other states of the state's claim to sovereignty enables it to enter into international agreements. Moreover, it needs a government to control its internal affairs. A more standard political-science definition of a nation state goes something like this: A state is an organised political community, occupying a territory and possessing internal and external sovereignty, which enforces a monopoly on the use of force. Max Weber, the political economist, defined the state as 'a human community that (successfully) claims the monopoly of the legitimate use of physical force within a given territory.'

Pakistan is a nation state by the above definition and must continue to remain one. In effect, it must be because it is! The cost of the disappearance or destruction of this nuclear-weapon state is too awful to contemplate. Pakistan can indeed become a nation; moreover, it will almost certainly become one in time. Although religion will certainly remain an important part of Pakistan's social reality for the foreseeable future, it must seek new roots lying within the country's social reality rather than religion.

Look at it this way: rain inevitably grinds down stony mountains over centuries, and ultimately creates fertile soil. Similarly, nations are inevitably formed when people experience a common environment and live together for long enough. How long is long enough? In Pakistan's case, the timescale could be fairly short. Its people are diverse, but almost all understand Urdu. They watch the same television programmes, hear the same radio stations, deal with the same irritating and inefficient bureaucracy, use the same badly written textbooks, buy similar products and despise the same set of rulers. Slowly but surely a composite, but genuine, Pakistani culture is emerging. Of course, stable nationhood is still not guaranteed. Both the Soviet Union and Yugoslavia broke apart after seven decades. If Pakistan is to stay together and chart a path to viable nationhood, it must identify its most pressing problems and seek their amelioration. What might be a suitable manifesto of change?

First, Pakistan needs peace. This means that it must turn inwards and devote its fullest attention to ending its raging internal wars. The sixty-year conflict with India has achieved nothing beyond creating a militarised Pakistani security state that uses force as its first resort even when dealing with its own people. Attempts to solve the Kashmir issue militarily have bled the country dry, leaving it completely dependent on foreign aid. The army's role must be limited to defending the people of Pakistan, and to ensuring that their constitutional and civil rights are protected. Indeed, given that the country could otherwise be rapidly overwhelmed by extremists who openly declare their disdain for democracy, the army is obligated to fight its progeny—the Taliban. There should be no illusion that extremism can be defeated by purely peaceful means. Indeed, the way ahead must be subtle and complicated. How can one develop the Federally Administered Tribal Areas (FATA) and ameliorate the anguish of their people when the insurgents are out to stop development, bomb schools and kill doctors? In such a situation, Pakistan must say yes to negotiations, but no to surrender. It currently appears that the future will be one of 'talk, fight, talk, fight'.

Second, Pakistan needs economic justice. This is not the same as flinging coins at beggars. Rather, it requires organisational infrastructure that, at the very least, provides employment but also rewards according to ability and hard work. Incomes should be neither exorbitantly high nor miserably low. To be sure, 'high' and 'low' are not easily quantifiable, but an inner moral sense tells us that something is desperately wrong when rich Pakistanis fly off to vacation in Dubai while a mother commits suicide because she cannot feed her children.

A welfare state in Pakistan is a distant ideal. India abolished feudalism upon attaining independence. But the enormous pre-Partition landholdings of Pakistan's feudal lords remained safe and sound, protected by the authority of the state. The land reforms announced by Ayub Khan and Zulfikar Ali Bhutto were eyewash. In later years, with the consolidation of military rule in national politics, the army turned itself into a landlord-and-capitalist class. Military officers own assets that have no relation to national defence. This includes vast amounts of farm lands and valuable urban real estate, banking, insurance, advertising companies, cement and sugar industries, airlines and ground transportation, cornflakes and commercial bottled water. Most countries have armies but, as some have dryly remarked, only in Pakistan does an army have a country.

Third, Pakistan must shed its colonial structure of governance. Different historically constituted peoples must want to live together voluntarily, and see the benefits of doing so. A giant centralised government machine sitting in Islamabad cannot effectively manage such a diverse country. The demand for creating more provinces should be carefully examined and not peremptorily rejected, as is currently taking place. Having smaller administrative units does make sense, especially due to the rapidly rising population. On the other hand, to fan the flames of nationalism can hardly be a good thing.

As in India, Pakistan should be reorganised as a federation in which provinces and local governments hold the critical economic and social powers, while defence and foreign affairs are held in common by the Centre. In particular, Islamabad's conflict with Balochistan urgently needs resolution, but using political sagacity rather than military force. Blaming India will not achieve anything—the Baloch are angry for good reason. At a recent lecture to senior Pakistan civil-service officers in Peshawar, this writer was taken aback at the intensity with which senior officers from Balochistan spoke. They said that Baloch wounds are too deep, and that the time for healing and reconciliation with Pakistan had passed. A decade ago, one would only have expected this language from student radicals—now, it is the mainstream Baloch who articulate such sentiments.

Fourth, Pakistan needs a social contract and economic justice. This is a commitment that citizens will be treated fairly and equally by the state and shall, in turn, willingly fulfil basic civic responsibilities. But today, Pakistanis are denied even basic protections specified in the Constitution. The poor suffer outright denial of rights—such as personal security and access to water in cities—while the rich are compelled to buy these. Rich and poor alike therefore feel no obligation to fulfil their civic duties. Most do not pay their fair share of income tax, leading to one of the lowest tax-to-GDP ratios in the world. Seeing that the rulers flagrantly flout the very laws they claim to espouse, it is no surprise that the common citizen does the same.

Fifth, the country's education needs drastic revision in the means of delivery and content. Money goes some way towards the first—better school infrastructure, books, teacher salaries, etc. But this is not enough. Schools teach children to mindlessly obey authority, to look to the past for solutions to today's problems, and to be intolerant of the religion, culture and language of others. Instead, students need to be taught to be enquiring, open-minded, creative, logical, socially responsible, and to appreciate diversity. Pakistan paid a very heavy price because its leaders could not understand that a heterogeneous population can live together only if differences are respected. The imposition of Urdu upon Bengal in 1948 was a tragic mistake, and the first of a sequence of missteps that led up to the awful slaughter of Bengalis by the West Pakistani military in 1971. A myopic education system is squarely responsible for the fact that ethnic and religious minorities are viewed with suspicion and disdain by the majority. This must change.

In the end, for Pakistan to succeed, it must want to become a nation held together by mutual interests rather than by some abstract Islamic ideology. This is the only way to deal with the multiple civil wars that have started in the country. The path to creating a Pakistani nation is doubtless difficult. As the population explodes, oceans of poverty and misery deepen, limbless beggars in the streets multiply, water and clean air become scarce, education is stalemated, true democracy remains elusive, and the distance from a rapidly developing world increases. One is strongly tempted to step aside, give up and admit helplessness.

But surely that is wrong, for what we fear will then actually come to pass. The political philosopher Antonio Gramsci spoke of 'pessimism of the intellect, optimism of the will'. Indeed, with the pessimism of the intellect, one must calmly contemplate the yawning abyss up ahead. But then, after a period of reflection, one should move to prevent falling into it.

Chapter 21

A Tibet of the mind

Himal, December 2010

Tenzing Sonam

Like most Tibetans born and brought up in exile, I grew up, in India, with a certain idea of my homeland, one that was informed by two extreme but inseparable views. On the one hand was an idealised state of grace that existed before the Chinese invasion; on the other, the violated and transformed land— a veritable hell on Earth—that it had since become. We were taught that we, the exiles, were the keepers of the true flame of Tibet's national identity, the guardians of its culture and traditions, which, as far as we knew, were being destroyed in our homeland. And we were also raised to believe that one day we would triumphantly return home, that the entire *raison d'etre* for our displacement was to fight for that moment.

Over time, this lofty aspiration lost some of its bearings, instead becoming simply another component of our lives as refugees. Our world evolved its own particular reality; we were neither Tibetans in the way that our parents were—and Tibetans in Tibet still are—in the sense of having a physical connection to our land, nor were we truly a part of our adopted countries. Our peculiar in-between lives seemed to demand the expectation of returning to our spiritual homeland for sustenance, but not necessarily its fulfilment. As far as we knew, this was our life—being an exiled Tibetan, inhabiting an ersatz Tibetan world.

For the first two decades of exile, we had very little communication with our homeland. China, then in the throes of the Cultural Revolution, was closed to the outside world, and the ensuing shroud of silence fell even more heavily over Tibet. We had no idea what had befallen our families back home, and the occasional snippet of news only confirmed our worst fears. Tibet seemed to be undergoing horrors that we could not remotely imagine; the very fabric of its existence seemed to be in the process of being dismantled. This knowledge gave us the impetus to rebuild our lives in our new home in exile. The preservation of Tibetan culture, especially its Buddhist traditions, and the development of a modern education system for the younger generation, became the Dalai Lama's most pressing concerns. And in this, helped by India's generous accommodation and the support of many international agencies, we proved remarkably proficient. Within a few years, we were able to create a parallel Tibetan world, complete with our own religious establishments, educational and cultural institutions, settlements and, most importantly, our own government, headquartered in Dharamsala. We became, in the words of one academic study, 'one of the most resilient and successful refugee groups in the world'.

In the early years, however, the belief remained strong that, sooner or later, we would be returning to Tibet. For people of my father's generation, this goal was a very real one. They retained strong memories of home, and the thought of one day being able to go back sustained them through the trauma of escape and relocation. But with each passing year, this hope became remote and unattainable. By the time my father died in a Delhi hospital, in 1999, most people of his generation had already passed away. The expectation of return thus shifted from being a credible goal to an abstract ideal. By this point, the majority of us had only ever known the state of exile as our home. Over the years, as fewer and fewer of us had any direct memory or link with Tibet, we drifted further away from the reality of its contemporary situation. Instead, we retreated deeper into the cloistered world we had created for ourselves, an alter-Tibetan universe that was validated by the existence of the Tibetan government-in-exile and the various religious, educational and cultural institutions we had established. But above all, it was the presence of the Dalai Lama that gave us a kind of moral justification, a redeeming reason for our continuing existence as refugees.

Sarjorwa sustenance

Oddly, the more successful we became at creating a new Tibet for ourselves, one that we believed was an authentic mirror of the original, the more we faced the danger of losing touch with the real Tibet. The latter, of course, had by now not only suffered and survived the ravages of the Cultural Revolution, but was itself in the throes of rediscovery and reinvention. And this gulf between the exile and the homeland would certainly have widened had it not been for a number of developments that began to impact our hermetic world from the early 1980s onwards. The relative liberalisation that took place in China in the period following Mao Tse-tung's death suddenly allowed us to communicate directly with our homeland. For the first time in two decades, we established contact with our long-lost relatives and learned first-hand what they had undergone. At the same time, the opening-up of the country to tourists meant that Tibetans in Tibet became exposed to the larger world and, crucially, to news of the Dalai Lama and the exile community. By the end of the 1980s, Lhasa saw a series of pro-independence protests, the Dalai Lama won the Nobel Peace Prize for his efforts at finding a peaceful solution to the Tibet question, and Tibet itself became an international *cause célèbre*. These events marked the beginning of another phase in our lives as exiles.

As China loosened its grip on Tibet, the floodgates opened to a second wave of Tibetan refugees who streamed across the Himalaya and down to the Indian plains. They included a diverse range of people who came from all three provinces of Tibet: educated youths, aspiring monks and nuns, young children, former political prisoners, and pilgrims of every background, nearly all united by their fervent desire to pay their respects to the Dalai Lama. We called them *sarjorwas*, the newcomers, but after the initial excitement of seeing so many of them, the cultural differences began to make themselves felt. The newcomers dressed funnily, their reference points were unfamiliar, even their speech—in the strong native dialects of Amdo or Kham, a distinction that more than two decades of exile education that used a version of the Lhasa dialect had eradicated—was incomprehensible to most of us. They preferred Chinese pop music over the Bollywood songs that we liked, and they watched Chinese TV serials, which we could not understand. We began to assume an attitude of moral superiority over them, even though these were the very people on whose behalf we were supposedly struggling: Tibetans who had actually lived under Chinese communist rule and who, more often than not, had risked life and limb to come to India.

I remember a particularly striking event that exposed this attitude. One day in 1996, Dharamsala woke to the shocking news that a young Tibetan girl had been raped and murdered. Her naked body was found in a bush near Gangchen Kyishong, where the offices of the Tibetan government-in-exile are located.

While the hunt was on for the killer, the community was rife with rumours and speculation; there was consensus on only one point, that the culprit must be an Indian. From my own conversations I gathered that he was variously a Gaddi (an Adivasi group), a taxi-driver or even an itinerant *sadhu* who was reported to have come into town the previous day. That the murderer might have been a Tibetan was inconceivable. Then came the news that he was, in fact, a Tibetan. The shock of this disclosure was only mitigated when it transpired that the man was a recent arrival from Tibet, a *sarjorwa*. We could relax again because, in a sense, he was an outsider—a Tibetan from Tibet.

Our sense of self-importance and moral superiority was also shaped by the growing fascination of the West with Tibet and Tibetan Buddhism, and its expectation of what Tibetans were supposed to represent as a people. By this measure, we were an almost otherworldly race, spiritually evolved, naturally compassionate, peace-loving and with the good of all sentient beings always at heart. We began to take this idealised view of ourselves seriously, and remade our history in its image. The wars we had fought in the past with our neighbours, the factional infighting, the court intrigues and political assassinations, the system of cruel punishments sometimes meted out by the state, the banditry that was commonplace in many parts of the country, even the fact that many thousands of Tibetans had not so long ago taken up arms against the Chinese invasion—these were all airbrushed out in favour of a reinterpretation of Tibet as a mythical Buddhist land of peace and harmony, governed by compassion and inhabited by the morally upright and ethically pure.

Of course, faith in Buddhism and the values it taught had always deeply influenced our way of life. But these characteristics were now being defined in starry-eyed Western terms, which allowed no room for shades of grey. Our political struggle took on a spiritual tinge, and coincided with a growing emphasis on non-violence. It also presaged a change in the goal of our struggle from total independence to one that could be accommodated within the People's Republic of China. A curious corollary of this transformation was the belief that we were now fighting not for the freedom of a nation, but for the benefit of the entire world.

In an interview in 2008, the Tibetan prime minister in exile, Samdhong Rinpoche, explained to me this revised worldview. 'Universal responsibility of Tibet as a nation is to preserve and promote its inner sciences, and that is unique and that is very much beneficial to the entire sentient beings,' he said, explaining that by 'inner science' he meant what others referred to as spiritualism, including Buddhism. He continued: 'So therefore, many people say that the humanity cannot afford to let the Tibetan heritage and the inner sciences die ... our responsibility is [thus] to promote and preserve the inner sciences of Tibet, which is not available with any other nation.'

The influx of new refugees continued apace throughout the 1980s and 1990s, and by the end of the millennium they had become a significant presence in our society. No longer could we apply the distinction of their being *sarjorwas* with any moral authority. In our exile monasteries, for instance, the newcomers were soon in the majority. This raised the disturbing question of what would have happened to these religious establishments—one of the prime examples of our community's successful rehabilitation—had their population not been replenished by the fresh intake of monks and nuns from Tibet. Even in the key exile centres of Dharamsala and Majnu ka Tila in Delhi, the change in the demographic makeup became apparent as more and more newcomers participated actively in every aspect of exile Tibetan life. Their growing influence in our lives could no longer be ignored.

Bod-pas means everyone

In March 2008, when a group of nearly 300 Tibetan exiles set out on a march from Dharamsala to Tibet to call attention to the plight of their compatriots under Chinese rule, the majority were recent arrivals from Tibet. That same month, when demonstrations broke out in Lhasa and then spread across the Tibetan plateau, quickly turning into the largest uprising against Chinese rule since 1959, it was the newcomers who kept us in constant touch with the unfolding situation there. They had the contacts in Tibet, and were in constant communication via mobile phones and the Internet. And they were the ones who received and made public many of the only images of Chinese retaliation against the protesters that the world eventually saw. Unlike previous protests in Tibet—most notably the last full-scale demonstrations in Lhasa, in the late 1980s—this time we had a sense of immediacy. Suddenly, it was no longer a hypothetical struggle; we were directly involved in the uprising in Tibet. The sarjorwas had invigorated our exile society by restoring crucial personal links to our homeland.

The impact of the second wave of refugees had consequences in Tibet as well. Some returned to their homes after spending a few years in exile. They took back with them a renewed sense of Tibetan nationalism and the dream of *rangzen*, or independence, which had remained strong among the exile community despite officially having been abandoned as a goal. The concept of

Bod (Tibet), as a nation that comprised *cholkha-sum*, the three traditional provinces of U-Tsang (Central Tibet), Dotoe (Kham) and Domed (Amdo), was a unifying ideal that had been developed and promoted in exile. In Tibet, before the Chinese occupation, Bod had referred to central Tibet, and bod-pas only to its inhabitants. People from Amdo or Kham did not see themselves as such. In exile, however, the notion of Cholkha-sum took root, eventually becoming the key defining concept of our identity as Tibetans.

We all thought of ourselves as Bod-pas, regardless of our provenance. When we as exiles said we were fighting for rangzen, we meant independence for all of Tibet and not just its central province. This was a crucial distinction in light of the fact that the Lhasa government had no jurisdiction over large parts of Kham and Amdo when the People's Liberation Army invaded in 1950. Even when the goal of Tibet's struggle was revised to that of seeking genuine autonomy, it was still for all three provinces under one administrative entity. This spirit of pan-Tibetan nationalism seeped back into Tibet with the refugees who returned. Popular singers from Kham and Amdo began to sing about the importance of the unity of the three provinces. Tibetans across the plateau began to refer to themselves as Bod-pas; during the uprising of 2008, Khampas and Amdowas from the furthest reaches of Qinghai, Gansu and Szechwan provinces were heard to shout for *Bod rangzen*—i.e., for Tibet's independence.

After 2008, the numbers of new refugees escaping to India was dramatically reduced, as China beefed up its border controls. Movement between the exile community and Tibet has also been curtailed. Nonetheless, the links that were established during the previous two decades remain vibrant and resilient. In the meantime, the Tibetan diaspora has spread across the world. Relatively large communities have taken root in New York, Toronto and various other cities in the US and Europe. For these Tibetans, home no longer automatically refers to Tibet. For all intents and purposes, it usually means Tibetan India, with its capital in Dharamsala, an indication of how strongly entrenched the exile Tibetan world has become and how separate its identity is to the homeland it set out to recreate and preserve.

The strength and depth of this affinity to a home away from home was vividly illustrated by an encounter I had in eastern Tibet in the summer of 2006. I was travelling with my family through the Kham areas of Szechwan and Yunnan. On the streets of one dusty town, I was startled to hear my name being called out. A young monk I knew from Drepung monastery in South India was excitedly greeting me from across the road. He had escaped to India as a teenager, and had now returned home for a visit after nearly 15 years. Thrilled to meet a fellow Tibetan from India, the first thing he said was, 'You must be missing sweet tea! I brought some with me. Come home and I'll make you some.' As anyone who has travelled in Tibet or China knows, outside of Lhasa and some of the larger towns in central Tibet, sweet tea made in the Indian style is a completely unfamiliar concoction. Later, in the security of his home, he told us how much he missed India, not just the relative freedom that he enjoyed in his monastery but also the simpler pleasures of life, such as eating dosas and vadas. Although he was happy to have met his family after so many years, he said he could hardly wait to go back to India. 'Home', even for this second-wave refugee, was no longer his birthplace, but rather an abstract construct that had its physical roots in a foreign land.

Purpose of exile

As we enter the sixth decade of exile, one thing seems to be clear: the exile Tibetan world we built will continue to exist in some form for the foreseeable future. But will it slowly lose its moorings and drift away from its mother ship, a fully formed satellite with its own orbit and gravity? What, then, will be the continuing purpose of our exile? Where, in the unfolding narrative of a Tibet that has been a part of China for more than 50 years, will our place be?

The goals that our parents set out for themselves when they left Tibet were clear: to restore Tibet's independence and to return with the Dalai Lama as our rightful leader. Politically, we have long since given up the goal of independence. Returning home no longer has the same immediate relevance to us as it did to our parents' generation, nor does it seem likely to happen anytime soon. In fact, many of us would probably be ill-equipped to live in Tibet, even if we were given the chance. So, as Samdhong Rinpoche maintains, is our primary function now only to preserve and keep alive 'the inner sciences of Tibet'? Or is there some deeper responsibility that we need to fulfil, which will continue to maintain our bond with our homeland and give our lives relevance as exiles?

To Tibetans in Tibet, Dharamsala has always been the symbol of hope and freedom. As long as this symbol remains strong, the exile Tibetan world, no matter in which direction we evolve, will remain significant in Tibet. But the moment this influence begins to fade, we will become irrelevant. The danger, of course, and one that Beijing officials are counting on, is that this is exactly what will happen as soon as the Dalai Lama passes on. Therefore, I believe our primary responsibility as exiles in the next, upcoming phase of our development is to ensure that the symbolic significance of what we have achieved survives the passing of the Dalai Lama, and remains a unifying force and a source of hope for the people of Tibet.

This can only happen if the government-in-exile, even without the Dalai Lama, continues to represent an ideal and a goal that is shared by all Tibetans. And in order to redefine this, we must remember once again the fundamental reasons why we came into exile in the first place, and why we have remained there for five decades as a distinct community: because China invaded and occupied our country, it continues to rule it as a colonial power, and will do everything necessary to maintain its authority. No matter how effective we are in preserving our own parallel world in exile, it will be the beginning of the end for us if we lose sight of these facts.

Chapter 22

Subsumed by history and nation

Himal, January 2011

Afsan Chowdhury

Faiz Ahmed Faiz remains one of the great unsolved enigmas of Southasian literature. Where does Faiz the poet end and Faiz the politician begin? Where does the pan-Southasian Marxist end and the Pakistani begin? His engagement with these contradictory identities constitutes a painful puzzle for his admirers. This becomes all the more complex because Faiz never seemed to have belonged fully to any one land—the boundaries of his literary, political and cultural life are fluid, flowing and overlapping.

The issue becomes even more complex for a Bangladeshi admirer such as this writer, who was born in the 1950s and to whom Faiz offers a complex identity and a bonding to great ideals crossing all borders. He is one Pakistani whom Bangladeshis have looked upon with the greatest possible admiration and affection. Yet what challenges this bond is the Faiz of the period through and immediately after 1971. During those terrible days, Bangladeshis who knew about or of him would ask each other, *What is Faiz saying about all this?* He had become the 'Good Pakistani' in the eyes of those in the East. Yet, was Faiz ever a person who represented more than Pakistan? Was it possible for him to escape being a Pakistani and have a wider identity encompassing all the admiring nations of Southasia and beyond?

During the late 1960s, Munir Chowdhury hosted a literary television show in East Pakistan, during which he would discuss various writers of Pakistan. He was a legendary speaker, and employed his dramatic skills to present literary luminaries to a devoted public. In one show he talked about Faiz, his friend and fellow-traveller. Chowdhury focused on the poem '*Mujhse pehli si muhabbat mere mehboob na maang*', presenting Faiz as a social revolutionary and a poet of the oppressed. This presentation suited Chowdhury, who had been a Communist Party member, jailed in 1952 for his activism during the Bengali-focused Language Movement, and a lifelong literary activist who had become an icon of Bengali nationalism. He had moved on from his firebrand days, however, to become more a writer than a politician, an unparalleled teacher and East Pakistan's leading dramatist.

Most importantly, Chowdhury's love for Faiz's poetry was real. His introduction was one of the memorable moments of my life, an introduction to a poet of passion and beauty whom I admire to this day. Though I understand little of the literary tradition that Faiz upholds or the magnificent language of his poetry, I appreciate it—somewhere, there is a deep bond that transcends poetic pursuits. Yet my affection is also tinged with pain, as I see Faiz nationalised, regionalised, made language-specific. This is a tragedy for a poet who once spoke to all of us.

Defanging the revolutionary

During the 1940s, Faiz was certainly a Marxist. At that time he was in then-undivided India and had gone to war as an officer of the British Indian army, but returned home to become a journalist. He was married to Alys, a British sympathiser of the communists, whose sister was married to an Indian who taught in Aligarh. During this period, as the nation-states of Pakistan and India came into being, the Communist Party (CP) told its members to choose countries according to their religions. Thus, many communists in India and Pakistan emigrated across the new border obeying the party diktat. Many critics argue that the Communist Party went 'communal' even before that, when it asked cadres to join the Muslim League or Congress as per their respective religious identity. Harnessing India's political will proved to be quite beyond the capacity of the party, and the CP was relegated to a marginal role.

After Partition, Faiz, who had earlier worked on both sides of the new border, chose to live in Pakistan. Was this because he believed in the political structure and state ideology of the new country, one that subsequently moved increasingly towards becoming what was obvious in its charter—a state for one faith alone? Faiz was never a Muslim Leaguer, nor even a 'Muslim', so why then would he choose Pakistan? Perhaps it was never more than a move to his homeland, which by all standards was much less open than India. It is difficult to pinpoint the exact reasons that attracted him to Pakistan, but the new country's ideals certainly would not have been guiding his decision—maybe, going home was all it was about.

In Pakistan after 1947, Faiz was known for his views and activism, a man clearly a part of the left. He was involved with trade unionism, which even in those early days in Pakistan was considered an activity almost treasonous. In 1950–51 Faiz was arrested, along with Communist Party leader Sajjad Zahir and a few military officers led by General Akbar Khan, for planning a military takeover. There was a period of prolonged incarceration and a trial followed by a four-year sentence.

What was Faiz trying to do? Gen Akbar, leader of what has since become known as the Rawalpindi conspiracy, was a rabid Pakistani nationalist. He wanted to take over Pakistan—not because he wanted a new form of the state, but because he was frustrated with the Pakistani leadership, considering it too moderate in dealing with India. How did Sajjad Zahir and Faiz get involved with such a person? Where was the common space? I have not come across any material on the motives of the participants, or of the deals that must have been made between these two completely disparate groups, the communists and the ultra-nationalists, to achieve this alliance.

Around the world, communist parties generally tend not to be pro-army when out of power. But there has always been a fatal attraction among communists towards the military, in the belief that a coup can deliver revolution in a quick stroke, rendering organisational work and resilience unnecessary. This has been tried in Africa with a marked lack of success, as in Ethiopia and Mozambique; and so too in Bangladesh, where a one-legged War of Liberation hero, Colonel Abu Taher, came to power for a few hours in November 1975. He led his Marxist activists in an anti-officer uprising, which was to deliver socialism. Along with many others, he was hanged. History has also shown that attempts by communists to use the military path to power usually end in failure.

There seems to be no satisfactory explanation for the left involvement in the 1950 Pakistan coup attempt. But Faiz was involved, or we assume he was, because no 'confession' exists. Soon after the imprisonment, his active political life also began to fade and, anyway, the CP was banned in 1954. In the public mind, Faiz gradually became many other things: one of the great poets of our time, a friend of the Sufis of Pakistan and, finally, the safest and most innocuous, an outspoken lover of alcohol. Faiz was transformed and fitted into the benign identity of a great poet who does not challenge the state. Yet the fact remains: he did challenge it, albeit unsuccessfully.

Poets as communists

The identities of poet and communist do not always go well together. Poets usually tend to be people of words and passion, moved to politics by the power of the heart, not ideology. Over time, the two identities can become contested, if not came into direct conflict. The Chilean poet Pablo Neruda was always a better poet than a Marxist revolutionary, but he did try to cultivate a mix of both identities. Bangladesh's national poet, Nazrul Islam, was jailed for sedition and was a fellow-traveller of the Communist Party; he even ran the party's official newspaper in Bengal but drifted away over time, as his poetry and songs began to take priority. Also his inter-faith devoutness, believing in the mystic constructs of Islam and Hinduism (hardly a Marxist attitude, whichever way you look at it) became increasingly important to him. Early senility robbed him of his faculties when barely past forty, and things therefore never really reached a point where this conflict could grow larger.

Faiz had a better formal education than Nazrul, and also had a better knowledge of Marxist dogma and its application. He was also more middle-class and *shareef* (genteel). His poetry's roots and tools were the fine wine of Urdu and Persian literature; even his most famous poem *'Mujhse pehli si muhabbat'*, was written in the language of a chosen few, a highly stylised articulate Persian-Urdu that would be meaningful only to the well-educated. He was in many ways far more representative of the CP leadership's class and cultural roots than was Nazrul, who came from a peasant background.

Yet that only underlines the original question: Where could Faiz's politics find space in Pakistan? Unlike East Pakistan, where the communist tradition was deep and its politics itself spurred on by Marxist intellectuals and cultural activists, West Pakistan was almost completely bereft of such impulses, united in hatred for India but not much more. One could name Mian Iftikharuddin and Wali Khan, but these politicians were more Pashtun than Marxist, and much of the left nationalism was limited to NWFP and Balochistan. The Punjabis of Pakistan were not known for their leftist leanings. Was Faiz's much vaunted loneliness merely a poetic expression, or did it go deeper?

As children in Dhaka, we heard about Faiz's refusal to write a laudatory editorial in the *Pakistan Times*—the paper owned by Mian Iftikharuddin and edited by Faiz—about the martial law imposed by Gen Ayub Khan in 1958. Soon the paper was taken over by the government and Faiz had to leave. For some reason, the political Faiz went missing after that defiant stand, at least as far as pan-Pakistani politics was concerned—the kind of politics that could also resonate in East Pakistan. Faiz was from then on just a poet, not a socialist poet.

Meanwhile, the Pakistan that Faiz wanted to transform in the image of his ideals ended in 1971. During the days after the crackdown on Dhaka on 25 March of that year, as people wondered how the people of the Western half felt about the bloody events in the East, they heard a chorus of approval, led by Zulfikar Ali Bhutto saying, 'Thank God! Pakistan is saved!' This was a famously premature statement, of course, as all of Bhutto's machinations ran out of momentum in the end, with Pakistan collapsing in ignominy in December of that year. During those days, those who knew would ask, *What did Faiz say? Did he protest? Did he give a statement saying it was wrong?* In fact, we do not know what Faiz did. But we do know that this was one man many Bangladeshis expected to stand up for them. Of course, it was unfair to expect that Pakistanis who wished to express dissent could do so in a martial-law governed Pakistan. Very few could, and those who did went to jail or paid an even higher price. But Bangladeshis were demanding all this from the person—poet and politician—they imagined Faiz to be, rather than the person of flesh and blood who lived in Pakistan. In a way, Faiz had become a prisoner of the history of Pakistan.

As the war reached a gory climax, Bengali supporters of Pakistan, particularly those belonging to the Jamaat-e-Islami, went around the curfewed city, picking up as many poets, academics and intellectuals as they could find. It was always their view that Bengali nationalism was produced by these people, the so-called Hindu-loving secularists and cultural activists. If the crackdown on 25 March 1971 was the beginning of the end, the day when most intellectuals were picked up, 14 December marked the explosive end of the carnage. Many bodies could be seen dumped in the swampy killing fields, but few could be identified due to the advanced state of decomposition. Corpses with arms tied behind their backs, bearing marks of torture and missing eyes, have become the visual memories of the torture and murder of 1971. Among the many who disappeared and were never found was Munir Chowdhury, the man who introduced me to Faiz.

Friends and strangers

Faiz did visit Bangladesh in 1974, as part of an official delegation, in the capacity of an advisor on culture. He met with his friends but the closest ones like Shahidullah Kaiser, Munir Chowdhury, Zahir Raihan, all writers and CP activists, had disappeared. Others were uneasy with Faiz, as memories, unshared history and the reality of two distant states came between friends. He clearly missed the warmth of their friendship. In one of his most painful and beautiful poems, '*Hum ke thehre ajnabi*' (We who have been rendered strangers), Faiz summed up his personal agony—and that of many Pakistanis and Bangladeshis whose friendship had been torn asunder by the war. The final lines are:

> *Unse jo kehne gaye thhe Faiz, jaa sadqa kiye*
> *Ankahi hi reh gayi vo baat, sab baatoon ke baad*

> Faiz, that one thing which I went there to say with all my heart
> That very thing was left unsaid, after so much had been spoken

Friendship is a much more complicated matter than one imagines, for in Southasia politics can burn friendship with the flames of conflict. Faiz's politics died in Pakistan soon after he was jailed in 1950; only his poetry remained. With each day, though, his status as a poet soared, while admiration for him spread throughout the Subcontinent. Eventually, Faiz had become among the greatest legends of all. One could ask whether he left the building of his people—the somewhat fuzzy definition of 'people' which Southasian socialism imagines existing beyond borders—as after 1947 his world was determined by the country in which he lived. His socialist imagination was encircled by Pakistan's politics, and the very politics he wished to change overcame his resolve.

Faiz's personality was much more than just that of a poet. Indeed, that is the root of my sorrow—an unreasonable feeling, I concede. We have also seen how people who are unable to change politics sometimes become depoliticised beings. Munir Chowdhury once lamented publicly that he was defeated by the temptations of life—he gave up the life of a party cadre to become a teacher. I am not sure what path Faiz followed, but I hope he found peace in supporting political causes in Pakistan.

It might be heretical to say this, but perhaps Faiz would have been happier in the more politically variegated soil of India, where his poetry is as much admired as it is in Pakistan. In India, only a crippled form of socialist politics breathes, but at least it exists. I concede that to suggest another home for Faiz, particularly India, will be tantamount to committing blasphemy in the eyes of some. It is cruel to Faiz, too. He lives on wherever Urdu remains alive. And yet, it is important to remember one more time that Faiz grew into adulthood and recognition in an undivided Subcontinent amid its dreams.

The communist, the rebel, the secularist, the romantic poet, the happy lover of alcohol—all had in the end become a Pakistani. So it was that when he visited Dhaka in 1974 with Bhutto, it was only to find that many of his friends had been killed or disappeared by the same forces he represented in Bangladesh. The chasm became infinite and complete: he visited accompanied by those with whom his Bangladeshi friends could no longer associate.

People who dream of a better world are often condemned to become what history demands of them.

About the Editor and Contributors

Editor

Kanak Mani Dixit, writer and activist, was educated in Nepal, India and the USA. He is the founding editor (1987 to the present) of *Himal Southasian*, a high-quality, independent, monthly journal that offers informed critical commentary on social and cultural issues.

Alongside the journal, Dixit plays an influential role in a wide variety of cultural disciplines. He founded the Film South Asia (FSA), a documentary festival, which has become an important platform for local creativity, stimulating innovative local filmmaking on topics such as gender, child labour and water scarcity. Dixit also organises public lecture series and conferences involving regional and international speakers—including, recently, a Cartoon Congress incorporating a Southasian cartoon competition. He promotes research, writes children's books and co-owns a publishing house that disseminates books and translations of great value to Nepali society. He is the author of *Peace Politics of Nepal: An Opinion from Within* published by Himal Books in 2011. He was one of the co-founders of the post-2005 Civil Society Platform, plays a key role in the pro-democracy campaign, challenges repression and promotes freedom of expression. Among other awards, he was awarded the Prince Claus Award in 2009.

Contributors

Eqbal Ahmad (1933/34–1999) was a Pakistani writer, journalist and public intellectual. During the 1960s, while in the USA, he became one of the founders of the anti-Vietnam War movement. He was strongly critical of America's West Asia strategy as well as what he saw as the 'twin curse' of nationalism and religious fanaticism in countries such as Pakistan.

Khaled Ahmed is the director of the South Asia Free Media Association, in Lahore, Pakistan, and consulting editor for the *Friday Times*. His books include

Pakistan: Behind the ideological mask (2000); *Pakistan: The state in crisis* (2001); *The Musharraf Years: Religious developments* (2010); *Musharraf Years: Political developments* (2010); *Sectarian War: Sunni Shia conflict and its links to the Middle East* (2011) and *Word for Word* (2011).

Sirivayan Anand is the publisher and cofounder of Navayana, an independent publishing house that focuses on issues of caste and marginality. In 2007, Anand won the International Young Publisher of the Year award of the British Council–London Book Fair. Before turning to publishing full time, he was a print journalist for 10 years and has worked with *Outlook*, *The Hindu*, *The New Indian Express* and *Telheka*. He is the co-author of *Bhimayana*, a graphic biography of Dr B R Ambedkar. He lives in New Delhi, India.

Manisha Aryal is a media-development specialist based in Washington, DC. She started her journalism career as a reporter with *Himal Southasian* two decades ago, and did in-depth investigative stories from India. She has also been a broadcast reporter, doing stories from across Southasia for international media outlets. She is the founding director of Antenna, a successful radio-and-television production house in Nepal, has launched a multi-faceted media-development project in Pakistan with Internews Network and now works globally on media-development issues.

Sanjib Baruah is professor of political studies at Bard College, Annandale-on-Hudson, New York. He has written extensively on Northeast India, including *Durable Disorder: Understanding the politics of Northeast India* (2005), *India against Itself: Assam and the politics of nationality* (1999) and the edited volume *Beyond Counterinsurgency: Breaking the impasse in Northeast India* (2009).

Afsan Chowdhury has worked as a journalist for the *Dhaka Courier*, the *Daily Star*, the BBC and other media groups. Currently, he is the consulting editor for *bdnews24.com* and a research associate at York University, Toronto, Canada. He has authored and co-authored over two dozen books on history, human rights and the media, as well as five literary works, apart from producing a dozen documentary films.

Shruti Debi is a senior literary agent and director of Aitken Alexander Associates, India. She started her career as an assistant editor at *Himal Southasian*, from where she went on to head the editorial side of Picador India.

Ramachandra Guha is currently (2011–12) Phillipe Roman Professor in History and International Relations at the London School of Economics, UK. He normally lives in Bangalore in India. His books include *India After Gandhi* and *Environmentalism: A Global History.*

Sanjoy Hazarika is currently the director and chair of the Centre for North East Studies at Jamia Millia Islamia, New Delhi, India, and also managing trustee for the Centre of North East Studies and Policy Research, which is based in Assam. His innovative boat clinics are regarded as pioneers of health outreach to the vulnerable island populations on the Brahmaputra Valley, and reach half a million persons in 13 districts with sustained health care. A former reporter for the *New York Times*, Hazarika is the author of four books, including three on the Northeast India, and is working on a fifth. He is a columnist and essayist and winner of numerous awards and international fellowships, and has made over a dozen documentary films on the Northeast.

Pervez Hoodbhoy teaches at the School of Science and Engineering (LUMS), Lahore, as well as at Quaid-e-Azam University, Islamabad. He received his BS, MS and PhD degrees from the Massachusetts Institute of Technology, USA. He is the author of *Islam and Science: Religious orthodoxy and the battle for rationality*, and leads a major translation effort to produce books on modern thought in Urdu.

Rajan Hoole was attached to the University of Jaffna, Sri Lanka, as lecturer in mathematics and was one of the founders of the University Teachers for Human Rights, Jaffna. In order to continue the work, he was forced to seek exile in the south after the LTTE assassinated another founder-member, Rajani Thiranagama (see, *uthr.org*). He is now back at the University. He has co-authored *The Broken Palmyra* with K Sritharan, Rajani Thiranagama and Daya Somasundaram, and authored *Sri Lanka: The Arrogance of Power.*

Prashant Jha is a journalist based in Kathmandu. He is the Nepal correspondent of *The Hindu* newspaper and a political writer for *The Kathmandu Post.* Jha has written extensively on Nepal's peace process, the evolution of the Maoists, politics in the Tarai and India–Nepal relations. Between 2007 and 2011, he was a columnist for the *Nepali Times.* Jha is a contributing editor of *Himal Southasian.*

C K Lal is a Kathmandu-based columnist and commentator. His book, *Human Rights, Democracy and Governance* was published in early 2010. In 2011, Martin Chautari published his 'thinking paper' on the future of Nepali identity, *Nepaliya hunalai…*, along with commentaries by more than 20 of the leading politicians and thinkers of Nepal. He also wrote the acclaimed Nepali play *Sapana ko Sabiti.*

Pratap Bhanu Mehta is the president of the Centre for Policy Research in Delhi. He has taught at Harvard, NYU and JNU, and has published widely in several fields including political theory, law, Indian politics and intellectual history. His recent books include *The Oxford Companion to Politics in India* (co-edited with Niraja Jayal) and *Burden of Democracy.* Mehta has done extensive policy work and is also a prolific columnist. He is the recipient of the 2010 Malcolm Adisheshiah Award.

Thant Myint-U was educated at Harvard and Cambridge and later taught history for several years as a fellow of Trinity College, Cambridge. He has also served on three United Nations peacekeeping operations, in Cambodia and the former Yugoslavia, as well as with the United Nations Secretariat in New York. He is the author of three books including, most recently, *Where China Meets India: Burma and the new crossroads of Asia.*

Meera Nanda was originally trained as a microbiologist, but later specialised in science-and-technology studies. She writes on Hinduism and science. She is a recipient of research fellowships from the American Council of Learned Societies (2000–01) and the John Templeton Foundation (2005–10). She was a visiting fellow (2009–10) at the Institute of Advanced Studies at Jawaharlal Nehru University, New Delhi, India. She is the author of *Prophets Facing Backward: Postmodernism, Science and Hindu nationalism* and *The God Market: How Globalization is Making India More Hindu.* She is currently working on an intellectual history of scientific rationalism and secularism in contemporary India.

Dilip Simeon is a Delhi-based historian and writer. He has worked on campaigns for communal harmony and human right, and has been a visiting scholar at universities in Surat, Sussex, Chicago, Leiden and Princeton. His publications include an academic monograph on labour history and a novel titled *Revolution Highway.* He is the chairperson of the Aman Trust, which works to understand and reduce violent conflict.

Tenzing Sonam is a filmmaker and writer. He was born in India to Tibetan refugee parents. He studied at University of Delhi, India and at the Graduate School of Journalism at the University of California, Berkeley, USA. His works includes award-winning documentaries, one feature film and numerous video installations. He is currently based in Dharamsala, India.